DIMENSIONS OF EDUCATION

DIMENSIONS OF EDUCATION

Prof. Dr. Akbar Husain
Prof. Dr. Noraini Idris

GYAN

Dimensions of Education

ISBN: 978-81-212-1031-7

Published in 2010 in India by
Gyan Publishing House,
23 Main, Ansari Road, Darya Ganj,
New Delhi-110002
Phones : 23282060, 23261060
Fax : 011-23285914
E-mail: books@gyanbooks.com
Website: www.gyanbooks.com

Lasser Type Setting by: Quick Media, Delhi
Printed at : Young Art Press, Delhi - 92

Contents

Preface

Education is the only means by which the personality of people and society can be developed. Education is responsible for the holistic health of an individual in terms of physical, social, mental, emotional, and spiritual development. Development in the field of education has provided human beings with countless means of ways to improving quality of life. Education is the means of purifying the world, and giving knowledge of the self, other, and various disciplines. The more education we have, the more we can contribute to the welfare of society. Education gives proper direction to our thoughts, actions, and feelings.

The fields of education have been revolutionized greatly enhancing our understanding in terms of teaching, research, practice, and training. The need to examine and explain these enormous advances and their significance for educators, researchers, and practitioners has necessitated an increase in depth and breadth of the subjects covered in this book. This book has covered some new fields of education. We have dedicated our efforts to retaining the strengths in terms of writing style, up-to-date information and references.

Our text is divided into six sections. In part I-Religious and Moral Education (Chapters 1 through 3), the authors have discussed the role of religious and moral education and their impact on human and societal development. Part II- Early Childhood and Higher Education (Chapters 4 through 8), the authors discusses the principles of primary education and suggested the strategies for child development. Part III-Creativity, Guidance and Counseling (Chapters 9 through 12) discusses the development of curriculum with particular attention to the domains of cognitive ability. In Part IV-Quality of Education and Learning (Chapters 13 through 17) the authors discuss how to enhance quality of education following certain principles of learning and to make important decisions about students. Part V- Science Education and Technology (Chapters 18 through 20) is devoted on counselor education and guidance that have relevance for practice and training. Part V1- Contemporary fields of Education (Chapters 21 through 26) discuss at length those topics that illustrate applications of concepts that provide a different perspective of familiar material.

In each chapter, the authors have raised issues and suggested the potential solutions of the problems. All of the chapters have focused issues, directions and innovations in the new topics that demand our attention in the 21st century.

We would like to thank our contributors for providing and editing their chapters. The authors of the chapters in this book are experts in the respective areas. We hope this book will serve as a reference for general educators and researchers. This book will also contribute to your students' knowledge in understanding the scope of the fields of education. It will stimulate further researches in various fields of education.

Akbar Husain

Noraini Idris

List of Contributors

Akbar Husain, Ph.D is Professor in the Department of Educational Psychology and Counselling, Faculty of Education, University of Malaya, Kuala Lumpur, Malaysia.

Ananda Kumar Palaniappan, Ph.D is Associate Professor, in the Department of Educational Psychology and Counselling, Faculty of Education University of Malaya, 50603 Kuala Lumpur, Malaysia.

C.S. Singhal, Ph.D is Professor at the Centre for Human Resource Development National Institute of Rural Development, Rajendranager, Hyderabad, India

Daryl S. Paulson, Ph.D Scholar at large, is the President and Chief Executive Officer of Bio-Science Laboratories, Inc. U.S.A

Dennis Karney, Ph.D is Ned N. Fleming Distinguished Professor, University of Kansas, U.S.A

Fauziah Hanim bte Abd. Jalal, Ph.D, is a Sr. Lecturer at the Universiti Pendidikan Sultan Idris, Perak, Malaysia.

H. L. Kaila, Ph.D is Professr and Head, Department of Psychology, S.N.D.T. Women's University, Mumbai-India.

Jasim Ahmad, Ph.D is Assistant Professor,Teaching of Biological Sciences, Department of Teacher Training and Non Formal Education (IASE), Faculty of Education, Jamia Millia Islamia, New Delhi, India

Jasvir Chahal, Senior Lecturer in Education, Government College of Education, Chandigarh and Fellow, Panjab University Chandigarh, India.

Loh Sau Cheong, Ph.D is Senior Lecturer in the Department of Educational Psychology and Counselling, Faculty of Education, University of Malaya, Kuala Lumpur, Malaysia.

Manisha Dasgupta, Ph.D is Lecturer, Department of Psychology, University of Calcutta, India.

Mariam Mohamed Nor, Ph.D is Associate Professor and Head of Language Studies University Tun Abdul Razak, Kuala Lumpur, Malaysia

Mary Wee Siok Choo is a Postgraduate student, Faculty of Education, University of Malaya, Kuala Lumpur, Malaysia.

Melati bte Sumari, Ph.D is Sr. Lecturer in the Department of Educational Psychology and Counselling, Faculty of Education, University of Malaya, Kuala Lumpur, Malaysia.

Muhammad Faizal A. Ghani is Lecturer in the Department of Educational Management, Planning and Policies, Faculty of Education, University of Malaya, Kuala Lumpur, Malaysia.

Nilanjana Sanyal, Ph.D is Professor and Former Head, Department of Psychology, University of Calcutta, India

Nishat Afroz, Ph.D is Lecturer, Department of Psychology, Mahila Mahavidyalaya, Banaras Hindu University, Varanasi, India.

Noraini Idris, Ph.D is Professor and Dean Faculty of Education, University of Malaya, Kuala Lumpur, Malaysia.

Peter Wong Sin On is Lecturer, Department of Psychology and Counselling Faculty of Management and Economics, Universiti Malaysia Terengganu, Kuala Terengganu, Terengganu, Malaysia

Priya Kayastha Resarch Scholar, Child and Adolescent Mental Health Unit, Department of Mental Health and Social

Psychology, National Institute of Mental Health and Neuro Sciences (NIMHANS), Bangalore, India.

Ranjana Mittra, Ph.D is Reader, Department of Psychology, Mahila Mahavidyalaya, Banaras Hindu University Varanasi, India.

Rohaida Mohd. Saat, Ph.D is Sr. Lecturer, Department of Mathematics and Science Education, Faculty of Education, University of Malaya, Kuala Lumpur, Malaysia.

Rohit Bhandari, Lecturer, Dev Samaj College of Education, Chandigarh, India

Selva Ranee Subramaniam, Ph.D is Senior Lecturer in the Department of Mathematics and Science Education, Faculty of Education, University of Malaya, Kuala Lumpur, Malaysia.

Shabeshan Rengasamy, Ph.D is Lecturer in the Faculty of Education, University of Malaya, Kuala Lumpur, Malaysia.

Shahril @ Charil Bin Hj Marzuki, Ph.D is Professor in the Department of Educational Management, Planning and Policies, Faculty of Education, University of Malaya, Kuala Lumpur, Malaysia.

Sharifah Norul Akmar Syed Zamri, Ph.D is Associate Professor in the Department of Mathematics and Science Education, Faculty of Education, University of Malaya, Kuala Lumpur, Malaysia.

Stanley Krippner, Ph.D is Professor of Psychology, Saybrook Graduate School and Research Center, U.S.A

Swaha Bhattacharya, Ph.D is Reader, Department of Applied Psychology, University of Calcutta, India

Tee Meng Yew, Ph.D is Senior Lecturer in the Department of Curriculum and Instructional Technology, University of Malaya, Kuala Lumpur, Malaysia

Uma Hirisave, Ph.D is Additional Professor in the Department of Mental Health and Social Psychology, National Institute of Mental Health and NeuroSciences (NIMHANS), Bangalore, India.

Vishalache Balakrishnan, is Sr. Lecturer in the Department of Foundations of Education, Faculty of Education, University of Malaya, Kuala Lumpur. Currently she is pursuing Ph.D program at the Victoria University of Wellington, New Zealand.

Yeo Swee Lan_is the Coordinator of United Voice *(Self-Advocacy Society of Persons with Learning Disabilities Selangor and Kuala Lumpur)* since 2002.

Thoughts of the Great Educators

"The aim of the higher education is not mere extension of knowledge; the conversion of a soul from study of the sensible world to contemplation of real existence." —Plato

"Only that a noble child by its own natural disposition and not by coercion, may be induced to receive perfect instruction in sciences." —Elyot

Education is not a preparation for Life; education is life itself. —John Dewey

"By education, I mean the all-round drawing out the best in child and man-body, mind and soul." —M.K. Gandhi

"Education is the complete development of individuality of the child, so that he can make his original contribution to human life according to his best capacity." —T.P. Tun

"We are currently preparing students for jobs that don't yet exist ... Using technologies that haven't been invented . . . In order to solve problems we don't even know are problems yet." —Karl Fisch

"We can't solve problems by using the same kind of thinking we used when we created them." — Albert Einstein

SECTION 1 : RELIGIOUS AND MORAL EDUCATION

1

Religious Education for Human and Societal Development

Akbar Husain

Introduction

The two great World Wars have led the people to realize the defects of the neglect of spiritual and moral values in man's life. People began to feel the need of religious education in the society again. They thought that the scientific and technological progress would not lead the man to achieve a goal of perfect happiness, nor the progress in physical and material culture alone would be sufficient for the human development. The realization of this fact led the Malaysian people to think for the development of moral and spiritual values in the society. They began to pay more and more attention to religious observance and religious education. In this chapter, the author discusses the role of religious education in human and societal development.

Meaning of Religion

Religion is a complex concept, and it has a variety of connotations. But the divergent views regarding religion may be reduced to the fundamental conflicts between two opposing schools of thought. According to one school, the supernatural element, the sacredness and holiness of a supreme power are included in the concept of religion, while according to other; religion is reduced to a social phenomenon devoid of sacredness and divinity.

Men like Radhakrishnan, Martineaue and Frazer belong to the school of thought which considers supernatural element to be the essential element of religion. Dr. Radhakrishnan (1966) defines religion as the "Summon to spiritual adventure". He considers different religions to be different aspects of one truth which is 'universal and timeless in its validity'. Siquerra (1943) regards religion as the whole attitude of man to God. Frazer (1890) views religion as a faith in the power of a Supreme Being whose Characteristics are forgiveness and toleration. By religion Frazer means a brief in a power superior to man, which directs the courses of nature, and of human life. For Martineaue (1888) religion is concerned with man's belief in an ever living God Who rules the Universe.

Pratt (1945) has attempted to define religion by adopting psychological approach. For him religion is concerned with the social attitude of men towards a Supreme Power, which man conceive as having ultimate control over their 'interest' and 'destinies'. For Thouless (1923) exclusion of superhuman element from the concept of religion is hardly justifiable. He considers religion as a felt relationship between man and what he believes as a Supreme Being. Tylor (1971), Jastrow (1901), Gallowey (1914) and Bertholet (1934) all regard religion as man's faith in Supernatural Being.

A remarkable definition of religion comes from Emile Durkheim (1916). Although he does not include any supernatural power in his concept of religion, yet the element of sacredness occupies a chief place in it, he writes: "A religion is a Unified System of beliefs and practices relative to sacred things that is to say, things set a part and forbidden beliefs and practices which unite into one single moral community called a church, all those who adhere to them".

Feurbackh (1957-Trans.) takes an extreme position and views religion as an illusion spun by men. McTaggort (1923), according to Thoughless (1923) regards religion as an emotion "resting on the conviction of harmony between man and the Universe." These thinkers exclude the Supernatural element from the conception of religion.

In his remarkable book, 'The New Education and Religion', Paul William (1946) reduced religion to a mere social phenomenon; Deities or Gods do not find any place in his conception of religion. By 'religion', he means, "all those social patterns—ways of believing and behaving—by which men attempt to relate themselves to what they believe to be the totality of things, those faith—and what one does about them—which are fundamental to thinking and living." According to this conception of man acts religiously whenever he acts in harmony with what he believes to be the central reality of the Universe. Thus, every normal and sane person does possess religion. Even the materialist can be said to religious if he moulds his behavior in accordance with his beliefs that matter is the ultimate reality of the universe and that the secrets of the world can be known through scientific techniques and methods. Bertrand Russell (1968) has also regarded religion as one of the social aspects of our life. Science and Religion are both aspects of social life.

Whitehead (1925) and Russell (1968) are the two most influential representatives of this school of thought. The divine and Supernatural elements do not find any place in the conception of religion proposed by Whitehead (1925). Bertrand Russell (1917) has described 'devotion to nation' as an essential element of religion. According to Russell "Devotion to nation," "is perhaps the deepest and most widespread religion of the present age."

Elements of Religion

There are three essential elements of religion. First, every religion has its own conceptions regarding the purpose of creation of the Universe, the nature of Heaven and Hell, the punishment and the reward in the next world, the origin and history of certain people having certain beliefs, the relationship between deity or Supreme Being and the mankind, and the part played by Prophets and Saints in the society and so on. They are written in what is called 'Sacred Books', or "Scriptures'.

Secondly, every religion has certain rituals and forms of worship. The purpose of the worship is to help the individual to seek the blessings of Deity or Supreme Being. This aspect of religion deals with the ways and manners of conducting our prayer and worship.

Thirdly, every religion has its own ethical system or rules of conduct for its followers. This system tells how one should behave in society and what rules and ethical principles one should follow in order to have a better life in this world and a good reward in the next world.

Meaning of Religious Education

Corresponding to the two above-mentioned schools of thought, two kinds of approaches have been made to the conception of religious education. According to one approach religious education is instruction designed to give the pupils the knowledge of the Supreme Being. His sacred and divine attributes, the art played by Prophets in human societies, the day of Judgment, the purpose of creation of man and the Universe by God, the conception of sin, and heavenly reward and punishment. The advocates of this view aim, through religious education, at character formation of the pupils and molding their behavior.on the patterns of lives of the Prophets and saints so that they may be equipped for a decent and virtuous life on the earth and a happier form of existence hereafter. For these people moral education is different from religious education.

The other approach to religious education identifies it with moral and ethical education. Exponents of this view aim at character formation, but to them character means avoidance of anti-social behavior. They aim at producing good citizens and preparing the pupils to adjust themselves socially, morally and culturally to the changing circumstances of the world.

In his 'Modern Philosophies of Education' Brubacher (1962) has discussed the philosophies of religious education of the three schools of thoughts: the Humanists, the Supernaturalists and the Secularists. The Humanistic approach to God is through human experience. The Church for the humanist is a community and the religious education is a preparation therein. According to Supernaturalists the entire religious education should center on the relationship between God and man. The aim of education for the Supernatralists should be to fulfill God's purpose in creating man, that is, to worship Him and obey His commands.

The Secularist approach, according to Brubacher (1962) has a theory of moral education of his own which involves no religious point of view. Under the programme of moral education, the secularists include the teaching of loyalties to academic freedom, and civil liberties, and placing the confidence in the abilities of man to mould his own destiny.

Supernaturalistic View of Religious Education

Supernaturalist religious education refers to those undertakings which are designed to inculcate in the new generation the attitudes, beliefs and practices of a particular religion. Cassidy (1950) defines religious education as the instruction designed to inculcate religious beliefs in the children and youth and to acquaint them with Church as religious institutions. Raichur (1951) maintains that religious education has two aspects—the speculative and functional. At the speculative level it deals with the various intellectual concepts that make theology, with scripture that constitute ecclesiasticism, and with the practices, which form rites, ceremonies and festivals. Functionally it is concerned with practical issues of life—i.e., intellectual well being of men and the general welfare. Hook (1946) has included the truth about the world, man and God in his concept of religious education.

Those who identify religious education with morality take a different view of religious education. Whitehead and Williams may be considered as the representatives of this school of thought. Whitehead (1929) considers the inculcation of a sense of duty and reverence in the children as the salient features of religious education. According to Whitehead (1929) religious education, "is an education which inculcates duty and reverence." Williams (1946) views religious education as the education which attempts to make the children understand their relations to whatever they believe to the vital, supreme reality in the Universe. Thus, any thinking or living which any one conceives of as dealing with ultimate values is religious for him.

Islamic Religious Education in Malaysia

According to Hassan (1983), traditional Islamic education existed in Malaysia since the fourteenth century. Historical documents such as the *Sejarah Melayu* (Malay Annals) and the Hikayat Abdullah (Abdullah's story) provide evidence of the continuation of traditional Islamic education into the early nineteenth century (Brown, 1970; Hill, 1969). The Islamic education system evolved from an informal—pondok-type institution in the middle of the nineteenth century to the more organized and formal *madrasah* system in the early twentieth century (Kim, 1980). These *pondok* and *madrasah* types of learning institutions were founded by individuals, mostly *ulama* (religious scholars), or by the local community. Educational institutions in Malaysia such as *pondok* and *madrasah* had a common goal of producing virtuous Muslims who would obey the religious commandments and be useful to society (Hashim, 2004).

Neglect of Religious Education

The progress of science coupled with the 'Industrial revolution' in the 18th Century resulting in new discoveries, and emergence of new values weakened man's faith in religion and its values. The works of Huxley, Newton, Darwin, Rousseau, Kant and Hegel influenced the human mind tremendously. The people all over the world began to look towards the new horizon of science and technology with new hopes. Increasingly greater emphasis came to be laid on learning science and technology. Religion gradually receded in the background and educationists began to consider it as stumbling blocks in the progress of man. People attended religious institution less frequently and religious festivals were observed either merely as tradition or as a social function devoid of any religious spirit. Intellectuals and educated people became more skeptics towards religion. They would consider religion as serving no useful purpose in man's life. Rich and well off persons, in general, became indifferent towards religion. Having a religious faith was considered a sign of backwardness (Herberg, 1955). Church membership declined. Argyle (1959) reported that in America a decline in the membership of the Churches from 55% to 51%

in 1916, but again rising to 64% in 1950. This rise was due to what Benson (1960) called as "social pressure". He held the view the people were persuaded or pressed to join church because of social pressure rather than 'spiritual incentives' from within. Herberg (1955) considered that most people would participate in the religious performances and accept church membership because of the desire to be social.

The decline of religious education was also noticed in the late 1950s in Malaysia. The indifferent attitude of the people towards religion has also affected the status of religious education. It does not occupy the same place in our curricula as it used to have earlier. But in the 1970s interest again developed with the resurgence of Islam in Malaysia (Nagata, 1984).

Consequences of the Neglect of Religious Education

The neglect of religious education has led to the negative effects on the human development and society. It has produced various evils and vices in the society. The spirit of defeatism may be seen in many spheres of human activity. Loss of spiritual values, worship of science and exaltation of competitive rather cooperative values are some of the most outstanding characteristics of the modern age. Norm erosion and moral degeneration appears to have reached to the highest peak. Social disorders are increasing in numbers. Not only do the illiterate, immoral and irreligious persons are involved in commit crimes, even the educated youth and cultured persons are also involved in committing crimes in large number, and violating moral principles and defying laws in every country of the world.

The loss of religious faith resulting from the neglect of religious education has affected our value system. Our moral and religious values are badly affected. People do not hold the same system of values, which was earlier, considered as very important. The neglect of moral and religious education has caused a serious threat to democracy. According to Raymond (1952), the neglect of religion in any democracy may either result in anarchy or in 'regimentation,' which seeks to preserve law and order by force. In either case there is an end of democracy.

Moreover, the neglect of religious and moral education has also helped the development of communistic attitudes and ideas among the people. Raymond (1952) considers the development of communism as the result of this neglect.

Need and Importance of Religious Education

Religion plays an important role in human life. An individual behavior, i.e., thinking processes, motives, emotions and feelings, and attitudes are largely influenced by his religiousness. His social, political, economic and other values are also governed by his religious sanctions. Hence, there is a great need to provide the children proper guidance and training following the religion. A religion deals with fundamental values of life and provides the right path for healthy living. If we recognize that religious education is a process that can provide us with codes of conduct and frames of references, the importance of religious knowledge in our society cannot be denied.

Religion is an essential part of our culture. If any aspect of our cultural heritage is ignored, our educational system cannot be said as complete and sound. By neglecting the religious aspect of our cultural heritage we provide our children with a type of education that leaves many important elements of our culture unaccountable.

Religion is concerned with those positive virtues and values which men have cherished as the most excellent, worthy and desirable. Such values are compassion, justice, freedom, truthfulness, cooperation, love, peace, honesty and so on. Prophets, saints and religious leaders have laid great emphasis on the inculcation of these values in the minds of their followers. The realization of these values leads the individual development not only to have adjustment in the society, but it also enhances the progress of the society at large. It is religion which helps us to realize these values.

Religion is of great value to the human development. It provides meaning and purpose of life to an individual. Religion deals with certain goals which are ultimate aims of life. The religious goals are important in relation to our sorrows and happiness and furnish criteria by means of which we can do the reversal from non-essentials to essentials. Religious education furnishes standards and norms by means of which one can judge the significance of an individual in the society. Education, no doubt, helps the individual to aspire and struggle for higher position in life. But it fails to prepare an individual to cope with the failures or frustrations in his life. But the religion helps the individual to cope with the stressful life events. 'Hence, there is a need for sound religious system of education which can prepare the individual to face the defeat courageously. Religion can furnish stronger motives for struggle. Of the many motives that impel individual to work none is stronger than the belief that 'I do the will of God'. Such belief or faith brings more sustained efforts, and can works more enthusiastically and energetically.

Religious education is also important in relation to the development of personality. Coe (1928) suggests some of the ways in which prayer and worship can promote growth of personality. They are as follows:

[1] Prayer and worship can replace worries and fears by calm self-possession.

[2] Prayer and worship help us in facing our faults as they lead to repentance and modification of our behavior.

[3] Prayer and worship can help us in promoting fellowship with other worshippers, and they can unite a group in support of a cause.

[4] Prayer and worship can intensify our devotion to a cause.

Religious education has a great social value in so far as it helps the society to decide what the primary aim of communal living is. As pointed out by Williams (1946) we can shape the fundamental values of a society and allegiance of the people through religious education.

Place of Religious Education in Malaysian Society

Religion has always played an important role in the lives of Malaysians. Even today we find religion having a great hold over the people of Malaysia. Hindus, Muslims, Sikhs, Buddhist and Christians lead their lives based on their own religious creeds. Religious attitudes and religious outlook dominates their whole lives. Prayers and worships are carried out with full devotion. Orthodox rites are performed with utmost zeal and greatest sanctity. Religious festivals and ceremonies are observed with all solemnity and sincerity. Religious institutions occupy a central place in the personal lives of Malaysians. Their thoughts, feelings and actions are all directed and governed by the religion, they profess. The teaching of religion in Malaysia is not confined to the educational institutions only, even family starts providing religious knowledge to the child right from its early childhood.

In the past as well as in the present the educational system is religion oriented. At present religious education of other than Islam is imparted to some private educational institutions and worship places.

After Malaysia became independent in 1957, it adopted a secular and democratic constitution based on freedom, equality and justice. The constitution grants religious freedom for adherents of other faiths (Sheridan & Groves, 1987). Every man is free to worship and preach the religion he professes. Although the constitution allows Islamic religious education in any educational institution which is being run by Government, but at the same time it does not prohibit the provision of religious education in any institution run by any religious community or private individuals. Islamic community has its own schools and colleges, which provide education to the children.

Conclusion

Thus in a long and chronicled history, we can notice that religious education had considerably been spread in Malaysia. The religious education not only slacked the intellectual thirst of the people but also played a vital role in the human and societal development. The most important aim, which was fulfilled through religious education, was the propagation of Islamic religious principles. From the viewpoint of administration, it was essential on the part of the rulers to acquaint their subjects with their religion, civilization and language.

REFERENCES

Argyle, M. (1959). *Religious behaviour.* New York: Free Press.

Benson, P.H. (1960. *Religion in contemporary culture: A study of religion through social sciences.* New York: Harper & Brother Publisher.

Bertholet, A. (1934). 'Religion'. *Encyclopaedia of Social Sciences,* Vol. 13. New York: Macmillan Company.

Brown, C. C. (1970). *Sejarah Melayu* or Malay Annals, an annotated translation. Kuala Lumpur: Oxford University Press.

Brubacher, S.J. (1962). *Modern Philosophies of Education.* New York: McGraw Hill.

Cassidy, F.P. (1950). 'Religion'. *Encyclopedia of Educational Research,* W.W. Monroe (Ed.). New York: Macmillan Company.

Coe, G.A. (1928). *The motives of men.* New York: Charles Scribner's Sons.

Durkheim, E. (1916). The elementary forms of religious life: A study of Religion and Sociology. Translated by J.W. Swaine, London: George, Allan & Unwin Ltd.

Feurbach, L. (1957-Trans.) *The Essence of Christianity,* translated by George Elliott, New York.

Frazer, J.G. (1890). *The Golden Bough : A study in Magic and Religion.* Macmillan and Company, Reprinted in 1963.

Galloway, G (1914). *The Philosophy of religion.* Edinburgh.

Hashim, R. (2004). *Educational dualism in Malaysia- Implications for theory and practice.* Kuala Lumpur: The Other Press.

Hassan, A. J. (19830. Islamic education in Malaysia. *Muslim Education, 1,* 81-4.

Herberg, W. (1955). *Protestant, Catholic, Jew.* Reprinted by Doubleday Company, Inc., New York: p. 72-73.

Hill, A. H. (1969). *The Hikayat Abdullah: The autobiography of Abdullah bin Abdul Kadir* (1797-1854), an annotated translation. Kuala Lumpur; Oxford University Press.

Hook, S. (1946). *Education for modern man.* New York: The Dial Press. P. 109.

Jastrow, M. (1901). *A study of Religion.* New York: Charles.

Kim, K. K. (1980). Perkembangan Pelajaran Agama Islam (The development of Islamic religious education0. In A. H. Salleh

(Ed.), *Pendidikan ke arah perpaduan* (Education for unity), Kuala Lumpur: Penerbit Fajar Bakti, p.1.

Martineaue, J. (1888). *A study of religion.* Oxford: Clarendon Press.

McTaggort (1923). Some dogmas of religion. In R.H. Thouless: *An introduction to psychology of religion.* London: Cambridge University Press.

Nagata, J. A. (19840. *The reflowering of Malaysian Islam: Modern religious radicals and their roots.* Vancouver: University of British Columbia Press.

Pratt. J.B. (1945). *The religious consciousness: A psychological study.* New York: The Macmillan company.

Radhakrishnan, S. (1966). *Religion and society.* London: George Allen and Unwin Ltd.

Raichur, S.S. (1951). Religion in public education in India. *The Indian Journal of Educational Research.*

Raymond, A.W. (1952). The role of religion in higher education. *School and Society.*

Russell, B. (1917). *Why man fight.* New York: Century, p.116.

Russell, B. (1968). *Religion and Science.* London: Oxford University Press.

Sheridan, L. A. & Groves, H. E. (19870. *The constitution of Malaysia.* Singapore: Malayan Law Journal, Chapter 3 (1).

Siquera, T.M. (1943). *The education of India: History and problems.* Humphry: Milford Oxford University Press. P. 169.

Thouless, R.H. (1923). *An introduction to psychology of religion.* London: Cambridge University Press, (1961 Ed.)

Tylor, E.B. (1971). Primitive culture: Research into development of mythology, philosophy, religion, art and custom. London: Murray.

Whitehead, N.A. (1925). *Science and the modern world.* New York: Macmillan, pp. 257-68.

Whitehead, N.A. (1929). *The aims of education – and other essays.* New York. P.23.

Williams, J.P. (1946). *The new education and religion.* New York: Association Press

2

Religious Education : What is it for ?

Daryl S. Paulson

Introduction

The search to know Being has been a major preoccupation of humans ever since they could consciously differentiate themselves from their environment and, thus, be forced to leave "Eden" by waking up. Our forebears must have pondered, as we ponder, these questions: What made the universe. What is my relationship to it? Is there a deeper reality than just the physical "stuff" I see? What is the purpose of life? What is my purpose? Why is there so much suffering? What is death? These questions are important to us, but we move on to other, more pressing issues. Am I loveable, successful, powerful? Am I fitting in? Am I popular enough? Am I able to pay my bills?

As members of a progressive society, we are obsessed with fashion and style, racking up credit card debt to support compulsive needs to be in style. We scour fashion magazines for the latest trends to follow, focusing far more on what one is wearing than who one is. Michelle Lee, a contributor to many female fashion magazines, has labeled fashion-obsessed women as "speed chicks." Like hamsters running on an exercise wheel, they are stuck on the fashion wheel in an endless cycle of trying to be "in." Feeling "in" provides them a temporary high, but soon a "low" enshrouds them, prodding them to search for the next style.

There is nothing wrong with this glitter, except it promotes an action that does not work for humans, to completely overlay feelings of inadequacy with superficial remedies (Angyal, 1965). The superficial remedy is to buy ourselves into being adequate through glamour. But it does not work. Those brave souls who look inside for a moment find that they are riddled with self-doubts about being "enough," that is, looking good enough, acting good enough, and feeling good enough. This often triggers needs deeper than being enough. Deep human needs are to be loved, to be accepted, to be appreciated, cherished, and valued (Firman, 1996). But being aware of these deeper needs throws up even more self doubt, so we "don't go there," not until we have become so unhappy that dealing with our issues in psychotherapy becomes the only way out. And at this point, we are forced to encounter our being and its meaning. To feel the naked presence of ourselves in front of ourselves is very painful at first, but under the guidance of a competent and caring therapist, it can be the way to a new, authentic, and meaningful life course (Bugental, 1965).

Generally, we do not search for this – at least not until we have suffered and hurt, been betrayed, taken advantage of, or fired from a job, or seen parents, friends, and others die, and we can no longer hide the pressing reality that yes, we, too, will die. These crises have a way of serving as wake-up calls, pressing us to deeper "spiritual" exploration. Discovery of ways to nourish ourselves, throwing the superficial junk food of glitter and glamour away and begin to feed our souls with real substance is absolutely critical. But where does one start? Interestingly enough, it is generally in the intersubjective, shared values of organized religious groups.

Religions

Religions have been vitally important to humans throughout their history in providing meaning, purpose, and direction to their lives. Religions are grounded in the teachings of specific individuals – Shankara, Jesus, Moses, Mohammed, Buddha, Zoroaster – as well as specific spiritual groups. These teachings, over the centuries, have achieved mythic status and are probably best viewed from that perspective (Campbell, 1968). This does not mean religions are "made up," but rather they are best understood allegorically, rather than literally.

Mythic meaning operates not only in our conscious awareness but our unconsciousness, too. Religion resonates with both the conscious and unconscious in non-threatening ways, allowing us to stand back psychologically from our day-to-day lives to achieve deeper meaning by perceiving the timeless. Myths provide meaning to our past, purpose to our present, and positive direction to our future (Feinstein & Krippner, 1988). In many ways, myths are more real to our psyches than are objective facts, for they enable us to make sense out of the world by adding a container to hold these facts and explain them in ultimate terms. Myths, then, enable humans to describe, at least partially, that which is beyond description (Edinger, 1972).

Mythic meaning occurs on a continuum of psychological levels simultaneously, deep to surface. At deeper levels, religious myths address our deepest concerns, our highest aspirations, concerning existence (Anthony, Ecker & Wilber, 1987). At the surface levels, each religion portrays specific images of deities, as well as providing specific practices, personal and cultural. Religious myths attempt to reveal aspects of existence beyond mere physical survival. All myths, including religious myths, however, need to be revised periodically to remain relevant for humans in changing cultures such as ours, or they become mere dogma.

Brahma, Allah, God, Jehovah, and Tao represent shared images or concepts of the "Being of Beings" (Assagioli, 1965). The Being of Beings enables humans to derive positive meaning from life and the Beings have a connection with Being, providing purpose and direction. With purpose and direction, humans feel their existence is more than random chance where billions of humans try to survive each day, in the face of complete and utter absurdity. The vast amount of disease, hunger, suffering, indifference, hatred, violence, and injustice among humans is staggering (Brown, 1993). Many humans, particularly in third world countries, from the time they are born until they die, are fated to be without hope for more than a base physical existence, lacking adequate amounts of food, safe drinking water, medical treatment, education, physical protection from violence, or any way to transcend their life condition. The overwhelming inequalities seen in human life and utter poverty can motivate a person to give their life for at least some cause they perceive as noble and honorable. As in the medieval crusades, where one religion was the enemy of another, that same mindset occurs today for the "true believer" (Campbell, 1968). Religion, then, is the "life blood" providing meaning for billions of earth's inhabitants. Many contemporary intellectuals do not hold a shared belief in any deity or underlying purpose of the Universe as depicted by traditional religions. Even the hardest core, card-carrying scientists do not live by biochemical reactions alone, but through meaning (Grof, 1998). Science, for them, is "God," perhaps a substitute God, but a God nonetheless, who provides meaning to their lives. For most humans, religion also provides a "ready-made" ethical/moral system by which to live. Followers regulate, or try to regulate, themselves based on these teachings, telling them right from wrong. For the masses of people, external guidance in moral behavior is clearly warranted.

Outsiders

The world's greatest spiritual beacons promoted care and concern for human beings, social status, wealth, or race. When their compassionate insights were venerated, their inclusive, open altruism was restricted to the religious group, a situation that exists to this day. It occurs when members of a religious group demonstrate care and concern exclusively for that group's members and, at best, indifference to those outside the group. Often, the outsiders are viewed as "enemy."

Pitram Sorokin, in the 1950s, was very concerned about this phenomenon he termed "tribal altruism." In his words, "an exclusive tribal solidarity – known as tribal patriotism, tribal loyalty, and tribal altruism – has mercilessly set man against man, and group against group. It has killed more human beings and destroyed more cities and villages than all the epidemics, hurricanes, storms, floods, earthquakes, and volcanic eruptions taken together. It has brought upon mankind more suffering than any other catastrophe" (1954, p. 461).

Look around; you can see the rampant effects of tribal altruism: political regimes struggle against political regimes, religions against religions, races against races, and cultures against cultures. Although religious intolerance has not mellowed globally, weapons of mass destruction have become easier to obtain, and religious zealots who would use them against the competition – other religions – seemingly have proliferated, it is in humanity's best interests that individuals – not clergy or clerics – return to the sources of these spiritual truths and interpret them for themselves. Seekers would discover that these truths are about caring, not vengeful actions, which, although real, are generally anecdotal incidents then used as propaganda for religious and political purposes. As the planet becomes more crowded, it is important, not just for quality of life, but human survival, to get beyond petty and exclusive in-group religions. Perhaps a meta-religion – a religion of religions – that encompasses all religions would be useful (Rishabhchand, 1959). A very difficult undertaking this would be, particularly because it would force entrenched dogmas to change, and that would be threatening to the many closed religions. But to continue on as we are is no longer an alternative. Take, for example, the often hostile relations of Christianity, Islam and Judaism. These three religions are fundamentally related, splitting off centuries ago down different paths, each proclaiming itself to be absolute truth. The founders, Christ, Mohammed, and Moses, predominantly promoted peace, equality of justice, tolerance,* and understanding, but the religious bureaucracies evolved into formal sects that became (and still are) as brutal as any nonreligious group has ever been. These groups see violent means as fulfilling the ends; it is God's will to slay nonbelievers. This is shallow mockery of God. God created the universe, keeps the planets on course, develops complex life forms, and is surely beyond the reflective Freudian superego view based in human intolerance, cultural prejudice, and self-righteous emulation (Jacoby, 1985). It is utter religious narcissism.

Religions could not exist without providing groups something. That something, all too often, is security at the price of one's personal responsibility to engage life authentically (Whitmore, 1991). Shared meaning is much stronger than personal meaning, which can give way to agonizing existential anxiety, the anxiety of not knowing for sure what is. Now this, in no way, condemns intersubjective culturally shared values and meaning. For a vision to manifest, it often requires that like-minded individuals constantly reinforce each other's meaning, which is precisely what occurs in groups.

This can be both beneficial and destructive. Many destructive issues, concepts and theories are collectively shared, which, from a Jungian point of view, are termed shadow material. That is, they are consciously unacknowledged, even denied, views projected psychologically onto others. A classic example is the shadow material projected onto Jews who became scapegoats for the Nazis to justify the problems – economic, political, and cultural – that Germans faced. The United States' foreign policy has projected its own darker (unexamined) side onto many third world states, including those in the Middle East. For example, waging a war on Iraq to free the enslaved citizens is the acceptable persona image. But, in reality, more sinister motives – oil, removing governments we do not like, promoting our form of democracy over the world, and attempting to fragment opposition – all are parts of the shadow mix. We certainly are not the only ones to do this. France is trying to carve a position of power in the European Union by trashing the United States and aligning with Germany and Russia. Israel does this to the non-Semitic Arab states, and Arab states do it to Israelis. Nothing is as it is presented; it is always self-preserving and self-fulfilling to each nation. This is a continuous problem of recurring nationalism made worse because the countries projecting their shadows onto other countries stir the masses. A new enemy is always on the horizon (Emmons, 1999).

Group or collective actions can be tremendously beneficial from a religious perspective. Much of the early settling in the United States by the Europeans was based on collective action. But it, too, can be detrimental. It can lead to forcing one's religion onto others, who are content with their own. For example, much of the aid given to Iraq by Christian aid groups included proselytizing Christianity by including bibles. Who said Iraq needed Christianity?

At this time, it is not political systems against political systems, but religious systems against religious systems that cause the greatest strife (Boorstein, 1997). A true believer can commit nearly any atrocity in the name of religion, and a society of "true believers" can wreak worldly havoc.

Collective religious behavior can be very positive, but it can just as easily be destructive. Spurred on by pious self concepts, religions are particularly prone to acting out their shadows. The Catholic Church's Inquisition in the Middle Ages is a prime example. This pogromic behavior has been repeated recently in the form of Catholic and Protestant inter-religious violence in Ireland, the ethnic murder of the Serbs by Croatians in the Balkans, Israeli violence against Palestinians, and their violence against Israelis, and on and on and on. One wonders if humanity might have been better off without any religions; this is something to ponder seriously and openly.

Inter-Religious Strife

Let us now change focus from inter-religious strife and look at some specific intra-religion problems, particularly with personality disordered leaders. The Catholic Church recently has been plagued with revelations of priests committing sexual offenses, often homosexually with boys. Although such acts in no way condemn the religion, they do point to serious psychological disorders among the clergy (Carson, Butcher, & Mineka, 2000). Advocates of priests marrying argue that there are a disproportionate number of clinical level psychopathologies, as presented in the DSM-IV-TR Axis I: Clinical Syndromes. They argue most heterosexual/homosexual persons prefer to have regular sexual relations with consenting partners. Complete abstinence from sex, while not always, can be an indicator of sexual disorders.

There is certainly no assurance that high levels of piety assure low levels of sexual misconduct. Perhaps the Catholic Church's absolute failure to deal with sex other than as a means of procreation, and its utter dogmatic stance against most forms of birth control, opens it to denying the existence of its sexual shadow (Jung, 1962). It does not appear that this will change any time in the near future, so perhaps priests will be forced to go further underground, continuing to hide psychopathology by denial, bureaucratic maneuvers, and censorship.

Charismatic Leaders

Let us now turn our attention to religious groups centered on high-profile charismatic leaders. Most recall Jerry Falwell's repeated sexual misconducts, as well as the greed and opulence of Jim and Tammy Faye Baker. But let us discuss a more egregious incident (Anthony, Ecker, Wilber, 1984).

By far, one of the most shocking incidents occurred in Jonestown, Guyana, in 1978, when about 900 followers of Reverend Jim Jones committed mass suicide. Jones, a dynamic and energetic individual with tremendous personal charisma, had instituted many positive initiatives and shared values among the members of his group, the People's Temple. But slow subtle changes occurred community-wide, as members became ever more isolated from the greater society and from outside friends and culture. By accepting Jones' sociopolitical ideology, group members, over time, became increasingly fearful of outsiders, which promoted greater isolation. When a visiting U. S. Congressman was killed at the airport by Temple guards, the long-standing decree by Jones of a noble death was enacted: drinking cyanide-laced Kool-Aid.

Religious problems like this are reasonably common. It is important, then, that humans not turn themselves over, heart and soul, to religious systems or leaders. This form of independence is possible only when people accept responsibility for their lives. But, this is a tremendous burden and responsibility. It is far easier to turn one's life over to another through what Rollo May (1953) has termed "the divine right to be taken care of." It does not work.

Material Aspects

Let's turn our attention to the personal objective level – the material aspects of religion – one's body and one's behavior. For many, the body is but a vehicle for sins; for others, it is a temple most high, to be cherished and appreciated during this earthly life. In truth, it has both aspects. At variance within the body are religious beliefs and biological drives, personal and interpersonal shared subjective interpretations versus hard-wired biological imperatives. Religious beliefs, like all beliefs, are constructed human concepts and interpretations. The body and its drives are biological pregivens. Viewed exclusively from one domain – subjective or objective – the other domain becomes the enemy. So from a subject religious view, my sexual drives to have sex with any woman who appeals to me is outright lust, driven by Satan. So I split my good self (religious self) from my evil self (biological, amoral self). I then live as a religious persona, denying my biological shadow self (Jung, 1962). The shadow self does not vanish, but instead, operates outside of my awareness. It rears its head in social situations when I encounter desirable women. But I then push all the harder to keep my biological self out of awareness. I soon am at war with myself. And to my chagrin, by denying my biological self, I allow myself to occasionally act out my sexual drives, rationalizing it as sharing spiritual insights, pleasing a desperate woman, or perhaps even "crazy wisdom."

Conversely, from the biological perspective, my religious self may be viewed as a hang-up, a Puritanical remnant that must be purged. My biological drives are natural and, thus, I should express them. But as I strive to eat well, play well, and make love well, I tend to feel off balance or lacking something. I feel full after eating, bored after playing, and tired after sex. My life becomes a series of meaningless circular events. So to counter this, I pick up the pace. To my horror, I feel empty and without meaning beyond sensation.

Neither of these extremes works well; I need both. I need to take care of my biological needs, but they need not be my sole focus. I also have psychospiritual needs as important to my well-being as biological needs. I need, as Maslow stated, to feel loved and cared for as I am. I need to feel a sense of contribution, to feel I am somehow aiding humanity and, because I am alive, the world is a slightly better place. I need to feel a connection with the mystery of being. Perhaps I am just an assemblage of the rocks and mud of this planet. But as an assemblage, I am rock and mud aware of itself and aware of being aware. I am that portion or aspect of the universe actually aware of the universe. Perhaps I am on an external path of self-discovery and will discover I, like everything else, am absolute spirit in form. But I need to do this from the perspective of a Great Adventure. I need to see and experience for myself and form my own relationship with the Mystery of Mysteries (Grof, 1988). There are people everywhere telling me what is, what to believe, how to act, how to think, and how to attain truth. On my great journey, I know these people and systems to be partially helpful, but not the focus of the great journey. I do not go to the Grand Canyon to see the world's largest snake at a Mom and Pop's four-animal zoo and buy trinkets. I don't need someone else's system to define the great journey. They are but hints, some valuable and some not, on my search. For me, then, being a mortal, limited human being, the grand purpose of life is intricately woven into the great journey. Like a trip to Taj Mahal, each individual on the great journey forms his/her own relationship with the terrain – the Mystery of Mysteries.

But self-absorption into a subjective relationship with the Mystery of Mysteries cannot be the exclusive goal. Grounding insights into service is also important (Assagioli, 1965; Vaughan, 2000). It is the body that provides humans a vehicle to serve others with applied wisdom in action. Clearly, the existent world is in need of grounded insightful service. It is easy to talk of contributing something of oneself to make a better world; it is another to pursue it through objective action. Over the long history of human development, some individuals have done so, in error. The Buddha, Mohammed, Christ, and Theresa of Avilla are examples. These heroic individuals did not isolate themselves from the existent world but, as Goodrich (1962) has stated, engaged it on their own terms. These were people who made things happen. They were in touch with the Mystery and acted on its call, not to slaughter humans, but to give them hope and meaning. They were not concerned about opinion polls, staging, pretending, or ulterior motives. They were beacons of light in life's storms, and oases for true spiritual nourishment.

Subjective Experience

One's subjective phenomenological experience is crucial to a well-lived life – how one experience and interprets the world, what provides meaning, what causes joy and sorrow, one's ethical and moral grounding, and one's spiritual views and aspirations. An often minimized concept of spirit is existential spirituality. While it includes spiritual gnosis or direct experience with Being via a peak experience, meditation or an altered state of consciousness, it is not limited to these. For example, looking into the heavens on a clear night, seeing the countless glowing orbs and being awe-struck can be a spiritual experience (Underhill, 1930). Sitting on a stream bank, watching the stream cascading over the rocks, smelling the wet earth, the moss, and hearing the flies buzzing overhead can be a spiritual experience.

I use the term spiritual experience, instead of religious experience, for authentic subjective insights are one's experiences of Being. There are no props, no shoulds, no explanations, just experience. Countless numbers of individuals have discovered and developed an authentic relationship with God or the Universal Spirit in this way (Hillman, 1996).

There is no reason that all humans cannot experience an authentic encounter with Being. Many do not pursue that course, however, leaving their spiritual experience to the religious group to which they are bound. Those individuals who have had authentic spiritual experiences seem to emanate a groundedness, stability, and a knowing that others do not. Those experiencing Being describe it as not separate from themselves, but their very core essence. For example,

- The Kingdom of Heaven is within you (Christ/ Christianity).
- He who knows himself knows God (Mohammed/Islam).
- He and he become one entity (Abulafia/Judaism).
- You are It (Yanti, Roshi, Zen).
- Look within; You are Buddha (Nakashima/Buddhism).
- You (Atman) and God (Brahmin) are the same (Vivekananda/Hinduism) (Chaudhuri, 1965; Cortright, 1997).

Now I doubt if any of those just-quoted viewed himself as God in totality. Instead, they viewed Universal spirit as at once self and other, as well as beyond humans. It is transcendent and eminent (Fingarette, 1963).

The Great Search for the Mystery often begins as an outward search. Initially, we try to find it in our "perfect" ideals (Daniels & Horowitz, 1976). We seek it in our parents when we are young, in our teachers and friends in grade school, in boy/girlfriends in junior high and high school, in romance and sex and money after college, in our marriages and careers, and in affairs, bouts with drugs, and perhaps even several changes in religion later in our lives. Vivekananda (1953) stated our situation profoundly:

> After long searches here and there, in temples and in churches, on earth and in heaven, at last you come back to your own soul, completing the circle from where you started, and find that He whom you have been seeking all over the world, for whom you have been weeping and praying in churches and temples, for whom you were looking as the mystery of all mysteries, shrouded in the clouds, is the nearest of the near, is your own Self, the reality of your life, body, and soul. That Self is your own nature. Assert it, manifest it. You are not to become pure; you are pure already. You are not to become perfect; you are that already (pp. 214-215).

This certainly does not mean that all our actions are perfect. Instead, our true core Being is perfect right now. The problem is most individuals do not know it exists, let alone are aware of it. Our being is said to be layered like the skins of an onion. The "surface" self is the most familiar to us. It consists of a series of roles or personas, each required for certain social situations. One may be a husband, a wife, sexy, tough, intelligent, sophisticated, a parent, a child, or a victim, depending upon the situation. This surface level is absolutely critical to smooth interpersonal functioning. For example, an employee role is beneficial when at work dealing with one's supervisor. One knows how to survive, even thrive, in the constructed rule/role work system. Without it, it is doubtful if one could even have a job. One would constantly challenge the system (Paulson, 1993).

Beneath the surface, self is the personal self. It is the part of us that chooses what role to play in a life situation. For far too many people, it is unknown, for the most part. Instead of attempting to discover what we like, want, and perceive in the world, we attempt to fit in and blend. In point of fact, the personal self is foreign. We do not feel comfortable with it, because we do not know it. And there is another reason. To know ourselves, we must deal with ourselves, and that means acknowledging and dealing with repressed and suppressed aspects of our being that we deny exist – for they are not acceptable (Bandura, 1997). However, if one works through this level, one's deeper Self, transpersonal Self, or Soul, the next level, becomes available.

Another important subjective aspect is self-volition. In life, unless we direct our insights to action, nothing happens (Bridges, 1980). Neutral insights do not have emotional energy, so the project never gets done. It is important for each individual to discover what is worth doing and even dying for, if required. This search is like Nietzche's "will to power," or will to self-direction, or self-empowerment. For example, if we are unhappy, feel at a dead end, or in a rut, no one can change our lives other than ourselves. No change occurs until one steps forward in spite of gut-wrenching fear and sets an authentic, original life course for themselves. This is tough, particularly in that it raises anxiety over change. Any change – positive or negative – tends to create anxiety (Beck & Emery, 1985).

Many individuals who have set an authentic course find a new problem: control. They strive to stay in control of their life situations, which is positive. This aspect is so important that many counselors focus their efforts on helping clients learn how to control their lives. Sometimes, people become control addicts and will go to great lengths to maintain control, no matter what (Shapiro & Astin, 1998). But this is self-defeating, because no one can be totally in control over anything. Individuals can learn a valuable control strategy using both active and "letting go" control. Active control is used in situations one can directly affect, and "letting go" control is release in situations that are beyond their direct influence (Shapiro & Astin, 1998). Yet, letting go is not having no control. Instead, it is the control of accepting, or letting go into one's sense of "Being." So, while we try to protect ourselves, we also realize we can only do so much. In letting go of personal control, when appropriate, we acknowledge that life has its own demands, and we put ourselves in the hands of the Way, or the Force, or "Being." In doing so, we are less likely to cling to the way life should be and, instead, adapt to life situations as they are encountered.

Violence

The world is a violent place. Both violence and the fear of violence have increased dramatically over the years (Hall & Whitaker, 1999; Whitaker, 2000). Individuals fear the all-too real drive-by shootings, hate crimes, gang wars, school killings, and the new threat – terrorism on one's own soil.

The purpose of terrorist acts is not so much overt destruction as to create fear, uneasiness, tension, and paranoia. And as lulls occur, when no violence takes place, it does not reduce anxiety but makes us apprehensive. We wait for the other shoe to drop, to experience what violence is next. Because people are not sure who the terrorists are, nearly everyone becomes a suspect.

It does not take long to see the widespread effects specific incidents of terrorism produce throughout our population, nor does it take long for the security and predictability we desire from life to vanish. Chaos appears to be the only truth, as positive meaning, values, and feelings of permanence evaporate.

Human Suffering

The Upanishads argued that much human suffering is due to making permanent in one's mind what is impermanent, and clinging to that impermanence, as though it were permanent. For example, many of us feel we will be rewarded (i.e., have a good life) for hard work, saving money, raising children, and being responsible. A good life for most of us is being respected, feeling safe, feeling loved, and being financially secure. But the reality for the vast majority of us is an unexpected divorce, an accidental death of a spouse, loss of a job, children who reject not only our values, but us as well, little money on which to retire, and death by a lingering and expensive illness. Not surprising, when these life events occur, we strive to make up for the loss, believing we can alter events and re-make our lives the way they are "supposed to be."

Truth is, there is no permanency in our earthly lives. Our lives are influenced by innumerable outside agencies, most we do not even perceive, much less control. Life actually is not this or that pregiven course, but instead, whatever circumstances we face at the moment.

This, in no way, means that we should not plan our life's course and look forward to the future. Instead, it means it is a fallacy to project permanence onto what is not. We should plan and work for a "desired life" but deal with our life circumstances as they arise (Daniels & Horowitz, 1976).

Many psychologists, theologians, and philosophers have taken this view. As Martin Heidegger (1962) stated, in encountering "Being," one must learn to accept "what is." One simply cannot live authentically according to what "should be." This existential worldview is also a fundamental one in cognitive psychotherapy and counseling. One may worry about all sorts of perils and problems that can occur, but one can deal only with the actual issues one faces in living.

As our own society becomes ever more ethnically and culturally diverse, and the world society is brought into our living rooms with many different cultures, we are challenged to receive different worldviews with tolerance, acceptance, and respect. It was not that long ago that most of us dealt mainly with Christian worldviews, but no longer. We now are increasingly exposed to Buddhists, Muslims, Hindus, and Judaists, who bring aspects of their core religious beliefs to our world. Humans are capable of developing psychospiritually beyond a fundamentalist level in order to tolerate different religious viewpoints without being personally threatened. We are able to work through our fear that, if my religion is not the "absolute and, therefore, only truth," it is nothing. One way to approach this problem was presented by Roberto Assagioli (1973), the founder of Psychosynthesis, modified from Hegel's work. He found an effective way to work with individuals of different religious beliefs was through a synthetic process, integrating the opposite belief poles to a higher—more inclusive—level, that of synthesis (see Figure 1). This is the Socratic method of the dialectic process – thesis, antithesis, and synthesis.

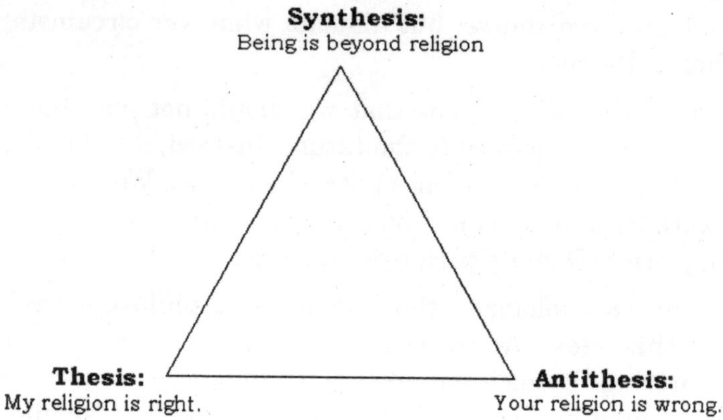

Fig. 1. Dialectic Process

For example, a person may view his/her own religion as the whole truth (thesis), and the other religions as false (antithesis). From this position, with no common ground, there is an impasse. What is needed is transcendence of this adversarial, thesis-antithesis position such that all religions can be included at the level of "Being." For it is Being for which we really search. At this more inclusive level, one sees that all the major religions – Hindu, Buddhist, Zen, Taoism, Islam, Judaism, and Christianity – come together in valuing the experience of Being, as well as providing creative, expressive channels for Being.

Conversely, elimination of the spiritual domain from life – a relatively common practice – is, in my view, repressing the sublime. The result is the loss of Soul, or one's essence, a condition so prevalent in these postmodern times.

Those who have succeeded in dealing with their psychospiritual issues generally become more spiritually integrated, grounding their personal, temporal lives in the stability and security centered in Being (Paulson, 2001). Many of these individuals are not "religious," clinging to a traditional belief, but instead, having experienced "Being" directly, report it to be larger, more real, and more meaningful than their personal, mundane lives.

As discussed earlier, the self-Being relationship is perceived in a variety of ways. For example, it has been perceived as being at one with the infinite, as aligning one's purpose with the Universal Force or Way, or even as recognizing a deeper, more inclusive relationship with oneself. The self-Being connection is not a cognitive construction, but a phenomenological reality. Those who have experienced this relationship *know* that they have gnostically connected with their source of Being. But recognition and experience of Being are generally not enough. Many experiencers also strive to ground and apply gnostic insights gained from experiencing Being into their daily lives. Being infuses them with the strength to help not only themselves but others. Additionally, once individuals connect with Being, their life values tend to change. They tend to do less "political" staging and more authentic connecting with the environment, others, and themselves.

Ironically, individuals who have consciously discovered this Self-Being connection often find it in a "place" of psychological pain. It was difficult at first to experience "Being," they say, because they were not only unaware of its existence, but also, that to reach Being, they had to deal with their psychological pains, fears, vulnerabilities, aloneness, depression, self-hatred, guilt, or feelings of meaninglessness (Moore, 1992). But, many state, it was in this very pain and aloneness that they discovered a "full" place within themselves, a place of "Being."

One of the greatest side benefits afforded those who have found "Being" is that "old plans" for living fall away. Rather than demanding a very predictable, safe life, they are better able to accept whatever life situations they encounter. Like others, they want their plans to work out and their lives to be happy at all times, but they do not cling to these wishes. They view good and bad, right and wrong, as relative positions, instead of being absolute, diametrically opposed conditions. That is, events do not exist in independent, absolute categories of good or bad. Instead, they are relative, dependent upon one's viewing point in life. So, for example, a nice sunny day may be termed good for a picnic, but bad for a farmer in need of rain.

Another characteristic worth mentioning is that these individuals tend to view life as if it were a school in which they learn, experience, and grow (Assagioli, 1965). This perspective is vastly different from that of individuals who desire to escape the unpleasantries of life.

Individuals who have aligned with Being are also less concerned about being killed, for example, in terrorist plots, or in a drive-by shooting. That is not to say that they have no fear of death. They do. But they also are infused with Being, which provides them a greater sense of meaning and purpose, so worrying about death is not a high priority. Their lives have meaning, and channeling this meaning into purpose is what matters most to them.

Interestingly enough, individuals who have aligned with Being are not necessarily above committing violence, themselves. If they are attacked, they will fight back. They have no fear of using firearms, physical force, or larger actions to prevent and eliminate violence, when they feel it appropriate. But they are not psychologically stuck at this level, either. They willingly look to transcend violence and work actively at solving differences in ways mutually satisfying and beneficial to those involved.

The Flow of Subjective and Objective Components in One's Personal Life

While most appreciate the value of theories, integral religion, to a large degree, deals with Dasein, being in the world. This requires facing at times the hard issues of life: the unfairness of life, the finality of death, the despair of divorce, the pain of betrayal, the grief of losing an intimate other, the anguish of trying to establish a quality life after a felony conviction, and the terror of facing a terminal disease. And who has not tried to console a friend, to help him/her grow psychospiritually, only to watch him/her drift back into a worldview of meaninglessness—back to where he/she began. Such times are hard, particularly when feeling one is in a "spiritual desert," not knowing where to go for nourishment. And even those who do find positive meaning through religious fellowship run a real risk of splitting their lives into two compartments, spiritual and mundane, thereby making it very difficult to live authentically and impossible to live integrally. Finding satisfying answers to these difficult problems are not usually easy, because one often does not completely perceive the situation.

Most find their personal and cultural psychological defence mechanisms incapable of masking both their awareness and their pain. This is rarely the situation of the general public, who are secure in the established roles, rules, and taboos of the culture – that is, until they have a close brush with death, confront a serious illness, or lose their life's meaning. Then their cultural and personal defences no longer work for them either. Individual psychotherapy and group counseling can be immensely helpful in assisting these "wounded" individuals and so can a religious grounding.

Humans commonly will not directly confront "Being," unless they are in crisis. In these cases, one is open to a deep encounter with "Being," or more generally, "what is." Encountering "Being" is a quest for self-understanding, allowing one to understand "Being" directly. Several core themes are often encountered in the search for "Being." First, the encounter is authentic and personal and, at once, imminent and transcendent. The shared group beliefs to explain "what is" no longer satisfy. Instead, one needs to encounter "what is" directly. And, in order to do this, one must allow whatever material is present in the unconscious to emerge to consciousness. This is can be a very painful process. But it not needless suffering. It is working through one's shadow.

Additionally, most persons, at least in western industrialized cultures, have been over-enculturated. They have literally been programmed to act the "right way," to go to the "right places," and be with the "right people," in order to gain or retain social status. While there is much value in enculturation—in fact, it is necessary—it can be overly restrictive to a person's authentic sense of being.

To counteract this, a person needs to listen to one's own authentic voice for counsel (Arbuckle, 1975). Many listen to the superego—society, parents, or other authority figures—in order to make decisions, to act, and to feel responsible. This is fine for some individuals, but for those who are in touch with "Being," it is not satisfying.

Paul Tillich (1952), an existential theologian, stated that authentic spirituality is a passion for encountering the Infinite – one's ultimate concern. Existential encounters with "Being" are not centered outside oneself, but within one's "being." And these experiences have little to do with academic or religious cognitive knowledge but, rather, occur through a direct phenomenological experience with "Being." Authentic encounters with one's Self require a committed, conscious relationship with the very source of one's "Being."

In seeking a direct encounter with "Being," one is advised to begin the search where one is in one's life, instead of where one thinks one should be. And where one is in one's life depends upon one's previous encounters with Being, if any, as well as one's inner values, beliefs, life experiences, life goals, and present aspirations.

In searching for one's own truth, it is important to respect the "great ones" – Krishna, the Christ, the Buddha, and the Prophet Mohammed, for example – but also, to acknowledge that one must find out for oneself "what is." In this process, one experiences, often for the first time, what it feels like to be oneself authentically—down to even what one's arms, legs, and teeth feel like from within. Additionally, what one authentically feels and values in one's life is critically important to finding positive meaning. And it is important to be honest in how one feels about this or that, not how one should feel.

Some people claim that, as their encounters with "Being" progress, they are metaphorically able to "rest"—to let go—into this being and to just "be." When issues surface to consciousness, one is free to attend them or not attend them, depending upon one's choice. And, over time, as previously suppressed and repressed painful emotional issues surface to consciousness are dealt from a position of where one is, genuine insights from one's source of "Being" also surface to consciousness, making the entire process deeply valuable to self-acceptance and understanding.

Direct conscious confrontation with ultimate concerns and ultimate meaning usually generates tremendous amounts of anxiety, for one does not know for certain where this exploration will lead: Will I find any positive meaning at all, or will I be sent into a spiralling, downward trajectory to meaninglessness and utter despair. And these become critical concerns. Many seekers, at this point of exploration, feel utterly alone, as if they were in a blinding snow blizzard or surrounded by a thick, heavy, dark fog, unable to perceive anything clearly, and unable to gain any sense of groundedness (Jung, 1962). This anxiety situation is not just tension; it is total gut-wrenching and all-consuming terror and confusion. There appears to be nowhere to go for escape, for one is stuck in a no-exit situation. At this point, one has gone too far to turn back. There is no ready-made belief system to which to subscribe now, only confrontation with the unknowable, absolute aloneness, and complete despair (Vaughan, 1995).

This period of the exploration has been called the "Dark Night of the Soul" or the "Night Sea Journey," for one is not only alone, but "all" is unknown (Campbell, 1971). A common metaphor reported is feeling as though one is on some dark planet in a dark and cold corner of the universe, where one is utterly alone and totally abandoned. There is no one to know how one feels or that one even existed (Angyal, 1965). One's meaning, direction, and purpose evaporate. Nothing makes sense. All appears to be lost. Yet one must continue the journey into the unknowable (Campbell, 1968).

Raw courage is needed just to breathe. One knows he/she cannot go back either. It is at this point where traditional existential encounters stop. That is, one is stuck in the closed jaws of the universe that has no meaning, no purpose. In this universe, one clearly moves forward every day to annihilation. One must face this death and destruction alone in a meaningless world with which they have no way of communicating. Yet in this utter aloneness, one is free to choose the way one faces the absurdity of life.

I, personally, do not think traditional existentialists went far enough in exploring this encounter with "Being." A surprising number of individuals have found that, within this apparent chaos and aloneness, a deeper, more solidly grounded Self emerges, like the Phoenix from its own ashes. This deeper Self knows things "for sure," and the individual, through the ego, comes to know that the Self does know things for sure. Individuals experiencing the Self ultimately perceive the day-to-day egoic self as being a part of this larger Self, with which they can communicate, and that knows their fears, hopes, aspirations, and values (Assagioli, 1965). This Self, while not generally interpreted as the "Ground of Being" in any absolute sense, is perceived to be a direct link to, as well as a part of the Universal All (Washburn, 1994, 1995). In fact, many individuals no longer feel a need to contact any Absolute Ground of Being, once they discover this aspect of themselves. They feel connected "enough" with "what is" through this Self-sense, a relationship that provides not only relief from groundlessness, but also an existential *knowing* of "what is." That knowing is sufficient not only to bring meaning into their lives, but literally to infuse their lives with it.

When one is in connection with this deeper Self, to one's amazement, one realizes there is no set of spiritual goals to pursue, directions to follow, or techniques to use. There is, however, a growing ability to experience this Self sense directly and ultimately as one's own Being. This is not a symbolic form of oneself, but a constantly emerging "Being-ness."

This deeper Self sense is not perceived by the experiencer as emotionally needy, controlling, directing, judgmental, or self-righteous. In fact, an overwhelming majority of subjects I have studied report that this Self-sense seems not to care if one even listens to its voice (Paulson, 1995). But those who do take the time to listen hear its soft, friendly, and accepting voice, clear in revealing truth.

This Self sense is not bound by tradition, sets of rules, roles, or taboos, nor does it make them. It is creative, authentic, and wise, knows what troubles the individual, and is accepting. Direct contact with this Self sense is truly a sublime event, but also a mundane event. Through this Self sense connection, one intuits or, rather, knows that *everything* is as it should be.

Some individuals state that this deeper Self sense becomes greater than the individual self. They prefer to call this their *Source of Being*, which they generally state is the "life-giving mystery" beyond any Self-sense, yet not separate from it. By merely becoming aware of that mystery directly, they feel grounded and solid within their lives. It is like being fed or supplied nourishment from the "river or spring of life."

Authentic Spirituality as A Rite of Passage

While there are no directions on the wall one must follow in the spiritual process of discovering "Being," there is a general viewing frame that seems to be useful to those individuals I have studied (Paulson, 1994). This perspective greatly assists the seeker in dealing with unknown circumstance over an unknown period of time (Campbell, 1968; Feinstein & Krippner, 1988; Paulson, 1994; Vaughan, 1995; Walsh, 1990). It is that of viewing the path to the discovery of "Being" as an initiation or a rite of passage. When a person's life situation is viewed as a rite of passage, that perspective can aid in self-discovery (who one is), in life direction (where one is going), and in purpose (why the passage is necessary) (Feinstein & Krippner, 1988; Paulson, 1998). Charles Taylor (1989) argues that without a framework or horizon to orient oneself in life, one is essentially adrift and disoriented. Such frameworks are absolutely necessary for humans, according to Taylor. And the perspective of a rite of passage provides that frame.

Meaning operates not only in one's consciousness, but outside it as well. The meaning carried outside our awareness has a powerful effect on how we feel, think, and act. The way in which we act or live may be thought of as our personal mythology (Feinstein & Krippner, 1988). In the sense in which I use myths, they are not mere stories, but constellations of beliefs, feelings, and behaviors organized around a central, core theme. These constellations may help or hinder us in comprehending our lives in meaningful ways, but they can also provide connection to the universe (Edinger, 1972).

Many mythological stories portray a central person (the hero) as going through a rite of passage, or initiatory experience, alone. To a large degree, those trying to uncover an authentic spiritual path also feel alone. Some individuals often will not understand their feelings or the significance of going through the journey's experiences. But they will identify with the hero in mythic stories, and so be able to better understand their own situation and its meaning.

As Jungian analysts have long argued, when one is given an analogy or a story to help explain their life situation, they can stand away from the drama of their lives and better incorporate useful personal meaning from the story. Viewing the life experience as a "rite of passage" does not make the experience any easier, but it provides meaning, and the strength to move into and engage the experience, instead of avoiding it.

Throughout life, humans experience many periods of joy and pain. Usually, people are so afraid of losing control and being gobbled up by painful experiences that they do not learn anything of value from them, except avoidance (Peterson & Nisenholz, 1999). For example, Ann, a 39-year-old mother of two, discovered that her husband of 19 years was "in love" with a 21-year-old woman and had been having an affair with her for over a year. Ann wanted to work it out, but her husband complained she was no longer exciting and told her he wanted a divorce. Ann was devastated. Her husband was her life. She panicked; what would she do? She was terrified that she would be *alone* for the rest of her life and unable to support herself and her children. She searched frantically for another man to fill the void and remarried within nine months. Now, three years later, she is unhappy, fearful of rejection, obsessed with looking good and doing the right think. Ann learned nothing from her experience, other than to avoid it. She continues to block any emotional or conscious mental contact with the experience.

Ann chose to avoid emotional suffering, but periods of suffering are often very valuable. During these times, important, unique lessons are learned, helping one to grow psychologically as well as spiritually (Egan, 1998). By coping directly with the pain, not just feeling it, one can develop new, more effective abilities for dealing with life, build self-confidence by handling difficult problems, and ultimately, achieve wisdom.

Christian (and non-Christian) spiritual leaders, over the centuries, have considered human life a "school" (Harvey, 1998; Underhill, 1930). Here, on this earth in our human bodies, we have the opportunity to learn to handle a variety of life situations, many with which we initially felt unable to cope. Yet, life continually pushes us on to further growth, particularly in learning the futility of clinging to any set view, situation, or experience. From this viewpoint, life is not conquered; instead, it is experienced fully and dealt with as it arises.

Rites of Passage

Literature across all cultures abounds with rites of passage stories or mythologies (Campbell, 1949, 1968; Goodrich, 1962; Metzner, 1988). For example, the search for the Holy Grail has been an inspiring Christian myth for centuries, usually overlooked by modern scrutiny. Jungians, however, have resurrected it recently, and it can be quite useful. It is important to understand that use of myths is not about mysticism, which attempts to transcend human life. Myth and mythic living, instead, connect spirit and body to live more fully in this life (Bridges, 1980). This concept is aligned with the works of Thomas Moore (1992) and James Hillman (1996) on soulful living—that is, seeing the spiritual in day-to-day life.

Joseph Campbell (1968) discovered that rites of passage consist of three sequential and invariant stages: (a) the separation or call, (b) the initiation, and (c) the return.

The Separation

The separation phase—also known as the call to adventure—signifies that destiny has called the individual to move from his or her present life situation into another. The call or separation phase consists of leaving the known and familiar and entering a transitional period, consisting of new and unknown aspects of life. One can either heed the call and go into the adventure, or refuse the call, as Ann did. Refusal does not necessarily mean one has regressed; it may mean simply that one is not ready for a life passage; one is not ready to move ahead.

All of us are "called" in life to face various life challenges or passages (Hillman, 1996). The call may take the form of going back to school, leaving an unfulfilling job, leaving a bad marriage, or trying to put one's life back in order after being betrayed and rejected by a loved one.

Often, one does not choose the life passage; it is literally thrown into a person's life. J. R. R. Tolkien's *The Hobbit* (1978), I find, is a wonderful source book for mythic living. Bilbo Baggins, a Hobbit and the main character, was utterly content to reside in Bag End, smoking pipeweed, unconcerned with knowing or experiencing any more of life. When Gandalf, the wizard (one's inner, greater, spiritual Self, also known as the Soul) visited him and tried to recruit him for an adventure, Bilbo quickly dismissed it, stating he did not want one. Yet, deep within, Bilbo wanted to go out into the world, to experience life beyond the Shire. He wished to see the great mountains, experience the pine trees and the waterfalls, explore caves, and wear a sword and shirt of mail. He was "called," and although he was scared, ultimately, he did accept the call. So it is with us. A new situation in life is unfamiliar, and therefore, by definition, it is threatening. We have grown comfortable with our behavior patterns and do not wish to change them. The call is a very anxiety-producing time, and, as pastoral counselors know, the divorced man or woman, beginning to date after twenty years of marriage, will tell how frightening it is. Yet, it is an exciting time, filled with a sense of adventure and expectation about what lies ahead (Bridges, 1980).

The Initiation

Once one has accepted the call, the initiation period begins. This period, very appropriately, has been called the "Dark Night of the Soul," "the Night Sea Journey," and the "Journey through

Hell" in Christian/Jungian literature. It truly can be a descent into the depths of despair, aloneness, and feeling abandoned, riddled with anxiety, meaninglessness, and, to appearances, is a "no-exit" situation. The initiation is the period during the rite of passage when one is faced with tests, obstacles, challenges, and battles. One is in a "new country," one is now alone with "Being." One also has no personal experience in meeting the new challenges thrown at them – the old ways no longer work. One must find effective ways of dealing with life, such as finding credible and reliable support people, counselors, and, eventually, "oneself" – one's personal "existential" Self, and that Self's connection to Being. So often, one is alien to one's true Self and, when it is glimpsed, the tendency is to withdraw, for it seems threatening (Assagioli, 1965). It is not recognized as "self," the real "Self." What we have been calling ourselves is usually a "false self," because it is a mixture of others' values that we believe to be our own.

During the initiation, when we are forced to act authentically in new ways, we feel naked, unsure of ourselves, and tentative about what direction to take. We no longer know what we value, whom or what we can trust, or where to put our faith. Religious literature, psychotherapy, meditation, physical exercise, accepting friends, and prayer can be of immense value during this period (Boorstein, 1997).

The initiation period is not a period when one feels good; one is not supposed to. One of the most problematic perceptions held by contemporary people is that handling a bad situation well should feel good (Shapiro & Astin, 1998). Not so! A bad situation, well-handled, will still feel bad. Just realizing this allows many individuals to gain confidence in their ability to handle new life situations, for they do not burden themselves with "false expectations" (Angyal, 1965; Fenichel, 1945).

Many people try to avoid life and its messiness, for example, by excelling in school so they can get a good job and bypass the problems of life faced by "the masses." Or, they may focus on being glamourous to get a "good spouse," one who will make them happy. And, to complete the cycle, they choose to send their children to private schools so that they, too, may avoid dealing with the messiness in life. Yet, for good or bad, we are all part of the human family—we are truly brothers and sisters.

The Return

Once the initiation has been completed, a person often thinks his or her life should get better "automatically." Usually, it does not, unless one integrates and grounds the initiatory experience in his or her daily life. Integration, then, is a critical phase that cannot be achieved until one stops avoiding one's life and participates in it fully. Fortunately, we can then learn valuable lessons from even the most tragic of circumstances.

Shirley, 40, and a mother of two teenagers, had just gotten off work about 5:15 p.m. It was a beautiful spring evening, and she was excited about attending her daughter's band concert. Just as she entered a two-lane highway headed toward home, she was hit head-on by a pickup truck that had drifted into her lane. Shirley was killed instantly from a crushed chest when the impact slammed her body into the steering wheel.

Her husband, Frank, was devastated when we met to discuss the accident. But Frank was not only grief-stricken by her death, he was guilt-ridden. He had "gone out with the boys" the week before, met a young woman, and, as one thing led to another, had sex. Unfortunately, to complicate the story, the woman had become pregnant. She told Frank she would go public unless he gave her $50,000.

Frank told his children about the affair so as not to be blackmailed, and settled with the woman for $5,000, plus an abortion. At this time, Frank was seriously contemplating suicide. But, fortunately, he chose to face his problems head-on. He dealt with his children as best he could, although they have yet to forgive him. He performed a series of visualization rituals in which he told his deceased wife how sorry he was for his mistake, and how much he still loved her. He learned that one-night-stands were not for him. Frank has gone out of his way to ground the lessons from the experience into his life by sharing with various people, for example, the importance of living in the "here and now" with their spouses, for it can all be over in a flash. Frank has authentic guilt and pain from the experience and has grown to become a different person—a more compassionate and understanding one. He is committed to giving something back to the world, instead of just taking from it.

The return phase of the life passage is not only an integration period, but one during which the person shares his or her new-found knowledge with others, as Frank has done. It is a period of service. One recognizes clearly that one is an integral part of the world, connected to God.

So it appears necessary that one learn to balance one's personal subjective (spiritual) life with shared views of others (religion), and ground or apply this knowledge in the world. Few of us are in the position to personally make a direct "world-changing difference," but each one of us can influence others close to us – family, friends, and co-workers. We can live with the integrity of living life based on our own truths, yet allow others to have their truths without belittlement, control, or coercion.

Conclusion

In conclusion, the works of Ken Wilber (2006) is a good place to stop. Wilber has incorporated three phases of spiritual life, first person, second person, and third person. These correspond to meditation, communing with God, and being in nature. In direct meditation, we can awaken as spirit. In a direct relationship, we can commune with Spirit. Finally, in contemplation, we notice and feel the entirety of this vast Kosmos. We truly have the three phases of spirit.

REFERENCES

Angyal, A. (1965). *Neurosis and treatment*. New York: John Wiley.

Anthony, D., Ecker, B., & Wilber, K. (1987). *Spiritual choices*. New York: Paragon.

Arbuckle, D. S. (1975). *Counseling and psychotherapy.* Boston: Allyn & Bacon, Inc.

Assagioli, R. (1965). *Psychosynthesis: A manual of techniques*. New York: Hobbs, Dorman.

Assagioli, R. (1973). *The act of will*. Viking: New York.

Bandura, A. (1997). *Self efficacy: The exercise of control*. New York: Freeman.

Beck, A. T. & Emory, G. (1985). *Anxiety disorders and phobias: A cognitive perspective*. New York: Basic.

Boorstein, S. (1997). *Clinical studies in transpersonal psychotherapy*. Albany: State University of New York Press.

Bridges, W. (1980). *Transitions*. Menlo Park, CA: Addison-Wesley.

Brown, M. (1993). *Growing whole*. New York: Harper-Collins.

Bugental, J. T. F. (1965). *The search for authenticity*. New York: Holt, Rhinehart, Winston.

Campbell, J. (1968). *The hero with a thousand faces*. Princeton, NJ: Princeton University Press.

Campbell, J. (1971). *The portable Jung*. New York, Viking Press.

Carson, R. C., Butcher, J. N., & Mineka, S. (2000). *Abnormal psychology and modern life*. Boston: Allyn and Bacon.

Chaudhuri, H. (1965). *Integral yoga*. London: George Allen & Unwin, Ltd.

Cortright, B. (1997). *Psychotherapy and spirit*. Albany: State University of New York Press.

Daniels, V., & Horowitz, L. J. (1976). *Being and caring*. San Francisco, CA: San Francisco Book Co.

Edinger, E. F. (1972). *Ego and the archetype*. New York: Putnam's Sons.

Egan, G. (1998). *The skilled helper*. Pacific Grove, CA: Brooks/Cole.

Emmons, R. A. (1999). *The psychology of ultimate concerns*. New York: Guilford Press.

Feinstein, D. & Krippner, S. (1988). *Personal mythology*. Los Angeles: Tarcher.

Fenichel, O. (1945). *The psychoanalytic theory of neurosis*. New York: Norton.

Fingarette, H. (1963). *The self in transformation*. New York: Basic.

Firman, J. (1996). *Self and self-realization*. Palo Alto, CA:

Goodrich, N. L. (1962). *Myths of the hero*. New York: Orion.

Grof, S. (1988). *The adventure of self-discovery*. Albany: State University of New York Press.

Grof, S. (1998). *The cosmic game*. Albany: State University of New York Press.

Hall, H. V., & Whitaker, L. C. (1999). *Collective violence*. Boca Raton, FL: CRC Press.

Harvey, A. (1998). *Son of man: The mystical path to Christ*. New York: Tarcher.

Heidegger, M. (1962). *Being and time*. San Francisco: Harper.

Hillman, J. (1996). *The soul's code*. New York: Random House.

Jacoby, M. A. (1985). *Longing for paradise*. Boston: Sigo Press.

Jung, C. G. (1962). *The collected works of Carl G. Jung*. Bollinger Series XX. Princeton, NJ: Princeton University Press.

Laquer, W. (1999). *The new terrorist*. New York: Oxford.

May, R. (1953). *Man's search for himself*. New York: W. W. Norton.

Metzner, R. (1988). *Opening to inner light*. Los Angeles, Tarcher.

Moore, J. (1992). *Care of the soul*. New York: Harper-Collins.

Nikhilananda, S. (1953). *Vivekananda: The yoga and other works*. New York: Ramakrishna-Vivekananda Center.

Paulson, D. S. (2001). The hard issues of life. *Pastoral Psychology*, 49(5), 385-394.

Paulson, D. S. (1993). Authentic integral living: The search for the real self. *Journal of the American Academy of Psychotherapists*, *30*(3), 58-65.

Paulson, D. S. (1994). *Walking the point: The Vietnam experience*. Plantation, FL: Distinctive Publishing.

Paulson, D. S. (1995). Integration of esoteric and transpersonal psychologies. *Journal of Esoteric Psychology*, 9(2), 118-131.

Peterson, J. V., & Nisenholz, B. (1999). *Orientation to counseling*. Boston: Allyn and Bacon.

Shapiro, D. H., Jr., & Astin, J. (1998). *Control therapy*. New York: John Wiley.

Sorokin, P. (1954). *The ways and power of love*. Boston: Beacon Press.

Taylor, C. (1989). *Sources of the self*. Cambridge, MA: Harvard Press.

Tillich, P. (1952). *The courage to be*. New Have, CT: Yale.

Tolkien, J. R. R. (1978). *The hobbit*. Boston: Houghton-Mifflin Company.

Underhill, E. (1930). *Mysticism*. New York: E. P. Dutton.

Vaughan, F. (1995). *Shadows of the sacred*. Wheaton, IL: Theosophical Publishing House.

Vaughan, F. (2000). Personal communications. Mill Valley, CA.

Walsh, R. (1990). *The spirit of shamanism*. Los Angeles: Tarcher.

Washburn, M. (1994). *Transpersonal psychology in psychoanalytic perspectives*. New York: State University of New York Press.

Washburn, M. (1995). *The ego and the dynamic ground*. Albany: State University of New York Press.

Whitaker, L. C. (2000). *Understanding and preventing violence*. Boca Raton, FL: CRC Press.

Whitmore, D. (1991). *Psychosynthesis counseling in action*. Newbury Park, CA: Sage Publishing.

Wilber, K. (1995). *Integral spirituality*. Boston: Integral Books.

Tolerance, in terms of religious acceptance, was often more liberal than social status or gender. Upper social class men clearly had more privileges than others, a situation which dominates most of humanity.

3

Moral Education : Are we there yet?

Vishalache Balakrishnan

Introduction

Moral Education (ME) is a core subject in the Malaysian education system and has been taught right from preschool up to university level. In secondary schools, ME is taught through from Form One to Form Five. Right up to Form Four, students undergo school based assessment and in Form Five they sit for a written centralized examination plus complete a Project Work component which is started in Form Four itself. During the initial stages of implementing Project Work in 2004, teachers and students were quite confused with this alternative assessment and some initial responses which were received were disturbing like this one :

We the Moral Education teachers don't really know what the Ministry wants us to do in the Project Work. So after the students' final examination, I planned a few social service projects and got my students involved. I collected reports and got students to prepare the portfolios. If it can be used for alternative assessment I will use it next year when they are in form five. (Moral Education teacher).

As for the students, they were equally as confused as their teacher. They were not briefed of any changes in the assessment method but heard that there are some other components which would be assessed in ME. This was a response received four years ago from a form four student.

We have been informed that we need to complete a project work for Moral Education but until now my Moral teacher has not briefed us. I see my friend from another school going to the Recycle Centre every weekend and he says he's doing a Moral project. I asked my teacher but my teacher said the project work will come later (16 year old Moral Education student).

ME in Malaysia has undergone various transformations since it was implemented in the late 1980's in secondary schools. Being a very dynamic and 'live' subject, there is the challenge of trying to formulate a syllabus and assessment system which focuses on the three dimension of morality as focused in the Malaysian Moral Education syllabus. In order to analyze why the subject faces so many challenges compared to other academic subjects, it is worth looking at the history of the birth of ME in Malaysia and how the syllabus has transformed since then.

History and Purpose of Moral Education (ME)

One important event for the history of ME was the cabinet Committee of Education requesting that the Ministry of Education set up machinery for the development and formulation of a moral education curriculum. The requirement stated was the curriculum should cover the 11 year of schooling period and be focussed on non-Muslim students because at that time, Muslim students were already having Islamic Religious Knowledge in their school curriculum. The new ME syllabus was required to be examinable since the *Ugama* syllabus was an examinable subject (Report of the Cabinet Committee, 1979, para. 127.1). This statement explains why ME is being assessed at Form Five level. Being a directive from the Cabinet itself, there is no way ME examination at SPM level would be abolished unless the issue goes back to Parliament. However, the method of assessment can be reviewed from time to time to keep in par with latest methodology for assessment for ME. All activities in regards to ME were based on the 1979 report of the Cabinet Committee on Education to review the implementation of education policy. In this report, it was stated that:

> "To build a disciplined, cultured and united society, it is recommended that while Muslim students study Islamic Religious Knowledge, and this includes other pupils who choose to follow this subject, Non-Muslim pupils should be taught moral and ethics education. All pupils who study this subject, Moral and Ethics Education, must take it in the examination. In both these subjects, respect for individual, freedom to embrace any religion in a multi-religious society must be cultivated" (para 127.1 p. 49).

Thus, when ME came into existence, it brought along the assessment package as well. It is clearly stated that all students who study ME must take it in the examination and since all non-Muslim students have to study ME subject they all have to sit for the centralized examination at the end of the 11 years of formal education. Now the issue is what would be examined in the exams? Until 2004, all ME matters were assessed through written examination. There were many complains from parents, media and the ME students themselves. Comments like 'You can't judge the morality of an individual based on what she or he writes on the Chapter' or 'Getting an A for ME examination does not determine that an individual has good morality' could be heard in media, in schools and in public. Ironically, if we look at the objectives of ME, it is holistic and not 'Chapter and pencil' oriented.

ME focus on the effort to instil spiritual and moral strength through experiential and daily virtues of Malaysian society that is found in religion, traditions and cultural norms of the various ethnic groups in Malaysia. Thus, students can build a way of life which enables them to be moral individuals. This also enables them to be socially and morally responsible in any decision or action taken. The whole effort is practical because finally what is expected is for students to be part of a proud, uplifted nation. They can be rational in their thinking and make a difference to their feelings and action because of the process they have undergone. The ME curriculum in Malaysia enables students to:

1. Understand and internalize values which are needed to be virtuous;

2. Realize and accept the importance of harmony between man and environment and strive to sustain it;
3. Enhance the understanding and cooperation by sustaining a peaceful and harmonious life in a democratic Malaysia;
4. Develop matured thinking based on moral and spiritual values and use them when making moral decisions and solving problems;
5. Develop initiative to act morally based on justice and altruistic in line with the noble values of the Malaysia community.

(Moral Education Syllabus for Secondary Students; 2000, p. 3, my translation)

With the five big notions above, the responsibility of educating students through ME becomes a holistic mission. However, teachers of ME are caught up between two ends and most of the time they are more concerned about assessment and grades rather than making their students moral citizens of the nation. On one hand, teachers are supposed to assess students like assessing any other academic subjects but on the other hand, teachers have to ensure that the ME curriculum is acquired by the students by the end of the formal schooling years. What a challenge? When too many complaints were put across about the centralized assessment in Sijil Pelajaran Malaysia (equivalent to GCE O-level) examination in Form Five, the Malaysian Examination Board came up with a formative assessment package which aimed to guide, develop and expand the moral values learnt in classrooms to be evaluated through project work.

Moral Education 1225/2 Chapter: Project Work

The Malaysian Examination Board, Ministry of Education Malaysia (2004), formulated a Moral Education 1225/2 package which is a formative assessment which aims to guide, develop and expand the moral values in students according to their individual capacity. The evaluation is to be carried out through two ways.

(*i*) *Sahsiah* (Personality)—reporting on the moral feeling and act while communicating, making decisions and solving matters.

(*ii*) *Iltizam* (Commitment)—involvement and being responsible in carrying out daily work and social service. Reports from daily activities and social service will be compiled and documented as a folio.

In January 2004, all secondary schools were sent the directories to implement Moral Education Project Work in secondary schools. The teachers were not trained but provided with a booklet in which they are to understand the whole assessment procedure and implement what was stated. It was stated that the Project Work is in collaboration with the Malaysian Examination Board, State and District Education Departments, school administrators, heads of social science departments and the ME teachers. Though the objectives of the Project Work was good where the main aim is to assess the achievement of ME holistically but were the teachers of ME prepared to carry out such a responsibility? Were they trained to assess the moral affective and moral action component for ME? All these while, teachers have been teaching by the syllabus and assessing based on moral thinking through written tests and examinations. Were they ready to instill good virtues among students and provide them with ample opportunities to bring out their strengths and self development in the process of carrying out the project work as propagated by the Malaysian Examination Board, 2004? It is realistic to reflect upon such matters now as Project Work is into the fifth year of its implementation.

In implementing the Moral Education Project Work, the Ministry of Education stated that the Project Work would be criteria for all students who will be sitting for the Moral Education 1225/1 as a prerequisite for certification purposes. The Project Work would be executed at school level starting from form four till students complete their form five. Students would have to complete their Project Work as required and verified by the school administrator. Evaluation and assessment would be carried out by teachers teaching Moral Education.

These teachers would have to plan the process and activities for the Project Work for all the students whom he or she is teaching. Evaluation will be based on the format given by the Malaysian Examination Board. The students will be assessed twice in form four and twice in form five for recording purposes but teacher can evaluate students according to his or her schedule. The issue that I would like to bring out here is the responsibility of the teacher to plan the process which the students would be carrying out. If four years ago when the programme was first implemented and the researcher carried out her first research, the teachers did not even know how to carry out the assessment, what has happened today?

As expected it is carried out for the sake of assessment. Being in a top-down educational system, whatever is brought down as directives will definitely be implemented by those in the system. However, the question to ponder upon after four years of having implemented Project Work is 'Are we there yet?' The answer is 'NO'. Why because as mentioned earlier the assessment is carried out for the sake of following directives. ME teachers and ME students are not ready to handle such a process and they have not been given enough exposure and experience to handle such a big responsibility.

A number of principles underpinned the process and product of the Project Work. From the outset, the Project Work provides ample opportunity for students to develop their level of *sahsiah* and *iltizam* in line with the aims of the ME for secondary schools in Malaysia. The Project Work also intends to be seen as producing good practice rather than perceived as another means of assessment. However as mentioned earlier the main flaw is insufficient training for teachers conducting the whole Project Work assessment. And the other question is how do they assess if they do not teach? Is it not being unfair to the end group called students? In any assessment system, teaching needs to take place before assessment is done. Do the teachers of ME teach the students how to carry out Project Work before they are assessed of do they (the teachers) need to be taught before they can teach? These are some questions that need to be reflected as I proceed with my case.

In the following discussions, explanation on the frustrations of students in carrying out such an assessment would be deliberated followed by some recommendations on how the Project Work component in ME can be salvaged at least for the moment. Focus would be on the students of ME who undergo Project Work and what it means to them.

METHODOLOGY

Demographically, two states and one federal territory in Peninsular Malaysia where ME is taught to more than 50 percent of the students in secondary schools was covered for the research. The federal territory school was an all boys' school whereas the students from the two states are from the all girls and co-educational schools.

The school in the state of Perak would be called Rose and it is a town school. Students attending Rose are mostly living in suburbs except for a few who still come from nearby villages and estates that are in existence. Students come to school by public transport or chauffeured by their parents.

The school in Selangor which would be called Orchid is situated in a rural area. Though the town is developed, access to outside world like the cities is quite limited. Students here mostly walk to school as their houses are nearby or use the school bus and public bus services. Several students travel with their parents who are teachers or government office workers whose offices are located nearby to the school.

The third school involved in the research is located in the centre of a federal territory where the hustle and bustle of life is at the maximum. This school would be named Jasmine. Students in this school are exposed to city life and keep up with the latest development in the heart of Malaysia. Students here come from different types of household depending on the family background and economic status. Some live in bungalow houses, double storey terrace etc and the others live in flats, apartments and several do still live in slum areas and the few shanty towns still existing in the outskirts of the federal territory.

In all three schools where the research was conducted, research methodology like participant observation and interviews were carried out.Participant observation is both an overall approach to inquiry and a data-gathering method (Marshal and Rossman, 2006). It is more ethnographic and provided a picture of the process of Project Work done during the study. According to Lofland and Lofland (1995) participant observation is a process where researcher communicates and forms a many-sided long-term relationship with a human association in their natural setting for the notion of developing an understanding that is association based and scientific. In all three schools researched, the researcher had the opportunity to see the ME students in action when being involved in their Project Work or explaining about it.

The second method that was used was interview. Interviewing may be defined simply as a conversation with a purpose (Berg, 2004; p. 75). This standard definition of interviewing has been stated by Denzin (1978), Patton (1990), Nachmias and Nachmias (1992). Recently, Denzin (2003) suggested that interviews today should be more than mere information-gathering devices. They need to be reflexive and reflect the perfomative aspect of life and the social sciences. It is usually between two people where one person-the interviewer-is seeking responses for a particular purpose from the other person: the interviewee (Gillham, 2000). Interviews are carried out in research to obtain information and understanding of issues relevant to research questions and other general aims of the research. All interviews were carried out in informal settings like the school canteen or the cafeteria nearby. This was to ensure that students were more relaxed and not threatened by the interview process.

Case Story 1: Rose

Rose has about 80 Form Four students and 76 Form Five students who need to fulfil the Project Work for their ME assessment. During observations in Rose, students in Form Four were carrying out recycling projects like newsChapter collection and cleaning the teacher's staffroom. As for the Form Five students they did not come out of class for any Project Work within the school compound. Instead they were being drilled with values and content areas based on the syllabus and the textbook. Here is an excerpt with my Form Five participant from Rose who spoke about the Project Work.

I: What have you done so far for Project Work?

Rose 1: I am not sure but every time my moral teacher asks us to write four freaking essays, long and tedious one. It's actually quite ridiculous. We have to choose from one category from the silly moral Chapter to write an entire folio on it. Not only that but we need stupid evidence like photographs and letters or certificates to prove we've actually done something. Why won't the government just realise that no matter how many essays we write, it won't change anything. In fact most students just copy from past years folios.

In just the short excerpt above, it is clear that as a ME student, Rose 1 is doing some deep reflection about Project Work and the issues brought out like writing an entire folio based on one category, providing evidences for grading purposes and the impression that nothing will change in spite of all the effort put into the Project Work. What does this imply? First thing there is no preference for the process involved but more for the product (essays, pictures, certificates etc). To assess a student holistically is no longer there but the focus is to assess the student's written work and provided evidences of undertaking a project. Isn't this actually going back to the assessment of moral thinking of how well a student can write four essays and able to collect other data for the assessment purpose. The notion of assessing the process that ME students undertake is practically lacking and needs serious considerations.

Case Story 2: Orchid

In Orchid, the system of carrying out Project Work is structured by the ME Head and department of social science. ME teachers plan the projects and students become participants of a planned Project Work. How do students feel about it? Here are some of the responses.

Orchid 1: I do the project for my teacher not for myself. If given a choice I would like to do something

I enjoy and find it meaningful. For example we are asked to do recycling of newsChapters. We don't but Chapters at home and I have to go to neighbours house to find for newsChapters which I don't like doing. I'd prefer to clean the school garden or plant herbs in the 'Herbal Garden'.

Orchid 2: We are treated like robots for the Project Work. We are given instructions and we follow. We are asked to do work and we do. We are asked to smile for photographs and we do. That's what Project Work is. We are just following instructions to get grades for Moral.

In the above scenario, the students are frustrated with their Project Work and the way it is handled because they do not have choices to make about what projects they can do and every thing is planned for them. This again is against the principles of Project Work where ME teacher and ME students are supposed to discuss, collaborate and come up with projects which are of interest and is meaningful to them. Where did the student or the teacher go wrong? Project Works are implemented but it does not make an impact on the students. They feel like robots following instructions. Is that what we want out of our ME students after 11 years of learning about values and becoming holistically moral? Are we there yet?

Case Story 3: Jasmine

Jasmine is a school where Project Work is integrated into other subjects and teachers of other subjects also become part of the theme. For example during my observation, Sports Day was carried out and Speed Day was also during the same duration. Even before this two annual school events, ME teacher discusses with students if they want to carry out any of their Project Work during that duration. Interested students give their names and other teachers who are in-charge of different responsibilities like mike system, decoration, food and drinks etc invite students who have give their names for some responsible task on the separate events. Here is an excerpt with ME students who had completed their project in school.

Jasmine 1: We don't find the project work tiresome because it is part of our responsibility towards our school. What I find good about it is I get to do my responsibility and at the same time complete my Project Work. Last year I helped with the Speech Day but this year I am in-charge of the PA system. That's a lot of fun but hard work. My teacher is happy with me and my ME teacher assess me on my performance. Now I can write my essays and submit my folio to my ME teacher.

Jasmine 2: Its fun doing project work here in our school. Teachers appreciate us and give us a treat at the end of the day though we don't expect it. We work as a team and our school photographer does all the clicking for our photography evidences. We get our certificates from the Headmaster and that makes us really proud.

Jasmine is the only school where the researcher found the ME students not being frustrated about the Project Work. They have a school culture which gets every one involved and it makes the process smooth and the product something to be proud of for the ME students. The ME teacher is being creative in using the school functions as grounds for the ME students to do their projects. Not only do they complete their projects successfully but they are also recognized for doing a good job.

Rose, Orchid and Jasmine: A Comparative Analysis

Now if we go back to the three schools that were researched, it is obvious that all three schools have different ethos and its worth looking into them. Rose concern is academic achievement because being a premier school; the focus is on grades and ranking. Because such a climate is created, students too focus on product rather than process. But students are not static, they are thinking beings who know what is going on and feel that such a way of handling Project Work is of no use to them. According to Abdul Rahman (2008), moral education must also involve inculcation of virtues, the code of ethics, rules and regulations to develop 'moral automaticity' among pupils, but at the same time there must be discussion on moral issues and dilemmas to facilitate development of moral reasoning capacities among pupils (p. 7). If students are not involved in the process for Project Work then they do not actually learn anything by producing the products (their folio, their essays etc.). This is a serious issue and need to be evaluated.

In the case of Orchid, they do implement the Project Work but everything is carried out with formalities without students of ME having any part in the decision-making or the choosing of the projects they would like to indulge in. Should the ME students be involved in the prior decision-making and choosing of projects? It is definitely a big 'YES'. In fact in the Project Work booklet it focus upon *sahsiah* (personality) and *iltizam* (commitment) which talks about assessing moral feeling and moral action while communicating, making decisions and resolving problems that arise. It does not work that way in Orchid. This is because it is their pre planned project and they are the 'robotic' ones are carrying out the whole process and producing the products needed for the Project Work assessment. In the Project Work package there are guidelines which state that teachers of ME would have to plan the process and projects for all students of ME who he or she teaches. Won't it be more meaningful for both parties if the process and project is planned collaboratively? Students would be enthusiastic and ME teachers would find it easier to assess them.

Since the whole process is planned by ME teachers, the students find themselves being treated like robots. It is a great issue to be reconsidered because one of the ME objectives is for students to 'Develop matured thinking based on moral and spiritual values and use them when making moral decisions and solving problems'. If they are not given the opportunity to be in such a democratic situation where are they going to find opportunity to resolve problem and make moral decisions? This type of regimental system of conducting project Work would only leave students in the confused stage and later argue that ME never taught them anything.

Jasmine is a good example of how the ME teacher has collaborated with other teachers and the administration to manage the Project Work. Initially the ME teacher together with ME students need to plan out events and activities in school that they can be involved to complete their Project Work. Then students are given the choice to choose which activity they want to be involved in. Choice is necessary because, to be a moral student, one must have more than one course of action available, as well as both the authority and the competence to choose which course of action to follow (Boostrom, 1998). ME students need choice in their daily lives to be able to consider pros and cons and come up with good moral decisions.

In comparison with Orchid, where students are even delegated to do their task according to the instructions of the ME teacher, Jasmine has a more democratic system which the ME students appreciate and adhere to. To have an opportunity to make moral choices, one must have more than one course of action available, as well as both the authority and the competence to choose which course of action to follow. When the ME teacher gave the students' names to the different teachers for the different events, students had choice to make on which responsibility they would like to shoulder. This again makes them reflect upon the role they want to undertake and how they would later construct their Project Work. All in, it is a collaborative effort between the school administrator who later appreciates the students through presentation of certificates and tokens. In countries like Canada and Australia, the Mayor of the local regions is also involved in appreciating and celebrating the success of students when they complete a certain project or community service.

Are we there Yet?

Based on Project Work research initially carried out in 2004 and now in 2008, there are a few issues that would be highlighted. When the Project Work was first implemented in 2004, the directives came direct from the Examination Board and teachers and students of ME were in the dark. Creative teachers carried out trial runes to familiarize students with the formative styles of assessment but most ME teachers followed the instructions in the Project Work booklet and implemented the task. The main question here is, is it fair to assess the students before teaching and guiding them through a process for the Project Work.

As in the case of Rose where ME teacher tells students to write essays even without them carrying out any project is really an unfair task. Students would have to imagine and cheat that they have done a project to complete their written assignment. Some even copy from previous year's folios to complete their Project Work. If this is what is happening in most schools, then Project Work is a failure. But students or teachers of ME should not be blamed for taking such short cuts. Where is the exposure for the teachers to handle such a challenging task? Where is the guidance for the students to complete their Project Work before they go to the written assignments? Were the school administration helpful to ME teachers who knew nothing about the whole task because they were relieve teachers of simply put to teach ME?

There are so many flaws in the implementation of Project Work that it becomes a mockery among students of ME. One student from Rose says she forges her certificates and gets her mother to take shots of her as if she is doing a task at home but its all deceit. Again, ME is taking a negative turn in reality because instead of making good moral citizens out of students, the system and implementation of Project Work is making students cheaters, liars and forgers? Are they to be blamed? No. The whole assessment system needs to be evaluated. Even before Project Work was implemented, trial runs should have been carried out to find the weaknesses of the assessment and most importantly the key players who are the ME teachers should have been trained to handle the responsibility. Curriculum Development Centre under the Ministry of Education should have key personals to train and guide ME teachers' nation wide to handle Project Work. Networking should be established through the net and *Pusat Kegiatan Guru* (Teacher Resource Centers) to help with the ongoing challenges in the process of managing Project Work. Thus, the answer to my earlier question of 'Are we there yet?' is a big 'NO'. But we cannot regret and complain over spilt milk. We have to keep going and think of innovative ways to improve flawed systems because we are dealing with the lives of students and formations of their identities in the moral domain. Now what can be done?

How to Salvage Project Work?

It is easier said than done to bring in school, parents, communities and all to be part of the Project Work and happily end with a note that with all their collaboration and cooperation we can have an ideal assessment process for Project Work. In reality after five years and based on initial and present research, it is evident that in most cases parents and those around the ME students are helping the student in wrong ways which we do not want to go on. So what should be done? Firstly is to go back to the structure of the Project Work and analyze the process required within the Project Work. This has to be done at the level of the Examination Board with collaboration with Curriculum Development Center. As explained earlier, testing without teaching is a very unethical thing to do especially in a subject like ME. Feedbacks should be obtained from all parties involved such as the ME teachers, administrators and most importantly ME students. Without analyzing their responses and feedback, the whole process of evaluating and restructuring the Project Work would again be challenged in different ways.

Next is to look into the ME syllabus itself. At the moment great emphasize is given to values and content that need to be taught for examination purposes. Though the Parliament directive for ME is that it should be examinable, there is no directive stating that cognitive or moral thinking assessment should be the main focus. Since its implementation, ME evaluation has been focused upon Chapter and pencil but by right the weight age should balance between moral thinking, moral feeling and moral action assessment. Mind sets of teachers and students of ME should change and be rational that if we study the three moral domains of thinking, feeling and action in ME then assessment should also be in the three domains. What is happening in reality is that ME teachers who produce good grades in their students are made into Master teachers and promoted. They even go around the nation giving seminars on how to produce students with good grades in ME. It again brings mockery and frustrations to the ME subject and those involved in ME. All these again defeat the purpose of ME and should be brought up again at the ministry level to see the implications of 'Chapter chase' for a humanistic subject like ME. As my Rose student said, "By providing a complete folio with beautiful pictures, you can't measure the morality of students. What is important is what they learnt by doing that Project Work if they ever did one honestly?'

Finally it comes down to the ME students themselves. They need to be given the awareness that ME is unique and different from all the other academic subjects they are dealing with in school. ME gives them an avenue to grow in mind, heart and action which does not occur in other subjects. The Project Work implemented was focused on the mind and action but based on my findings it has lost its original objectives and needs to be restructured for the future good of ME.

Process Versus Product

As a lecturer in the field of ME and previously a ME teacher for more than a decade, the researcher is most concerned with processes of implementations rather than product in ME. As a ME teacher, the researcher focused on educating the three domains of ME. ME students who were mentally good were given plenty of exercises to reflect upon their moral feelings and actions. Hands on activities were given to bring out their three domains. And most important, classroom activities were always linked with their lives outside the school. In this way even the weakest ME students saw significance to studying ME. What surprised the researcher most was these groups of weak ME students started to pay attention to their written work and slowly started to perform better in the written assessment. The main point here is when students find meaning to what is being taught, their academic achievement will also show progress. On the other hand if students are forced to memorize values and content areas they end up feeling choked and find ME a real torture in school life.

The skill of balancing between teaching and assessing the three ME domains (moral thinking, moral feeling and moral action) is essential for every ME teacher. It is challenging and the ME teacher has to be creative and reflective. It also deals with the identity and personality of the teacher because in most cases 'Values are caught and not taught'. ME students are always observing their ME teachers and reflect upon their teachings and character in school and at times outside the school ground. It is a vice versa reaction on the teachers part too. But when ME teachers focus upon the process of Project Work then they may be able to see avenues to improve their assessment and appreciate their ME students better.

Conclusion

Project Work in ME was implemented with the good intention of assessing ME based on the three domains taught during ME lessons and to reduce the focus on the written examination. It was also to provide the ME students an opportunity to utilize values learnt within the four walls of the classroom outside the classroom. A way of bridging theory into practice as Vygotsky (1978) puts it. However, with all the current complains upon Project Work, it still can be salvaged if all parties involved become more reflective and critical in ensuring that ME attains the objectives mentioned earlier. Realizing that Project Work has failed to fulfill the requirements of alternative assessment is the first step but to re-evaluate and work upon the flaws that are taking place within Project Work is a smart and moral step.

REFERENCES

Abdul Rahman Md. Aroff (2008). Character Building and Education. In C. L. Hoon, N. M. Salleh, W. H. W. Mamat & Vishalache B. (Eds.), *Asia-Pacific Moral, Civic and Citizenship Education*. Kuala Lumpur: University of Malaya Press.

Berg, B. L. (2004). *Qualitative Research Methods For The Social Sciences* (5 ed.). Boston: Pearson.

Cabinet Committee Report (1984). *Report of the Cabinet Committee on Educational Policy 1979*. 4th Ed. Kuala Lumpur: Dewan Bahasa dan Pustaka.

Denzin, N. K. (1978). *Interpretive interactionism*. Newbury Park, CA: Sage.

Denzin, N. K., & Lincoln, Y. S. (2003). *Strategies of Qualitative Inquiry*. Thousand Oaks: Sage Publications.

Gillham, B. (2000). *The Research Interview*. London: Continuum.

Lickona, T. (1991). *Educating for character: How our schools can teach respect and responsibility*. New York: Bantam Books.

Lofland, J., & Lofland, L. H. (1995). *Analyzing social settings: a guide to qualitative observation and analysis* (3rd ed.). Belmont, California: Wadsworth.

Marshall, C., & Rossman, G. B. (2006). *Designing Qualitative Research*. California: Sage Publications.

Ministry of Education Malaysia (2000). *Moral Education Syllabus for secondary schools Malaysia*. Kuala Lumpur: Curriculum Development Centre.

Nachmias, C., & Nachmias, D. (1992). *Research methods in the social sciences*. New York St. Martin's Press.

Patton, M. Q. (1990). *Qualitative evaluation and research methods (2nd ed)*. Newbury park, CA: Sage.

Vishalache, B. (2004). *Project Work in Teaching Moral Education: A Malaysian Review*. Chapter presented at the Association for Moral Education International Conference.

Vygotsky, L. S. (1978). *Mind in Society*. Cambridge: Harvard University Press.

SECTION 2 : EARLY CHILDHOOD AND HIGHER EDUCATION

4

Abolition of Child Labour and Universalisation of Primary Education through Gram Panchayat—Case Studies

C.S. Singhal

Introduction

As per an official estimate about 17 million children are working in India, of whom 2 million are employed in hazardous occupations. The real number is much higher. The children are employed in agriculture and allied area, variety of industries, informal sector and as bonded labour. The high participation of children in the labour force leads to low enrolment and school dropout. As per 2001 census nearly one third population is illiterate, and about 20 per cent of children in the 6-14 age group do not go to school. Out of the enrolled, more than one third was dropouts before completing primary school.

To abolish the child labour and universalisation of Primary Education M.V. Foundation is working in about 6000 villages in India, since 1991. Out of these over 1000 villages are child and bonded labour free. About 3,70,000 children have been mainstreamed to schools and over 10 lakhs children including the school going and non school going children are monitored regularly under the programme of MVF. All this has been possible with the massive support and involvement of the Gram Panchayats apart from the child rights protection forums and other committees operating at the village level.

In order to prevent children from joining the labour force and also to reach out to girls, MVF looked at the issue of abolition of child labour as an issue of children's right to education. Consequently, MVF evolved multiple strategies to withdraw children from work and to retain them in schools. In the process it involved the active participation of different sections of the community including institutions such as Gram Panchayats. The MV Foundation experience shows that gram panchayats can play a significant role in controlling and evolving new processes involving the community at large towards the protection of children's right and strengthening of the school system. This is in accordance with the 73rd constitution amendment which envisages far greater devolution of powers than ever before to these institutions.

The Gram Panchayats have been playing an important role in support of children's right to education. As local bodies, they are the essential link between the community, the school and the government. They are actively engaged in planning, implementation and monitoring of the schools. The Gram Panchayat have enhanced their capacities towards this end and built accountability to the Gram Sabha/community. The local bodies or the Gram Panchayats have taken upon themselves to engage in strengthening of the schools.

Protection of child's right through Gram Panchayat in the M.V.F. Project area have developed several innovative approaches by way of co-ordination with several community based organizations like child right protection forum, schools education committee (youth/mother committee).

The main objectives of the study were:

(a) to study the role of Gram Panchayat and its impact in eradication of child labour and universalisation of primary education;

(b) to prepare the case studies of successful Gram Panchayats in the process of their convergence with community based organizations and;

(c) the role of stakeholders at the village level for eradication of child labour and universalisation of primary education.

METHODOLOGY

Study Area

The study was conducted in Ranga Reddy and Nalgonda Districts where M.V. Foundation Project has undertaken several activities to abolish child labour and universalisation of Primary Education with the involvement of GPs are in the implementation. The villages for the study were:

1. Rangareddy District : Bulkapur, Poddetor, Solipet
2. Nalgonda district: Patha Suryapet, Midthanapally, Dacharam, Bibigudem, Vathikum Pahad.

Procedure

The data were collected through interview schedule from elected representatives of Gram Panchayat, parents, children, members of several committees like school committees, child right protection forum, youth volunteers and project staff of the M.V. Foundation officials. About 20-25 people from each village were contacted and interviewed individually, and in-group after establishment of rapport with them. The secondary data were collected from reports of census, M.V. Foundation and Serva Siksha Abhiyan reports.

CASE STUDY OF BULKAPUR VILLAGE

Village Profile

The Bulkapur village in Shankarpally Mandal was about 2 km. from Mandal Head Quarters. There were about 695 households in the village. The total population was about 3715. The considerable number of population belongs to other backward castes (1259) and scheduled castes (868). The majority of people (>901) were earning their livelihood through agriculture and allied activities. The majority of household (330) in the village belonged to small farmers (2.5 – 5 ac.), followed by marginal farmers (120; <2.5 ac.), big farmers (75; > 5 ac.) and considerable number of household (120) were landless labours.

There are upper primary school (1) upto 7th class, anganwadi centres (2), cooperative society (1), DWCRA groups

(22), youth clubs (4), post office, sub health centre, road, and electricity facilities available in the village.

When the task of identification of child labour, bonded child labour and school dropouts was undertaken by M.V. Foundation with involvement of Gram panchayat in 1992, there were 237 children (6-14 years) were out of school (127 boys; 110 girls) and 310 children were going to school (185 boys, 125 girls) where as in a follow up survey in 2007-08, 407 children (207 m: 200 F) were going to primary school and 12 were non school going.

Profile of Gram Panchayat

The Gram Panchayat consisted of a Surpanch (Mr. G. Laxma Reddy, 47), Dy. Surpanch Shri K. Rajasekhar and nine Ward panchs. Of these, three were females, five panchs belong to other backward community, and three were scheduled caste. The Surpanch was educated upto Intermediate and 2 lady panchs were illiterate. The main occupation of G.P. members was agriculture.

The Gram Panchayat has contributed immensely in mainstreaming children to the school as informed by Shri G. Laxma Reddy, Surpanch of the village.

Surpanch and other ward members of Gram Panchayat were aware about Child Labour Act, role of GP as per PRI Acts related to universalisation of primary education informed the G. Laxma Reddy, Surpanch.

The Gram Panchayat members reviewed the survey work undertaken by M. V. Foundation in 1992, and further co-operated in doing the door to door survey work to find out the enrolled children in the school. The Gram Panchayat along with Child Rights Protection Forum, Youth Clubs, women groups and volunteers of M.V. Foundation motivated parents to enrol their children and employers to discuss the child labour issues. The present Surpanch G. Laxma Reddy remembers fondly that in 1992 when M.V. Foundation started the work in his village he was president of a youth club. For educational awareness there was motivation campaign for parents. The Gram Panchayat along with youth clubs and all other community organizations organized school children's rally for motivation of parents and all villagers for awareness about importance of education. In the nights, cultural programmes were organized to collect money for construction of a room of a school building. The village youths were teaching as and when there was shortage of teachers in the village primary school not for getting salary or even any honorarium.

The Gram Panchayat along with youth clubs and other community organizations constructed boundary wall of school with free *sramdan (free labour)*.

Mr. G. Laxman Reddy, the surpanch on date informed that the former surpanch Mr. M. Bikshapathy cooperated with community based organization, motivated parents and threatened them to cancel their family ration card that employ their ward as child labour.

Initially lot of resistance was enforced from the parents as they were not aware but subsequently most of them understood the importance of education.

Role of Education Committee and School Management Committee in Abolition of Child Labour and Universalisation of Primary Education

Gram Panchayat's education committee This committee has the following constitution:

Structure of Gram Panchayat Education Committee

Chairman	Sarpanch
Members	Ward Panchs (2)
Convener	Youth (2)
	Head Master of Primary School (1)
	Mandal Parishad Territorial Candidate

Structure of School Management Committee

Chairman	Sarpanch
Members	Parents (2)
Convenar	Youth (1)
	Representatve of
	DWCRA (1)
	Head Master of Primary School (1)

Sarpanch informed that during discussion in Gram Panchayat's Education Committee they decided to find out the dropouts and try to change that it reduces. The responsibility to educate the dropout children were given to respective ward punch. Sarpanch proudly informed that there was no drop out now in the village and all ward punch and parents were vigilant about the child absenteeism problem.

The second main concern was to improve the quality of education. The Sarpanch informed that he himself checked the reading and writing abilities development among the school children. Besides, Gram Panchayat viewed that children were able to read news Chapters, property land Chapters, land pass books, etc. The teachers were also given necessary instructions by Sarpanch to improve the quality of education.

The Sarpanch informed that in School Management Committee, the main agenda was how to utilize school funds, identify and solve day to day school problem and improve school infrastructure. The School Education Committee's meeting held regularly and all the members were participating in the meeting.

The Surpanch donated Rs.1500/- for giving award to meritorious children, and plates and glasses for mid day meals. It was informed that Gram Panchayat didn't get any fund for development of school infrastructure. The school infrastructure needs to be improved in the village as it was only up to 7th class. The school was with 5 teachers and there was no play ground in the school. The sufficient furniture also required in the school. The Gram Panchayat provided drinking water and toilets facilities in the school, but it was not in use as the door of toilets was broken and not properly maintained. There was a need of 2 more rooms as classrooms, one room each required for Head Master's and Library Room in the school.

The Gram Panchayat was aware of child marriage problem and demotivating parents so as not to get trapped by legal action by passing on the information to police whenever required. Gram Panchayat was active in Health and Anganwadi Committees. Sarpanch takes-up the matter at "Mandal level

Committee" regarding school infrastructure, play ground etc. whenever required.

Apart from this, Sarpanch and ward members regularly visit school, checking the attendance of children and teachers. Whenever teacher is absent made record in register and ask them to come in time, as a result of active participation of Gram Panchayat with other community leaders/organization the teachers were coming regularly and timely, the child drop out reduced to nil, the quality of teaching improved. The Head Master got motivation. With the cooperation of all stakeholders several maps and other teaching aids were developed and displayed in the wall of school for improvement of overall quality.

One teacher *Vidhya Volunteer* kept out of the fund available under *Serve Sikshal Abhiyan* and one employed out of donation by Surpunch shows his interest in the improvement of primary education.

The Sarpanch informed that the education committee members regularly meet the parents of absentee children and try to motivate them. But many parents wanted their children to work in Agriculture field/household 2-3 days in a week at least owing to their economical poverty. Few children were engaged in running autos after class 10th. Gram Panchayat was seriously deliberating on these issues of how to motivate the parents and children to bring to mainstream education.

Another problem Sarpanch stated was that in the nearby Sankarpally Mandal Govt. school was available only upto Class 10th. For class 11 & 12 only Pvt. College was available, they charge Rs. 4000-5000/- per annum. Many parents can't afford to shed down the same; hence children withdraw from taking up further education.

RESULTS

Gram Panchyat's Support for Awareness and Motivation Campaign

The elected representatives were supporting and involved in awareness and motivation campaign. In several villages GP is supporting motivation campaign by undertaking *pad* yatra, *nukkad natak, drum beating* and *wall writing,* cultural programs by villagers and youth leaders of *Child Right Protection Forum* (CRPF) initiated by MV Foundation to make people aware about abolition of child labour under the Act. The elected representatives as community leaders addressed community and motivated them to get rid of the problems of child labour and made them understood about the importance of universal primary education.

The elected representatives were motivating parents in Bulkapur village for abolition of child labour and universalisation of primary education. The GP was supporting the CRPF, women groups in this regard.

In Bibiguda village

- The employers of child labour who leave the child labour practice were honoured publicly to motivate others not to employ children.
- GP served notice to owners of rice mills to release all working children within 15 days. The GP threatened them if children were not released than they will inform department of labour and police for taking necessary action against them.

Quality of Educational Improvement

GP was concerned about improvement of quality of education, school enrolment, and monitored regularity of teachers; motivate children to participate in sports. GP assisted MV foundation in conduct of survey, established norms in the villages that children should not work and education is necessary to alleviate poverty.

GP in Bulkapur village

- Decided to withdraw the *ration card* of parents who were not sending their children to school.
- Established social norms that all children must study in the village.
- Assist in abolition of child labour by motivating parents, facilitated *pad yatras* in different villages.

School Education committee (SEC) was headed by *sarpanch*. In Bulkapur village the responsibility to educate the dropout children was given to respective ward punch. As a result there was no drop out as the ward panch and parents were vigilant about child absenteeism. SEC utilizes school funds, identify and solve day to day problems, improve school infrastructure. The meeting of SEC held regularly and all the members participated in it.

Sarpanch is reviewing the functioning of the school to improve the quality of primary education, besides there was GP education review committee headed by *sarpanch* as its chairman. The *sarpanch* invites various development functionaries like Head Master, ANM, Anganwadi Workers, *Prerak* of continuing education etc. The review meeting was held quarterly.

The School Monitoring Committee headed by *sarpanch* see the school drop out, long absentees if any and attended the day to day problem informed the *Sarpanch* of Poddetor village. *Sarpanch* and *ward members* regularly visited schools, checking the attendance of children and teachers. Whenever teacher was absent, record was made in register and they were asked to come in time. As a result of active participation of GP with community leaders /organizations teachers were coming regularly and timely, the child drop-out reduced to nil, the quality of teaching improved.

The *sarpanch* and ward members were concerned about the functioning of school as well as the infrastructure development and toilet availability.

In an another instance in Bibiguda village when a teacher was not coming regularly to school GP has suspended him by reporting at higher level and in his place a volunteer was engaged to teach children. GP arranged tuition for primary school children last year in Bibiguda village. In the year 2007, they were planning the same for improvement of the quality of education.

In Pathasuryapet village ward punch investigate the reason of school dropout and take up the matter with respective parents for correction. They supervise text books distribution.

The *sarpanch,* Bulkapur village, was concerned about the improvement of the quality of education. The *sarpanch* informed that he himself was checking the reading and writing abilities developed among the school children. The teachers were given necessary instructions by *sarpanch* to improve the *quality of education.*

In another village (Poddetore) the members of GP were playing pivotal role in appointment of *vidhya volunteers* and in such cases where number of teacher were in short GP was bearing the cost of *Vidhya Volunteers* thereby directly contributing to the improvement of quality of primary education.

In another GP (Midnapally) School Education Committee headed by *sarpanch* decided to send children on picnic and arranged cultural programme to attract children to school.

GP Contribution in School Infrastructure

GP was arranging donation for development of school infrastructure. *School Management Committee* was concerned about up-keep of school infrastructure, provision of drinking water and regularly monitoring various activities informed the sarpanch of Poddetore GP. *Sarpanch,* Poddetore village arranged to get white wash of village school spending Rs.30,000/- collected as donations from *Pragati Resort* (a real estate private company) , arranged water tap in the school and arranged to get constructed boundary wall of primary school with free labour of the village community in Bulkapur village. The *sarpanch* helped in arranging sports material and contributed Rs. 2,000/- in 2007 towards school improvement fund.

The Dy.Sarpanch, Poddetore village would be constructing an extra room in high school for the use of computer lab as expression of the commitment towards education in the village.

In another village (Solepet) sarpanch

- Got repaired the school toilet and gave prize worth Rs. 2,000/- to school children on special occasion like independence day.

- The *school parent committee* headed by *sarpanch* could arrange to get clean the surroundings of the school.
- Panchayat gave donation for purchase of land and arranged to get cleanliness of surroundings of school at their own.

The *sarpanch* of Bulkapur village -

- Donated Rs.1500/- for giving awards to meritorious students and plates and glasses for *mid day meals.*
- With the cooperation of all stakeholders several maps and other teaching aids were developed and displaced in the wall of school for improvement of overall quality.

GP (Midanapally) along with other stakeholders arranged to get donation of Rs. 1.5 Lack from parents and others to get purchase of 2 Acre land for school. They were in the process of negotiation for purchase of this land adjacent to school building.

One *vidhya volunteer* employed out of the donation by *sarpanch* shows his interest in the improvement of primay education.

Advocacy by GP

GP has represented the issues of augmentation of infrastructure and increase the number of teachers to improve quality of education to the districts and *Mandal* level officials and elected representatives at higher level.

In Pathasuryapet village *sarpanch* gave petition to officials at mandal and district levels and got approval of a subject teacher and school up gradation up to high school. Another petition for assistance to improve rural water supply was also given.

Lobbying for Abolition of Child Labour

Political parties had meeting and decided to abolish child labour irrespective of the party affiliation. The leaders of political parties organized *dharna* and GP representatives lobby in front of parents who engaged their children as child labour.

Other Monitoring Activities of GP

GP members facilitate and monitor the *Mid Day Meal*. Sarpanch (Solipet GP) informed that he even some time test the meal served to the children to ensure the quality. In some occasion the GP pressurize school administration to admit children without any fees as they were poor.

GP (Pathasuryapet)

- Provide and maintain plantation in school premises.
- Arrange to get utensils (plates) for *Mid Day Meal* through "*Varavi Club*" a Voluntary Organization.

Suggestions and Implications

- The involvement of GP in school management could bring very positive change in improvement of the quality of primary education in the villages. Hence, PRIs should be given grater responsibility to run grassroots level institutes smoothly.
- Government should issue clear guidelines about the structure and functions of School Management Committee.
- To improve the quality of education and to supplement the teaching staff government has sanctioned *Vidhya Volunteers* on consolidated honorarium of Rs. 1500/- pm. The most of the Vidhay Volunteers were not trained and were only 10th class pass. Secondly, delay in release of their honorarium causing lack of motivation and increasing their attrition rate. Hence their amount of honorarium needs to be periodically reviewed based on the performance and funds to be released in time.
- There are lacks of infrastructure in school which need to be strengthened by contribution of all concern. Besides government should increase funds to strengthen school infrastructure along with participation of GP and community in large by involvement of civil society organization like MV Foundation.
- The attitude of all stakeholders needs to be changed by community mobilization through involvement of civil

society organization and training to all concerned to abolish child labour and expansion of education.

- GP members need periodic training in child labour Act and Universalisation of Primary Education with special reference to their role in it.

Ultimately, it is the level of awareness, attitude change towards education will make people to abolish child labour and facilitate improvement of quality of education. The involvement of GP, youth activist (CRPF), NGO like MV Foundation will make all the difference in abolition of child labour and universalisation of primary education. The GP members need to be empowered for greater say in functioning of village organizations like the school and they could change the outlook of the society and could bring positive change. GP could contribute significantly in the abolition of child labour and universalisation of Primary Education by ensuring the proper functioning of the school system in the selected villages with the activation of GP through CRPF and other volunteers of MV Foundation and if given proper training and expose for further strengthening at grass roots level.

5

Early Childhood Education

Priya Kayastha and Uma Hirisave

"As the twig is bent, so is the tree inclined"

Introduction

Recent years have seen an increasing recognition of the importance of Early Childhood Education. The word education has a very wide connotation. It holds different perspective for an educator, an artist, an economist, a philosopher, a psychologist and a sociologist. Etymologically the word education is derived from the Latin word.

'EDUCARE' which means 'to draw out', to nourish', implying education is a process of drawing out and leading out something from within the individual through bringing up, nourishing, raising and training.

Early Childhood Education regards education in the early stages of childhood. According to the National Association for the Education of Young Children (NAEYC), it spans the human life from birth to age eight. Early Childhood Education (ECE) has been defined as "guidance and training imparted through specifically designed programme in carefully controlled and stimulating environment with the explicit purpose of enhancing child's physical, mental, emotional and social development". ECE programme are developed according to child's needs, competencies and ability to grasp along with suitability to environment, thus ensuring their growth and development. A well planned programme plays a vital role in emphasizing and raising the standard of ECE because it enables children to acquire pre-literacy skills which facilitate further education. Thus the above mentioned saying "As the twig is bent, so is the tree inclined" confirms that whatever values, attitudes, desired traits and habits we cultivate in a child are reflected in her/his personality as an adult. ECE is essential for human resource development.

"Early childhood education" is interchangeably used with other terms such as "early childhood learning", "early care," and "early education.", "Montessori education", "Kindergarten education" and "Balawadis". Before going into the details of early childhood education it is important to briefly understand its relation to normal child development

Normal Child Development

Development is an ongoing process. It takes place in stages and each stage influences the next. The normal child development takes place from infancy through childhood to adolescence in the areas namely motor, cognitive, language, emotional, social, moral and sexual. All the aspects of development are inter-related and one aspect affects the other.

Earlier the child was considered to be born with a mind like "clean slate" and was supposed to learn everything from their interaction with adults. However the current understanding based on the research in child development demonstrates that children are born with enormous capacities of the brain and the mind to acquire skills soon after the birth. Play is very important for holistic development of children. The abilities of infants and toddlers should not be underestimated as they have the capacity to learn about themselves and others though observation and trial and error method. All we need to do is provide the child with environment that is conducive for playful activities. By exploring and using various materials of different shape, size and color around us, the child can use his/her imagination and creativity to engage in playful activities that promote language ability, physical, psychological and social development in them. Table 1 gives guidelines for adults to observe children during play and assess development in various domains.

Table1. Assessing a Child in Play or Child Initiated Activities

Personal, social and emotional development
Disposition and attitudes : who initiated the play/ activity? Did the child introduce new ideas- if so what? Did the child select or create any thing to use- if so what? How involved was the child-did she/he show persistence/determination? How confident did the child appear?
Social development **:** was there any new evidence of building relationships, negotiating skills, sharing and co-operating with others? Was there evidence of respect for others and growing cultural awareness?
Emotional development **:** how did the child express feelings and/or respond to the feelings of others? Was there evidence of growing control over own behavior- if so how was it shown?
Communication, language and literacy **:** What type of language was evident? For example- talking about present, past or future events, sustaining a conversation with adults or child; using language to express imaginary or real ideas ; using language to create or add to a storyline; using language to question or clarify thoughts.
(*Source:* Hutchin, 2003)

From Theory to Practice

Early childhood education has a long history rich with tradition. The efforts of past religious leaders, reformers, educational theorist, philosophers have helped to shape contemporary thinking about young children. Critical events have a role in shaping the history of early childhood education. E.g. the founder of play-way method- Froebel's own unhappy childhood inspired new way of teaching called kindergarten and introduced first educational toys which he termed as 'gifts'. Similarly the passion and struggle of Dr. Montessori convinced the world that slum children can succeed and learn.

In the field of psychology early childhood development theorist (Ainsworth1974) and Bowlby (1969) found human relationship,central to the care and education of children. Later Piaget (1951) focused his theory on inseparability of cognitive

& affective development whereas Erikson (1963) explained the early years as crucial and healthy for psychosocial development establishing the trait of trust, autonomy and industry. The current view of highly influenced socio cultural context is renewed by the interest and work of Vyotsky (1978) work. For Vyotsky the social context i.e. individual's family, social and social expectation shape the child's development.

The work of twentieth century theorist John Dewey, Maria Montessori, Jean Piaget & Lev Vygotsky attracts a great deal of educators and has influence on the ECE. Dewey, a student of Stanley Hall was one of the first American to significantly impact in educational theory and practice. He is regarded as the founder of the school of "Progressivism" .His approach emphasizes on the child interest and prevalent theme of the teacher directed subject oriented curriculum. According to Dewey, learning flowed from the interest of the child instead from the activity chosen by the instructor. Dewey coined the term "Child Centered Curriculum" and "Child Centered School". Consistent with Dewey's belief ,the purpose of school was to prepare the students for the realities of the world and not just prepare for the future. In Dewey's classroom the children were socially active free in discovering what the objects were. They were continually provided with opportunities to explore and discover opportunities for experimentation. He did not abandon the subject matter or skills. Instead, the child interest was favored as the subject matter of instruction. Thus, from Dewey's perspective we learn that subject or curriculum cannot be established in advance. Educators are to guide activities, observe, monitor and offer encouragement and assistance as needed. They are not to control students.

As we examine the work of early childhood education the work of Maria Montessori stands out. Her contributions to early childhood education are significant. Her initial work with children having mental retardation was then considered indistinguishable from mental illness lead her to conclude that mental education rather than medical treatment could be a more effective strategy. She formed her theory of working with children which is similar to the philosophy on which early childhood education is built. The physician turned educator Dr Montessori believed that child's intelligence is not fixed / static but could be influenced by ones own experiences. She developed activity based sensory education model on which youngsters who were initially considered unachieving were successful. Children learn best by direct sensory experiences. She was further convinced that the children had natural tendency to explore & understand their world.

Dr. Montessori used dyadic material and fully allowed children to do things by themselves. She was convinced that children are capable of teaching themselves through interaction with carefully planned material and environment. She identified this concept as "Auto Education". Teachers in Montessori are facilitators and monitor child activity by using skillfully crafted lessons. Ideas are presented to the children in small steps built on previous experiences which form basis for next skill development.

Piaget stage theory helped educators structure learning opportunities that involve the ability to use symbol, reasons about quantities, classification and the perspective of others. From Piaget point of view the main accomplishment of preschool period (pre-operational stage) involve the development of symbolic abilities, language, imitation, symbolic play and drawing. For Piaget young children's thought take place in here and now and on the perceptual level. Similar views are shared by Vygotsky. Vygotsky's lack of training in psychology was an advantage to his understanding about child development. As an outsider he looked psychology with a fresh perspective. He proposed that children are influenced by socio and cultural worlds when they come in contact with parents, teachers and peers. Social experiences were very important to him because he believed that higher cognitive processes such as language and cognition necessitate social interaction. In his writing he has integrated physical and psychological world of the youngsters. Vygotsky believed that social interaction not only fosters intellectual development but is also vital for the development of social competence.

Significance of Early Childhood Education

The importance of early education is complemented by the fact that infants and toddlers experience life more holistically than any other age group. Children are born with natural curiosity and a strong exploratory drive. Their inquisitive nature feeds their development and learning. They seek active experiences through manipulating objects and play. They possess wide range of skills which helps them to explore as well as tune their finer skills and shape them by interacting in enriching environment.

The first five years of the child's life is crucial in determining their future development. During this period the architectural structure of the brain's connectivity is being formed. The nature and quality of stimulation and interaction will determine the child's capacity to learn in the long term and the associations they make between learning and pleasure.

There are developmental phases that all children go through but the individual progress is shaped by their culture and experience.

In social context, with the fading of traditional joint family system and increase in number of working mothers, many young children lack the required stimulation for development at home. The early childhood education is especially important for these children as a supplement to the home and mothering. It is well established fact that childhood stage is the most impressionable period during which vital foundations are laid down for optimum development. The formative years are decisive in unfolding the psychological abilities and capabilities of the children. Presently it has been observed that parents are pre-occupied with day to day hassles and worries. They lack knowledge about the child development and thus are unable to provide enriched and stimulating environment to their children at home. Researchers view the parents and/or families as an integral part of the early childhood education .Thus, early childhood educators attempt to bridge the child's two worlds: school and home. It is during early years that foundations for future learning are set and form the building block years. ECE often focuses on a child learning through play.

The main aim of ECE is promoting psycho-social development in children with focus on cognitive stimulation. The objectives of early childhood education are:

1. To address and foster the child's interest and curiosity through opportunities to explore, investigate and experiment in his/her environment.
2. To encourage independence and creativity by providing the child with sufficient opportunities for self expression
3. To develop child's competence to express his /her thoughts and feelings spontaneously, clearly and accurately.
4. To develop adequate gross and fine motor skills and visuo-motor coordination
5. Encourage in developing desirable social skills and attitudes, to facilitate healthy group participation and being sensitive to needs and rights of other individuals.
6. To develop emotional maturity by guiding the child to become aware, control and express his/her emotions in appropriate manner.

Who Needs Early Childhood Education?

What do children need to develop optimally? At the minimum all children have physical, social and emotional and cognitive needs. Physical needs include food, clothing , shelter and medical care. Social and emotional needs include consistent and predictable relationship with an attentive and caring adult and experience a strong peer relation. Minimal cognitive needs include the ability to communicate thoughts and feelings, to process information in a meaningful way, to engage in constructive problem solving and experience success in both school and in community.

Children who grow up with their basic physical and emotional needs met are more likely to trust themselves and their community, and build an inner resources to participate in society. They are likely to develop inner sense of confidence and competency in family, school and community endeavors as a result of successful coping experiences. On the other hand children who grow up without these basic needs met are at a clear disadvantage of starting healthy life. Many of these children exhibit particular behavioral and developmental characteristics. (e.g. developmental disabilities, poor school performance).

Children who are at risk of developmental disorders or belong to disadvantaged background are ideal participants for programmes aiming at early development of skills. Cole, Cole and Lightfoot (2006) has reviewed risk and protective factors associated with childhood problems. The factors are at different levels: child characteristics (temperament, cognitive abilities, attachment, self-esteem, and social relations), microsystems (child rearing skills, family environment), exosystem (neighborhood and community services) and macrosystem (culture, racism). From these factors it is evident that inputs are necessary at each level to bring about holistic changes that can be sustained. Programs such as Head Start, Perry preschool project, the Houston Parent Child Development Project, the Brookline Early Education Program and Interpersonal Cognitive Problem Solving in the United Kingdom, the Integrated Child Development Services (ICDS) in India, PANDAI project in Indonesia, Integrated Programme in Thailand (WHO, 1999) are all governmental initiatives to promote physical and/ or psychological development of preschoolers from disadvantaged backgrounds. Programs such as Sure Start and Head Start are commendable holistic efforts at promotion of well- being of children from disadvantaged backgrounds.

Primary prevention efforts with children have emphasized the importance of the first three years of children (WHO, 1999). However in an attempt to use the existing infrastructure of schools for service delivery or as an entry point for service delivery preschoolers (4-6 years) may be chosen as an appropriate group for work. The normal child development shows that the preschool period is significant for several reasons. The preschool period encompasses rapid growth in all developmental domains, including biological, cognitive, linguistic, emotional and moral development (Clyman, 2003). The growing cognitive abilities can enable acquisition of pre-academic skills. Linguistic development can assist promotion of communication skills which are important in both their social and emotional realms of interaction. Regulation of emotion is a principal development task of the preschool years (Cole, Cole & Lightfoot, 2006). Emotional regulation and effective social skills are crucial for maintaining positive peer relations (Sigelman, 1999).

Methods of Early Childhood Education

ECE takes into account the characteristics of children in the age group of 4-6 years. It follows the play-way approach which includes the following activities:

- Play (free and structured)
- Rhymes/songs
- Story telling
- Conversation
- Puppet play
- Doll's play

- Dramatization
- Indoor & outdoor games
- Nature walk
- Music & rhythmic exercises
- Languages and cognitive activities with manipulative material
- Experiments at the child's level

(such as water play, fun/magnet /balancing toys)

Family Participation

Families play an important role in promoting the healthy development of children. Thus supporting family's capacity in healthy development of a child is the efficient way to improve child outcomes (Powell, 2006).

Every facet of early learning program is related to parent and family dynamics. Family provides children with their most powerful learning arrangement. This includes modeling of behavior and disposition, the way members relate to each others and the kind of learning opportunities family members provide as children grow and develop.

Parents are needed in guiding young children. Many early childhood programs are promoting "parents as leaders" philosophy in order to encourage parents as effective problem solvers and nurturers of their children. This promotes parents being capable caregivers thereby increasing parent-child efficacy. When families are involved in their children's early childhood education, children may experience greater success once they enter elementary school (Miedel & Reynolds, 1999).

There are three important processes by which parents become involved in their children's kindergarten; those that build forms of confidence, skill, knowledge, and connection essential to family involvement in education (see figure below)

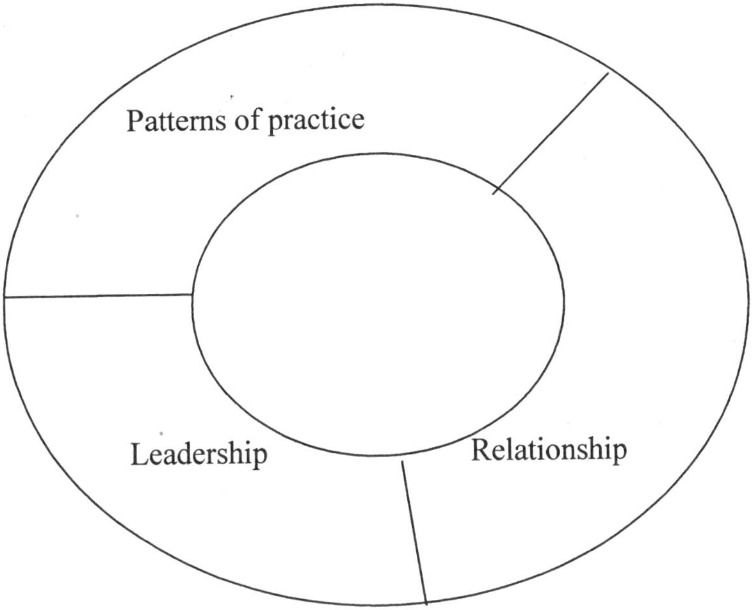

Processes that help Parents for Involvement in Kindergarten

- Information and guidance give them knowledge in how to help their child.
- Leadership opportunities give them a sense of efficacy about getting involved.
- Patterns of practice established early give parents skills for later involvement.
- Trusting relationships help parents connect with other educators later

Parents can Facilitate ECE......few Suggestions

- Developing a positive attitude towards learning right from beginning of schooling.

- Understand the importance of the pre-school period for acquisition of pre-academic skills and how cognitive development takes place. There is a need to recognize the role of critical period in learning and why it is important for child to receive basic inputs at this time.
- Parents need to utilize the curiosity of the child to help them know more about their environment.
- Exploring methods of making learning enjoyable and effective.
- Being innovative and creative in using naturally available material and resources.
- Understand the principles of learning such as starting with what the child knows, teaching at the child's pace, acknowledging child's efforts and using mediational and incidental approaches of teaching.
- Spending 'Quality Time' with the child and making him / her feel loved and secure.
- Giving proper guidance to the child.
- Taking the child outdoor and making him / her feel and aware of his/her surroundings. Draw the child's attention to the changes taking place around him / her in the environment.
- Respond to the child's queries and encourage him / her to explore. Avoid scolding the child even if he / she questions repeatedly.
- Let the children learn from their own experiences by touching, smelling, tasting and examining things carefully.
- Meeting the teachers regularly for feedback about their child's progress in learning. They can get specific ideas about learning activities which they can engage in and support learning at home.

Activities and games at home provide children maximum opportunities for interaction with parents and other adults at home. The child benefits in the following ways by spending quality time with the elders at home:

- Feels secure
- Becomes aware of his/her identity
- Learns to adjust with others
- Reposes confidence in others
- Becomes self-confident
- Gets opportunities for self expression
- Becomes curious and motivated
- Becomes sensitive to others

Role of Early Childhood Educator

Most of the teachers have a false notion that children can only learn when they are taught by their teachers. Often children are compared to lumps of clay or empty vessels which the teacher shapes or fills up. Conventional teaching methods contribute very little to the overall development of the child, while play-away and child- friendly methods promote overall development. Theoretically teachers claim that they are familiar with 'joyful learning' methods but in reality they have very little idea of how it works as they have not witnessed it. It is important to realize that all children are well equipped to learn about the world, if given a chance. Teachers should appreciate that children can be skilled, creative, imaginative and communicative and can demonstrate a new world of experience to their teachers.

In guiding young children's learning and development, early childhood educator must possess the knowledge, skills and sensitivity to interact successfully with the child. They need to realize that children are different in their temperament; some are shy, irritable, friendly, happy, active or dull. Hence each child requirements and expectations differ. They must make attempts to work closely with parents, guardians, paraprofessionals, community organizations and others whose actions affect child's development

Effective Educators of Young Children Possess the Following Qualities

- Establishes rapport with children, shows empathy and unconditional regard for them.
- Ensures pleasant learning environment for the children.
- Maintain a neutral stance and not be biased in approach towards children.
- Help young children explore and interpret the world around them in a way that makes sense to them.
- Takes interest in child's activities and feelings.
- Has knowledge of principles and domains of child development.
- Uses knowledge of how young children differ in their growth, development, and approach to learning.
- Uses knowledge of child development to facilitate the next developmental step for each child in the group and works with developmental specialists and special educators as necessary.
- Creates and modify environments and experiences to meet the individual needs of all young children in an inclusive educational setting.
- Utilizes various locally available resources to provide a suitable learning environment.
- Sets goals which reflect developmentally appropriate expectations.
- Focuses on child's special talents, competencies and achievement.
- Teaching the child difference between right and wrong. It is necessary to know this for the development of healthy habits and social interaction.

- Provides positive reinforcement for the child's efforts and recognizes the role of motivation in children's growth, development, and learning.
- Works in close association with children parents and caregivers and provides adequate support to them.

Differences between Type of Early Education for Privileged and Disadvantaged Children

In particular the living arrangement and psychosocial situations of children from disadvantaged backgrounds is different from their counterparts. The constellation of various dimensions in their environment are inherent and are potential risk factors that can influence the child's normal development trajectory .The dimensions such as inadequate parental supervision, lack of quality time, inadequate living arrangements, poor parental mental health, frequent conflicts at home and hostility towards the child indicates the presence of definite psychosocial risk factors in child's immediate environment. The mothers of such children are low on the positive parenting parameters such as warmth, reasoning, use of democracy and responsiveness (Nithya, 2007). These children go to government run school where teachers lack basic training and awareness about child's growth and development. The school lacks basic facilities and resources to provide opportunities for child to learn pre-academic skills. Keeping in mind the contrasting background of children from disadvantaged families as compared to children from more functional families, the programmes targeting early childhood education in children would differ in their focus to facilitate child's early learning. The children from privileged background and well educated families have more favorable conditions in their home and environment and are less exposed to stressors in life. The programmes designed for such privileged class would focus on helping parents to gain knowledge about child development and understand various strategies to facilitate child's learning. However the components of education for disadvantaged families would largely focus on promoting mental health of children and parents by helping them deal with stressful life situations and develop better coping skills. The programme emphasizes on normative child development with key focus on positive parenting, communication skills and shaping positive behavior in children. To promote early learning in children attempts are made to cultivate positive attitude in parents towards academics and discuss methods to make learning an enjoyable experience through play.

Evaluation and Recommendations

Children can be the resource for promoting their own psychological development. In the contemporary context of developmental psychology, emphasis is given to creative, flexible and child centered approaches.

In developed nations, for schools catering to the middle and upper strata of society this approach can widely be practiced due to available resources of manpower and expensive toys and equipments. Programs such as Sure Start and Head Start are commendable holistic efforts at promoting the well- being of children from disadvantaged backgrounds. However such innovative programmes all over the world have been questioned and discarded on the question of sustainability and applicability when tried out on a nationwide scale. In developing countries implementing such educational programs in schools is far from reality for disadvantaged population. Most of the schools follow traditional teaching method, where teaching is unilateral, from teacher to the child. The other problems include poor organization of educational services, poor infrastructure of the schools, high teacher-student ratio, lack of trained staff and inadequate training facilities, lack of knowledge and understanding about children's developmental patterns.

Lack of preschool facilities in government schools is a major setback for children belonging to disadvantaged population. This puts them at a disadvantage right from the beginning since they are expected to learn complex academic skills within short time after joining school. On the other hand teachers find teaching difficult and pressurizing. It is the need of an hour to acknowledge that ECE comes before primary education; every primary education centre must set up an early childhood centre. Incorporating school mental health program within the existing educational system would be helpful as suggested by Kapur (1997).

ECE is a special type of education and is different from education at all other levels. Therefore organizations working in ECE should cooperate actively in order to make it more effective. It is important to involve Ministry of Welfare to initiate change at larger level. One of the innovative methods to reach the needy population is conducting an opinion poll among the prospective recipients to know what their actual needs are. This would give an idea about setting the priorities while planning the programmes for children and their families. Respect for participants and equality of power in service delivery are needed for healthy engagement. Where minorities are targeted, the focus in the programs should be on strengthening their resources rather than highlighting their weaknesses.

In many developing countries though there are established governmental services to attend to the needs of children, there is definite potential for enhancement of resources at the individual and family level. Successful liaison between health service providers, educators and families is required for effective change to occur.

REFERENCES

Bowman B. T., Donovan M .S. & Burns M .S. (2000). *Eager to learn: Educating Our Preschoolers,* National Research Council, National Academy Press, Washington, DC, United States of America.

Clyman, R.B. (2003). *Preschool Development.* In A. Tasman, J. Kay, & J.A. Lieberman, (Eds), Psychiatry, (2nd Ed),Vol I (pp 118-132).Chichester: John Wiley.

Cole , M., Cole, S.R., & Lightfoot, C.(2006).*The development of children.* (5th Ed), (pp. 243-275), New York: Worth Publishers

Gargiulo, R.M., Kilgo, J.L. (2005).*Young Children with Special Needs.* New York, United States of America:. Thompson Delmar Learning,

Hutchin, V. (2003) *Observing and Assessing for the Foundation Stage Profile*. London: Hodder & Stoughton Educational.

Kapur, M. (1997). *Mental health in Indian Schools*. New Delhi: Sage Publication

Kapur, M. (2007). *Learning from children: What to Teach Them.* New Delhi: Sage Publications, INDIA.

Miedel, W. T., & Reynolds, A. J. (1999). Parent involvement in early intervention for disadvantaged children: Does it matter? *Journal of School Psychology*, 37(4), 379–402.

Nithya, P. (2007).Efficacy of Promotive Intervention with Lesser Privileged Preschoolers. *Unpublished PhD thesis submitted to NIMHANS*, Bangalore, India.

Powell, D.G. (2006). Families and Early Childhood Intervention. In Renniger, K.A. & Sigel, I.E. (Eds), *Handbook of Child Psychology*, (*6th edition*) Vol.4: *Child Psychology in Practice* (*pp 548-584*). New Jersey: John Wiley and Sons Inc.

Sigelman, C.K. (1999). Life-Span Human Development, (3rd Ed) (pp 2-22). CA:Brooks/Cole Publishing Company.

WHO,(1999). *A critical link: Intervention for physical growth and psychological development.* Switzerland : Department of Child and Adolescent Health and Development, World Health Organization.

6

The Basic Ingredients of Education for Children

Nilanjana Sanyal and Manisha Dasgupta

Introduction

In this planet, one of the significant qualities of life is its educational embellishment. Life is offered with rustic inherited traits or inclinations that need polish of civilization and marks of progression through "education", the environmental means of reaching to the desired points in life itself. Technically, educational qualifications are "stamps" of achievements – the password for entry into higher social frames of life. Philosophically, it is absorption of experiential knowledge into the system so that realization modes get uplifted and humane qualities are established in behavioural context. The former one needs admission into former courses of education, the latter ushers in the tendency of curving the path for deeper knowledge, values and virtues in life. The aim of life is just not material achievements and attainments of enjoyable frames of social life with greater number of available facilities, but reaching a point in spirit that can bring harmony in life, being connected with other elements of life and life-beyond. The tunes of life will tingle there, making the human soul taste the freedom of thoughts, feelings and experiences.

This is higher philosophy, not easily understandable by the general mass of the society. In daily doldrums of life, we need education to proceed further towards achievement processes. There, the values are different, realization coatings are of different shades. It is high time then to analyze the situation in terms of our educational practices, their implications and coming down to the point of assessment of what we are doing and why we are doing so. The chief concern is initiating children in formal educational processes, trying to help them in life progression. The results need to be analyzed in terms of exhibited outcome and then reverting to the point of probing into "why" and "how", if the outcomes are not of our choice. Citation of certain clinical cases would help to establish certain issues in the context.

8-year old Sayan has become very impulsive, restless, and at times, abusive towards authority that has prompted the parents to bring him to the psychotherapist's chamber. Record shows he is the only child of a nuclear family, where the father holds a most ordinary job and the standard of home life is of very moderate quality. From the beginning of Sayan's school life, he has been proved to be meritorious. His performances in the class situation are always of being "topper" in grade and hence a special place of recognition by teachers as well as other guardians of his batch-mates. The parents also started enjoying the fact and openly appreciating his merit. Sayan's sense of "I" got so inflated that in the annual examination of the previous year, when he had been placed in the second position because of obtaining one mark less than another boy, he could not bear it and gradually started showing the disturbed features in his behaviour. Parents were worried, and sad over his little less score points and unruly behaviour. They were not aware that their disappointment was one of the factors behind Sayan's emotional turmoil. Is this the education we plan to offer our children? Let us think...

In the play school, 3-year old Risha has urinated in the classroom for three consecutive days. Other than receiving prompt scolding, on the fourth day, she has been detained in the school for an extra hour after the school hour as a token of punishment for the same. Her phobic response to school set up has ultimately brought her for therapeutic intervention. The school demands well-trained toilet habits, the child fails..how can we educate her then?

7-year old Anup has a small brother of 5 years of age. Anup is a sensitive child and enjoys "nature" very much. While trying to complete a set of sums, he gets lost at times in the clouds of the sky and the birds flying there. Sums get mixed up, followed by scoldings or other punishments. Over his poor academic performance, he is being criticized through comparison with the younger brother who is considered to be very sharp intellectually. Extreme exposures in the process have ultimately made him withdrawn socially and emotionally. Are we really trying to educate him or pushing him down into darkness of failure? Is it an attempt of education or negligence of uneducated mind?

14-year old Aahan gets enmeshed in football fantasy being at study table. The problem is, he is being allowed to watch boys playing football from three-storied verandah for half an hour in the evening, but not allowed to play with them to save energy for studies. His energy is physically saved but what about saving mental energy for it?

A very regular scenario in the after school hours of renowned school areas is parents talking to their wards while collecting them from home. A close observation of their constant interaction reveals getting information from them regarding the day's performances in the school. Such conversation mostly meet parental comparisons with other students and their annoyance over his/her ward's not satisfactory performance. The query is, "Is this educational platter that a child should have to grow up being 'educated'?" The discussion needs clarification of the word, "education".

The English word, "education" etymologically means "drawing out." It refers to an endeavour to develop our latent talents. Hence, "education" can mean "unfoldment." It involves picking up something from one's own experiential fold, thereby giving a fresh "meaning" to experiences themselves.

1. Concept of Education

- Education encompasses teaching and learning specific skills, and also something less tangible but more profound: the imparting of knowledge, positive judgment and well-developed wisdom.

- Education has as one of its fundamental aspects the imparting of culture from generation to generation.
- Education means "to draw out," facilitating realization of self-potential and latent talents of an individual.
- It is application of **pedagogy,** a body of theoretical and applied research relating to teaching and learning and draws on many disciplines such as psychology, sociology and anthropology (Achilles et al., 1989).

1.1 Behavioural Elements of Education

- Education is utilizing one's own inner resources, both physical and mental, in the best possible way, without stressing or stretching the child as per the desire of the adults, so that he/she becomes a healthy, happy human being.
- Education is the prompter of openness of the self to the self-free states of life also to be able to enjoy the ultimate vision of life.
- Education is being aware of external as well as internal reality.
- Education is relating ability – cognitive assimilation and emotionally concept contextualization.
- Education is feeling-based realization.
- Education is picking up values.
- Education is practicing positivity.
- Education is finding out roots of non-materialistic energy-bound self-existence.
- Education is developing effective action plans to reach one's destination in life.
- Education is developing proper set of values that initiate stable developmental changes in character, leading a child to be a matured being in the years to come.

Psychologically, education is aiming to produce a human being who is intelligent, knowledgeable, hard-working, efficient, disciplined, smart, successful and hopefully a leader in his field of endeavour.; The real responsibility of education, in this perspective, is to reveal to the child all the beauty in art, in literature, in science, in mathematics, in music, in games and sports, in nature, and in relationship – indeed in every aspect of life.

2. Folds of formal education

A. Initiation of formal education is needed for:

Habit Formation

Children are simply bundle of physical as well as mental energy. Owing to immaturity and hence lack of reality-knowledge, they are unaware of the utility of adopting social control – being impulsive is the "norm" with them. To be in the arena of matured life in years to come, they need to be taught regular habits through the system of following caregivers' instructions. Cuddling them, pampering them, catering to their wishes are part pleasures in life – helping them in true sense requires teaching them curtailments, waiting, and keeping patience.

Routinization of Life

The spectrum of life to children means activity-involvement and seeking pleasure. The activities of these sorts are mostly stray and not goal-oriented. At least a significant length of activities needs to be target-oriented to enjoy smoothness in life – needs to be taught to them that needs support routinization of their life. This system is expected to open the vistas of good time management to them in later years.

Learning Discipline

A consequent educational element of the above two points is "disciplining" children. This is partly harnessing their bubbling energy to their own benefits; otherwise life seems to meet just the waste of their physical-mental resources in terms of being unruly, indisciplined, erotic in character pattern and neurotic at times in temperamental orientation. The net result is lack of education in the respect, producing a maladjusted unhappy child (Moyer, 1974).

Exposures to Different Subjects

Children need formal school set-up bound educational exposures. This is their access to different "subjects" – the ultimate route to develop personal interests in any or multiple contexts of them. The exposures, not forced impingement of different curricular and extra-curricular subjects are expected to help the child to develop personal tastes that may ultimately culminate in serious involvement and persuasion in the regard. The earlier the exposure, the earlier the interest-training – the better quality of involvement is expected in adult years.

Helping Children to be Motivated in Life

Life is just not an effort-adoption task scheme. Life has enjoyable aspects and elements both in external reality as well as in inner frames of mind and should be the proved lesson to children. Being involved in something, doing something just for the sake of enjoying it can also be a definite point of motivation in life. "I do these things, may be as routine tasks or else on the basis of my desire, I complete them and feel nice," may serve a permanent yardstick for assessing one's self-esteem and positive self-concept not to impart the idea of following them, but to prove the evidences of possibility in life contexts.

Helping Children to Develop Study-habits

Withdrawing mind from varied pleasure points and concentrating on comparatively drab "print materials" for intellectual information are difficult tasks for children. But without developing concentration habit, no education can become successful for anybody. Hence, initially with support, later on letting them being on their own, children need to have steady study-habits to develop positive approaches in life, toward information-seeking, and hence, rather than becoming victims of impulsive behaviour and inviting patches of depression-darkness in life (Sheoran & Kalia, 2005).

Value Education

Value education for children appears to be the call for the day for instilling the seedlings of education in the young. In fact, Living Value Education (LVE) envelops 12 key personal and social values to be developed for a better world and better life. The values are:

- Cooperation;
- Freedom;
- Happiness;
- Honesty;
- Love;
- Peace;
- Respect;
- Responsibility
- Simplicity
- Tolerance;
- Unity;
- Humility;

Value education implies that "fruitful education" is the kind used for our own welfare as well as that of others.

B. Training in physical health:

In the second fold of educational measures for them, training in physical health seems most essential. That maintenance of health is crucial as baseline for doing any other thing with full vigour and must be taught at very young age In this respect, three-fold orientations need to be maintained for them.

(a) Indoor games—Practices in such games are expected to bring greater concentration and restfulness in them. Sharing, cooperation and utility of cohesion seem to be extra attainments.

(b) Outdoor games—to develop participatory habits, cooperation and self-confidence, these are needed.

(c) Yogic exercises—These have multi-fold benefits for any child. Stabilization of inner physical resources and acquisition of energy to be productive in life comes from these sources. Children must realize that such involvements are basic and most essential requirements in life. Yoga seems to help them restore the inherited physical resources and help them develop fighting strength against environmentally-induced anomalies (Kochargaonkar, 2005, Swani, 2005).

C. Management of Anger and Anxiety

In the third fold, children need behaviour-oriented educational mould to be effective social member. In the respect, they need to be aware of basic social responsibilities in life and should be exposed to certain social practices from early stages. For example, helping elderly people physically or helping parents by being self-dependent in daily chores of life or being helpful to friend – should be there in their experiential realms. In the context, they should be made aware of their self-resources as well as environmental resource availabilities, so that with maximum maturity in their system, they can maximally utilize the available resources of outer reality in their achievement processes as well as in their processes of attainment of "personal meanings of life". In this sequence, a point of high importance seems to be "teaching them anger and anxiety management."

Anger Management

Individual differences in irritability, emotional susceptibility and dissipation versus rumination following an aggression-eliciting stimulus have been linked to differences in aggression among children and adolescents (Caprara et al., 1994; Collins & Bell, 1997). Moreover, hostile attributional bias, ie., the tendency to interpret others' behaviour as hostile, has also been found to predict aggressive behaviour (Burks et. al., 1999). Finally, a new perspective on the role of self-esteem claims that it is not low but unrealistically high self-esteem that makes individuals vulnerable to aggression (Baumeister & Boden, 1998). Individuals holding inflated and/or unstable views of themselves are more easily threatened in their self-esteem and are more likely to show aggression to restore positive self-appraisal (Baumeister & Boden, 1998).

Hence, the utmost necessity of helping children to manage their aggression and keep their self-control to facilitate them to acquire emotional maturity so as to unfurl the fruits of education.

Managing Aggression in Children

An important first step is to understand the underlying cause of the aggression. Dealing with the source will have a more long-term effect in addition to dealing with the here and now situation.

Secondly, identifying triggers to the aggression can help the adult head off a problem before it starts. Knowing what triggers the response allows for planning, even discussing the situation with the child and asking, "What would be the best way?"

Probably the most important part of handling an aggressive incident is to keep calm. Children need role models of adults who are able to handle their own feelings. It gives the child a sense of security to know that even though he may be out of control, the adult can maintain his own self-control. Many children respond to a soothing touch, but others just get more upset. So it is important to know what works with each child.

If time-out method is used, it should not be referred to as a punishment, but as a useful tool to help a person to cool off. It is important to model to the child that the parent uses time-out himself/herself when s/he feels stress coming on. The child may also be helped to find words to express his/her feelings rather than using his/her fists. The child may also be asked after an aggressive incident to think of as many ways as he can of what he could do differently if the circumstances were repeated. Some other measures of managing aggression in children are as follows:

- To plan schedules and physical space to reduce the frustrations that cause aggression;
- To use humour to defuse a difficult situation. Using a light approach can often deflect a power struggle that may deteriorate into aggression.
- Being more appreciative and positive in one's relationships and being assertive.
- Taking the stance of respecting life, people and other approaches; being proactive and not reactive.
- Avoiding gender-biased attitudes, categorizing and generalizing; describing instead of interpreting.

Anxiety Management

Anxiety is inevitable in our life. As we all are self-willed to a great extent, having myriads of personal desires, we ought to face frustrations and failures in life. The situation calls forth anxiety. A child wanting to be the topper in class, captain in school cricket team, champion in carom or a good dancer or painter – can at any moment suffer from anxiety. They need to be shown that a bit of anxiety is a motivation prompting factor in us, but too much of it spoils our attention on "present" and drags us to "future" which is not within our control. Hence, there should be a conscious practice of attending task at present, rather than thinking of what may come in future. Additionally, children should be given the fact that a failure does mean disappointment but that is not an "end" point in life. Hence, overcoming anxiety means being more active and enjoying the fact of being active, not taking our mind to future consequences.

Accepting "Nature" as Learning Canvas

In the fourth fold, a need is fėlt to educate *children to be connected with "nature"*. That we all are part of nature like other elements there, opens up a canvas of extended existence-platter. This helps in identification with human, non-human elements and increases the spectrum of pleasure in many respects. Since we all are earth-bound creatures of a fast growing technological world, we are bound to be materialistic. But those materialistic pleasures are comparatively temporary pleasure pots that many times invite competition-bound stresses and enormous feelings of negativity in us – need to be explained to them in many respects. Comforts in life are material-bound and they are needed in life, no doubt about it, but that mental comforts, which are long-lasting, if present in a person as an orientation in oneself, are also attainable in life, should be taught to them. These non-materialistic pleasures are simple self-pleasure points that cannot be destroyed by any external force. Enjoying beauties of life in so many different respects being non-interfered, seems to be a passion-glory for us. A flower-pot in someone's garden, a painting of depth touching one's heart, a soft tune that tingles in one's mind, a patch of soothing greenery in vision can be sources of enormous pleasure. No touch of competition and stress can be evident there. They can be simply "mine" and "my spirits". Can there be any stress-reducing factor of higher intensity? Doubt seems to cast its vote. A proper and harmonious blend of intellect, heart, and soul (our spirit) is the requirement of the making of a balanced being. Other than being ritualistic, little bit of orientation in spiritual education is expected to bring greater peace and harmony in mind, lesser anxiety and suspicion and may usher in a trend of mind to seep in inner experiences from time to time to touch upon the fathomless layers of life...the life in experience with all its fragrance.

Conclusion

Children are "tiny beings", waiting to be moulded by expert hands. This moulding process is education for them. Education is not just intellectual flare; it ought to have an emotional flare of understandability, acceptability and accommodativeness regarding life in the whole. Broadening of mental spectrum, developing higher quality of identification, having greater enjoyability-rim of mind is the required education for today's children – the residents of a technology crafted, competition-win hungry world of great chaos. The concept of power and position is in the air, the vibes of inner tranquility is missing. Education for children needs to be information curving intellectual enrichment process, but together with this the emotional education of absorbing deeper qualities and values of life should be its other wing. A child in such a blend will inhale the balanced vibes of dynamic life, be peaceful and contributory to the wealth of the magnificent experiential context of life and life only...

REFERENCES

Achilles, C.M., Linz, M.N. & Wayson, W.W. (1989). Observations on building public confidence in education. *Educational evaluation and policy analysis, 11(3)*, 275-284.

Baumeister, R.F., & Boden, J.M., (1998). Aggression and the self: High self-esteem, low self-control, and ego-threat. In R.C. Geen and E. Donnerstein (Ed.). *Human aggression: Theories, research and implications for social policy* (pp. 111-137) San Diego, CA: Academic Press.

Burks, V.S., Laird, R.D., Dodge, A., Pettit, G.S., & Bates, J.E. (1999). Knowledge structures, social information processing and children's aggressive behaviour. *Social Development, 8,* 220-236.

Caprara, G.V., Pergini, M., & Barbaranelli, C. (1994). Studies of individual differences in aggression. In M. Potegal and J.F. Knutson (Eds.) *The dynamics of aggression* (pp. 123-153). Hillsdale, NJ: Lawrence Erlbaum Associates Inc.

Collins, K., & Bell, R. (1997). Personality and aggression: The dissipation-rumination scale. *Personality and Individual Differences, **22,*** 751-755.

Kochargaonkar, S.H. (2005). Effect of Vipassana on subjective well-being and academic performance among adolescents. *Indian Journal of Community Psychology, **1(2),*** 181-186.

Moyer, K. (1974). Discipline. In K.Moyer, *You and your child: A primer for parents* (pp. 40-61). Chicago: Nelson Hall.

Sheoran, A., & Kalia, A.K. (2005). A study of depression, study habits and academic anxiety of urban and rural scheduled caste adolescents. *Indian Journal of Community Psychology,**1(2),*** 213-222.

Swani, P. (2005). Science of breath: Neorophysiological effects of Pranayam. *Indian Journal of Community Psychology, **1(2),*** 165-170.

7

A Review of Indian Schools for Child Development

H.L. Kaila

Introduction

Creating natural environment in the school as well as the classroom is getting increased impetus due to inclusion of environmental studies as compulsory Chapters under various courses of study. The school campuses and the classroom are a getting the natural and the greener outlook. The participation of students in creating natural school environment is also getting momentum. Teachers, parents and students at all levels get involved in the practical projects on the environment related issues so that the school becomes a centre for creating awareness about protecting natural habitats. The environment has many sides to study such as physical, social, political, cultural and the psychological. This Chapter has particularly focused on the socio-psychological environments with special focus on mental health issues of school children.

While taking a review of child mental health in Indian schools, the following issues come to the forefront such as segregation, children voices not being heard, teachers' punitive behaviour, and children being sexually abused. Students are also seeking democracy in school as in other places around the world. It is increasingly being realized that teachers can change schools. Mental health professionals are actively propagating mental health care of children in schools in India. A concept of happy schools is emerging.

METHODOLOGY

This Chapter particularly highlights a brief rapid review of research studies as conducted by the author between the years 1997 and 2007, and also his professional experience and interactions in the field of school psychology for nearly 15 long years.

The Findings and observations

Negative classrooms

It is much "easier" to run large schools with fear and a rod. John Loflin[14]

Indian Schools are fundamentally very strong that they believe in teaching discipline and character building but lack in imparting values in the classrooms; teachers teach non-violence with a cane in hand. The 34.1% of male students and 18% of female students expressed that they were hit with a ruler, paddle, or something else a few times (Kaila et al., 2002).

Segregation in schools Segregation—discrimination on the basis of academic performance—and detention (just to reach a 100 per cent pass percentage in SSC, schools tend to detain students) impact young minds. Children start segregating among themselves. Bright students feel happy, they look down upon others. The average ones feel depressed and lack interest in studies. They lack confidence and feel mediocre, feel hatred towards discriminating teachers. "Schools do it without realizing the consequences. They are not aware of the ill-effects" (Kaila & Kushal, 2007).

Stress Schools in India have become homes of stress, schools are where stress resides. Competition, marks, exams are major features. Students' voices are unheard in classrooms (Kaila, 2001).

Victimization The 11.3% of male students and 6.6% of female students were not allowed to go to the bathroom a few times. 9.7% of students (nearly one out of every 20) reported a few times that 'I wished I were dead. 2% students were forced to have sex one time (Kaila, 2002).

Sex experience The 17.0% students in school experienced one time that someone talked about sex and they didn't like it. The 10.4% students experienced the same a few times. 5.2% students in school experienced that sexual comments were made about them a few times (Kaila, 2003).

Punishment 5.5% students (one out of every twenty) were locked in school one time in a closet or small room. The 28.0% of boys and 15.1% of girls experienced a few times. They were given a punishment that was not fair (Kaila, 2003).

Students beaten up 19.2% of male students and 13.1% of female students stated that they were beaten up a few times. 18.4% of male students and 6.3% of female students expressed that they were slapped a few times (Kaila, 2003).

Negative discipline Teachers victimize students in order to discipline their classroom, as they don't know better ways of managing the classroom. Teachers are not aware as to how they harm emotional health of children. Peers bully their friends as they seek fun and thrill, they are not aware as to how they are affecting their friends emotionally (Kaila, 2005).

Children voices not heard Largely in the Indian schools scenario, the children are not allowed to speak out or raise their voices. They don't speak out in the classroom, and teachers also don't let them speak out (Kaila, 2006).

Worst experiences There are 58 worst things that happened to male and female children and adolescents in their school times. There are 105 mental health symptoms the students experienced as a result of worst experience in school (Kaila, 2006).

Teachers punitive behaviour Some teachers have continued punishing or harassing children over the years, even to an extent that a father said, "this teacher has not changed, she used to ask me to stand on the bench, and now she is asking my son to do the same, isn't it disgusting" (Kaila, 2007).

Classroom management The major factor that triggers such misbehaviors of teachers was that they are not equipped or trained with knowledge or wisdom on how to manage the class without affecting an emotional health of children (Kaila, 2007).

Impact of victimization Though male students received victimization (such as slapped, pushed, shaken) significantly more than the girls, the girls seem to be more impacted (such as getting angry and nervous) than the boys as a result of worst experience in school (Kaila, 2007).

A Survey on academic pressur A new survey in Thiruvananthapuram, capital of the southern Indian state of Kerala, has confirmed that academic pressure is making life miserable for our school children. They also seem to think fathers are not of much help and prefer to confidential their problems to their mothers only (Kaila, 2007).

Children sexually abused at school A survey carried out this year by the union ministry of women and child development shows nearly 50 per cent of children between the ages of 5 and 18 in 13 states across the country are sexually abused at school, and 53 per cent say they have suffered some form of sexual abuse - at school or elsewhere (Kaila, 2007).

Democratic school An Australian child was asked, how do you feel in a democratic school, he replied, "I am accepted here, I asked what do you mean, he added, my personality is accepted here in this school"...This does not happen in Indian school. Democracy in schools means an experience of Love, Inspiration, Freedom, and Enjoyment (LIFE) by children, teachers, parents and everyone. Does school provide LIFE is a big question mark? Indian schools are so much adult and authority driven, syllabus-pressurized and marks-oriented that they don't even see whether democracy in schools is what the children are wanting. DAV Schools in Mumbai have given democratic orientations to their students and teachers (Kaila, 2007).

Children seek democracy Though teachers and children both are seeking democracy to exist in Indian schools, they aren't getting much opportunity to experience it. If we wish our children to be taken care of in schools, schools need to take care of teachers' emotional health (Kaila & Kushal, 2007).

A field observation What we observed is that the teachers did not allow democracy to children in classroom because school authorities did not allow democracy to teachers in their work practices. Child friendly education is being demanded and emphasized now. In the present context, a group of sensitive people attempting to sensitize schools, parents, children, teachers and the policy makers on the alternate methods of education which is largely child centric or child friendly (Kaila & Kushal, 2007).

Teachers view on children While working with schools in India, what is being increasingly realized is that it is crucial to change 'teachers' view on children' through interactive discussion and dialogues as a measure to reform schooling to be experienced by children as promoting their natural potentials and creativity (Kaila, 2007).

Ban the word 'Fail' in schools

When you give next step to someone; you move this world up.

When you fail someone; you hold this world back.

Because someone whom you fail or promote is a small part of this big world.

NCERT is Banning the word 'Fail' from schools (Kaila, 2007).

Teachers can change schools

Teachers can inculcate self-governance and self-actualization in children.

A teacher said that I feel so guilty to ask for searching bags of every child when a child loses a pen in the classroom.

A democratic teacher said, "Why don't you allow children to decide how to find out the lost pen of a child"..this will resolve your guilt feelings (Kaila, 2007).

A Case

Two students were caught smoking in a school, out of fear, they ran away and returned after 4 days, the school principal asked them to make a presentation in front of the students /

teachers about what they experienced in 4 days, many students / teachers almost cried while listening to their worst experiences ..an insight came across as to how such a behaviour of students need to be dealt with (Kaila, 2007).

Major Thrust in Schools

Indian schools are now majorly working on teachers' re-training on dealing with learning, emotional and behavioural issues of children and adolescents. Parenting classes in schools are being held. Mental health professionals are actively propagating mental health care of children in schools (Kaila & Kushal, 2007).

Concept of Happy Schools

According to Vijayam Ravi (2007), Director of Singhania School, "School is a place where there is a lot of people activity. It comprises of children, teachers, management and parents" A school will be happy if there is an excellent networking among all these categories. Unfortunately, in schools today only teaching and examination take place and no learning! Partly the Principals and teachers and parents are responsible for this.

A school in which every teacher is emotionally secure and transmits this security to the students he/she interacts with is a happy school.

A school in which every one is motivated to give off their best is a happy school. A school in which everyone feels a sense of belongingness, love and takes ownership is a happy school.

The marushalas (desert schools) of western Rajasthan exist where there are no other schools. Pioneered by an NGO called the Urmul Trust, this unique alternative desert school is any urban pupil's fantasy. There are no classes in the accepted sense of the term. No corporal punishment, no stress-inducing tests. Instead, a relaxed learning environment, where children were looking forward to coming to school.

Teachers from these schools visit homes regularly to brief parents upon their child's progress. This also enables them to identify children not attending school. Although fees are not mandatory, parents can pay a sum voluntarily.

Principal Ranjini Krishnaswamy (2007) says that Happy Teachers make a happy school. Children interact most of the time with their teachers. If teachers are happy automatically their happiness rubs into the children.

Alka Lokre (2007) Principal, JHA Petrochemicals English Medium School, Nagothane shares that Happy schools are those who make happy children, who create positive attitudes and creative hands, who introduces the difference between the good and bad and inculcate in children the capacity to differentiate the two at right point and give courage to act accordingly, who create minds with empathy and thoughts with commitments.

A School Experience

I asked a class of 40 teachers to be honest as to what methods do they use to deal with difficult children in the classroom. They said the following ways:

(a) All of them agreed, they used cane, ruler of the children to punish them

(b) Scolding

(c) Giving remarks

(d) Warning

(e) Kneel down (one teacher showed how children do so)

(f) Asking them to stand for 20-30 minutes (even for KG children)

(g) Putting tag around their neck writing 'I am a bad boy'

(h) A 2-3 teachers gave some responsibility to naughty child to improve

(i) One of them used hugging the child

(j) A Catholic teacher said, it's written in the Bible "spare the rod, spoil the child".

(k) A Maharashtrian teacher says "chadi lage cham cham vidya aye gam gam"

Conclusion

Though the environmental studies have been added in schools as compulsory Chapters, we have yet to research and know as to how these natural and the green environments of the school have soothing and positive impact on the mental health of children. As far as the socio-psychological environments and its impact on mental health of school children is concerned, the Indian school and the classroom environments need a paradigm shift in view of the democratic schooling perspectives for which one could refer to www.educationrevolution,com for having an idea on a variety of democratic schools existing in different parts of the world. The democratic school environment encourages an individual child to recognizing and enhancing an inner potential and strengths for evolving a meaningful and satisfactory life.

Democratic school system is providing new meaning to the education system. It is going to provide a new step to the child development. Freedom schools, citizenship, free and alternate schools are some names given to democratic schools. There are democratic schools in USA, Israel, Japan, Thailand, England, Russia, Canada, and other countries. Democratic schools believe that the teacher needs to model joy, interest, excitement, and innocence of the children. Teacher needs to be transformational in her approach rather merely transactional. It is important to respond to the emotions of children. It's more important that the teacher learns how to manage her own emotions.

Informal and formal environments of the school do impact the child's learning and the way they imbibe values, which they would unconsciously use when they grow adults. According to a scholar, "I would be happy to see a school producing a street cleaner rather a neurotic scholar".

The students need a big positive change in schools on their socio-psychological environments with special focus on mental health issues. The education and the learning processes are killing the creative potentials of young people. The children are searching for baseline meaning for their life. They need an open environment in which they can express and experiment with their original and novel ideas. The present institutions and its teachers are unable to tap and develop the scientific attitudes and creativity in students, which is in abundance in them. Schools need to be democratized where the students have the rights to decide over matters that concern them in learning and education. The world needs democratic schools where students no longer suppress themselves but instead feel free to experience life the way they wish, and develop their natural potentials they are endowed with.

Indian schools have a long way to go as far as bringing about a radical change as needed by all those stake holders of school education. The child in school is to be heard for his / her choices and concerns, some schools are trying their best efforts as the globalizing and competitive society is impelling them to constantly change their curriculum and the methodology they adopt for its delivery to the students and also listening and responding to the concerns of parents. The teachers' sensitivity towards children remains an area of concern for which school teachers need regular cognitive and behavioral re-training towards holistic well-being of children. The school authorities and teachers need is also to constantly think and plan on as to how creating natural environments can contribute in improvement of the psycho-social environment in school education for enhancement of creativity in children.

REFERENCES

Kaila, H.L. (2001). Social Development of Teenagers. *Social Welfare, 48*, 31, 18-23.

Kaila, H.L. (2002). School Mental Health in Mumbai City: Review and Alternatives. *New Quest, 149*, July-September, 38-43.

Kaila, H.L. et al (2002). *Counseling for Growth*. New Delhi: Himalaya Publishing House.

Kaila, H.L. (2003). *Parenting Function*. New Delhi: Icon Publications Pvt. Ltd.

Kaila, H.L. (2003). School Based Approaches of Child Guidance and Counselling Services in Mumbai City. *Journal of Psychological Researches, 47,* 2, 57-60.

Kaila, H.L. (2003). School Mental Health in Mumbai City: Review and Alternatives, *Journal of Psychological Researches, 47,* 1, 31-35.

Kaila, H.L. (2005). *Educational Culture in Urban Cities. Health Administrator, XVII*, 2, 20-26.

Kaila, H.L. (2006). *Counselling in Schools*. New Delhi: Icon Publications Pvt. Ltd.

Kaila, H.L. (2006). Worst experiences of children in schools, Bihar Journal of sustainable Development, 2, 2, 67-87.

Kaila, H.L. (2007). Victimization of School Children. New Delhi: Icon Publications Pvt. Ltd.

Kaila, H.L. (2007). Worst experiences of children in school—A study in Mumbai. The Urban World, July-Sept, I, 2, 75-85.

Kaila, H.L & Kushal, K.B. (2007). Guidance and Counselling—New Perspectives. Ambala: The Associated Publishers

Krishnaswamy, R. (2007). A personal communication from a school Principal, Mumbai.

Loflin, J. (2007). A personal communication from a school educator. Indiana, USA.

Lokre, A. (2007). A personal communication from a Principal, JHA Petrochemicals English Medium School, Nagothane, Maharashtra.

Vijayam, R.(2007). A personal communication from a Director of Singhania School, Thane, Maharashtra.

World Health Organization (1997). Young People and Their Families: A cross-cultural Study of Parent/Adolescent Discord in Cote d' Ivoire, India, and Nigeria. Geneva. Switzerland.

8

Higher Education and Professionalism : Through the Lens of Self-Actualizing Potentials

Nishat Afroz and Ranjana Mittra

Introduction

Self-actualization is the prime motivation of a healthy person. It is a person's desire for self-improvement, or actual use of potentials, talents and capacities. Self-actualization need not take the form of creative and artistic endeavours. A parent, an athlete, a student and a teacher may be actualizing potential in doing well in respective pursuits (Maslow & Lowery, 1998). The individual must feel that they are an important and useful specimen of the nature and is made for the work they are doing. They have adequate potentials to do the job and can achieve success in that profession.

According to Maslow (1954), the highest human values are said to be associated with self-actualization. He admits that self-actualization can be defined in various ways but essentially, self-actualizers (a) accept and express the inner core or self (b) imply minimal presence of ill health, neurosis, psychosis, of loss or diminution of the basic human and personal capacities and (c) are motivated by some values which they grope for, and to which they are loyal (Maslow, 1968; Maslow, 1971). It is, according to Maslow, the striving for health, the search for identity and autonomy, and the yearning for excellence. It is the need for the development of the essential human nature; a pressure toward a unified personality, toward identity and full individuality (Maslow, 1970), the need for the attainment of full humanness (Maslow, 1971).

Education is one of the highest fields of human endeavour, which has helped human beings understand themselves, their life, and their society, and has trained them to become a productive member in particular area of human life. Education and self-actualization are parallel processes. Both require personal investment and are defined by their progressive nature (Merriam & Caffarella, 1998).

It is often assumed that education may be enriching for individuals and a mode for enhanced learning, self-actualization, personal growth as well as national cultures in general. It is assumed that higher education may function, in a highly complex fashion, as a catalyst in initiating social change, stimulating economic growth and increasing people's overall sense of life-quality (Steir, 2004). Developing learning experiences that facilitate self-actualization and creativity is among the most important goals of our society in preparation for the future. To facilitate deep understanding of a new concept to facilitate learning, learners must have the opportunity to develop multiple and flexible perspectives (Winslow, 2005).

Self-actualization, "the desire to become more and more what one is, to become everything that one is capable of becoming" (Goble, 1970), as stated in Abraham Maslow's theory of basic needs, is fundamentally equivalent to the goals for education, learning environments, and creativity, espoused by notable educators and psychologists. Notable educators and psychologists agree that learning is enhanced when it is pursued as a creative and self-actualizing passion. These goals emphasize learning in relation to creativity, incubation, play, imagination, analogy, flexibility, optimal experience, joy, well-being, and adequate challenge. There is agreement not only that learning and creativity are essential to self-actualization, but also that self-awareness, intrinsic motivation, and self-actualization are fundamental to learning and creativity as well, there is a synergistic cycle (Amabile & Kramer, 2003; Csikszentmihalyi, 1996; Faure, et.al., 1972; Torrance, 1965; Childs, 2003).

Many investigators (Schostac, 1989; Cangemi, 1987; Wacks, 1987; McAlindon, 1981; Smith & Meek, 2000; Fletcher, 1998) have put forward the view that education is a creative source which will help in attaining self-actualization. Banaras Hindu University is a different kind of educational institution that provides professional as well as general education at the same campus. Its academic programs and professional courses provide students with optimal conditions for realization of one's real self and achieve individual integration and growth. Assuming that appropriate conditions and other prerequisites of self-actualization are available in the educational and professional settings, the present study proposes to examine whether professional and non-professional career orientation has an effect on the development of the need for self-actualization.

An assumption of the present study was that higher education along with attendant learning, skill training, and highly placed professional and non professional careers would provide the subjects with many growth enhancing conditions that may enable them to achieve self-actualization. Based on the studies carried out in different societies, it was hypothesized that there would be greater number of self-actualized individuals in the professional group than in the semi-professional group, or in the group of academicians. It was also hypothesized that self-actualized professionals would score higher on the POI as compared to semi-professionals and academicians.

METHODOLOGY

Sample and Design

The study was conducted on 100 professionals, 100 semi-professionals and 100 academicians. The present study has operationally differentiated between professionals, semi-professionals and academicians. Professionals represent those individuals who pursue a career that allows them to apply and observe the effects or outcomes of their knowledge and skills in creatively dealing with everyday demands and solving problems of their career. Semi-professionals represent those individuals who pursue a career that mainly involves teaching as a full time faculty member at a university. To some extent they are also able to practice their knowledge as part-time consultant doctors, consultant engineers, and management consultants. Academicians represent those individuals who pursue a career that involves teaching and research as full time faculty members of the university. Their high knowledge and learning do not have an immediate impact on the society.

In the present study practicing doctors, engineers, lawyers, architects and managers represented the professional group. They were selected from the city of Varanasi. Semi professionals were selected from the Institute of Medical Sciences, Institute of Technology and Faculty of Management Sciences of Banaras Hindu University, Varanasi. The academicians were selected from the Faculty of Arts, Faculty of Sciences, Faculty of Social Sciences and Faculty of Commerce, Banaras Hindu University, Varanasi. All the groups included male and female participants.

Table 1: Sample Distribution

	Professional [N 100]		*Semi-professional [N 100]*		*Academician [N 100]*	
	Male	Female	Male	Female	Male	Female
N	85	15	91	9	66	34
Mean Age	33.82	32.13	46.70	36.44	48.30	41.44

TOOLS

Biographical Data Sheet

The sheet was prepared to provide necessary demographic details of the selected subjects. Special efforts were made in collecting data regarding people's social contributions, awards, recognitions in their respective fields of work and participation in extra-curricular activities.

Personal Orientation Inventory (POI)

Personal Orientation inventory developed by Shostrom, (1964) was used to select respondents who are self-actualized and those who are not self-actualized. It was a 150 two-choice item, self report questionnaire which reflects the values and behaviour of major importance in the development of a self-actualizing person. The items are scored twice, first for two basic scales of personal orientation, inner directed support (127 items) and time competence (23 items) and second for ten subscales each of which measures a conceptually important element of self-actualizing: (1) self-actualizing value (SAV), (2) existentiality (Ex), (3) feeling reactivity (Fr), (4) spontaneity (S), (5) self-regard (Sr), (6) self-acceptance (Sa), (7) nature of man (Nc), (8) synergy (Sy), (9) acceptance of aggression (A), (10) capacity for intimate contact (C).

Results

The data were analyzed using Mean, SD, Tukey's test of significance, one way analysis of variance and t-test. The overall results indicate that professionals and semi-professionals are generally able to function effectively and have the requisite level of competence or ability to develop towards a higher level of self-actualization. Academicians, on the other hand, though highly educated and settled in respectable career, are not able to self-actualize like professionals. They do not function at an effective level to move towards self-actualization.

Table 1: Mean, SD and F-ratios for Professionals (N = 100), Semi-professionals (N = 100) and Academicians (N = 100) on the POI Scale.

POI Scales	*Professionals*		*Semi-Professionals*		*Academicians*		*F value*
	Mean	*SD*	*Mean*	*SD*	*Mean*	*SD*	
1. Time Competence (Tc)	15.32	2.60	14.10	2.60	13.78	2.29	10.54**
2. Inner-Directed (I)	77.83	9.23	77.39	8.91	74.27	6.53	5.44**
3. Self-actualizing Value (SAV)	18.66	3.04	18.51	3.09	17.54	2.59	4.33**
4. Existentiality (Ex)	16.52	3.96	15.32	4.28	15.70	3.37	2.47
5. Feeling Reactivity (Fr)	13.45	2.88	13.31	2.80	12.60	2.48	2.78
6. Spontaneity (S)	11.22	2.24	10.03	2.22	10.80	1.87	8.08**
7. Self-Regard (Sr)	12.40	1.86	11.93	2.03	11.47	1.82	5.91**
8. Self Acceptance (Sa)	14.02	3.42	13.41	3.06	13.94	2.21	1.26

POI Scales	Professionals Mean	SD	Semi-Professionals Mean	SD	Academicians Mean	SD	F value
9. Nature of Man (Nc)	11.75	1.82	11.79	1.77	11.25	1.64	2.95*
10. Synergy (Sy)	6.62	1.40	6.14	1.51	6.26	1.26	3.19*
11. Acceptance of Aggression (A)	14.61	2.57	13.97	2.92	14.19	2.62	1.43
12. Capacity for Intimate Contact (C)	15.86	3.74	14.71	3.54	15.82	3.06	3.54*

**P <.01, *P <.05

Table 2. Tukey's Test of Significance across Means of three groups on the POI

Variable	Category		Mean difference
Time competence	Prof.	Semi-Prof.	1.22*
		Acad.	1.54*
	Semi-Prof.	Acad.	.320
Inner-directed	Prof.	Semi-Prof.	.440
		Acad.	3.56*
	Semi-Prof.	Acad.	3.12*
Self-actualizing value	Prof.	Semi-Prof.	.150
		Acad.	1.12*
	Semi-Prof.	Acad.	.970*
Spontaneous	Prof.	Semi-Prof.	1.19*
		Acad.	.420
	Semi-Prof.	Acad.	.770*
Self-regard	Prof.	Semi-Prof.	.470
		Acad.	.930*
	Semi-Prof.	Acad.	.460
Nature of man	Prof.	Semi-Prof.	-4.00
		Acad.	.500
	Semi-Prof.	Acad.	.540
Synergy	Prof.	Semi-Prof.	.480*
		Acad.	.360

Variable		*Category*	*Mean difference*
	Semi-Prof.	Acad.	–.120
Capacity for Intimate	Prof.	Semi-Prof.	1.15*
Contact		Acad.	.000
	Semi-Prof.	Acad.	–1.11

**P <.01, *P <.05

Table 1 presents the mean score and SD of professional, semi-professionals and academicians on various subscales of the POI. ANOVA revealed significant difference (F = 10.54, p<.01) in scores on the scale of time competence (Tc). Tukey's test (Table 2) revealed that professionals with a mean of 15.32, were more time competent as compared to semi-professionals (Mean = 14.10) and academicians (Mean = 13.78). While the difference between semi-professionals and academicians were not significant.

On the scale of Inner-directedness (I) a significant variance (F = 5.44, p<.01) was found. Professionals with a mean of 77.83, were more inner-directed as compared to semi-professionals (Mean = 77.39) and academicians (Mean = 74.27). While the differences of professionals and semi-professionals with academicians were significant. The difference of professionals with semi-professionals was not significant.

These findings indicated that professionals with a higher mean score on both the scales were more time competent and inner-directed (a necessary requirement for self-actualization) as compared to semi-professionals and academicians who had relatively lower mean scores on these scales. This suggests that these groups did not have enough time competence and inner-directedness to be able to self-actualize like the professionals.

Analysis also indicated that the three groups differed significantly (F = 4.33, p <.01) on the scale of self-actualizing value (SAV). Professionals with a mean of 18.66 were higher on self-actualizing value as compared to semi-professionals (Mean = 18.51) and academicians (Mean = 17.54). The differences of professionals and semi-professionals with academicians were significant. This suggests that the professionals and semi-professionals hold on and live by self-actualizing values more than do academicians.

A significant variance (F = 8.08, p<.01) was found on the scale of spontaneity (S). Professionals having a mean of 11.22 were higher on this scale as compared to academicians (Mean = 10.80) and semi-professionals (Mean =10.03). The difference between professionals and academicians was not significant. While semi-professionals and academicians differed significantly on the Scale of spontaneity.

On the scale of self-regard (Sr), professionals, semi-professionals and academicians differed significantly (F = 5.91, p<.01). Professionals with a mean of 12.40, were higher as compared to semi-professionals (Mean = 11.93) and academicians (Mean = 11.47). Professionals and semi-professionals did not differ significantly on this scale. While the difference between professionals and academicians were significant. This suggests that professionals and semi-professionals have more self-worth as compared to academicians.

A significant variance (F = 2.95, p<.05) was found on the scale of nature of man (Nc). Semi-professionals with a mean of 11.79, held a more constructive view of the nature of man as compared to professionals (Mean = 11.75), and academicians (Mean = 11.25). However, groups did not differ significantly from each other on the Tukey's test.

On the subscale of synergy (Sy) a significant variance (F = 3.19, p<.05) was found. Professionals with a mean of 6.62 tended to demonstrate the ability to see the opposites of life more meaningfully related as compared to semi-professionals (Mean = 6.14) and academicians (Mean = 6.26). The difference was significant between professionals and semi-professionals. While the differences of professionals and semi-professionals with academicians were not significant.

A significant variance (F = 3.54, p<.05) was found on the scale of capacity for intimate contact (C). Professionals with a mean of 15.86 revealed greater ability to develop intimate relationship with other human beings as compared to academicians (Mean = 15.82) and semi-professionals (Mean =

14.71). The difference between professionals and semi-professionals was significant. The differences of professionals and semi-professionals with academicians were not significant.

No significant variances were found on the scales of existentiality (Ex), feeling reactivity (Fr), acceptance of self (Sa) and acceptance of aggression (A). The mean differences were too small to reach the level of significance. On the subscales of existentiality (Ex), professionals (Mean = 16.52) were slightly more flexible than semi-professionals (Mean = 15.32) and academicians (Mean = 15.70). On the subscale of feeling reactivity (Fr) professionals (Mean = 13.45) were slightly higher than semi-professionals (Mean = 13.31) and academicians (Mean = 12.60). This suggests that professionals were slightly more sensitive to needs and feelings as compared to semi-professionals and academicians.

Findings also revealed no significant difference on the scale of self-acceptance (Sa), though professionals (Mean = 14.02) showed more ability to accept self in spite of weaknesses or deficiencies as compared to academicians (Mean = 13.94) and semi-professionals (Mean = 13.41).

Analysis also indicated professionals having a slightly higher score (Mean = 14.61) on the scale of acceptance of aggression (A), than that of academicians (Mean = 14.19) and semi-professionals (Mean =13.97), but again the difference was not significant. These findings reveal that professionals were generally higher on the POI scales than semi-professionals and academicians.

Table 3. Mean, SD and F-ratios on the POI Scales for Self-actualized Professionals (N =50), Semi-professionals (N = 28) and Academicians (N = 19)

POI Scales	*Professionals*		*Semi-Professionals*		*Academicians*		*F value*
	Mean	*SD*	*Mean*	*SD*	*Mean*	*SD*	
1. Time Competence (Tc)	16.94	1.25	16.92	1.38	16.00	1.29	3.96*
2. Inner-Directed (I)	85.10	4.77	85.53	4.57	83.52	3.25	1.23
3. Self-actualizing Value (SAV)	19.92	2.05	19.78	2.28	19.42	2.77	.3[illegible]1

POI Scales	*Professio-nals*		*Semi-Professionals*		*Academi-cians*		*F value*
	Mean	*SD*	*Mean*	*SD*	*Mean*	*SD*	
4. Existentiality (Ex)	18.66	3.28	17.67	3.96	16.84	3.41	2.02
5. Feeling Reactivity (Fr)	14.46	2.47	13.78	2.18	15.26	2.37	2.20
6. Spontaneity (S)	12.34	1.82	11.00	2.05	11.78	1.54	4.73**
7. Self-Regard (Sr)	12.78	1.48	12.57	1.97	12.84	1.86	.182
8. Self Acceptance (Sa)	15.82	2.98	15.00	2.81	15.84	2.11	.876
9. Nature of Man (Nc)	12.40	1.53	11.57	1.34	12.15	1.70	2.67
10. Synergy (Sy)	7.18	1.02	6.53	1.37	7.21	1.08	3.23*
11. Acceptance of Aggression (A)	15.88	1.82	14.07	2.95	15.15	2.77	5.13**
12. Capacity for Intimate Contact (C)	18.14	3.16	16.57	2.65	17.94	2.46	2.74

**P <.01, *P <.05

Table 4. Tukey's Test of Significance across Means of Self-actualized Professionals, Semi-professionals and Academicians on POI

Variable		*Category*	*Mean difference*
Time competence	Prof.	Semi-Prof.	1.14
		Acad.	.940*
	Semi-Prof.	Acad.	.928*
Spontaneous	Prof.	Semi-Prof.	1.34*
		Acad.	.550
	Semi-Prof.	Acad.	–.789
Synergy	Prof.	Semi-Prof.	.644*
		Acad.	–3.05
	Semi-Prof.	Acad.	–.674
Acceptance of Aggression	Prof.	Semi-Prof.	1.80*
		Acad.	.722
	Semi-Prof.	Acad.	-1.08

**P <.01, *P <.05

Table 3 compares the mean scores of self-actualized professionals (N = 50), semi-professionals (N = 28) and academicians (N = 19) on various dimensions of self-actualization. ANOVA revealed that the concerned groups differed significantly (F = 3.96, p<.05) on the scale of time competence. Tukey's test (Table 4) revealed that both professionals (Mean = 16.94) and semi-professionals (Mean = 16.92) scored higher and differed significantly from academicians (Mean = 16.00). The difference between professionals and semi-professionals was marginal and statistically not significant.

A significant variance (F = 4.73, p<.01) was found on the scale of spontaneity. Professionals with a mean of 12.34, showed a higher ability to express feelings behaviourally as compared to academicians (Mean = 11.78) and semi-professionals (Mean = 11.00). Professionals scored higher and differ significantly from semi-professionals. The difference between professionals and academicians and between semi-professionals and academicians was not significant.

On the subscale of synergy self-actualized professionals, semi-professionals and academicians differed significantly (F = 3.23, p<.05). Professionals (Mean = 7.18) and academicians (Mean = 7.21) scored higher than semi-professionals (Mean = 6.53). The difference between professionals and semi-professionals was significant. The difference of professionals and semi-professionals with academicians was not significant.

The self-actualized professionals, semi-professionals and academicians differed significantly (F = 5.13, p<.01) on the subscale of acceptance of aggression. Professionals (Mean = 15.88) and academicians (Mean = 15.15) with a higher mean revealed that they had a higher ability to accept anger or aggression as compared to semi-professionals (Mean = 14.07). Table 4 indicates that the difference of self-actualized professionals with semi-professionals was significant. While the difference of professionals and semi-professionals with academicians were not significant.

No significant differences were found among self-actualized professionals, semi-professionals and academicians on inner-directed (I), self-actualizing value (SAV), existentiality (Ex), feeling reactivity (Fr), self-regard (Sr), acceptance of self (Sa), nature of man (Nc) and capacity for intimate contact (C) scales. The trend of mean scores in general indicated professionals to be higher on inner-directed, self-actualizing value, existentiality, spontaneity, nature of man and capacity for intimate contact scales as compared to semi-professionals and academicians. The mean scores also indicated professionals and academicians to be close to each other with respect to self-regard and self-acceptance, while semi-professionals scored lower on these two scales.

The overall findings revealed that the three groups of self-actualized subjects differed significantly on the scales of time competence, spontaneity, synergy, and acceptance of aggression. The professionals scored higher than semi-professionals and academicians on all those scales. They were more time competent, had more ability to express feelings behaviourally, saw man as essentially good, and accepted anger or aggression within oneself as natural. On the remaining scales the groups did not show significant differences.

Discussion

An assumption of the present study was that higher education along with attendant learning, skill training, and highly placed professional and non professional careers would provide the subjects with many growth enhancing conditions that may enable them to achieve self-actualization. The results indicated that professionals and semi-professionals were generally able to function effectively and had the requisite level of competence or ability to develop towards a higher level of self-actualization. Academicians, though highly educated and settled in a respectable career, were not able to self-actualize like professionals. They did not function at an effective level to move towards self-actualization.

Findings of the study suggested some effect of professionalism on self-actualization. A comparison of self-actualized professionals, semi-professionals and academicians revealed that self-actualized professionals and semi-professionals were superior on some scales as compared to academicians and the number of self-actualized people was higher in professional group than in semi-professional and academician groups. Other researchers had also indicated that self-actualization was positively and significantly related to the degree of professionalism. It reflects a leader's potential to excel. In theory, reaching this level includes finding fulfillment in individual accomplishments, as well as recognizing the potential to stand out as a change agent and lead others to see and do the same. (Fetzer, 2003; Hamric, et. al., 2000; Schindler et. al., 1986; Gundersheim, 1982; Rotella et. al., 1980; Carlson et. al., 1980; Steir, 2004).

Self-actualization needs have been rated as important by Indian managers, regardless of differences in their occupational levels (Venkatraman & Anantharaman, 1991). Indian managers, including officers, have been found to be more oriented towards higher level needs than non-managers and clerks (Kulkarni, 1981). Officers attach greater importance to growth needs than do clerks who in turn attach greater importance to existence needs than do officers (Rao & Kulkarni, 1998).

Professionals and semi-professionals of the present study clearly show that the professional aspect of their career is helpful in functioning effectively and having the requisite competencies to develop towards a self-actualizing person. On the other hand, academicians who were equally educated and placed in respected careers were not able to achieve as high level of self-actualization as did professionals and semi-professionals. The number of self-actualized academicians was also small. Findings similar to those of the present study have been reported in other studies too. Hankins and Clarks (1989) found that teachers were less self-actualized as compared to education majors.

Some studies have reported teachers (Hankins et al., 1989), university professors (Hampton & Kerasotes, 1978), and managers (Mathur et. al., 1987) to be less self-actualized than was hypothesized. Professionals, semi-professionals and academicians of the present study were highly learned and educated. The general environment and opportunities for all subjects were more or less the same but only half of them were able to actualize their potentials. Others failed to attain the required level of time competence and inner-directedness to be able to self-actualize. One possible reason could be that most of us are generally not aware of our hidden potentialities and capabilities. We tend to remain satisfied with whatever we have achieved. Maslow notes that people will grow and actualize their potential only if the environment is right (Ulrich, 2003).

Findings discussed in the previous pages reveal that in spite of all growth enhancing environment, the respondents of the present study were not able to achieve a higher level of self-actualization. Professionalism facilitates the process of self-actualization, but to a limited extent. Maslow (1971) suggests that the need for self-actualization is natural, inborn and present in all of us, but very few people are able to realize this. The subjects of the present study had reputed careers with national and international recognition of their academic contributions, and were the recipient of various prestigious awards. Thus, all prerequisites of self-realization were present among them.

Facilitative environmental factors, skills and knowledge training, and reflection upon experiences and beliefs are regarded as important factors in teacher development. In spite of all these, however, only a limited number of subjects were able to self-actualize, and those who were able to self-actualize, also did not cross the mean standard score for each scale. In an unpublished Chapter, Maslow notes that, 'So far, I have been studying self-actualization via autonomy, as if it were the only path. But this is quite Western, and even American' (cited in Hoffman, 1988). He was concerned that the theory of self-actualization might not apply to relatively poorer countries, where only few people can find self-fulfillment through their livelihood. This could be a reason. It is difficult to specify reasons for it, however, we may look at it in terms of differences in cultural orientation (Eastern vs. Western), domain specificity of self-actualization (work vs. family), and the appropriateness of the POI as a tool of measurement of self-actualization. Therefore, the inability of these three groups needs to be viewed in a different context.

REFERENCES

Amabile, T, & Kramer, S., (2003). The Best (and Worst) Days in Creative Project Teams: Some Preliminary Results; SESP Groups Pre-Conference, Harvard Buisness School, October 2.

Cangemi, J. P. (1987). Education and self-actualization. *Journal of Instructional Psychology. 14,* 4, 164-175.

Carlson, J. M., & Hyde, M. S. (1980). Personality and political recruitment: Actualization or compensation. *Journal of Psychology 106,* 1, 1117 - 1120.

Childs, M. (2003). 'Father of Creativity' E. Paul Torrance Dead at 87; The College of Education: Online News. The University of Georgia. Monday, July http://www.coe.uga.cdu/coenews/2003/EPTorranceObit.html

Csikszentmihalyi, M. (1996). *Creativity: Flow and the Psychology of Discovery and Invention.* Harper Collins Publishers, New York, NY.

Faure, E., Herrera, F., Kaddoura, A., Lopes, H., Petrovsky, A., Rahnema, M., & Ward, F. (1972). Editors, *Learning To Be: The World of Education Today and Tomorrow*, UNESCO, Paris.

Fetzer, S. J. (2003). Professionalism of associate degree nurses: the role of self-actualization. *Nursing Education Perspectives, 24,* 3, 139-143.

Fletcher, S. (1998). Attaining self-actualization through mentoring. *European Journal of Teacher Education, 21,* 21, 109-118.

Goble, F. (1970). *The Third Force: The Psychology of Abraham Maslow A Revolutionary New View of Man.* Pocket Books, New York, NY.

Gundersheim, J. (1982). A comparison of male and female athletes and non-athletes on measures of self-actualization. *Journal of Sport Behaviour, 5,* 4, 186-201.

Hamric, A.B; Spross, J.A. & Hanson, C.M. (2000). *Advanced Nursing Practice: An Integrative Approach* (second ed), W B Saunders Company, Philadelphia.

Hampton. J. D., & Kerasotes, D. L. (1978). Faculty level of SAZ in relation to student rating instructors. *Educational and Psychological Measurement, 39*, 971-975.

Hankins, N. E., & Clark, H. (1989). Self-actualization: Do teachers need it? *Journal of Human Behaviour and Learning. 6,* 2, 7-13.

Hoffman, E. (1988). *The right to be human: A biography of Abraham Maslow*. New York: McGraw-Hill.

Kulkarni, A. V. (1981). Reward expectancies in relation to cognitive styles. Unpublished Ph. D. thesis, Nagpur University.

Maslow A. (1954). *Motivation and personality*. New York: Harper and Row.

Maslow, A. (1968). *Toward a psychology of being*. New York: Van Nostrand.

Maslow, A. (1970). *Motivation and personality*. New York: Harper and Row.

Maslow, A. (1971). *The farther reaches of human nature*. New York: Viking.

Maslow, A., & Lowery, R. (1998). *Toward a psychology of being* (3rd ed.). New York: Wiley & Sons.

Mathur, P. & Yadava, S.R. (1987). Managerial effectiveness, leadership styles and SAZ, orientation of middle level managers in public sectors organizations in India. *Social Science International*, *3,* 2, 1-12.

McAlindon, H.R. (1981). Education for SAZ. *Training and Development Journal,* 35, 10, 85-91.

Merriam, S. & Caffarella. (1998). *Learning in Adulthood: A comprehensive guide*. San Francisco: Jossey-Bass.

Rao, P. U. B., & Kulkarni, A. V. (1998). Perceived importance of needs in relation to job level and personality make-up. *Journal of the Indian Academy of Applied Psychology, 24,* 1-2, 37-42.

Rotella, R. J., Gansneder, B., Ojala, D., & Billing, J. (1980). Cognitions and coping strategies of elite skiers: An exploratory study of young developing athletes. *Journal of Sports Psychology, 2,* 350-354.

Schostac, J. (1989). The play of education. Special issue: New directions for educational theory:II. Conceptualizing the problems of educational change. *Cambridge Journal of Education. 19,* 2, 207-223.

Schindler, T. M., & Waters, M. (1986). Athletic involvement and aspects of self-actualization. *Journal of Sport Behaviour, 9,* 2, 59-69.

Shostrom, E.L. (1964). Edits manual for POI. *Educational Industrial Testing Services*. San Diego, California.

Smith, M. C., & Meek, G. (2000). Teachers' value orientations and their compatibility with the National Curriculum for Physical Education. *European Physical Education Review, 6,* 1, 27-45.

Stier, J. (2004). Taking a critical stance toward internationalization ideologies in higher education: idealism, instrumentalism and educationalism. *Globalisation, Societies and Education,* 2, 1, 1-28.

Torrance, E.P. (1965). *Rewarding Creative Behavior: Experiments in Classroom Creativity.* Prentice-Hall, Inc., Englewood Cliffs, NJ.

Ulrich, B. (2003).The nursing shortage and potential solutions: An overview. *Nephrology Nursing Journal,* 30, 364–376.

Venkataraman, S., & Anantharaman, R. N. (1991). Need satisfaction and need importance among managerial personnel. *Journal of Psychological Researches, 25,* 15-20.

Wacks, V. Q. (1987). A case for self-transcendent as a purpose of adult education. *Adult Education Quarterly, 38,* 1, 46-55.

Winslow, B. (2005). Developing creativity, motivation, and self-actualization with learning systems. *International Journal of Human-Computers Studies,* 63, 4-5, 436-451.

SECTION 3 : CREATIVITY, GUIDANCE AND COUNSELING

9

The Social Construction of Creative Children

Stanley Krippner

Introduction

Societies have constructed an assortment of terms to describe activities that resemble what Western psychologists refer to as "creativity." The first hexagram of the Chinese "Book of Changes," *I Jing*, is *Ch'ien*, "the Creative Principle." Most Oriental, African, and Native American traditions used creative imagination to enrich and enhance everyday life; novel, original contributions were typically seen as gifts from deities or spirits who used humans as "channels" (a formulation not unlike B.F. Skinner's notion that the creator adds nothing to creation but is merely the "locus" through which environmental variables act). Yet, in some of these societies an individual who conceived or produced something unprecedented (e.g., a mask) would have been censured for breaking with tradition. In Western civilization, not all people have had equal opportunities for creative expression, e.g., women's creativity was not valued or encouraged and they were given few occasions to develop the skills (e.g., critical thinking) or life circumstances (e.g., solitude) on which creative productivity often depends (Krippner, 1999a, 1999b).

The English word "creativity" is linked, historically and etymologically with the concept of origin itself (consider the related term "originality"). Some psychologists require *products* to be of social value or to have attained some other type of consensual agreement if they are to be called "creative," while other psychologists focus on the *process* by which these products come into being. Other attempts at definition conceptualize creativity as a unique *achievement*, *ability*, and/or *attitude* of a person or consortium of people. In each of these outlooks, there can be levels of accomplishment, utility, or originality. From the Western psychological perspective, "creativity" is a term that can be used to describe the process of bringing something new into being by becoming sensitive to gaps in human knowledge, identifying these deficiencies, searching for their solutions, making guesses as to a potential solution, testing one's hypotheses (sometimes modifying and refining the result of these examinations), and communicating the final product (Krippner, 1999a, 1999b).

These steps may be linear or overlap, may occur in a planned sequence or spontaneously, and/or may be intentional or largely unconscious. And even though creativity is constructed differently in disparate societies, an individual's genetic propensity and biological status act as constraints on social construction, expanding or limiting the way that creative activities can be expressed. Hence, "creativity" can be conceived as a judgment made as a result of a social dialogue. Some creative people, such as the American novelist, Alice Walker (1993), stress the biological antecedents of creativity; perhaps metaphorically, she once remarked, "The world is made of stories....I still remember in my genetic memory having been owned, being somebody's slave....I have gone back, in *The Temple of My Familiar*, to reconnect with the very first ancestors."

It could be said that people, groups, or cultures are "creative" during those periods of time when they exhibit activities—innovative for a given group—that yield concepts, items, or behaviors that address human needs (e.g., for survival, for enhanced work performance, for enjoyment, for esthetic satisfaction, for enriched quality of life) in ways considered valuable by a social group. These novel concepts, objects, and behaviors (e.g., a scientific discovery, a mathematical theorem, a philosophical insight, an artistic masterpiece, an innovative sports performance, a technological product, a military victory, a diplomatic accomplishment) can also be termed "creative," although one social group might arrive at a different consensus than another group. In other words, the term "creativity" is a social construct used to describe various social outcomes. If this social construct is studied from a systems perspective, the interaction of person, environment, process, and product needs to be the topic of disciplined inquiry.

Family Experiences of Creative Children

In attempting to understand how the creative child is socially constructed, his or her family can be studied from a systems perspective that focuses on both the individual members and the family unit itself. What are the components of a family system that will foster or stultify creative behavior? One of the most basic systems research designs would identify four clusters of antecedent variables in creative activity: *biological variables* (e.g., genetics, health status, gender), *interpersonal variables* (e.g., family members, peers, authorities), *cultural variables* (e.g., socioeconomic status, ethnic and religious backgrounds, setting and opportunity), *spiritual variables* (e.g., transcendent experiences, moral codes, ethical decisions). From a systems perspective, there is no simple cause-and-effect explanation of creativity; the same cause can have several outcomes.

Usually more than one of these variables impinges on any given situation, producing an outcome that might nurture or stultify creativity. When a preschool child is given the opportunity to draw, to mold, to dance, to cook, to perform athletically, to assume social leadership, or to look through a telescope, his or her response will be related to various combinations of these antecedents. A girl who was born with a club foot will be less likely to participate in dance or sports than a girl who is physically agile. A boy from a social background that imposes rigid gender roles will be unlikely to partake in cooking or artistic activities, while his sister will be less likely to take apart a machine than siblings from backgrounds which do not draw the gender lines as tightly. When there is an opportunity to volunteer for a field trip, a child's decision might be decisively influenced by his or her mood, health status, time constraints, or the perceived social climate. As the child's creativity undergoes the process of social construction, his or her actions are not isolated or independent from the behavior of other family members; everybody who matters influences and is influenced by everybody in the family, positively or negatively. Home and family variables are present in the conditions many investigators consider important for creativity; they range from solitude, inactivity, and daydreaming, to opportunities for creative play and thought, the availability of unstructured play materials, interactions with parents and siblings in experiences involving problem-solving, and positive reinforcement of children's attempted creative behavior.

Children's creative thinking skills can be elicited in many ways, e.g., providing toys, books, and other materials that encourage creative play; providing unstructured play materials such as blocks, clay, and paint, that enable children to develop their imagination; providing experiences such as story-telling and open-ended questioning that help children to form imaginative mental images; helping children to solve their own problems instead of giving them ready-made answers, demonstrating that sometimes there are alternative solutions; allowing time for contemplation, thinking, and imagination; encouraging children to record their ideas through drawing, tape recording, or even using simple computer, film, and video technology; displaying children's drawings, designs, and other creative products; helping children find creative ways of problem-solving, resolving disputes, and meeting their own needs while not negating those of others; helping them channel destructive energy into productive behavior through physical activity, fantasy, psychodrama, or discussion and debate.

E. Paul Torrance, the distinguished creativity researcher, has added that communication skills are especially important in facilitating creative development in the first six or seven years of a child's life. Torrance's suggestions are based on honoring the child's experiences. This can be done by encouraging them to talk with their toys, and entering into these conversations when appropriate. It can be done by singing to children, especially songs that express feelings and ideas. The child's experience can be honored by encouraging mutual story-telling, engaging in dance and movement, and using puppets, musical instruments, and "make-believe" television.

Torrance observes that socialization in the early years can be achieved without sacrificing creativity. If children develop a concept of themselves as competent individuals, and if self-esteem is established at an early age, negative peer reaction to creative activities will not have the impact that it might if internal standards had not evolved. One's self-concept is socially constructed, and the family can arrange for the child to engage in enterprises that will build the attitudes and skills needed to withstand external assaults on behavior that a peer group might consider aberrant.

John Dewey, the pioneer psychologist and educator, wrote extensively on the ways in which a child's curiosity is developed, moving from the level of childish energy, to that of questioning, to an intellectual inquisitiveness. At any point, the child is at risk of having his or her curiosity dampened if the energy is inhibited, if the questions are rebuffed, or if the inquisitiveness is unsatisfied. Torrance states that studies of creatively productive people show that they enjoy a calculated risk in which success or failure depends upon their own ability. This willingness to take risks needs to be identified early in life and reinforced by helping children to estimate their limits accurately, and to attempt tasks of appropriate difficulty. Torrance's own research identified ways in which this could be done. Working in pairs was more effective than working alone; the least effective strategy was performing before the entire class.

Early School Experiences of Creative Children

Torrance has argued for the testing of creativity in preschool children, sadly observing that children who demonstrate creative behavior are frequently punished and discouraged by parents and teachers who find creative behavior inconvenient and difficult to manage. He developed a number of tests based on four guidelines: (1) The tasks in creativity tests should permit preschool children to respond in modalities appropriate to their developmental level, (2) The tasks should contain procedures for warm-up and motivation, (3) The tasks should sample the kinds of creativity that are important in the children's' lives; in other words, the test should make sense to them, (4) The tests should be easy to administer and score. In 1981, Torrance produced *Thinking Creatively in Action and Movement*, a splendid example of a creativity test that adheres to all of these guidelines, making possible the early identification of creative potential.

John Dewey reminds us of the plasticity of human nature. This plasticity underlies the pioneering work reported by Corals McCallister and Kay Queen (1991) at the Institute for the Gifted and Talented at Texas A&M University. The four assumptions on which this work is based are: (1) Creativity is continuous, not dichotomous; all young children are creative to some extent but children who excel in creative activities need to be identified if they are to retain these qualities and accept their creativity as part of their developing self-image, (2) Creativity is a dynamic, interactive, and multidimensional process; when children come to the classroom, they have already been learning for some time, and returning home they begin to interact with their family in new ways, (3) Creativity may encompass intentionality but requires awareness; children who extend their attention span when engaged in creative activities become *aware* that they enjoy these activities, (4) Creativity is a high order cognitive process, eventually involving various types of discrimination, proficiency, and judgments, and their emotional components.

These assumptions were tested and applied in several projects involving parent-child interactions. One of them, the Esperanza School, specialized in helping creative children who had social or emotional problems. Another was a summer preschool for creative children sponsored by Texas A&M University. Another was Kaleidoscope, a month-long model preschool which drew children from eight different countries. McCallister, Queen, and their colleagues learned that educational interventions for the gifted need to be keyed to the degree and variety of giftedness observed. They also discovered that the awareness of creativity must extend from the children to their parents and to their communities. In other words, the degree of creativity exhibited by a child might have biological constraints but for a "creative child" to be socially constructed, the process needs to involve the home and the community as well as the school.

McCallister and Queen found that sociological aspects of their pupils were critical important. Economic status impacts creative development in practical ways; a lack of funds limits the supplies for creative play, lessons in the arts and other creative activities, and educational materials and opportunities. This situation has been graphically portrayed by Jonathan Kozol (1993) who has stressed the importance of environmental factors in stultifying creativity: "The fact that once inner-city kids are racially isolated they get a message. The message...they get is that they are scorned, that they are shunned, that they are viewed as contaminated, that they are viewed as carriers of plague."

Some children begin to view themselves as creative even if their economic circumstances are inimical to the process. But in these cases there are supportive family members who give physical and emotional care to the child, as well as the time and attention needed to enhance self-esteem and creative behavior. Carl Rogers (1983) reminds us that a child who develops a sensitive openness to the world and who trusts his or her ability to form new relationships with the environment, is the child from whom creative products, creative processes, and creative living are most likely to emerge (p. 291).

McCallister and Queen conclude that the program development for young creative children is too often a solitary activity characterized by the devotion and interest of a single teacher. Now, however, there are theoretical models, worthwhile materials, and field-tested techniques that can assist both the school and the home in identifying and developing creative behavior in young children. Torrance has presented four guidelines for creativity testing at early ages. McCallister and Queen have proposed four theoretical assumptions that can guide program proposals for developing creative potential in young children. The practical enactment of these suggestions can result in the social construction of a larger number of creative children than is possible by haphazard methods. The notion that "creativity can not be stifled and will eventually come out" is based on a mystification of creativity that makes no sense to modern social scientists.

These principles, if put into operation, might ameliorate the distressing discontinuities in creative growth that have been noted at about age five and, again, between the third and fourth grades. Without discounting possible biological factors in this "slump," the social constructionist perspective would examine whether there was sufficient external stimulation of creative activity during those years that would reinforce the child's concept of him or herself as creative. Indeed, certain innovative programs in education have yielded encouraging results in maintaining a creative child's continued growth during those years.

Case Study

Martin was a 6-year-old boy living in Rhode Island who was disliked by his parochial school teacher because he asked too many questions. She told Martin's parents that their son was "defiant and hyperactive." The school physician took these reports into consideration, gave him the label of "attentional deficit disorder," and told Martin's parents that he should take ritalin to "slow him down" and make him more tractable in the classroom situation.

Instead, Martin's parents decided to request another opinion and had their child tested at the National Foundation for Gifted and Creative Children in Warwick, Rhode Island. Martin obtained an extremely high score on the Peabody Picture Vocabulary Test, and above average to high scores on the Torrance Tests of Creative Thinking. His verbal proficiency, wide range of knowledge, and curiosity were apparent in the interviews, and no attentional problems were observed.

Martin's parents were told that he was "potentially creative" and that he demonstrated "giftedness" in the verbal area. This was a very different set of labels than had been given Martin by his school teacher and physician. Based on this information,

Martin was transferred to a public school where the teacher was given the foundation's report. Special enrichment activities were arranged for Martin, and no aberrant behavior in the classroom was reported. Martin enjoyed his new school, and his parents began to plan various trips to zoos, museums, and historical points of interest to expand his educational horizons.

In this instance, Martin's school constructed him in one way, and he would have been medicated had the parents accepted this construction. A private foundation constructed Martin in another way, and his parents' accepted this construction. Rejecting the labels of "hyperactive" and "disordered," Martin's parents endorsed the labels of "creative" and "gifted." This led to a change in schools and a series of family experiences that reinforced the new construction, one that appeared to be more beneficial to Martin's self-concept.

Conclusion

Like any other human capacity, creativity, in all of its forms, has a biological predisposition that may or may not fulfill its potential. The outcome is more likely to be favorable if deliberate action is taken to assist the child identified as potentially creative to think of him or herself in these terms, and to instill this concept in the child's family and neighborhood. This will be easier if creativity is presented in positive terms, making it a desirable trait rather than something that engenders jealousy, suspicion, and apprehension. Attitudes toward creativity, as well as creative activities themselves, are socially constructed. Educational intervention needs to consider the attitudes, biases, and opportunities present in each family and community.

Future research on preschool creativity needs to identify the genetic markers for creative behavior; reconcile personality, cognitive, and sociological research data in creativity; evaluate the part played by altered states of consciousness in creative ideation; determine the role of mental illness in blocking or facilitating creative expression; and specify what home and school variables are key factors in the development of highly creative individuals. The need for creative solutions to the world's many social, economic, and environmental problems reflects the importance of this field, and of the psychologists who dedicate themselves to understanding *I Jing*'s "Creative Principle" as it manifests itself in human life.

REFERENCES

Kozol, J. (1993, Spring). *Common Cause Magazine*, pp. 24-28.

Krippner, S. (1999a). Altered and transitional states. In M.A. Runco & S.R. Pritzker (Eds.), *Encyclopedia of creativity* (Vol. 1, pp. 59-70). San Diego: Academic Press.

Krippner, S. (1999b). Dreams and creativity. In M.A. Runco & S.R. Pritzker (Eds.), *Encyclopedia of creativity* (Vol. 1, pp. 597-606). San Diego: Academic Press.

McCallister, C., & Queen, K. (1991, August). Theoretical perspectives on teaching the young creatively gifted or talented child. Chapter presented at the 9th World Conference on Gifted and Talented Children, The Hague, Netherlands.

Rogers, C.R. (1983). *Freedom to learn for the 80's*. Columbus, OH: Charles E. Merrill.

Torrance, E.P. (1981). *Thinking creatively in action and movement*. Bensenville, IL: Scholastic Testing Service.

Walker, A. (1993, Winter). The world is made of stories. *New Dimensions*, pp. 7-21.

10

Creativity Dimensions : Self and Multi-talent Perceptions Across Culture

Ananda Kumar Palaniappan

Introduction

Creative Perception which refers to perception of oneself as being creative and capable of creative productions, is one of the most important personality traits related to creativity (Biondi & Parnes, 1976; Davis, 1983). This is further confirmed by Khatena (1977) when he said that "an individual who perceives himself as creative and with accuracy, is a person who can be expected to behave in creative ways" (p. 517). Studies have shown creative perception to be significantly related to creative performance (Ashton, 1974; Lindseth, 1980; Irby, 1987; Kalsounis, 1975). Multitalent Perception refers to a person's perception of his past activities and experiences in the areas of Leadership, visual-performing arts and the creativity correlates. This study intends to investigate whether perception of oneself in the areas of leadership, visual performing arts and the creativity correlates are related to perception of oneself as being creative and capable of creative productions.

Creativity Research

The word creativity has been used since the early writings in ancient Greece and Rome (Trefinger, Young, Selby & Shepardsen, 2002). But most of the empirical evidence of its existence seems to surface after Guilford's presidential address in 1950 where he presented his famous Structure of Intellect model (Guilford, 1967) which explained the existence of creativity as one of the major intellectual processes of the mind.

Creativity is a very complex construct. Despite more the six decades of research, there is no one definition that is accepted by everyone. However, research on these definitions has revealed four general consensuses on the definition of creativity–that creativity is a cognitive process, a constellation of personality characteristics very different from those who are not creative, a unique and useful product, or the environmental influences that facilitate creativity (Rhodes, 1961). Of these, four components, commonly called the 4 P's referring to the Process, Person, Product and Press. Creativity Process and creative Person have been researched rigorously for the past five decades (e.g. Barron & Harrington, 1981; Palaniappan, 1994; 2006). Findings have attested to the existence and the importance of these two factors in our everyday life.

Creative perception and multitalent perception have been investigated in several doctoral studies (Thomas, 1988, for example) and other published research. Thomas (1988) found that there is a significant relationship between talent as measured by Khatena-Morse Multitalent Perception Inventory (KMMPI) and Khatena-Torrance Creative Perception Inventory (KTCPI). In this study, the influences of creativity on physiological and psychological well-being of 143 Midlife women were investigated.

Khatena & Morse (1994) studied the relationship between KMMPI and SAM, a subscale of KTCPI, in their validation of the former instrument. The respondents comprised 700 adults and 1013 students. They found that the correlations between overall versatility index given by KMMPI and SAM ranged from .57 to .81 for Form A of the instrument and from .57 to .76 for Form B. On the factor scores of KMMPI and SAM, they found positive correlations between talent factors and the total SAM score as well as between Artistic and Artistry (SAM) (between .36 – .39 for children; between .44 – .46 for adults) while the correlations between Artistic and Environmental Sensitivity were very low (.01 for adults and .21 – .23 for children).

With regards to the correlations between KMMPI and WKOPAY, another subscale of KTCPI, these correlations were lower than those with SAM but were significant (.18 and .16 for children on Form A and Form B and .32 for Adults on each form). On the correlations between KMMPI and the factor scores of WKOPAY, they found that both Artistic and Musical factor scores did not yield significant correlations with WKOPAY factors. Higher negative correlations were obtained between the non-creative factor of WKOPAY, Acceptance of Authority and KMMPI factor scores as expected. Creative Imagination correlated moderately with Disciplined Imagination (.25 – .29 for adults and .18 – .22 for children). Similar correlations were observed for Initiative (.30 – .37 for adults and .19 – .24 for children). Leadership factor scores correlated significantly with Self confidence (.15 – .21 for adults and 16 – .20 for children) and Awareness of Others (.12 – .19 for adults and .12 – .18 for children).

Rationale for the Study

Giftedness has always been associated with creativity. But according to the United States Office of Education (USOE), giftedness can be classified as the intellectually gifted, the academically gifted, the creatively gifted and gifted in areas of leadership, visual-performance arts and psychomotor—there are at least six categories of giftedness. If this is the case, can a student classified as gifted in areas of giftedness other than creativity, also display creative behavior? Does he/she also perceive himself as creative? Do students, who are talented in leadership and visual-performing arts, possess distinct creative perception profiles?

Studies have also shown that talent in the areas of leadership and visual performance arts are gender dependent. There appears to be a significantly higher precocity for leadership among female students than male students (Khatena & Morse, 1994). Similarly there appears to be significant gender differences in talents in visual performing arts. (Khatena & Morse, 1994). However, very few studies have attempted to investigate that there are gender differences exist in the relationships between these talent areas and creative perception. Hence, this study intends to investigate whether there are significant gender differences in these relationships especially among Malaysian undergraduates.

For the purpose of this study creativity is assessed using creative perception measured by Khatena-Torrance Creative Perception Inventory (KTCPI) (Khatena and Torrance, 1976a b) and talents in the various areas is measured by Khatena-Morse Multitalent Perception Inventory (KMMPI) (Khatena & Morse, 1991).

These are few studies undertaken to investigate the relationships between talent perception and creative perception. Thus, there is a need for further study to examine these relationships.

Research Questions

This study will attempt to answer the following research questions that are aimed at understanding the level of creative perception of students talented in leadership and visual-performing arts:

1. What is the nature of creative perception and multitalent perception of students of selected Malaysian undergraduates ?
2. What is the correlation between creative perception and multitalent perception among these undergraduates?
3. Are there significant gender differences in the relationships between creative perception and multitalent perception?

Definition of Terms

Multitalent Perception, Creative Perception and their factors are defined in their respective manuals as follows:

(1) **Multitalent Perception** is the self-perception of past experiences relative to leadership, visual-performing arts (music and art) and creative talent. It is the total score obtained on the Khatena-Morse Multitalent Perception Inventory (KMMPI) (Khatena & Morse, 1987, 1990, 1991; Morse & Khatena, 1988) and is called the Versatility Index. Its factors are defined as below:

(*a*) *Artistic* relate to the expression of ideas, personality, and feelings in interesting and novel ways via art. It includes analytic and evaluative skill in addition to a proficiency in artistic rendition.

(*b*) *Musical* relate to facility in learning, modifying and singing or playing music, tunes or rhythms. Technical skill appears to be a strong component of this factor.

(*c*) *Creative Imagination* emphasizes a fluent, vivid imagination which can be used in accomplishing tasks. The characteristics of uniqueness, resourcefulness and inquisitiveness are found in this factor.

(*d*) *Initiative* relates to insight, flexibility and originality in a wide range of endeavor. It includes ability in self-expression and in one's activities.

(*e*) *Leadership* relates to earning of the respect of others, having and understanding effective relationships and possessing good communication skills.

(2) Creative Perception as measured by WKOPAY which is a creative personality measure, is based on the rationale that an individual has a psychological self whose structures have incorporated both creative and non-creative ways of behaving. Its factors are defined as below:

(*a*) *Acceptance of Authority* relates to being obedient, courteous, and conforming and accepting of judgments of authorities.

(*b*) *Self-confidence* relates to being socially well-adjusted, self-confident, energetic and curious, thorough and remembering well.

(*c*) *Inquisitiveness* relates to always asking questions, being self-assertive, feeling strong emotions, being talkative and obedient.

(*d*) *Awareness of Others* relates to being courteous, socially well-adjusted, popular or well-liked, considerate of others, and preferring to work in a group.

(*e*) *Disciplined Imagination* relates to being energetic, persistent, thorough, industrious, imaginative, adventurous, never bored, attempting difficult tasks and preferring complex tasks.

(3) Creative Perception, as measured by Something About Myself (SAM), is a creative achievement measure and is based on the rationale that individual creativity is reflected in creative characteristics possessed in the use of creative thinking, and in creative productions (Khatena & Morse, 1991). It gives measures of six personal factors which are defined as follows:

(*a*) *Environmental Sensitivity* relates to being open to ideas of others, relating ideas to what can be seen, touched, or heard; interest in beautiful and humorous aspects of experiences and sensitivity to meaningful relations.

(*b*) *Initiative* relates to directing, producing and /or playing leads in dramatic and musical productions; producing new formulas or new products; and bringing about changes in procedures or organization.

(*c*) *Self-strength* relates to self-confidence in matching talents against others, resourcefulness, versatility, willingness to take risks, desire to excel and organizational ability.

(*d*) *Intellectuality* relates to intellectual curiosity, enjoyment of challenging tasks, imagination, and preference for adventure over routine, liking for reconstruction of things and ideas to form something different, and dislike for doing things in a prescribed routine.

(*e*) *Individuality* relates to preference for working by oneself rather than in a group, seeing oneself as a self-starter and somewhat eccentric, critical of others' work, thinking for oneself, working for long periods without getting tired.

(*f*) *Artistry* relates to production of objects, models, paintings, carvings, musical composition, receiving awards or prizes or having exhibits, production of stories, plays, poems and other literary pieces.

Methodology

This is a survey investigating the relationship between creative perception and talents in areas of leadership and visual performing arts among selected university undergraduates.

Sample and Procedure

The sample of university undergraduates were drawn from the first and second year students enrolled in the University of Malaya in Malaysia. They major in counseling with the aim of becoming counselors in both the schools and companies. In the survey, two instruments were administered at different times to a class of 94 students but complete scores for only 57 were obtained. The mean age and S.D of the respondents were 21.4 years and 1.09 respectively. The students took about 30 minutes to complete this instrument.

Instruments

Khatena-Torrance Creative Perception Inventory (KTCPI) comprises two subscales, namely, Something About Myself (SAM) and What Kind of Person are You? (WKOPAY?).

The second instrument, Khatena-Morse Multitalent Perception Inventory comprises 50 items. It gives a measure of talent named versatility index and factors scores in Artistry (labeled as Multitalent Artistry to distinguish it from the Artistry factor in KTCPI), Musical, Creative Imagination, Initiative (labeled as Multitalent Initiative) and Leadership.

Data Analysis The data were analyzed using the SPSS Version 16 according to the research questions stated above. The results are as follows:

Results and Discussion

(a) The nature of the KMMPI scores of undergraduates : The KMMPI scores of the undergraduates are given in Table 1. In terms of normality in the distribution of the scores, the skewness and kurtosis of the Versatility Index and its factor scores except Creative Imagination indicate that the scores were all approximately normally distributed. The Creative Imagination

scores appear to be not normally distributed as the ratio of skewness and its standard error exceed –/+ 2.0.

Table 1. Statistics for KMMPI Scores (N = 57)

	Versatility Index	*Multi-talent*	*Musical*	*Creative Imagination*	*Multi-talent*	*Leadership*
Mean	26.96	4.46	4.91	7.74	2.95	3.11
Std. Deviation	6.782	3.196	3.037	1.951	1.231	1.080
Skewness	–.518	.598	.186	–1.516	–.135	–1.096
Std. Error of Skewness	.316	.316	.316	.316	.316	.316
Kurtosis	.828	.039	–.420	2.441	–.806	.291
Std. Error of Kurtosis	.623	.623	.623	.623	.623	.623
Minimum	11	0	0	2	1	0
Maximum	44	13	12	10	5	4

When compared to an American Adult sample (Khatena & Morse, 1990), it appears that the sample of Malaysian undergraduates have a slightly lower mean. (Table 2). For example, the Malaysian sample scored 26.98 for the Versatility Index whereas the American sample had an average of 31.04. The results were obtained for the factor scores as well. It appears that there are differences between Malaysian and American samples on KMMPI which may be due to cultural differences in the upbringing and the facilities available in Malaysia which may be different from those in America.

Table 2. Comparisons between Malaysian and American samples on KMMPI

		Malaysian (N = 57)	*American (N = 2414)*
Versatility Index	Mean	26.96	31.04
	SD	6.78	8.39
Artistic	Mean	4.46	4.96
	SD	3.20	4.20
Musical	Mean	4.91	7.63
	SD	3.04	3.74

		Malaysian (N = 57)	American (N = 2414)
Creative	Mean	7.74	8.30
Imagination	SD	1.95	1.91
Initiative	Mean	2.95	3.08
	SD	1.23	1.31
Leadership	Mean	3.11	3.19
	SD	1.08	0.94

Table 3 shows the means and standard deviations of the overall creative perception (SAM) scores and its factor scores. The skewness and kurtosis data indicate that all scores were approximately normally distributed except for Initiative and Intellectuality where the ratio of skewness and its standard error exceeds +/– 2.0. When compared with the similar American adults (Table 4) it appears that Malaysian students were higher on all measures of the except for Artistry. This indicates that Malaysian students appear to perceive themselves as creative based on their past creative performances compared to their American counterparts except on Artistry.

Table 3. Statistics for Creative Perception based on Something About Myself and its factor scores

(N = 57)

	Something About Myself	*Environmental Sensitivity*	*SAM Initiative*	*Self-strength*	*Intellectuality*	*Individuality*	*SAM Artistry*
Mean	30.93	4.86	1.72	6.68	7.28	4.09	1.68
Median	31.00	5.00	1.00	7.00	8.00	4.00	2.00
Std. Deviation	3.84	9.833	1.411	1.391	1.688	1.074	1.256
Skewness	–.268	–.303	.758	–.437	–.899	–.180	.294
Std. Error of Skewness	.316	.316	.316	.316	.316	.316	.316
Kurtosis	–.352	–.443	–.159	.043	.719	–.741	–.608
Std. Error of Kurtosis	.623	.623	.623	.623	.623	.623	.623
Minimum	23	3	0	3	2	2	0
Maximum	39	6	5	9	10	6	5

Table 4. Comparisons between Malaysian and American samples on SAM and its factors

		Malaysian (N = 57)	*American (N = 912)*
SAM	Mean	30.93	28.77*
	SD	3.85	7.42
Environmental	Mean	4.86	4.84
Sensitivity	SD	–.83	1.34
Initiative	Mean	1.72	1.41
	SD	1.41	1.36
Self-strength	Mean	6.68	5.43
	SD	1.39	2.15
Intellectuality	Mean	7.28	6.48
	SD	1.69	2.13
Individuality	Mean	4.09	3.53
	SD	1.07	1.27
Artistry	Mean	1.68	2.44
	SD	1.26	1.39

* N = 1277

Creative Perception as measured by WKOPAY and its factors scores were also analyzed. The data for skewness and kurtosis indicate that the scores are approximately normally distributed except for the scores for Inquisitiveness, Awareness of Others and Disciplined Imagination (Table 5). Parametric analyses were limited to scores that were normally distributed.

Table 5. Statistics for Creative Perception based on What Kind of Person Are You (WKOPAY) and its factor scores (N = 57)

	What Kind of Person are You	*Acceptance of Authority*	*Self-confidence*	*Inquisttiveness*	*Awareness of Others*	*Disciplined Imagination*
Mean	21.33	3.42	7.40	2.77	7.56	2.82
Median	21.00	3.00	7.00	2.00	8.00	2.00
Std. Deviation	4.024	1.463	2.095	1.881	1.648	1.824
Skewness	.606	.321	–.016	1.228	-1.862	1.185

What Kind	*Acce- of Person are You*	*Self-confi ptance of Authority*	*Inquisi- dence*	*Awar- tiveness*	*Discip- eness of Others*	*lined Imag- ination*
Std. Error of Skewness	.316	.316	.316	.316	.316	.316
Kurtosis	.201	–.387	–.353	2.480	6.928	1.350
Std. Error of Kurtosis	.623	.623	.623	.623	.623	.623
Minimum	15	1	3	0	0	1
Maximum	32	7	12	10	10	9

These Creative Perception (WKOPAY) and its factor scores were compared with those of similar American samples (Table 6). The American samples obtained higher means on all factors except on Self-confidence and Awareness of Others. There appears to be some cultural differences on these scores. There appears to be significant differences between the Malaysian and American samples on Awareness of Others. The Malaysians appear to have significantly higher ability to be courteous, receptive of ideas of others and prefer to work in groups.

Table 6. Comparisons between Malaysian and American samples on WKOPAY and its factors

		Malaysian (N = 57)	*American (N = 190)*
WKOPAY	Mean	21.33	26.68*
	SD	4.02	5.52
Acceptance of	Mean	3.42	4.27
Authority	SD	1.46	1.84
Self-confidence	Mean	7.40	7.01
	SD	2.10	1.64
Inquisitiveness	Mean	2.77	3.62
	SD	1.88	1.24
Awareness of	Mean	7.56	4.93
Others	SD	1.65	1.43
Disciplined	Mean	2.82	4.64
Imagination	SD	1.82	2.31

* N = 2920

(b) Correlations between Multitalent Perception and SAM as well as Gender differences in these correlations

To investigate the correlations between Multitalent Perception and Creative Perception (SAM), Pearson Product-moment correlations were undertaken. As is evident from Table 7 that there were significant correlations exist between the Versatility Index and Artistry factor scores.

Significant correlation was also found between Artistic (Multitalent) and Artistry (SAM) as expected.

Musical talent scores were also significantly correlated to Artistry (SAM).

Significant positive correlations were between Initiative (Multitalent) scores and the Overall SAM scores as well as the factor scores of Intellectuality and Artistry (SAM).

These findings indicate that students who perceive themselves as talented and versatile tend to also perceive themselves as talented in areas related to creativity such as photography, sculpture, music and imaginative writing (SAM Artistry). As expected students who perceive themselves as creative in Art (Artistic – Multitalent) and also musical in nature tend to also be talented in areas like photography, sculpture, music and imaginative writing. Those high on Initiative (Multitalent) who show great insight, flexibility and originality in a wide range of endeavor also tend to significantly perceive themselves as creative based on past experiences and prefer challenging tasks (Intellectuality) and also perceive themselves as creative areas like photography, sculpture, music and writing.

Table 7. Correlations between Multitalent Perception and Creative Perception (SAM) for the Overall Sample (N = 57)

	Versatility Index	*Multitalent*	*Musical*	*Creative Imagination*	*Multitalent*	*Leadership*
Samething About Myself	.177	.110	.158	.047	.286*	-.037
Environmental Sensitivity	-.124	-.043	-.195	.120	-.164	-.063

Versati-	*Multi- lity Index*	*MusicalCreative talent*		*Multi- Imagi- nation*	*Leader- talent*	*ship*
SAM Initiative	.036	.148	.069	-.105	.187	-.215
Self-strength	-.122	-.148	-.159	-.011	.032	.070
Intellectuality	-.035	-.206	-.040	.066	.308*	-.036
Individuality	.032	.191	.046	-.108	.017	-.116
SAM Artistry	.412**	.286*	.269*	.184	.266*	.143

** Significant at the 0.01 level (2-tailed).
* Significant at the 0.05 level (2-tailed).

Comparing the correlations for both male and female students (Tables 8 and 9) it appears that there are differences. Significant correlations were found to be negative (Artistic – Intellectuality and Leadership – Intellectuality), among males, whereas the significant correlations were fond to be positive among females. For female students there appears to be significant correlations between Artistry (SAM) and the Versatility Index, Artistry, Musical, Creative Imagination and Initiative but not for male students. Hence, gender differences existed in the correlations between Multitalent Perception and Creative Perception (SAM) among the Malaysian undergraduates.

Table 8. Correlations between Multitalent Perception and Creative Perception (SAM) for Male Students (n = 17)

	Versati- lity Index	*Multi- talent*	*Musical*	*Creative Imagi- nation*	*Multi- talent*	*Leader- ship*
Samething About Myself	-.436	-.380	.138	-.313	.040	-.379
Environmental Sensitivity	-.383	-.368	-.205	.123	-.162	-.017
SAM Initiative	-.440	-.251	-.186	-.244	.058	-.367
Self-strength	-.408	.079	-.388	-.290	-.350	-.124
Intellectuality	-.242	-.493*	.224	-.071	.427	-.487*
Individuality	-.086	.201	.137	-.292	-.056	-.119
SAM Artistry	-.234	-.090	069	-.241	-.068	-.184

*Significant at the 0.05 level (2-tailed).

Table 9. Correlations between Multitalent Perception and Creative Perception (SAM) for Female Students (n = 40)

	Versatility Index	*Multi-talent*	*Musical*	*Creative Imagination*	*Multi-talent*	*Leadership*
Samething About Myself	.330*	.260	.157	.172	.364*	.079
Environmental Sensitivity	-.038	.109	-.172	.114	-.196	-.099
SAM Initiative	.187	.301	.154	-.041	.252	-.144
Self-strength	-.049	-.187	-.077	.064	.094	.108
Intellectuality	.031	-.090	-.125	.120	.268	.130
Individuality	.054	.176	.008	-.048	.050	-.107
SAM Artistry	.612**	.419**	.378*	.366*	.401*	.286

** Significant at the 0.01 level (2-tailed).

* Significant at the 0.05 level (2-tailed).

(c) Correlations between Multitalent Perception and WKOPAY as well as Gender differences in these correlations

When Multitalent Perception was correlated with Creative Perception as measured by WKOPAY (perception of oneself based on creative personality characteristics) (Table 10), different results were obtained from those obtained with SAM (perception of oneself based on past creative performance) (Table 7) indicating the two creative perception measures measure two different dimensions of Creative Perception.

Correlations with WKOPAY (Table 10) indicate that Versatility Index was significantly correlated to Inquisitiveness only. This indicates that students who perceived themselves as versatile in their talents were also inquisitive. Another interesting finding was that talents relating to leadership were negatively related to WKOPAY and Disciplined Imagination but positively related to Self-confidence. This indicates that students perceiving themselves as leaders although have high self-confidence, may not perceive themselves as having creative personality characteristics and do not like challenging tasks.

Students talented in Music and high on Initiative tend to be significantly more Inquisitive.

Table 10. Correlations between Multitalent Perception and Creative Perception (WKOPAY) for the Overall Sample (N =57)

	Versatility Index	*Multi-talent*	*Musical*	*Creative Imagination*	*Multi-talent*	*Leadership*
What Kind of Person are You	-.072	-.006	.078	-.075	.115	-.448**
Acceptance of Authority	.163	.279*	-.253	.202	.122	.152
Self-confidence	.098	-.140	.067	.096	.188	.344**
Inquisitiveness	.317*	.172	.337*	.022	.272*	.082
Awareness of Others	-.153	-.066	-.054	-.087	-.082	-.004
Disciplined Imagination	-.084	-.099	.245	-.249	.004	-.335*

** Significant at the 0.01 level (2-tailed).
* Significant at the 0.05 level (2-tailed).

The correlations between Multitalent Perception and WKOPAY for male and female students were compared (Tables 11 and 12). There appears to be significant differences in some of these relationships. Versatile male students do not perceive themselves as creative (WKOPAY) and do not like challenging tasks compared to female students but the former are more accepting of orders (Acceptance of Authority) compared to their female counterparts. However, talented female students were significantly more inquisitive than male students.

While musically talented male students perceived themselves as not having creative personality characteristics, female students do. The latter were also significantly more inquisitive and like challenging tasks.

Surprisingly, male students who perceive themselves as leaders were more accepting of authority compared to female students. The latter were also significantly more self confident than their male counterparts.

Hence it appears that there were significant gender differences in the relationships between multitalent perception and creative perception as measured by WKOPAY.

Table 11. Correlations between Multitalent Perception and Creative Perception (WKOPAY) for Male Students (n = 17)

	Versatility Index	*Multitalent*	*Musical*	*Creative Imagination*	*Multitalent*	*Leadership*
What Kind of Person are You	-.486*	-.002	-.491*	-.160	-.048	-.655**
Acceptance of Authority	.619**	.389	.023	.380	.190	.681**
Self-confidence	.152	-.085	.557*	-.006	.011	.130
Inquisitiveness	.187	-.114	.168	.025	.380	.434
Awareness of Others	.050	-.125	.100	.056	-.060	.443
Disciplined Imagination	-.504*	-.108	-.185	-.485*	-.314	-.280

** Significant at the 0.01 level (2-tailed).
* Significant at the 0.05 level (2-tailed).

Table 12. Correlations between Multitalent Perception and Creative Perception (WKOPAY) for Female Students (n = 40)

	Versatility Index	*Multitalent*	*Musical*	*Creative Imagination*	*Multitalent*	*Leadership*
What Kind of Person are You	.085	.018	.343*	-.042	.158	-.383*
Acceptance of Authority	.020	.237	-.361*	.126	.102	-.062
Self-confidence	.085	-.158	-.115	.141	.249	.433**
Inquisitiveness	.343*	.242	.372*	.027	.270	-.010
Awareness of Others	-.202	-.062	-.103	-.127	-.079	-.119
Disciplined Imagination	.049	-.079	.420**	-.160	.088	-.372*

** Significant at the 0.01 level (2-tailed).
* Significant at the 0.05 level (2-tailed).

Conclusion

Although creativity is a multifaceted construct, it is still possible to investigate. It is based on the four main dimensions identified through the various definitions proposed in literature, namely, Process, Person, Product and Press (Rhodes, 1961). This study focuses on the Person dimension, specifically the creative perception and multi-talent perception. It indicates that the various personality and talent areas relate to creative person.

The relationships between multitalent perception and creative perception of selected Malaysian university undergraduates were investigated. When the multitalent scores (KMMPI) were compared to an American Adult sample (Khatena & Morse, 1990), the Malaysian undergraduates have a slightly lower mean. On creative perception as measured by SAM, Malaysian students obtained higher means on all measures except for Artistry. On WKOPAY, the American samples obtained higher means on all scores except on Self-confidence and Awareness of Others. This indicates that there may be cultural differences on Multitalent perception and Creative Perception.

On the relationship between multitalent perception and creative perception (SAM), significant correlations were found between the Versatility Index and Artistry factor scores. Significant correlations were also found between Artistic (Multitalent) and Artistry (SAM) as expected. Musical talent was also significantly correlated to Artistry (SAM). There were significant positive correlations between Initiative (Multitalent) scores and the Overall SAM scores as well as the factor scores of Intellectuality and Artistry (SAM). Gender differences were also observed in the correlations between Multitalent Perception and Creative Perception (SAM).

On the relationship between multitalent perception and creative perception (WKOPAY), the Versatility Index was significantly correlated to only one factor, namely, Inquisitiveness. Students perceived themselves as leaders although have high self-confidence, may not perceive themselves as having creative personality characteristics and do not like challenging tasks. Students talented in Music and high on Initiative tend to be significantly more Inquisitive. There were significant gender differences in the relationships between multitalent perception and creative perception as measured by

WKOPAY. These findings were based on the study of a selected university undergraduate. Hence, more studies need to be undertaken to further establish the nature of the relationships between Multitalent Perception and Creative Perception and the influence of gender on these relationships.

REFERENCES

Ashton, P. (1974). Personality characteristics associated with originality and elaboration. *Psychological Reports*, *34*, 651-657.

Baron, F. & Harrington, D. M. (1981). Creativity, Intelligence and Personality. *Annual Review of Psychology,* 32, 439-476.

Biondi, A. M., & Parnes, S. J. (1976). Assessing creative growth: The tests and measurement changes. New York: Bearly Limited.

Davis, G.A. (1983). *Creativity is forever*. Iowa, Kendall/Hunt Publishing Company.

Guilford, J. P. (1967). *The Nature of Human Intelligence*. New York: McGraw-Hill.

Irby, G. R. (1987). An examination of those relationships among students' concepts of their own creativity, students' concepts of their own creativity, students' personality type and the instructor observations of university Art students. *Dissertation Abstract International*, *47,* 364A.

Kaltsounis, B. (1975). Further validity on "Something About Myself". *Perceptual and Motor Skills*, *40*, 94.

Khatena, J. (1977). The Khatena-Torrance Creative Perception Inventory for identification, diagnosis, facilitation and research. Gifted Child Quaterly, 21, 517-525.

Khatena, J., & Morse, D. T. (1987). Preliminary study of the Khatena-Morse Multitalent Perception Inventory, *Perceptual and Motor Skills*, *64*, 1187-1190.

Khatena, J., & Morse, D. T. (1990). Additional evidence on reliability and validity for the Khatena-Morse Multitalented Perception Inventory. *Perceptual and Motor Skills*, *70*, 1276 – 1280.

Khatena, J., & Morse, D. T. (1991). *Khatena-Morse Multitalent Perception Inventory: Norms-technical Manual*. Bensenville, IL: Scholastic Testing Service.

Khatena, J., & Morse, D. T. (1994). *Khatena-Morse Multitalent Perception Inventory: Norms-technical Manual*. Bensenville, IL: Scholastic Testing Service.

Khatena, J., & Torrance, E. P. (1976a). *Khatena – Torrance Creative Perception Inventory*. Chicago, Il: Stoelting.

Khatena, J., & Torrance, E. P. (1976b). *Manual for Khatena-Torrance Creative Perception Inventory*, Chicago, Stoelting.

Khatena, J., & Torrance, E. P. (1990). *Manual for Khatena-Torrance Creative Perception Inventory for children, adolescents and adults*. Bensenville, IL: Scholastic Testing Service. (Originally published by Stoelting, 1976).

Lindseth, V. M. (1980). The relationship of creativity to the independent school achievement and the sex and value orientation of the student. Dissertation Abstract International, 41, 3491-3492A.

Morse, D. T. & Khatena, J. (1988). Evidence for validity of the Khatena-Morse Multitalent Perception Inventory as indicated by differential performance. *Perceptual and Motor Skills*, *66*, 591-594.

Palaniappan, A. K. (1994). A study of creativity and academic achievement among form four Malaysian students. Unpublished Ph.D dissertation, University of Malaya.

Palaniappan, A. K. (2000). Sex differences in creative perceptions of Malaysian students. *Perceptual and Motor Skills*, *91*, 970-972.

Rhodes, J. M. (1961). An analysis of creativity. *Phi Delta Kappan*, *42*, 305-10.

Thomas, D. N. (988). Influences Of Creativity, Depression, And Psychological Well-Being On Physiological And Psychological Symptoms In Midlife Women. Unpublished Doctoral Dissertation, Texas Woman's University.

Treffinger, D. J., Young, G. C.. Selby, E. C. & Shepardson, C. (2002). *Assessing creativity: A guide for Educators*, The National Research Center for the Gifted and Talented, University of Connecticut.

11

Evaluating the Effectiveness of a Guidance Program

Melati bte Sumari and Fauziah Hanim bte Abd. Jalal

Introduction

In this era of accountability, counselors are growingly being asked to give information to parents, administrators and stakeholders on the effectiveness of guidance programs. The goal of guidance program is to impart specific skills and learning opportunities through academic, career, personal/social and family development experiences in varieties of ways for all audiences. Thus, guidance outcome becomes potentially useful information for counselors in selecting and developing counseling intervention and guidance activities that have been shown to be effective. Counselors can starts to taking tasks, support change, and provide leadership whereby the counselors value the concept and nature of accountability and incorporate it into their daily performance in an almost automatic manner. Focusing on the outcomes is another means to evaluate the effectiveness of programs (VanZandt & Hayslip, 1993). Evaluating programs through measuring outcomes method concentrate on whether the program is producing the desired result, generating the greatest possible impact and making the most efficient use of public funds. It is an alternative evaluating guidance programs that can be implemented considering the developmental aspect of the audiences.

The Importance of Effectiveness of a Guidance Program

Evaluation is a vital part of a developmental guidance and

counseling program and ensures accountability. The idea of evaluation is to establish the value of the program, its activities and staff to make decisions or to take actions regarding the future (Henderson, 1987). The American School Counselor Association's (1984) guidelines and the recently published National Standards for School Counseling Programs suggested specific developmental domains to be considered in a comprehensive guidance program. Within each of these domains one would anticipate to see the following specific types of development delivered. Among the domains to be considered is cognitive, personal-social, and career (Campbell & Dahir, 1997).

Guidance program development is a process to plan, design, implement, and evaluate program effectiveness (Henderson, 1987). Measuring the effectiveness of the programs is the ability to identify and meet the changing needs of audiences. Therefore, the process provides for purposeful change and growth. A center which supports this process will see the relevance of the process for (1) designing new guidance and counseling programs, (2) improving existing guidance and counseling programs, and (3) evaluating and documenting guidance and counseling program effectiveness.

Evaluating Program using Logic Model

Logic models offer counselors in an agency, schools, or in a university with a road map describing the series of connected events involving the community's needs with the organization's desired impact. Mapping an organization's impact assist one to look and realize how human and financial investments can add to achieving intended goals and can lead to improvements in programs. Basically, the logic model is a picture of how a program will work. It uses words and/or pictures to illustrate the series or chain of activities thought to bring about change and show steps these activities are linked to the this model will gives a clear picture of cause-and-effect relationships—a systems approach to communicate the path toward a desired result. It is a concern as to how to control over complex outcomes as impact measurement is concerned. Setting up desired long-term outcomes, such as reduced teen-age violence, is tenuous because of the limited control we may have over the target audience, and complex, uncontrolled environmental variables. Thus, this model includes this issue because the necessity to be considered when planning such outcomes. Logic models relate the problem (situation) to the intervention (inputs and outputs), and the impact (outcome). In addition, the model helps to recognize partnerships critical to enhancing counselor's performance (Fig. 1)

The logic model process has been used successfully following the above sequence. However, according to Millar *et al, 2* logic models that begin with the inputs and work through to the desired outcomes may reflect a natural tendency to limit one's thinking to existing activities, programs, and research questions. Starting with the inputs tends to foster a defense of the status quo rather than create a forum for new ideas or concepts. To help us think "outside the box," Millar suggests that the planning sequence be inverted, thereby focusing on the outcomes to be achieved. In such a reversed process, we ask ourselves "what needs to be done?" rather than "what is being done?" Following the advice of the authors, we might begin building our logic model by asking questions in the following sequence.

(1) What is the current situation that we intend to impact?

(2) What will it appear when we achieve the desired situation or outcome?

(3) What behaviors need to change for that outcome to be attained?

(4) What knowledge or skills do group need before the actions will change?

(5) What activities should be performed to allow the necessary learning?

(6) What resources will be essential to accomplish the desired outcome?

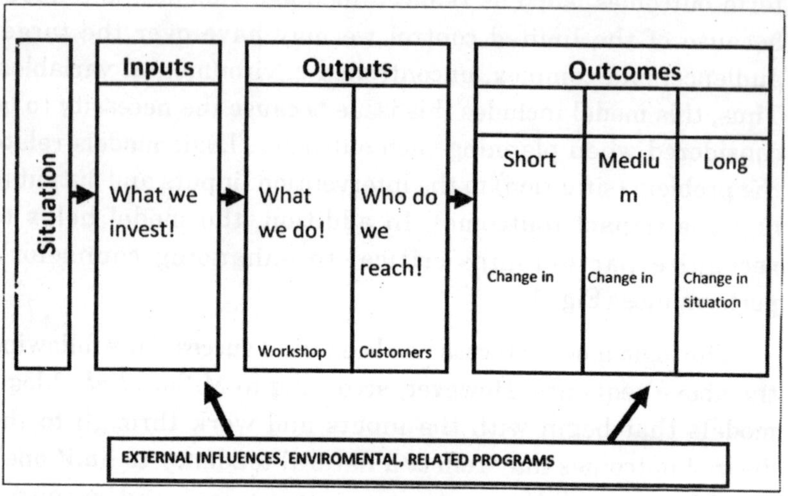

Fig. 1. Element of Logic Model

An example of a guidance program for family development.

Strengthening Families Program

Families with adolescent 13-15 years old

SECTION-1 : PROGRAM CONTEXT

In this section, creating a context means choosing a district or area or a group that needs to be involved in the program. It starts with creating a committee such as the School Counselors Committee to design a *"Strengthening Families Program"(SFP) aims to strengthening relationships in families in a chosen area. Next is having the rational of having the program. It might be to* protect and to sustain a stable family relationship and to assist families in identifying their strengths and building their own resources in facing the challenges of today's globalization and urbanization. Building strong and resilient families is one of the national goals as Malaysia becomes more industrialized (Mohamad, 1991). Along with the demand of the K-economy (knowledge societies), Malaysian families, in particular, will have to adapt themselves to living in changing and growing cities (Musalmah, 2003).

Also making a study on the area in term of the demographic, the geographical, and the social issues (i.e. divorce, the way of life, time spending of families, and juveniles activities) to the program is needed. The issues related to the problem facing by families such as working parents and spending time with their adolescents. More adolescent spend more time with their peers after school at the malls and other popular places such as cyber café. Other issues such as balancing work and life sometimes brings family stress due to lack of skills in overcoming it. Another issue is the conflict between parents and their adolescents' who want more independence and control of themselves.

Thus, the school counselors committee needs to identify the families and determine their needs and know how the program effectively helps the families to strengthening the family relationship with focusing on improving the families' communication, creating a positive and nurturing environment and alleviating risk factors and reduce stress among families from various economic, cultural and ethnic backgrounds in Seremban.

SECTION–2 : THE COLLABORATION FRAMEWORK

I. The Concept of Collaboration

In implementing this program, the organizing committee will involve all the local leaders, educators, experts, and officers from various organizations in Negeri Sembilan. This approach will help the families in Seremban becomes familiar with these people and easier access in the future. This type of communication will help both parties working together in a small communities but effective for the betterment of the families of the area. The Negeri Sembilan School Counselors Committee, the lead agency for the program, will create an Office of Strengthening Families to coordinate and implement projects and activities. It will coordinate six organizations from the government agencies, 5 non-governmental organizations (NGOs), and the local leaders in communities.

The Strengthening Families Office will engage in capacity building in a variety of ways to work effectively with other agencies and be part of a team working to solving problem in the community. This will reveal the importance of the Malaysian culture working together known as 'gotong royong' which is normally practice especially in family wedding, and festival. By collaborating with the other groups, the office is preparing them to share information, decision making, problems solving, feeling of engaging as part of the community and developing a common understanding of the problem (Kretzamann and McKnight's, 1993). This is supported by Vaughn (1994) that collaboration in program planning and development includes categories of human, purpose, environment, process, communication and resources. The process of getting the resources is central when involving the human dimension. By building the capacity of communities and groups to more effectively develop, deliver, and evaluate programs, stronger and more efficient community-based programming can be facilitate (Kretzamann and McKnight's, 1993).

The philosophy of "constructing active engagement" in collaboration engages the community in constructing positive activities as well as identifying and addressing the needs of children, youth, and families in their own communities. Thus, every groups in the collaboration should have clear knowledge of, and involvement by, the citizens who live in the community is imperative for effective programs. In developing programs, emphasis is placed on bringing together diverse perspective, experiences, and expertise of the, Negeri Sembilan School Counselors Committee, agencies and community.

Creating strong team work of community is appropriate with an African proverb says "it takes a village to educate a child" and understanding the basis that each locality knows their own challenges, strength, and weakness. Such collaborative approach is critically needed in the size of the unrelenting increase of problem in families of adolescents and diversity of Seremban population.

II. The organizations involved are:

(i) The government agencies:

- The Education Department - providing the guidance teachers as the facilitators, students and the Parents and Teacher Associations;
- The Department of Islamic Development -providing advice and information on Islamic matter of Moslem families.
- The Department of Social Welfare-giving advice and information with regard to the trouble families;
- The Police Department- providing information adolescent and delinquency;
- The Melewar Teacher Training Institute in Seremban – providing expertise in child development and family development;
- University Putra Malaysia, Selangor - providing expertise and researchers in child development and family development;

(ii) The non-governmental organization (NGOs):

- PEMADAM (National Anti-Drug Council)- providing information about adolescent involvement in drug and its impact, and volunteers;
- The Ibu Tunggal (single parents) Association- providing information about broken families and volunteers;
- Puspanita (Women Civil Servants Association) – providing information about career women and families and volunteers;

- Rukun Tertangga (Neighborhood Watchdog) – providing information in each localities and volunteers;
- Malaysia Youth Council, Negeri Sembilan Branch-providing information about youth and volunteers.

(iii) The local leaders in communities

are those who are respected in the community especially from the Malay and Chinese and Indian community.

III. The collaboration process

It is suggested that the collaboration involved the agencies and the community leaders in establishing a basis for the planning process.

Project Planning	-	The Negeri Sembilan School Counselors Committee
Program Activities	-	University Putra Malaysia and Welfare Department;
Training of Facilitators	-	Melewar Teacher Training Institute and school counselors
Participants	-	Education Department and Puspanita;
Volunteers	-	Neighborhood Watchdog and Youth Council;
Program Evaluation	-	Research Team of University Putra Malaysia;
Resources	-	The Department of Islamic Development, PEMADAM, Single Parents Assoc., Police Department, and local leaders.

SECTION–3 : TARGET AUDIENCE

1. Family Criteria

Two groups of population selected for this program (a) the

parents who has adolescent children age 13-15 years old and the children have shown behavioral problems in schools and having family problems (b) the adolescents age 13-15 years (lower secondary students) studying in the secondary schools showing the above criteria. Participants among the parents of adolescent who have the above criteria will be randomly assigned. Information about the families that has trouble adolescents is determined through the guidance teachers in secondary schools. Letter of invitation to the parents and their adolescent will be sent after they randomly assigned to all 24 secondary schools in Seremban. The number of the subjects will depend on guidance teachers should provide the information. This will involve the three ethnic families-Malays, Chinese and Indian. For this program about 200 parents and 200 adolescents in Seremban will be selected for this program.

2. Getting Resources from the families:

(a) The Personal Perspectives—the culture in raising the children and their ways of solving problems in the family.

(b) Assess Needs and Assets—assessment regarding possible strengthening family program for the community that this committee want to serve. A need assessment in a form of written survey about the families that could be used to help with the program and/or help solves the problems.

(c) Identify Problem or Issue—it involves collecting information from the families about demographic information and their knowledge about child development as well as indicators of family relationship with their teens such as parent-child relationship, conflict, coping mechanism, stressful life, time management in the family, attitude becoming parents, risk factors in families, self esteem, decision making, and communication skills. This document is for monitoring utilization and satisfaction of the resources given to them and modifying existing programs

SECTION–4 : GOAL AND OUTCOMES

Section 4 Goal and Outcomes

INPUTS →	**OUTPUTS**
Resources dedicated to or consumed by the program	**What the program does with the inputs to fulfill its mission**
• MWFD –family extension (1) family extension specialist (2) Assistant (3) research teams (10) technical, and administration and management staffs • (40) Facilitators from guidance teachers and other agencies • Experts in child Development and family development – higher institutions • Information resources – Police, *Pemadam*, *Puspanita*, Single Parents, Youth Council, Schools, Welfare Dept, Neighborhood Watchdog • Volunteers from the NGOs • Grant funds • MWFD annual budget • Meeting rooms • Curriculum and Video tapes • Counseling Staffs and Rooms •	• Guest speakers • Support groups • Parenting skills workshop and conferences • Camp • Seminar • Group Discussion • Youth and Family Camp • Family meeting • Family Games

OUTPUTS → OUTCOMES

OUTPUTS

The direct products of program activities

- No. sermons about family stress ,etc
- No. radio talks about family
- No. participants in Family Day
- No. campaigns products – buttons, posters, banners, etc.
- No of parents in the groups
- No teen in the activities
- No of girls/sons and mom in the family sessions
- No of boys and dad in the boys in the family sessions
- No of participants in workshops
- No of participants seminar

OUTCOMES

Benefits for participants during and after program activities

- Awareness of quality parenting
- Positive attitude toward self as parents
- Positive attitude towards self as sons/daughters
- Knowledge of adolescent development
- Knowledge of relationship with parents
- Parent-Teen relationship
- Communication skill parent-child
- Awareness of risk factor affect families
- Awareness of opportunities of protective factors in families
- Self esteem among participants – parents and teens
- Problems Solving Skills in marital and family relationship
- Decision Making Skill in marital and family relationship
- Conflict between families members
- Academic Achievement
- High risk families

Section 4: Goals and Outcomes

- Academic Achievement
- High risk families
- Parents file for divorce
- Betterment of community and the state

Longer-Term Outcomes (Environment social

- Parent-Teen relationship
- Communication skill parent-child
- Awareness of risk factor affect families
- Awareness of opportunities of protective factors in families
- Self esteem among participants – parents and teens increased
- Problems Solving Skills in marital and family relationship increased
- Decision Making Skill in marital and family relationship increased
- Conflict between families members reduced

Intermediate Outcomes (behaviors, practices)

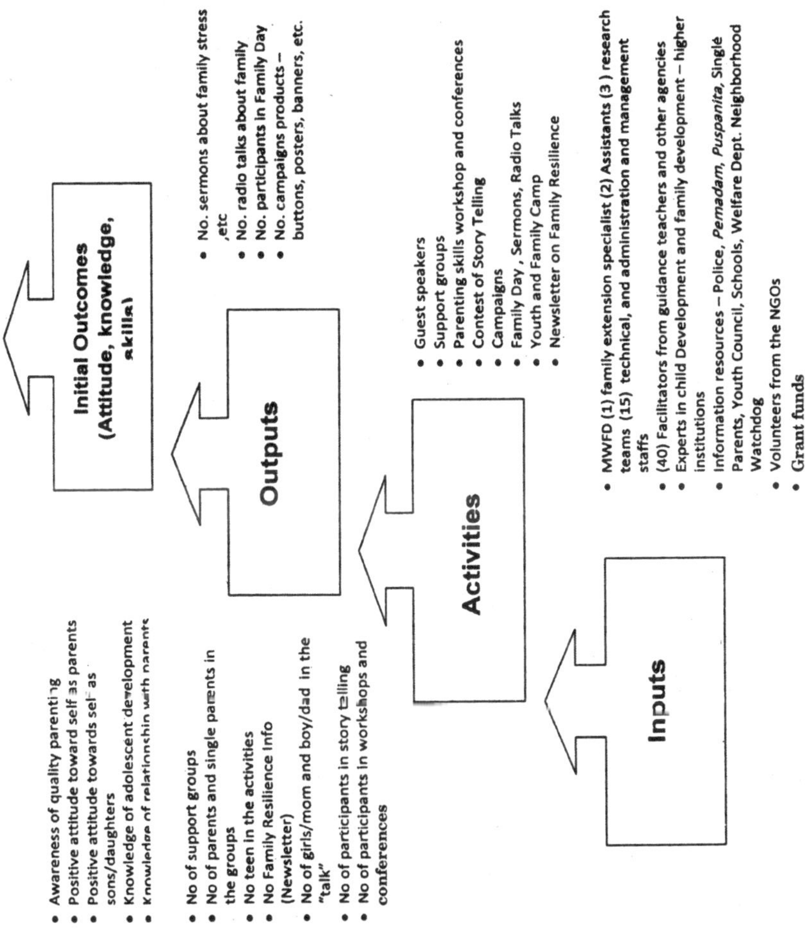
Initial Outcomes (Attitude, knowledge, skills)
Outputs
Activities
Inputs
• Awareness of quality parenting
• Positive attitude toward self as parents
• Positive attitude towards self as sons/daughters
• Knowledge of adolescent development
• Knowledge of relationship with parents
• No. sermons about family stress ,etc
• No. radio talks about family
• No. participants in Family Day
• No. campaigns products – buttons, posters, banners, etc.
• No of support groups
• No of parents and single parents in the groups
• No teen in the activities
• No Family Resilience Info (Newsletter)
• No of girls/mom and boy/dad in the "talk"
• No of participants in story telling
• No of participants in workshops and conferences
• Guest speakers
• Support groups
• Parenting skills workshop and conferences
• Contest of Story Telling
• Campaigns
• Family Day , Sermons, Radio Talks
• Youth and Family Camp
• Newsletter on Family Resilience
• MWFD (1) family extension specialist (2) Assistants (3) research teams (15) technical, and administration and management staffs
• (40) Facilitators from guidance teachers and other agencies
• Experts in child Development and family development – higher institutions
• Information resources – Police, Pemadam, Puspanita, Single Parents, Youth Council, Schools, Welfare Dept. Neighborhood Watchdog
• Volunteers from the NGOs
• Grant funds

SECTION–5 : PROGRAM DESCRIPTION

Strengthening Families Program (SFP) is unique and innovative program through which families and their adolescents are teamed with the local agencies to strengthen family relationship focusing participation in enhancing communication skills; creating a positive and nurturing environment; and alleviating risk factors and reducing stress in the families. This program will develop on research-based program design to meet the need of diverse audiences of families and teens. It will introduce strengths –based approach in the program. The Strengthening Families Program (SFP) involves secondary school school-aged children (13 to 15 years old) in youth training and development and their families in parenting skills training sessions. SFP will use family systems and cognitive-behavioral approaches to increase resilience and reduce risk factors for behavioral, emotional, academic, and social problems. It will take 2 months training for the program. It builds on protective factors by:

- Improving family relationships;
- Improving parenting skills;
- Improving communication skills
- Improving family environment;
- Increasing the youth's social and life skills;

The SFP curriculum is a 14-session behavioral skills training program of 2 hours uses for three groups – the parents, the children and the families. In this program it will offers incentives for attendance, good behavior in children, and homework completion to increase program participation.

SECTION–6 : PROGRAM ACTIVITIES

Parent Session - 6 sessions

Parent Activities—Parents meet separately with group leaders for one hour to learn to increase desired behaviors in children by increasing attention and rewards for positive behaviors. They also learn about clear communication, effective discipline, substance use, problem solving, and limit setting.

1. *Parenting Workshop* I—3 sessions (3 hrs)

Format	1 day seminar
Times	10:00 am- 3:00 pm
Day	1st Saturday of the month
Objectives:	To understand the goal of marriage and having families
	To know the child development
	To realize parenting adolescents
Activities	Guest speakers, group discussion
Mode	Session 1- Family Life with Children
	Session 2- The characteristic of adolescents
	Session 3 –Parenting skills

2. *Parenting Workshop* II—3 sessions (3 hrs)

Format:	1 day workshop
Times:	10:00am -3:00 pm
Day:	3rd Saturday of the month
Objectives:	Identify parenting skills in handling stress in communication, loving and peer pressure.
	Know setting limit, problem solving, substance abuse, discipline
Activities:	Demonstration, Role Play and Group Discussion
Mode	Session 4 - Setting Limit
	Session 5 – Problem solving
	Session 6 - Positive communication

Adolescents Session – 6 sessions

Adolescents activities—Adolescents meets meet separately with adolescent's trainers for an hour, to learn how to understand feelings, control their anger, resist peer pressure, how to appreciate parents, comply with parental rules, solve problems, and communicate effectively. Adolescents also develop their social skills and learn about the consequences of substance abuse.

Youth Camp I - 3sessions (3 hrs)

Format	1 day camp
Venue	Camp site
Times	10:00 am - 3:00 pm
Day	2nd Saturday of the month
Objectives	Know how to appreciate parents
	Understanding Roles and Responsibilities as children
Activities	Talk, group discussion, games
Mode	Session 7- Appreciating Parents
	Session 8-Roles and Responsibilities
	Session 9-Reaching Out to Others

Youth Camp II - 3 sessions (3hrs)

Format	1 day camp
Venue	Camp site
Times	10:00 am- 3:00 pm
Day	4th Saturday of the month
Objectives	Know how to set goals with parents
	Identify coping skills in peer pressure, stressful, conflict
	Learn to control anger
Activities	Talk, group discussion, games
Mode	Session 10–Deciding your goal
	Session 11–Handling Peer Pressure I and II
	Session 12–Anger Management

Family Sessions - 2 sessions

Families Activities—Parents and children meet in another session after they have finished parents and adolescent sessions. In this session both will engages in structured activities, conduct family meetings, learn communication skills, practice effective discipline, reinforce positive behaviors in each other, and plan family activities together.

Youth and Family Camp – 2 sessions (2hrs)

Format	1 day dyads
Venue	Camp Site
Time	10:00 a.m. – 12:00 p.m.
Day	2nd Saturday
No. of participants	Father and son or daughter for a family Mother and daughter or son for a family
Objectives	To understand family strengths To appreciate family life To know each other more To identify listening and empathy skill
Activities	Dyads, Presentations and games
Mode	Session 13 - Building Family Communication Session 14 – Understanding Each Other

Family Dinner (Booster activity)

Format	Family Meeting
Venue	Home or any places such restaurants
Times	4 times a week
Day	Flexible
Activities	Eating together and sharing information
Objectives	To have time together Listening to each other

Section 7 Time Line

Program Activities	Jan	Feb	Mac	Apr	May	Jun	July	Aug	Sept	Oct	Nov	Dec	Jan	Feb	Mac-Jun
Meeting with the Ministry WFD (Internal)	■	■			■				■			■			■
Setting up SFP Office			■												
Contacting and Meeting with agencies, NGOs, local leaders (External)				■					■			■			■
Contacting Parents and Adolescents about the program.					■										
Getting Resources from subjects					■	■									
Training facilitators						■									

Training volunteers															
Adjusting Program Activities due Subjects Resources															
Pre-Survey to Subjects															
Parents Session – Parenting Workshop 1 (1st Saturday of the month)															
Parents Session- Parenting Workshop 11 3rd Saturday of the month)															

Strengthening Families Program -Time line of the programs in Seremban Community (contd.)

Program Activities	Jan	Feb	Mac	Apr	May	Jun	July	Aug	Sept	Oct	Nov	Dec	Jan	Feb	Mac-Jun
Youths Session- Youth Camp I (2nd Saturday of the month)															
Youths Session – Youth Camp II (4th Saturday of the month)															
Families Session Youth and Families Camp (2nd Saturday of the month)															
Family Dinner (4 times a week)															

Post- Survey – given after the program															
Telephone Survey for parents on program effectiveness (after 6 months program end)															
Interview Survey for youth on effectiveness at their schools (after 6 months program end)															
Evaluation the overall program															

SECTION–8 : PROGRAM EVALUATION

The evaluation process of Strengthening Families Program (SFP) involve the use of surveys, interviews, direct observation or the review of program records to assess the development and operation of the program. Common measures used in the evaluation of this program include;

(1) Number of parents attended for the parent session;

(2) Number of adolescent attended for the adolescent session;

(3) Number of father and their adolescent attended for the families' session;

(4) Number of family dinner the families have in a week

The outcome evaluations of family strengthening programs will be using a single group self-report pretest - posttest comparison. The program will be evaluated using a pre and post survey, observations by the project team. For the pre survey it will administering a questionnaire to participants when they enter the program to assess on factors such as family functioning, parent-child relationship, family strength, coping skills, and the family cohesiveness and stressful indicators, and family dinner survey, and adolescent peer pressure survey. The scores are then compared with scores on the same questionnaire administered again when the families exit the program. Telephone interviews conducted six months to the parents and interviews with the adolescents in the schools after participants had completed the program to see the effectiveness (Denzin & Lincoln, 1994).

Conclusion

Evaluation is a continuing process of program renewal. It starts with progress of questions to be answered by the evaluation and ends with building and acting on the recommendation generated by findings. Therefore, developing suitable and measurable indicators during the planning stage is the key to a good evaluation. Early recognition of indicators permits the program manager/team to learn what baseline data already may be obtainable to help evaluate the project, or to design a process to collect baseline data before the program is begins. The logic model is useful for ascertaining elements of the program that are mainly likely to yield helpful evaluation data and to identify an appropriate sequence for collecting data and measuring progress. In most cases, however, more work on a project will be needed prior finalizing the indicators. Outcome indicators to assess learning should be building on specific learner objectives that are described as part of the curriculum. Further, indicators to measure behavioral change should indicate which behaviors are targeted by the program. Outcomes for the medium-term and long-term outcomes may require a significant investment of time to link these two pasts. Better results can be achieved through the application of a targeted study or relevant research base.

REFERENCES

Brown, M, & Paolucci. (1979). What is Critical Theory and Critical Science? In Gentzler, Yvonne S. (Eds.). *Family and Consumer Sciences Teacher Education Yearbook 19*, (p. 25). AAFCS, Etd.

Caffarella, S.R. (1994). Planning Program for Adult Learners. San Francisco: Jossey-Bass Publishers.

Crabtree, B. (1996). Reflecting on our integrative nature and how our subject matter areas/specializations relate today to families, and consumers. In Crabtree, B. (Eds.). Integrating concepts from subject area specializations- Reaffirmation and impact of the 'Body of Knowledge'.for Family and Consumer Sciences.' *The Candle*, Spring, 14-15.

Crabtree, B. (2002). Integrating concepts from subject area specializations- Reaffirmation and impact of the 'Body of Knowledge'for Family and Consumer Sciences.' *The Candle*, Spring, 14-15.

Denzin, N. K., & Lincoln, Y. S., Eds. (1994). Handbook of Qualitative Research. Thomas Oaks, CA: Sage

Henderson, P. (1987). A comprehensive guidance program at work. *TACD Journal*, *15*(1), 25-37.

Kretzman, J.P. and McKnight, J.L. (1993). Building Communities from the Inside Out: A path Toward Finding and Mobilizing Communities Assets. In Martin, S. & Evans, B. (Eds). Available: ??www.unce.edu/Gateway/2003CYFProg Plan. pdf

Mohamad, (1991). *'Malaysia: The Way Forward'* . Speech presented by The Prime Minister, Dr. Mahathir Bin Mohamad in In The Inaugural Meeting Of The Malaysian Business Council On 28

February, Kuala Lumpur. Available: http://www.epu. jpm.my/ Bi/speech/vision2020i.html

Musalmah. (2003). Incorporating Life-Long Learning in K-Economy. Available:
http://www.mier.org.my/mierscope/muslamah5_4_2003.pdf

Rahim, Abd. (1997). *On Agenda Item 102: Social Development, Including Questions Relating to the World Social Situation and to Youth, Ageing, disabled Persons and the Family, Speech at the Third Committee of the 52nd Session of the United Nations General Assembly*, New York, on October 17, 1997. Available: http://www.undp org/missions /malaysia/3cte102.htm

Shukor, R. (1996). Lack of community spirit in urban areas. In Bunnell, T. (2002). *Kampung* Rules: Landscape and the contested government of urban (c) Malayness. *Urban Studies*, 39(9), 1685-1701.

Vanzandt, C.E. (1993). *Multidimensional model of guidance management*. Gorham, ME: University of Southern Maine.

Vaughn, G. G. (1994). Collaboration: Finding pathways for change. *Home Economics Forum,* Spring.

12

Spirituality in Counsellor Education

Peter Wong Sin On

Introduction

Despite the huge number of studies conducted on spirituality thus far, there is still no consensus on the definition of spirituality. For the purpose of this Chapter, spirituality is defined as "the motivational and emotional source of an individual's quest for a personally defined relationship with people and the non-human environment; for some, it includes a connectedness with a higher being leading to enhanced feelings of well-being, inner peace, and life satisfaction" (Wong, 2006, p. 624). Spirituality is differentiated from religion as every person can have his sense of spirituality, including an atheist. However, not everyone adheres to religious beliefs. At the same time, spirituality which covers a wider spectrum overlaps many aspects of religion. As far as this Chapter is concerned, there are numerous instances where spirituality and religion need to be addressed simultaneously when such a dichotomy is not always possible.

Religion and spirituality and its feud with psychology is still ongoing. A strong emphasis given on empirical measurements are frequently applied in the quantitative studies of human behaviour and there is comparatively little attention paid to the experiential part of the person which is considered the activities of the soul (Tam, 1993). Counselling is an art, as well as a scientific discipline based on modern psychology. Just as psychology and theology are not mutually exclusive, spirituality too has a place in counselling although finding such a place has taken a long time. Counsellor educator Gerard Corey (2006) writes:

> Effective counseling addresses the body, mind, and spirit. The field of counseling has been slow in recognizing the need to address spiritual and religious concerns. There is now widespread interest in the role of spirituality in both assessment and treatment. (p. 117)

The last two decades saw the momentum on both the quantity as well as the quality of research on spirituality. The consequential increase in the literature on spirituality has not been limited to healthcare, but across disciplines and this includes sports, business and the workplace as well. Within clinical disciplines, there has been growing attention of spirituality in primary care in medicine, psychiatry, psychology, sociology, epidemiology, alcohol and drug abuse treatment and prevention, public health, neurosciences, research design and so on (Morgan, 2007). Within healthcare domains, interest has gained momentum in recent years on the role of spirituality in coping with chronic illness (O'Connor, Guilfoyle, Breen, Mukhardt, & Fisher, 2007).

Turning the scenario to medical education, of the 129 medical schools in the United States and 17 medical schools in Canada which represent the American Association of Medical Colleges (AAMC, 2008), 80 percent of them offer one or more courses on spirituality. The introduction of the spirituality component in medical schools first started in 1991 when the George Washington University School of Medicine offered the course on spirituality and health to its students (The George Washington University Medical Center, 2008).

Currently, the counsellors see the need for addressing the issue of spirituality in counselling despite the difficulty to encompass the issues of spirituality due to their subjective and controversial nature (Everts & Agee, 1995). Similarly, counsellees have continued to touch on the spiritual dimension of their life in the face of everyday issues. While counsellors who have been adequately trained to handle spirituality in counselling no doubt exist, how many counsellors today, even among those who have been professionally trained, are able to properly handle the spiritually related issues of their clients?

Early Roots of Counselling

Very soon, we will witness the centenary of the posthumous publication of the book, *Choosing A Vocation* in 1909 by Frank Parsons, the chief architect of the guidance movement (Brown & Srebalus, 1996). Modern counselling can be traced back to a long tradition of soul care (Morgan, 2007) and more recently, with the evolution of the vocational guidance movement around the turn of the 20th century. Thus, guidance and counselling have always been closely linked despite the fact that guidance covers a wider spectrum which includes counselling, appraisal, providing information, consulting, planning, placement, follow-up, and evaluation (Shertzer & Stone, 1981).

Although counselling is often seen as a new field in mental health services, a century of development and evolution has taken the profession to greater heights, noticeably the appearance of numerous theories and approaches spearheaded by the many proponents within counselling, or borrowed across disciplines such as psychotherapy, social work, psychology, the behavioural sciences, and healthcare in general. Such evolution has enabled counselling to make adjustments and adaptations in many ways that withstands the test of time as well as making improvements so that it is able to serve the contemporary needs of the clients in an optimal manner.

The Significance of Integrating Spirituality into Counselling

Frankl (1965), says that the spiritual dimension of the person cannot be ignored, as this is what makes us human. Speaking of human life, counsellor educator Sandhu (2007) says that spirituality is the *summum bonum*, the highest good. For counsellor educator Morgan (2007), spirituality is a search for the sacred in which the process is cognitive, emotional, behavioural, and experiential in nature.

Spirituality can be understood in humanistic terms which include self-transcendence, connectedness, reverence for life, and ultimate meaning (ibid.). For humanistic psychologist

Stephen Schoen (as cited in Faiver, Ingersoll, O'Brien, & McNally, 2001), the counselling session is a sacred ground that signifies the counsellor who is concerned with the free flight of the client's soul. In the words of psychotherapist and counsellor O'Hanlon (2006), the soul is given the chance to integrate the disparate aspects of one's personality.

A person's religious affiliation can signify more than one's identity. To some, it is a way of life. Indeed, religion is one of the most influential factors in the shaping of humankind (Abdel-Khalek, 2007) while Novak (as cited in Abdel-Khalek, 2007) predicted the twenty-first century to be the most religious century. Frame (as cited in Morgan, 2007) reported that some 88 percent of the world's population is affiliated to some form of theistic belief system.

In a 1996 Gallup poll (as cited in Leseho, 2007), 90 percent of the adult respondents in the United States indicated that religion was important in their lives. The current scenario in Malaysia is not much different in essence. In a study of 100 adults who were pursuing their postgraduate studies at the University of Malaya, these students who were either affiliated to Christianity, Hinduism or Islam indicated that within the lives of Malaysians, spirituality plays a central role. These participants also conveyed that counsellors and psychologists could help the people to develop their spiritual orientation (Husain, Hshim, & Rosli, 2008). Both the practitioner and the counsellee need to be aware of one's own definition of spirituality and religion as well as its conceptual framework and practice. In fact, more and more clients' today request that their faith dimension be included in the counselling process (Fischer & Hart, 1994). In the Gallup poll conducted in 1992 in the United States, 81 percent of the respondents preferred some form of integration of their beliefs and values into the process of counselling (Morgan, 2007).

Kelly's (as cited in Kahle & Robbins, 2004) study of 479 counsellors from a randomly selected 1993 American Counseling Association membership list reported that 90 percent of the respondents indicated that they had some degree of spiritual or religious orientation. Of these counsellors, 70 percent of them indicated an affiliation with an organized religion. As such, there was clearly a wider profession of spiritual values than did religious values.

Integrating spirituality in counselling is not limited to theistic counselling but all forms of counselling, such as career and school counselling, even though there are several characteristics in the theistic approach to counselling. Richards and O'Grady (2007) propose several emphases be given to the nature of theistic counselling and psychotherapy. They write:

> 1. Establishing a spiritually open and safe environment for clients.
> 2. Assessing the spiritual dimension of clients' lives.
> 3. Setting spiritual goals for treatment.
> 4. Using spiritual interventions in treatment, and
> 5. Seeking divine guidance to assist in treatment and recovery. (p. 88)

Spiritual issues are no longer alien to secular counselling and they are seen as part and parcel of counselling today. Counsellor educator Gerard Corey (2006) writes:

> The major professional organizations are recognizing the importance of spiritual issues in counselling practice. Spiritual and religious matters are therapeutically relevant, ethically appropriate, and potentially significant topics for the practice of counselling in secular settings. Counselors must be prepared to deal with their clients' issues of the human spirit. (p. 117)

Although spirituality is increasingly important for counsellors in their everyday clinical practice, there are counsellors who either feel inadequately prepared or uncomfortable to cater to the spiritual issues of their clients. Under such circumstances, many counsellors choose to make referrals to appropriate pastoral counsellors, imams, priests, pastors, monks or other spiritual or religious leaders (Nutt, 2007).

The Inclusion of the Spiritual Component into Counsellor Education

Counsellor education is defined as "a process that prepares counsellors in both didactic and clinical aspects of counselling" (CACREP, 2007, p. 58) and is used as an operational definition as far as this Chapter is concerned.

In order to maintain the standards of counsellor education to be at par with its counterparts in the United States, the Board of Cunsellors in Malaysia has set its requirements to those of CACREP and the National Board of Certified Counselors (NBCC). At the same time, counsellors who are locally trained and wish to continue their training in counselling in America will find it easier to have their credits transferred for courses already completed (Md. Shuaib Che Din, 2004).

Leseho (2007), a counsellor educator who created and taught a graduate course on spirituality in counselling at the Faculty of Education, Brandon University located in Canada says:

> Counselling is a spiritual activity, so while a course that focuses on spirituality is ideal, so too is it necessary to include the spiritual in every counselling course taught. Just as we are introducing students to the importance of expanding the counselling session to include their client's spirituality, we too must see our classrooms as containers that expand to fit the wide expressions of spirituality. Within an environment that is supportive, caring and free of judgment, we may offer students the experience of tapping into their own spirituality and give permission to bring their own spiritual beings into the counselling session. (p. 452)

Hence, learning to integrate spirituality into counselling is more than simply passing the required spirituality related courses in a counsellor training programme. It is necessary to include the experiential dimension that involves the whole person as well. Consequently, an effective spirituality curriculum in counsellor education requires one to see spirituality, in the words of Kurtz (as cited in Morgan, 2007) as an attitude, rather than a method. It is a posture that enables one to see everything differently, instead of seeing different things.

Nevertheless, an effective counsellor education programme should be able to adequately equip future counsellors to provide proper interventions in their clinical work. Since counselling, including the incorporation of spirituality is more than a grab-bag application of technique, counsellors need to grow from the therapeutic encounter and all applications are uniquely applied within the context (Faiver, Ingersoll, O'Brien, & McNally, 2001). Counsellor educator Fukuyama (2007) recommends the following approach, which has been simplified for practical reason, for the training of counsellors on the inclusion of spirituality and religion in multicultural counselling:

1. Begin with self-awareness, understand the influence of family history, and resolve childhood issues and biases.
2. Learn about diverse religions and spiritual traditions, beliefs, and customs.
3. Discuss topics with colleagues and in supervision.
4. Have a personal spiritual practice.
5. Study a spiritual tradition in depth for a period of time.
6. Cultivate referral resources (religious leaders) who can serve as consultants.
7. Talk with a trusted colleague with whom you can "check yourself" related to power issues or cultural blind spots.
8. Be open to change.
9. Enjoy the process! (pp. 106-107)

Hence, it is not only essential that a counsellor educator needs to know the substance of spirituality in order to teach the subject, a personal awareness and understanding of one's own background, religious and spiritual orientation and practice are all too important to provide a role model which is vital to the professional development of the trainees.

Competencies Required for Spiritual Counsellor

The issue of competency of a counsellor is a vital one, as the ability of a counsellor in executing his tasks is very much determined by his training (Abdul Halim Othman, Md. Shuaib Che Din, & Sapora Sipon, 2000). Unfortunately, despite the need to integrate spirituality into healthcare, most healthcare professionals in various fields have limited training in the area of spirituality and religion, at least among the mental health professionals (Duba, 2007). Psychologist Lawrence LeShan (2004) says:

> It is not only the spiritual aspects of human beings that the modern therapist is rarely trained or equipped to deal with and to encourage and strengthen. It is also most of the other positive special aspects that make us more than animals and more than pathology. It is creativity and the love of the beautiful and of the true. It is 'honor and faith and a sure intent.' It is the search for the meaning of our existence. (pp. 125-126)

In a study of 52 students from 6 of the American Association of Marriage and Family Therapy accredited training programmes in the United States, half of these students indicated that spirituality or religion was not incorporated into their training (ibid.). Onedera (as cited in Duba, 2007) reported that only 12 of the 203 CACREP accredited counsellor education programmes have a course specifically addressing spiritual and religious issues.

Without adequate preparation, there is no way a counsellor can properly handle the spiritual or religious needs of the clients. Arveson (n.d.) suggests that most students are trained to be sensitive to the multicultural concerns, sufficient training in spiritual integration strategies and world religions are still lacking in counsellor training programmes. While most of the courses in counsellor education are already mandatory, it is likely that future counsellor training programmes will be more demanding as courses related to spirituality will be added and possibly made compulsory in time to come.

Competencies for Integrating Spirituality into Counseling have been suggested by ASERVIC (2006) based in the United States. They appear in the form of guidelines based on nine basic competencies as follows:

Competency 1—The professional counselor can explain the difference between religion and spirituality, including similarities and differences.

Competency 2—The professional counselor can describe religious and spiritual beliefs and practices in a cultural context.

Competency 3—The professional counselor engages in self-exploration of religious and spiritual beliefs in order to increase sensitivity, understanding and acceptance of diverse belief systems.

Competency 4—The professional counselor can describer her/his religious and/or spiritual belief system and explain various models of religious or spiritual development across the lifespan.

Competency 5—The professional counselor can demonstrate sensitivity and acceptance of a variety of religious and/or spiritual expressions in client communication.

Competency 6—The professional counselor can identify limits of her/his understanding of a client's religious or spiritual expression, and demonstrate appropriate referral skills and generate possible referral sources.

Competency 7—The professional counselor can assess the relevance of the religious and/or spiritual domains in the client's therapeutic issues.

Competency 8—The professional counselor is sensitive to and receptive of religious and/or spiritual themes in the counseling process as befits the expressed preference of each client.

Competency 9—The professional counselor uses a clients' religious and/or spiritual beliefs in the pursuit of the clients' therapeutic goals as befits the clients' expressed preference.

These guidelines demonstrate the kind of competencies required in practice what and how the issue of spirituality needs to be addressed. As such, the guidelines provide the extent spirituality needs to be covered as a human dimension and thus assist the course provider to adequately plan and execute the spirituality component in a counsellor training programme.

Although these guidelines have been formulated in the United States, they provide useful references for the training of counsellors in Malaysia. However, both counselling and counsellor education programmes in Malaysia are still very much American inventions. Malaysian values, local worldviews, and Eastern traditions need to be considered in this regard where it involves the lives of 26 million Malaysians. A fine tuning of these guidelines will enable the tasks of training local counsellors more viable where local context of multicultural counselling is addressed.

Though less specific on the nature of the competencies required, the 2005 Code of Ethics of the American Counseling Association spells out the ethical standard with regards to the issue of spirituality which concerns the counsellor. Counsellors are not permitted to "condone or engage in discrimination based on age, culture, disability, ethnicity, race, religion/spirituality..." (C.5. Nondiscrimination). Likewise, counsellors must "recognize the effects of age, color, culture, disability, ethnic group, gender, race, language preference, religion, spirituality..." (E.8. Multicultural Issues/Diversity in Assessment). The CACREP 2001 Standards require each counsellor education program to provide curriculum experiences and demonstrated knowledge and skills related to "the role of racial...religious and spiritual beliefs..." (Duba, 2007, p. 20).

Effective Implementation of the Inclusion of Spirituality in Counsellor Education

It is rather naive to assume that it is a simple and straightforward task to introduce the spirituality component into the counsellor education curricula within an institution of higher learning, be it publicly or privately funded. Several factors must fall into place for spirituality to be effectively integrated in the training of counsellors.

Firstly, one of the most essential requirements for anyone to be a professional is to acquire the necessary training that is required. Professional counsellors undertake accredited counsellor training at institutions where their programmes are recognised by the body that sanctions them. In Malaysia, the Board of Counsellors [Lembaga Kaunselor] is empowered by the Counsellors Act 1998 to regulate the training of counsellors and determine the qualifications required of counsellors (Statue 12). Hence, it would be helpful if the Board of Counsellors make it mandatory to include spirituality as one of the required components in counsellor education.

Secondly, it is important that the spirituality-related courses be taught by faculty members who are adequately prepared for such courses. Ideally, a teacher who handles the spirituality course has both the theoretical background as well as the experience in integrating spirituality into counselling practice.

Finally, spirituality cannot be taught through textbooks alone. Burke, Hackney, Hudson, et al. (1999) hold that spirituality can be learned in a profound way through the mutual sharing of its mystery, as they say, "Scientific dissection of its significance tends to distract from its authenticity as a decisive human emotion" (p. 253). They suggest proper techniques to teach spirituality which could include individual stories of students, case studies, interviews, and readings of diverse cultures in philosophy and literature. In addition, several demographic factors and cultural issues of the clients need to be considered such as ethnicity, religious background, superstitious beliefs, as well as the nature of the problems faced by the clients.

Conclusion

Taking a course on spirituality alone does not guarantee a counsellor is able to adequately integrate spirituality into practice when the need arises. Though intellectual knowledge on the subject is helpful, a practitioner needs to be convinced of the vitality of such integration that actually helps the client to address a very important dimension of life for without which many of the fundamental questions raised in counselling cannot be properly addressed.

Indeed, it is timely that the Board of Counsellors which is the agency entrusted to oversee the training of counsellors in Malaysia to seriously look into the integration of the spirituality component in counsellor education. At the first instance, a revised curriculum in counsellor education needs to be drawn up by the board followed by its implementation in all counsellor education programmes in Malaysia. In this regard, the Board of Counsellors will be required to ensure that faculty members are adequately prepared for such a task. Consequently, proper implementation will take its course and proper timeline needs to be monitored so that the overall quality of counsellor education is not compromised. As an implication for research, sufficient studies over time could be conducted to see how the revised counsellor education programmes are fare as compared to the previous programmes, as well as how far the integration of spirituality is able to help clients in Malaysia.

NOTE

1. The British English version of the words, "counsellor" and "counselling" are used in principle throughout this Chapter. Where quotations are made, the original texts are followed, including the use of the American English version of "counselor" and "counseling".

REFERENCES

AAMC. (2008). Website for American Association of Medical Colleges. Retrieved September 2, 2008, from http://www.aamc.org/medicalschools.htm

Abdel-Khalek, A. M. (2007). Religiosity, happiness, health, and psychopathology in a probability sample of Muslim adolescents. Mental Health, Religion & Culture, 10 , 571-583.

Abdul Halim Othman, Md. Shuaib Che Din, & Sapora Sipon. (2000). Latihan kaunseling di Malaysia: Satu ulasan dan cadangan [Counselling training in Malaysia: A commentary and suggestions]. Jurnal PERKAMA, 8, 137-151.

American Counseling Association. (2005). ACA code of ethics. Alexandria, VA: Author.

Arveson, K. R. (n.d.). A conceptual model for integrating spirituality into the diagnosis and counseling treatment plan. Retreived

September 16, 2008, from http://counselingoutfitters.com/vistas/vistas06/vistas06.23.pdf

ASERVIC. (2006). Website for the Association for Spiritual, Ethical, and Religious Values in Counseling. Competencies for Integrating Spirituality into Counseling. Retrieved September 8, 2008, from http://www.aservic.org/Competencies.htm

Brown, D., & Srebalus, D. J. (1996). Introduction to the counseling profession (2nd ed.). Needham Heights, MA: Allyn and Bacon.

Burke, M. T., Hackney, H., Hudson, P., Miranti, J., Watts, G. A., Epp, L. (1999). Spirituality, religion, and CACREP curriculum standards. Journal of Counseling and Development, 77, 251-257.

CACREP. (2007). Website for the Council for Accreditation of Counseling and Related Educational Programs. CACREP Standards Draft #3. Retrieved September 8, 2008, from http://www.cacrep.org/StandardsRevisionText.html

Corey, G. (2006). Integrating spirituality in counseling practice. Retrieved September 28, 2008, from http://www.counselingoufitters.com/vistas/vistas06/vistas06.25.pdf

Duba, J. D. (2007). Incorporating religion in your counselor education program. Retrieved September 7, 2008, from http://digitalcommons.wku.edu/context/csa_fac_pub/Chapter/1006/type/native/viewcontent/-

Everts, J. F., & Agee, M. N. (1995). Including spirituality in counsellor education: Issues for consideration, with illustrative reference to a New Zealand example. International Journal for the Advancement of Counselling, 17, 291-302.

Faiver, C., Ingersoll, R. E., O'Brien, E., & McNally, C. (2001). Explorations in counseling and spirituality: Philosophical, practical, and personal reflections. Belmont, CA: Wadsworth.

Fischer, K., & Hart, T. (1994). A counselor's prayer book. Mahwah, NJ: Paulist Press.

Frankl, V. (1965). The doctor and the soul: From psychotherapy to logotherapy. New York: Alfred A. Knopf.

Fukuyama, M. A. (2007). Weaving sacred threads into multicultural counseling. In O. J. Morgan (Ed.), Counseling and spirituality: Views from the profession (pp. 93-109). Boston: Houghton Mifflin Company.

Husain, A., Hashim, O. & Rosli, N. A. (2008). Spiritual orientation among Malaysians. In A. Husain, S. Jamaluddin, O. Hashim, L. S. Cheong, M. Md Nor, & H. Sulaiman (Eds.), Horizons of spiritual psychology (pp. 263-271). New Delhi: Global Vision Publishing House.

Kahle, P. A., & Robbins, J. M. (2004). The power of spirituality in therapy: Integrating spiritual and religious beliefs in mental health practice. New York: The Haworth Pastoral Press.

Kerajaan Malaysia. (1998). Akta Kaunselor 1998 (Akta 580)/ Counsellors Act 1998 (Act 580). Kuala Lumpur: Percetakan Nasional Malaysia Berhad.

Leseho, J. (2007). Spirituality in counsellor education: A new course. British Journal of Guidance and Counselling, 35, 441-454.

LeShan, L. (2002). The dilemma of psychology: A psychologist looks at his troubled profession. New York: Allworth Press.

Md. Shuaib Che Din. (2004). Ke arah mewujudkan struktur pengajian kaunseling di institusi pengajian tinggi: Beberapa saranan untuk pertimbangan. Dalam Abdul Ghani Sulaiman (Ed.), Hala tuju kaunseling [Direction in counselling] (m.s. 209-217). Tanjong Malim: Penerbit Universiti Pendidikan Sultan Idris.

Morgan, O. J. (2007). Counselling's fifth force. In O. J. Morgan (Ed.), Counseling and spirituality: Views from the profession (pp. 1-24). Boston: Houghton Mifflin Company.

Nutt, R. L. (2007). Counselling men: Necessary knowledge. Counselling and Spirituality, 53 (1), 53-80.

O'Connor, M., Guilfoyle, A., Breen, L., Mukhardt, F., & Fisher, C. (2007). Relationships between quality of life, spiritual well-being, and psychological adjustment styles for people living with leukaemia: An exploratory study. Mental Health, Religion and Culture, 10 (6), 631-747.

O'Hanlon, B. (2006). Pathways to spirituality: Connection, wholeness, and possibility for therapist and client. New York: W. W. Norton & Company.

Richards, P. S., & O'Grady, K. A. (2007). Theistic counselling and psychotherapy: Conceptual framework and application to counselling practice. Counselling and Spirituality, 26 (2), 79-102.

Sandhu, D. S. (2007). Seven stages of spiritual development: A framework to solve psycho-spiritual problems. In O. J. Morgan (Ed.), Counseling and spirituality (pp. 64-85). Boston: Houghton Mifflin Company.

Shertzer, B., & Stone, S. C. (1981). Fundamentals of guidance (4th ed.). Boston: Houghton Mifflin Company.

Tam, J. S. C. (1993). A review on the place of spirituality in counselling psychology. Asian Journal of Counselling, 2, 17-23.

The George Washington University Medical Center. (2008). Retrieved September 2, 2008, from http://www.gwumc.edu/healthsci/programs/shc-c/

Wong, P. S. O. (2006). Spirituality as a dimension in counselling. INTI Journal, 2, 624-630.

SECTION 4 : QUALITY OF EDUCATION AND LEARNING

13

Improving the Quality of Education in Malaysia : Issues and Challenges

Shahril @ Charil Bin Hj Marzuki, Mary Wee Siok Choo and Mohummad Faizal A. Ghani

In this Chapter we analyze the Vision 2020, Education Development Plan (EDP) (2001-2010), and Ninth Malaysia Plan (NMP)(2006-2010) which has become the core foundation for formulation of National Education Blueprint (2006-2010). Vision 2020 was announced in 1991 by the then Prime Minister of Malaysia, Tun Dr Mahathir Mohamad. It is aimed at making Malaysia a fully developed country by 2020. It is the mother plan. This does not only means that Malaysia is fully developed in the economic sense but fully developed in all aspects such as economically, socially, spiritually, psychologically and culturally.

Nine Strategic Challenges of Vision 2020

Vision 2020 outlines nine strategic challenges that the country has to overcome to achieve this vision. They are:

1. To establish a united Malaysian nation with a sense of common and shared destiny. This is to create a nation which is at peace with itself, territorially and ethnically integrated, living in harmony and full and fair partnership. Malaysia will be made up of one race i.e. one 'Bangsa Malaysia' with political loyalty and dedication to the nation.
2. To create a psychologically liberated, secure, and developed Malaysian Society.

Faith and confidence in itself are justifiably proud of what it refers to, of what it has accomplished, robust enough to face all manner of adversity. This Malaysian Society must be distinguished by the pursuit of excellence, fully aware of all its potentials, psychologically subservient to none, and respected by the peoples of other nations.

To foster and develop a mature democratic society

Practice a form of mature consensual, community-oriented Malaysian democracy that can be a model for many developing countries.

To establish a fully moral and ethical society

Strong in religious and spiritual values and imbued with the highest of ethical standards.

To establish a mature and tolerant society

Malaysians of all colors and creeds are free to practice and profess their customs, cultures and religious beliefs and yet feeling that they belong to one nation.

To establish a scientific and progressive society

A society that is innovative and forward-looking one is not only a consumer of technology but also a contributor to the scientific and technological civilization of the future.

To establish a fully caring society

A social system in which society will be for the welfare of the people will revolve not around the state or the individual but around a strong and resilient family system.

To ensure an economically just society, in which there is a fair and equitable distribution of the wealth of the nation

Full partnership in economic progress

To establish a prosperous society with an economy that is fully competitive, dynamic, robust and resilient (The Star, 3 May 1991)

Ten years later, in 2001, the Ministry of Education launched the *Education Development Plan,* which covers from 2001 – 2010. It takes into account the aims and aspirations of the

National Vision Policy to build a resilient nation, encourage the creation of a just society, maintain sustainable economic growth, develop global competitiveness, build a K-economy, strengthen human resource development and maintain sustainable environment development. The main aim of the Education Development Plan is to ensure all citizens have opportunity to twelve years of education.

Education Development Plan (2001-2010)

This Plan has 4 main thrusts and they are:

1. Increase Access in Education

- Education system to be restructured from 13 to 12 years (P12 i.e. 6+4+2).
- Institutionalized preschool education for children aged 5+ years.
- More schools/public universities /universities colleges, refurbishing dilapidated schools.
- Develop private higher education institutions – better prepare students for the job market.
- Expand distance learning education.
- Expand fully residential schools, vocational and technical schools, sports schools, special education schools and improve the quality of existing schools.
- Community colleges – promote lifelong learning and provide alternative routes for continuing education for school leavers, dropouts and local communities. To be built in each in every parliamentary constituency.
- Expand basic utilities i.e. water supply, electricity, telephone.
- Expand and improve: hostels, textbooks, teaching materials, resource centers, computers.
- Adequate physical facilities e.g., classrooms, labs, special rooms – to reduce double session schools and achieve 60:40 ratio of science to arts students.

2. Increase Equity in Education

- Conducive learning environment to be provided to all schools irrespective of type and location.
- Equal teaching and learning opportunities to be provided to students with special needs/from minority groups, esp. Orang Asli in Peninsular Malaysia and other ethnic groups from remote and isolated areas of Sabah and Sarawak.
- Educational inputs: teachers (esp. critical subjects such as English, Science and Mathematics), allocation of funds, teaching facilities and support services will be equally distributed to schools.

3. Improve Quality in Education

- Emphasize co-curricular activities and provide facilities to develop students' potential, talent and interests.
- Curriculum to enhance students' ability in languages, mastery of 3Rs, science and technology, and ICT
  - to meet the needs of the job market and industries
  - to attain K-economy, enabling the nation to face the challenges of globalization and competition from the global market.
- Trained and responsible teaching workforce are able to implement teaching and learning effectively and use the latest ICT-based pedagogical approaches.
- Achieve 50% and 100% trained graduate teachers for primary and secondary schools respectively by 2010.
- To improve teachers' welfare (staff quarters, car/computer loans).
- Evaluate content of textbooks, relevant to current development.
- Will equip Teacher Activity Centres, State Educational Resource Centres and the Education Technology Division with adequate personnel and facilities – to expose teachers with teaching aids and educational technology.

4. Improve Efficiency and Effectiveness of Education Management

- To strengthen the process of program monitoring and evaluation by increasing the number of trained Federal School Inspectorate (FSI) staff to ensure successful implementation of the Education Higher Quality Standard (EHQS).
- To integrate various databases and systems via data warehousing – more accurate information and strategic planning.
- To provide ICT infrastructure and application systems to all MOE agencies to support an efficient and effective management system.
- To raise the E&E levels of education management at Departments/Divisions, State/District/Division Education Offices, other MOE education institutions and agencies, schools to ensure all educational programs are successfully implemented, and achieve objectives with optimised resources.
- Expand empowerment at all administrative levels in schools to enhance efficiency and effectiveness of project management and to reduce bureaucracy.

(Ministry of Education, 2001)

On 1 April 2006, 5 years after the launch of the Education Development Plan, the fifth Prime Minister of Malaysia, Datuk Seri Abdullah Ahmad Badawi announced the 9th Malaysian Plan (9MP). The 9th Malaysia Plan represents the first 5-year blueprint of the National Mission (a 15-year phase from 2006 to 2020).

Ninth Malaysia Plan (2006- 2010)

The theme of the 9MP is "Together Towards Excellence, Glory and Distinction". This plan covers the country's developmental initiatives and is not just an education plan for the nation's education system.

In order to achieve the mission, 5 thrusts were outlined and they are:

To move the economy up the value chain

To raise the capacity for knowledge and innovation and nurture 'first class mentality'

To address persistent socio-economic inequalities constructively and productively

To improve the standard and sustainability of quality of life

To strengthen the institutional and implementation capacity

(Economic Planning Unit, 2006)

The bulk of the 9 MP relating to education is in the second "thrust" - to raise the capacity for knowledge and innovation and nurture a 'first class mentality'. There are 6 strategies identified in this second thrust.

These 6 core strategies are:

1. Improving the Access to and Quality of the Education System at All Levels

Curriculum and Teaching

At Pre-school Level

Implement a National Pre-school curriculum

Ensure standardization and quality

At School Level

Review curriculum and co-curricular activities

Review teacher training curriculum

Improve subject content

Enhance pedagogical skills

Enable greater ICT application

At Tertiary Level

Respond to market needs and reduce mismatch

Improve employability of graduates (to include internship and industrial training)

Improve curriculum

Other Education programs

Redesigned training programs to match the changing industry requirements

Establish the National Advisory Council on Education and Training

Set policies and strategies related to education and industrial training

Infrastructure and Facilities

Provide more pre-school classes especially in rural areas

Provide better facilities for primary and secondary schools especially in rural areas and Sabah and Sarawak

Build more classrooms for primary education

Increase the capacity of university education and advanced skills training

Making National Schools the School of Choice

Improve the quality of teachers

100 per cent of teachers in secondary schools to have 1st degree qualifications by 2010

25 per cent teachers in primary schools to have 1st degree qualifications by 2010

Provide more in-service training for teachers

Standardize national schools

Make all national schools smart schools through 'Program Pembestarian Sekolah'

Reduce the performance gap between rural and urban areas, various initiatives will be undertaken, including the provision of better educational facilities and basic amenities

Increase opportunities for children with special needs and learning disabilities in national schools.

Deploy more experienced teachers to schools in rural areas

Provide educational support programs to assist students from low-income families

Producing Tertiary Institutions of International Standing

Enhance quality of tertiary education

Benchmark against international standards

Introduce rating system for tertiary institutions

Set up Malaysian Qualifications Agency (MQA) to implement the Malaysian Qualifications Framework (MQF)

Improve quality of academic staff

More staff development programs

Increase academic staff with doctorate qualification in public universities to 60% by 2010

Collaborate with renowned international universities in research

Nurturing Top Quality Research and Development and Scientific and Innovation Capability

Strengthening Policy Commitment

Emphasize human resource capacity building

Strengthen the National Innovation System

Establish a National Innovation Council to provide leadership for formulating policies and strategies

Promote a culture of innovation

Enhancing Research and Development (R&D) Capabilities

Target a National R&D expenditure of 1.5% of GDP by 2010

Strengthen research and innovation capability

Increase number of researchers, scientists and engineers

Launch a National Brain Gain Program (start with science and technology human capital)

Set up centers of excellence in emerging technology areas

Increase R&D capacity in universities and research institutions

Provide more grants, scholarships and endowment funds for research

Develop innovative products for commercialization

Promoting technopreneurship and Technology-based Enterprises

Enhance the Technology Incubator Programme to develop a pool of technopreneurs and technology-based companies

Improve funding mechanisms

Encourage innovation, technology transfer and commercialization

Strengthen the existing intellectual property framework and shorten the IP approval process

Nurture a Bumiputera Science and Technology Community

Empowering Women and Youth

Greater participation of women in business

Increase education and training for women to increase employability

Increase number of women in workforce

Improve the access to funding for businesses

Provide childcare facilities, flexible working arrangements

Review existing laws which discriminate against women

Reduce violence against women

Development of Youth

Provide more youth programs to focus on problem youths

Improve access to education and skills training programs which focus on leadership, team-building and character-building training

Strengthen programs like Rakan Muda and National Service

Fostering a Society with Strong Values

Nurturing High Performance

Use of performance-based approach

Use of KPI (Key Performance Indicators)

Instilling a Progressive Outlook and Moral and Ethical Values

Refine and implement programs which encourage the development of a strong moral and ethical culture as encapsulated in the PIN [National Integrity Plan]

Intensify the promotion of Islam Hadhari as a foundation for a progressive developmental outlook

Expand j-QAF program for Muslim students in all primary schools

Provide Moral education for all students

Improve Sivik & Kewarganegaraan subject for all students in years 4-6 and all secondary schools (Economic Planning Unit, 2006).

National Education Blueprint (2006- 2010)

After the announcement of the 9MP, the Ministry of Education came out with the National Education Blueprint (NEB) or Pelan Induk Pembangunan Pendidikan (PIPP). This NEB was launched in February 2007 by the 5th Prime Minister of Malaysia, Datuk Seri Abdullah Ahmad Badawi. The NEB is a mid-term plan from 2006-2010 formulated based on the 9th Malaysian Plan (2006-2010), Education Development Plan (2001 – 2010) and the Vision 2020 (1991-2020). Its objective is to 'develop the nation's people'. This blueprint contains the strategies and plans on the national education system.

The two main aims are:

To complete unfinished tasks laid out in the 8th Malaysia Plan (2001-2005) which sought to provide everyone access to education and create a level of playing field for all students

To exploit fully schools' potential by having clusters of excellence so as to enable teachers and students to raise the standard of the system of learning in the country to be world class (Ministry of Education, 2006).

The 6 thrusts in NEB to hence quality of education and further strengthen the national education system are:

Building the nation and people that is united and proud of its national identity

Developing Human Capital that is knowledgeable and skilled with an appreciation of pure values

Strengthening national schools, making national schools the main choice without obstructing the development of vernacular schools

Narrowing the education gap in terms of location, socio-economic status and student abilities so that all schools and students will be given the same opportunities to achieve excellence

Improving the teaching profession

Accelerating excellence at educational institutions through cluster schools (which are centers of excellence) so that they will become showcase or model schools

(Ministry of Education, 2006).

This Chapter analyzes each of these six thrusts of the NEB and evaluate how each of this formulation is based on the Education Development Plan - EDP (2001 – 2010), Ninth Malaysia Plan – 9MP (2006 – 2010) and Vision 2020 (1991 – 2020). Generally these six thrusts of the National Education Plan or *Pelan Induk Pembangunan Pendidikan* are based on the Ninth Malaysian Plan, Education Development Plan and Vision 2020. This is because Vision 2020 is the mother of all plans and so whatever strategies and plans developed after 1991 would have to be in line with it so as to achieve the vision of being a developed nation. This NEB is also inline with the Education Plan as this plan was developed ten years after Vision 2020 which was very specific for the national education system. The Ninth Malaysia Plan was launched in 2006 which covers everything including the education system. It was covered in Thrust 2.

In 2006, the education system in Malaysia was divided into two ministries. Tertiary education now falls under the Ministry of Higher Education while the rest falls under the Ministry of Education. As such the NEB does not have any strategies and plans for tertiary education as in the past. Hence, the NEB has thrusts and strategies that focus on pre-school to upper secondary education and this is under the jurisdiction of the Ministry of Education. The Ministry of Higher Education recently launched the National Higher Education Strategic Plan and the National Higher Education Action Plan 2007 – 2010 outlining the strategies and action plans for this period in line with the Vision 2020.

The Implementation Of The National Education Blueprint in Malaysia (2006- 2010) is based on Vision 2020, Education Development Plan (EDP) and Ninth Malaysia Plan (9MP): Issues and Challenges.

In this section, we highlights some of the issues and challenges in the implementation of NEB in Malaysia...

Thrust 1 of NEB:

Building the nation and people that is united and proud of its nation identity

- Instill love and value Malaysia's heritage
- Strengthen Bahasa Malaysia as the national language
- Foster understanding of the content and needs of Islam Hadhari

This is in line with Strategy 6 of 9MP as this will foster a society with stronger values as well as Thrust 4, Core Strategy 7 to enhance the role of culture, arts and heritage and to pay more attention to greater attention to conservation and preservation of heritage products.

Though it is not directly a result of the 4 thrusts of the EDP, generally if the 4 thrusts are achieved, it will result in building the nation and people who are proud and united. It is with the high quality of education, high accessibility and equity and with effective and efficient management system that the people are educated and the nation can be more developed. (Ministry Of Education, 2001).

This thrust will help the nation to achieve the Vision 2020. If we can achieve this in 2010, we are on the road of achieving our Vision 2020 where we would accomplish the following strategies:

Strategy 1: Establish a united Malaysian nation with a sense of common and shared destiny,

Strategy 2: Create a psychologically liberated, secure, and developed Malaysian Society,

Strategy 3: Foster and develop a mature democratic society,

Strategy 4: Establish a fully moral and ethical society,

Strategy 5: Establish a mature and tolerant society,

Strategy 7: Establish a fully caring society

On the issue of strengthening Bahasa Malaysia as the national language, it is a good strategy to have our own national language but for the past 50 years, we have been promoting and encouraging the use of Bahasa Malaysia and yet today, we are not as united as we wish to be. Because of the changing demand of the global community, the government is promoting the use of English to make our people more compatible with the rest of the world and hence the teaching of Science and Mathematics in English is introduced. We feel proud and united to have a common national language. But in the competitive world and to meet the demands of the challenging world in order to be economically strong and survive the threats of the developed countries, we have to adopt the international language i.e. English.

In order to achieve this thrust, more character building programs can be introduced at all school levels such as teambuilding, camps, nation building activities to foster more unity among the different races. Students should be exposed more to our national heritage; bringing them to such areas and instilling in them this value could help. Exposing them to the different cultural differences and making them appreciate each of the differences can instill a sense of understanding and tolerance. If we start at the young age, we will be able to achieve this goal.

All students should be taught moral education instead of just the non-bumiputera students so that there is unity even in the school curriculum instead of the bumiputera students just doing Islamic Studies. We should include in the curriculum different religions in the world and not divide them in the classes.

The curriculum on history of Malaysia could be improved to make it more interesting and that will connect the students to our heritage instead of just memory work. Visits to historical sites and places of interest could be introduced to create the love and unity for our country.

Thrust 2 of NEB:

Developing Human Capital that is knowledgeable and skilled with an appreciation of pure values

- Motivate learning skills and competency among students in specific subjects including Mathematics and Science
- Roll out the Smart school Concept
- Strengthen the curriculum

This thrust is very much based on Thrust 2 of the 9MP based on the following core strategies:

1. Improving the Access to and Quality of the Education System at All Levels
2. Making National Schools the School of Choice
4. Nurturing Top Quality Research and Development and Scientific and Innovation Capability
6. Fostering a Society with Strong Values (Economic Planning Unit, 2006).

This thrust is also based on the EDP where it focuses on the following:

1. Increase Access in Education
2. Increase Equity in Education
3. Improve Quality in Education
4. Improve Efficiency and Effectiveness of Education Management

(Ministry of Education, 2001)

With this thrust of developing a knowledgeable and skilled human capital, we are on the road of achieving our Vision 2020 of being a developed nation. All the challenges of the Vision 2020 are being addressed by this thrust.

Building human capital is in fact not just starting at tertiary level. It is a right move to start from preschool to tertiary level to train and develop our people who are knowledgeable and skilled to meet this changing environment. We need to equip our next generation to access the wealth of knowledge in Mathematics and Science and to penetrate the technological, financial and commercial world in this millennium and this is being addresses by the teaching of Science and Mathematics in English to make our people more literate in English which is the global language of communication. The focus on motivating learning skills and competency among the students will make our people lifelong learners so that they can be up-to-date with the latest technology and advancement. Strengthening the curriculum will also help to improve the knowledge and skills for our people. We should not rely too much on outdated textbooks.

Clearer assessment and evaluation should be emphasized so that students are not just memorizing the facts rather than they should understand the concepts and their application. With the advancement of technology, students are exposed a wide array of information and hence, continuous evaluation and assessment could be introduced and not just the final examinations which really is a test of students' memory.

Strengthening the curriculum to put more focus on the application and skills will develop our students' knowledge and skill. The curriculum needs to be updated periodically and to include the practical use because of the demands of this fast changing world. We do not want our students to be left behind. Public speaking and oral presentation should be introduced to equip them with good communication skills. The reading habit should be instilled in the students at the young age so that they may become lifelong learners.

Thrust 3 of NEB:

Strengthening national schools, making national school the main choice without obstructing the development of vernacular schools

- Strengthen school leadership
- Develop school infrastructure
- Expand preschool programme (Economic Planning Unit, 2006)

Thrust 3 supports the core strategies 1 and 2 of Thrust 2 of 9MP which are to:

1. Improving the Access to and Quality of the Education System at All Levels
2. Making National Schools the School of Choice

This thrust fully supports the EDP which focuses on the 4 thrusts of:

1. Increase Access in Education
2. Increase Equity in Education
3. Improve Quality in Education (Ministry of Education, 2001).
4. Improve Efficiency and Effectiveness of Education Management

This also supports Vision 2020. If we can achieve this thrust, national schools are the main choice without obstructing the development of vernacular schools, and then our people will be happy and not focus on minor issues. With a strong school system, flexible curriculum and excellent infrastructure, our youth will be educated and that in turn will be able to help and develop our nation.

The issue here is how can the national schools be the main choice without obstructing the development of vernacular schools? Can we have schools that can cater to all the people's needs? There are so many thousands of schools in Malaysia and how can all the school principals be trained to take up more leadership roles in creating these strong schools? Do the principals have enough leadership training especially principals of rural schools? Are they ready to be empowered to compete towards excellence especially those in the rural areas where they do not even have their basic requirements to run the schools?

Chinese schools prepare their students well to perform much better than the national type school students. Many parents including non Chinese parents want to send their children to national type Chinese schools. The teachers of these schools are more committed in bringing out the potential of the students. The national school teachers should learn from these schools on how to encourage and motivate the students to excel in life.

Many private schools are mushrooming these days and 'the rich' can afford to send their children to these private schools. National schools should learn from the success of these schools. A one session school with longer schooling hours is preferred than a two session school. Is it possible to have a one session national school system? If national schools can have a one session schooling system, maybe the national schools can be the schools of choice. (Economic Planning Unit, 2006).

These private schools have better facilities to enhance the teaching and learning process. Thus, national schools should look into this in order to make our national schools the school of choice. National schools should have better facilities such as science and computer laboratories, well-stocked libraries, resource centers for students to discuss and share ideas, rooms or centers for activities and many more to not only provide students with academic knowledge but equip them with everyday living skills that can help them meet the challenges of the future.

The number of students per class can be reduced in national schools as currently, there are more than 40 students per class. We should look into the teacher: student ratio such that there is effective and efficient interaction between teachers and students.

International benchmarks or even local successful schools should be looked into to give a better picture of how national schools can be the schools of choice. Schools must be created in such a way that students develop willingness to go to school instead of withdrawing from there. More extra-curricular activities and co-curricular activities should be included in schools to build the character of the students instead of just concentrating on academic achievement. Soft skills should be introduced at an early age to build the students' character and personality.

Thrust 4 of NEB:

Narrowing the education gap in terms of location, socio-economic status and student abilities so that all schools and students will be given the same opportunities to achieve excellence

- Improve infrastructure and basic necessities for rural schools
- Increase the number of trained teachers and options in rural areas
- Improve the delivery system of assistance for poor students as well as those with special needs and minority groups (Ministry of Education, 2006).

Thrust 4 also supports the core strategies 1 and 2 of Thrust 2 of 9MP which are to:

1. Improving the Access to and Quality of the Education System at All Levels
2. Making National Schools the School of Choice

This thrust supports 3 of the 4 thrusts in the EDP They are:

1. Increase Access in Education
2. Increase Equity in Education
3. Improve Quality in Education (Ministry of Education, 2001).

This also supports Vision 2020. By providing universal education to al, intellectual poverty can be reduced. The government can address to so many social problems and can concentrate on building and developing our nation of healthy people who are financially sound and emotionally and spiritually developed.

This is an excellent strategy where the people of the nation will be provided with a good education regardless of race or social status (Hussin, 2004). If the gap between all schools can be narrowed, the national schools will be the schools of choice. However, there are schools especially on the hills and island areas and deep in the interior regions of the country which do not even have the basic facilities let alone the teachers. How would this be possible? How can these schools be provided with the necessary facilities and human resources for them to operate effectively and efficiently? How can the schools be given the same opportunities to achieve excellence?

The deployment of more experienced teachers to these schools is also an issue. The allowances given to these teachers are not enough to offset their cost of traveling to these schools and the hardship they have to endure. Will the extra allowance encourage experienced teachers especially those who are married with children to go to these schools and affect their children's education, forego their urban lifestyles and loss of opportunity in the urban areas. Can the allowance compensate for all these losses when these experienced teachers relocate to these rural schools?

It is difficult to provide all schools with the same facilities because Malaysia is so big and there are schools in very remote places such as the mountain ranges and interior of Sarawak and Sabah. To reach these schools is also a problem. There is no proper transport to go to these schools and they do not have the basic amenities and hence how can we narrow the gaps here? It is definitely a good move to improve the infrastructure and basic necessities for rural schools and increase the number of trained teachers and options in rural areas (Shahril @ Charil Marzuki, 2005).

Instead of opening the schools in the rural areas, children should be brought to schools nearer to the urban areas so that they may be given a conducive environment for studies. They would have a better exposure instead of staying in their rural homes without proper amenities. This may also cause some family problems because some poor families would want their children to help them at home.

Plans are giving weightage to minority students and students with learning disabilities or rather slow learners. Certain schools have classes specially to cater the needs of these students. More details specified to assist these students with special needs could be useful. However, provision for gifted students' education should be addressed too. In the past, students who were high in their academic achievements, were selected at year 3 for promotion to year 5 which was a good move. This is no longer in practice.

Thrust 5 of NEB:

Improving teaching profession

- Improve the identification of teachers
- Strengthen teacher training
- Improve career prospect for teachers
- Improve teachers' work environment

Thrust 5 also supports the core strategies 1 and 2 of Thrust 2 of the 9MP which are to:

1. Improving the Access to and Quality of the Education System at All Levels
2. Making National Schools the School of Choice (Economic Planning Unit, 2006).

This thrust supports strategy 3 in the EDP that is to improve the Quality in Education. The EDP aimed to have 50 percent of the primary school teachers as trained graduate teachers while the 9MP aimed only to have 25 percent of them by 2010. Since the EDP was formulated in 2001, it aimed to have that 50 percent but by 2006, when the 9MP was launched, it was reduced to 25 percent.

This also supports all the challenges in Vision 2020. With an improved teaching profession, students are educated to meet the challenges of the changing world. Malaysia then will be a developed nation.

The question now is with the NEB; would it be able to achieve the goals of having 25 percent primary teachers as first degree holders? The issue is that some primary teachers do not want to pursue a degree because having a degree would not increase their salary package. If the salary is not adjusted for degree holders, then how can the teachers be motivated to pursue their further studies? There should be an incentive for them to do so.

As for the secondary school teachers, some of them do not teach in the discipline they specialized or trained in. This is a real mismatch and the Ministry should look into it to ensure high quality of education.

Career prospects for teachers look more encouraging these days with the Ministry strategizing and planning for their career path. Master teachers and specialist teachers are created to encourage more teachers to improve themselves. Professional and self development courses are provided for teachers to make them better teachers but most of the time, their students are left unattended to when they are away for training. There must be standby or reserved teachers to relieve them so that the students are not left alone. Computer training and up-to-date or modern teaching techniques should be introduced to teachers to equip them to meet the needs of our modern generation.

Promotions for the teachers are mainly focused into the administrative roles. Good and experience teachers are promoted to be assistant principals and then principals. This looks like a good teachers move but then how many positions are there for these posts compared to the number of teachers in the nations. If good teachers are promoted to take up administrative duties, then we will be deprived of good teachers which we are lacking currently. This is not the right move in rewarding the experienced and excellent teachers.

The Ministry should consider this matter seriously i.e., how to reward excellent teachers and chart their career path in the teaching line. A school teacher starts his career as a teacher and retires as a teacher too. There can be different levels to differentiate the teachers such as Assistant Teacher, Junior Teacher, Senior Teacher, Master Teacher, Super Teacher, Principal Teacher and so forth. This will give the teachers some form of incentive and encouragement to drive them to higher levels of excellence.

Furthermore, the Ministry should look into the extension of the retirement age of the good and committed teachers. There are many dedicated teachers who are still capable but have to leave the teaching line because they have reached 56 years of age. If they are still healthy and strong, we should extend their retirement age to 65 years. These teachers are an asset to the teaching profession.

Yearly increments and bonuses based on performance or Key Performance Indicators (KPI) could also be looked into so that teachers will have more drive to move forward in this changing world. They then would not rest on their laurels and just teach the subject and not the students and collect their pay at the end of each month and receive their bonus and increment at the end of each year. With the introduction of performance-based appraisal or Key Performance Indicators (KPI), the leaders of each school would then be accountable for the yearly appraisal process together with the coaching and training schedules to ensure that the teachers are given the proper training for them to perform. Though this will incur a greater financial outlay, it will surely improve the teaching profession.

Teachers' work environment should be improved in terms of providing facilities in the staff rooms. Schools situated in the urban areas such as the Klang Valley, working conditions are not conducive for preparing their lessons. They should have better facilities to explore and implement new teaching methods.

Teaching and Learning Units should be set up in each school to assist teachers so that they may be well equipped with the latest pedagogical skills to enable them to improve the quality of education in the schools. These units should look into the different teaching techniques and share them with the teachers. They should also encourage the use of computers and Internet resources to help build their knowledge and skills. Today, the world is borderless and the teachers' role is no longer just to spoon feed the students with information. Teachers act as the facilitators and direct the students to use the right information and apply the knowledge they gather into their everyday lives.

Thrust 6 of NEB:

Accelerating excellence at educational institution through cluster schools (which are centers of

excellence) so that they will become showcase or model schools

- Ensure effective leadership
- Give more autonomy to cluster schools in several areas
- Create an accountability system
- Create standard and bench mark that can guide a country to developed status (Ministry of Education, 2006)

This thrust is quite similar to core strategy 2 of the 9MP that is to make national schools the school of choice. It is also in line with the EDP's thrusts 1 and 4 and the strategies 2, 3, 6 and 9 of Vision 2020.

The 9MP proposed to standardize national schools and make all national schools smart schools. Hence, to make them smart schools, the principals must have strong and effective leadership to run these schools (Economic Planning Unit, 2006). The concept may not be identical but the idea is similar. If we want to make all national schools the school of choice, then we should develop cluster schools rather than developing two types of national schools? Would it then create a gap in the provision of education between those of cluster schools and the rest?

The concept of cluster school is not well-defined and there are many interpretations of cluster schools in the world. Which concepts are we adopting? It would be good to name it as excellence schools. These cluster schools will become role models to other schools by challenging them to excel in their specific desired field. However, the implementation of cluster schools needs to be looked into so that before implementation, the selected schools will know what to do.

As mentioned in the NEB, clusters schools will be given autonomy in five main areas:

1 human resources

2 school funds

3 student intake

4 teaching and learning

5 examination and evaluation

Even with this autonomy, can the principal of the cluster school have complete full autonomy to run the school? There are many questions which the Ministry has to address and here are some of them:

- Are the school principals ready to take up this challenge?
- Do all the principals of these selected schools know what they need to do?
- Do they have the autonomy to hire and fire?
- If they have the autonomy to hire and fire, then would staff monitoring be allowed?
- Do they have the autonomy to take in students they like and refuse those students who do not meet their expectations?
- Would creating cluster schools increase the education gap between students from different schools?
- What is the level of autonomy given to these principals?
- Would the principals have the autonomy for expansion of the schools?
- Can they offer programs besides the national curriculum?
- Can these schools not follow the national curriculum and assessment and evaluation system?
- Where do they get all the extra finances to run these schools?
- Can they also charge students fees?
- These cluster schools will attract more students than they can accommodate. What can be done?
- What are the limitations of the principals of cluster schools? Is there any limit to what they can do?
- Who are they accountable to? The Ministry of Education, the parents, the community, the teachers, the students?

The principals of some selected schools have been sent to Kings College in the United Kingdom for training. Most of the principals are already near retirement age and hence, how many years more can they continue to run their schools? It is the policy that civil servants retire when they turn 58 years old. Therefore, they must have good succession plans such that the new principal will be equipped with these skills to take over once the old principal retires.

It may be good to have a pool of trainers in Malaysia to train the principals. These trainers could also train other principals to be equipped with all the necessary skills such they can steer their schools towards excellence.

The principals of those schools not selected as cluster schools may feel dejected and disappointed at not being selected. They may lose their motivation and commitment in running the schools. Can all schools be clustered in a while to help each other?

Cluster school systems in other countries such as Singapore use a different concept. A few schools in the same location are grouped together to form a cluster so that they can provide support to each other and not be seen as a threat to each other. Hence, they would grow and improve and this will provide the synergy for accelerating education excellence (Ministry of Education, Singapore, 2006). Malaysia wants to look at how other countries have set up cluster schools and adopt the best practices and not just re-invent the wheels that do not work in our education environment. From the cluster school concept in Malaysia, these schools are selected from near and far to be in clusters and so how can they support each other? A proper study has to be conducted before implementation takes place.

Some schools with more dynamic principals can bring the schools to higher levels of excellence. And this should be the objective for having this cluster school concept. However, some may feel so challenged that sharing with others may bring them down the rank. This kind of competition is not healthy and it loses its sight of accelerating excellence in schools.

Conclusion

The NEB basically supports the Vision 2020 which is the mother of all plans. The Vision 2020 is the long term plan for the development of the whole nation as a developed country.

The Education Development Plan is the education plan which is the mid-term plan of 10 years from 2001 – 2010. It has 4 main thrusts and all the strategies and plans to provide education to the people. This education plan supports Vision 2020 in developing education for the people so that we are a developed nation.

The 9MP is the mid-term plan for 2006-2010 and it covers everything for the 5 years. It also has a section on the education plan which is mainly in Thrust 2 and these are also in line with the Vision 2020 and Education Development Plan.

Because the Education Development Plan is for 10 years, a revision was brought in with the launching of the NEB which is basically to evaluate, amend and update all the mid-term plans such that they stay in line with Vision 2020. New strategies and plans are also added such as the introduction of the cluster school concept to push our education system to higher levels to meet the challenges of the changing global environment. The success of the National Education Blueprint depends on:

- The implementation and the process of implementation in all schools
- The effectiveness of the implementation
- The follow-up and evaluation
- Financial resources (budget for headmaster to run the school)
- Physical resources (school expansion, computers and other teaching aids required)
- Human resources (staffing and training) (Shahril Marzuki & Habib Mat Som, 1999).

It also depends on the commitment of everyone involved from the Ministry of Education down to the principals, teachers, students, parents and other stakeholders. It encompasses a lot of good and forward looking strategies to drive the education in the nation. If everyone understands all these thrusts and strategies and come out with workable and realistic action plans, we will be able to achieve the goals of the blueprint. Everyone must be willing to change their mindset, face the challenges of the changing world and take steps and actions to be creative and innovative to meet these changes which include technological advances. If we can achieve all these goals, we are on the way to achieving our Vision 2020 of being a developed nation.

REFERENCES

Economic Planning Unit. (2006). *Ninth Malaysia Plan 2006- 2010.* Putrajaya: Economic Planning Unit, Prime Minister's Department.

Ministry Of Malaysia. (2001). *Education Development Plan 2001-2010, Generating Educational Excellence Through Collaborative Planning.* Kuala Lumpur: Ministry of Education Malaysia

Ministry of Education Malaysia. (2001). *The Education Development Plan 2001 - 2010*, Kuala Lumpur: Percetakan Nasional Malaysia Bhd..

Ministry of Education Malaysia. (2006). *National Education Blueprint (2006- 2010)(Pelan Induk Pembangunan Pendidikan 2006-2010),* Kuala Lumpur: Bahagian Perancangan dan Penyelidikan Dasar Pendidikan, Kementerian Pelajaran Malaysia.

Ministry Of Education, Singapore. (2006). *Education in Singapore.* Singapore, Ministry Of Education Singapore.

Shahril Marzuki, Habib Mat Som. (1999). *Education in Malaysia: Issues and Challenges.* Kuala Lumpur: Utusan Publication & Distributors.

Shahril @ Charil bin Marzuki (2005). *Management of School Finance.* Kuala Lumpur: PTS Publication & Distributors.

Sufean Hussin (Ed.). (2004). *Education Development Policy in Malaysia.* Kuala Lumpur: Dewan Bahasa Dan Pustaka.

Taylor, S., Rizvi, F., Lingard, B., & Henry, M. (1997). *Educational Policy and thePolitics of Change.* London: Routledge.

14

Awareness Training Model—The New Age Guru for Enhancing Interpersonal Skills in Academic Settings

Jasvir Chahal and Rohit Bhandari

Temporal transition, when it was set in, was a big event for those who witnessed it. The millennium change was ushered in with great fanfare and it was believed that the ensuing times will not remain the same. And so has it happened, the predicted change could set in quite soon than it was expected. Barely a decade after the beginning of this fresh era the change is being perceived, felt and lived. The landmark historical testimony perhaps to this transformational transition is being set in by the embarkment of the Obamanism Era. The change is manifesting itself in tangible gains to the interest of the educationists. It is time to introduce and integrate the change in life patterns to the pedagogical circles before they become meaningless to us in our life-preparation-factories; our educational institutions.

"No man is an island in itself" is a dictum which is not purely confined to the fictional circles rather it seems to be transcending the mental imaginational boundaries of the philosophers and thinkers and in fact we all are living this changed life style. Each day, each event builds our faith stronger in the belief that in order to master life skills we need to be practitioners in successful establishment of healthy interpersonal skills. Building interpersonal skills within the pedagogical precincts is the new age challenge to the practitioners of the discipline of education. It is the onset of an era which is going to witness the instant crystallization of the fluid facts of life into the theoretical philosophies of life. Life will require extempore decisions and the ones who are used to this life style will be able to spell success for themselves. The social awareness philosophy which was spelled by the pragmatists can at no time be said to be a living reality than our very own times through which we all are passing currently. Today requires enhanced awareness, a conscious decision to lead one to awareness and to extend that awareness to become limitless in terms of its social quotient. Academic circles get an impetus out of the enhanced awareness and finer inter personal skills. The increased number of forums, groups and communities on internet, if they are any indicators to be considered are the testimony to the fact that realization of self today is getting more and more based into its social quotients as it is an age of heightened awareness not only of the self but of the others and the environment too. Spirituality, philosophy, science, sociology, psychology – all are becoming more and more intertwined and interdependent and we will like to label it as a situation of perfect amalgam when all blend in so perfectly that each seems inseparable component of the other. It is this age perhaps when ultimate knowledge of Art of Living life is going to dawn upon mankind and that our instrument in hand- Education- has to prepare us well for that moment of realization.

History always leads us to present and so has it done to us in its developmental sequence of the history of educational research and philosophy and technology of education too. About five decades back the need to have some models based into awareness enhancement were purported and also it was felt that Interpersonal skill development may as well be included into the domains of curriculum transaction. All that which seemed virtual reality then seems to be knocking at our doors today as a stark reality. Today's global village desires it to the level of necessity to possess increased awareness of self and surroundings so that one can master ones grip over the world not by merely making one an island of isolated knowledge but by having a shared control over each others emotions by mastering the skill of living together in a socialized situation which is gross reality of our existence. Together we survive, isolated we perish is the life instilling fundamental.

Of late, the lid which has been debarring humans from realization of their total potential, has went off and all around us we are finding a frenzy to have the realization of one's potential in all respects. The barricades are breaking one by one and the boundaries are melting; giving way to the true Brave New World of the writers imagination or for that matter the imaginations of so many of us combined. It is this collective consciousness which spells the cardinal principles of the movement which found its beginning with the thoughts being aired in the discipline of Education by Fritz Peris and later being chiselled to popularity by Schutz (1958). Human Potential Movement gave fullest expression to this Interpersonal Movement. We have chosen to focus on a model described by Schutz (1958), especially in FIRO: A Three-Dimensional Theory of Interpersonal Behavior: Joy; Expanding Human Awareness; and Elements of Encounter. Schutz's writings emphasize interpersonal training as a means of increasing personal awareness and joy, which he defines as the feeling that one is fulfilling one's potential (1960). There are so many Models of Teaching like concept attainment model by Jerome S. Bruner, Inductive Thinking Model by Hilda Taba and Inquiry Training Model by Suchman etc. but Awareness Training Model by Schutz has significant impact in the field of Social Sciences.

"Awareness Training Model is a model to create awareness and to increase self understanding of one's own behaviour and that of others, and also to help students develop alternate patterns for their personal and social development" (Schutz, 1958).

"Awareness Training Model presents a group with a task that involves exploration of an area in a warm emotional way, and in the extensive use of discussion where frankness and open expression of affect are encouraged" (Howard Lewis and Harold Streidfeld (New York), 1986).

Processes of Awareness Training Model (Schutz,1958)

1. Syntax : It consists of two phases. First is the posing and completing the task and second is a discussion or an analysis of what has gone on. First phase includes giving directions and ensure safe environment and second one includes emphasis on responsibility, feelings and feedback. It promotes honesty and openness.

2. Social System : The model is characterised by norms of mutuality, trust and openness. Low to moderate external structure is provided by the task sequences.

3. Principle of Reaction : It guards against overintensity, help individual to gain insight into their own behaviour and develop conceptual tools. It assists students to take responsibility and focusing on feelings.

4. Support system : The teacher should be an open person who has the requisite interpersonal and intrapersonal skills.

The Awareness Training Model has a great importance in developing curriculum, designing education and teachers have explored ways of incorporating so-called affective education in to the school curriculum and activities. It creates openness, honesty and capacity to take responsibility. It helps the students in developing or expanding their mental horizons by exploratory nature.

The definition of Awareness Training Model for now is an adoption of the definition given by Schutz (1958) which is depicted as follows:

Awareness Training Model

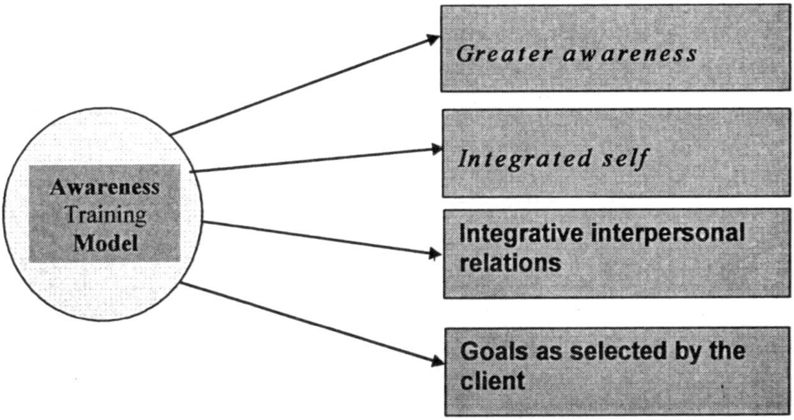

Fig. From Joyce, B.E. and Weil, M. (1985) "Models of Teaching", New Delhi, Prentice Hall of India Pvt. Ltd.

The above figure encounter open up to the "student" the possibility of development, but they do not lead him precisely toward pre-selected goals- he grows as he can in directions greatly determined by his readiness and his wishes.

1. Greater Awareness : Greater Awareness aims at promoting awareness in an individual about the self and environment. Many likes, dislikes, potential and weaknesses about one's self remain undiscovered in an average individual and the same is true to the school going children also. Greater Awareness makes a conscious measured effort in this direction.

2. Integrated Self : Integration by the various forces working within the self is essential to gain the maximum in today's competitive world. Philosophicaly contemplating realisation of the self, if that is a purpose of life, will remain incomplete without focusing and integrating all energies of the self. After discovering the self next logical step is to work for the coherence of the self.

3. Integrated Interpersonal Relations : The knowledge of the self, the awareness of the surroundings (living and non-living) and the integration of self ultimately is going to see an individual in harmony with his social surroundings. It is the next skill logically developed in the Awareness Training Model.

4. Goals as Selected by the Client : Control of the self and the environment converts an individual into a chooser and not a loser. Such an individual automatically gains control over the situation and thus is in a position not only chose the targets but to attain them also.

Interpersonal Skills

Skill is an art or way of expressing one's idea. Teaching can be considered as fifty percent knowledge and fifty percent interpersonal skills. That means while teaching teacher should not just maintain the quantity of lecture but also the quality of lecture. This quality of lecture can be provided with the help of interpersonal skills.

"Interpersonal skills have been defined as those responses which within a given situation prove effective and in other words maximise the probability of reducing, maintaining or enhancing positive effects for the interactor" (Bernard Shah, 2002).

This definition stresses a situational and interactional emphasis. Interaction is the basis of group process, thus a peer group approach as opposed to individual treatment should be the most appreciative on text for teaching and learning interpersonal skills.

"Interpersonal skills have been defined as those responses which with in a given situation prove effective and in other words maximise the probability of reducing, maintaining or enhancing positive effects for the interactor" (Brown, 2003). This definition stresses a situational and interactional emphasis.

"Interpersonal communication is the manner in which information is shared or exchanged between a small numbers of people. Healthy interpersonal skills lead to creative and effective approaches to solving problems and getting work done" (Kahn & Weiss, 2005).

'Interpersonal skills' is a way of interacting and happens always at all time whether you want it to happen or not.

Types of Interpersonal Skills

A number of interpersonal skills are needed to assist an individual as they interact with other. Various types are as follows :

- disclosure Communication skills
- Empathy
- Effective body language
- Silence
- Reflectiveness
- Self

Developing Interpersonal Skills

As students are the future of our nation, so the target has to be cultivating better interpersonal skills among students to make them better learners; the overall personality of students and thereby that of the nation can be improved. So interpersonal skills are very important part of our education system. We can develop interpersonal skills by various methods or techniques.

Interpersonal Skills

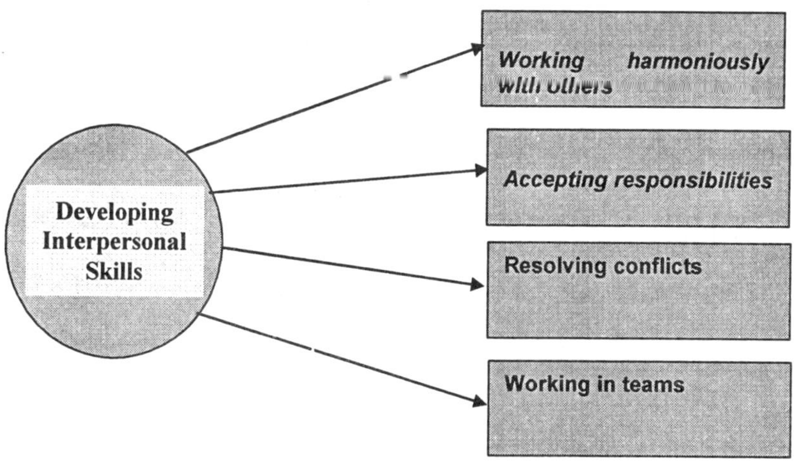

Fig. Adapted from matter found in Burnard, P. (2005) "Interpersonal Skills Training – A source book of activities", New Delhi, Prentice Hall of India Pvt. Ltd.

1. Working harmoniously with others

In order to work harmoniously and efficiently with others one should have :

- Tolerance
- Empathy
- Patient listening
- Adaptability
- Trustworthiness
- Mutual understanding
- Social adjustability
- Democratic attitude
- Openness of mind

2. Accepting responsibilities

In order to accept responsibility one should have :

- Leadership
- Dedication towards assigned tasks
- Accountability
- Perseverance
- Confidence
- Endurance

3. Resolving conflicts

In order to resolve conflicts in group one should have :

- Decision making capacity
- Problem solving capacity
- Farsightedness
- Management skills

4. Working in teams

One should have following skills to work in groups :

- Cooperation
- Effective communication
- Group dynamics
- Transparency
- Capacity to motivate others
- Understanding human psychology

In a study conducted in 2006 to measure the "Impact of Awareness Training Model on Interpersonal Skills and Academic Achievement" (Bhandari , 2006) in the subject of Economics it was found that Awareness Training Model has significant positive impact on Interpersonal Skills of +1 students and that Awareness Training Model has significant positive impact on Academic Achievement of +1 student.

In yet another study titled, "Awareness Training Model and Constructivism as related to Acquisition of Concepts of Commerce" (Kaur, 2008) it was found that Awareness Training Model has significant relationship with acquisition of concepts in Commerce. It was also found in the same study that Constructivism too, which can be assumed to be culling out of increased awareness, correlates significantly positively with the acquisition of concepts.

In order to make it more meaningful to have enhancement of academic domains and the social skills it is worth giving a trial to the Awareness Training Model as purported originally by its propagators or to modify and adapt it according to the local, regional variations as desired by the practitioners of education from time to time. Awareness otherwise also is one of the essential accomplices of the process of education and by doing so it will make us reach the essence of education; the education which liberates; the education which makes us the masters of the skilful handling of Art of Living Life!

REFERENCES

Bhandari, R. (2006). Impact of awareness training model on interpersonal skills and

academic achievement. M.Ed. dissertation (Unpublished), Panjab University, Chandigarh.

Burnard, P. (2005). *Interpersonal skills training – A source book of activities*. New Delhi: Prentice Hall of India Pvt. Ltd.

Gurinder, P. (2005) http://searchwarp.com/swa10270.html

Joyce, B.E. & Weil, M. (1985). *Models of teaching*. New Delhi: Prentice Hall of India Pvt. Ltd.

Kaur, A. (2008). Awareness training model and constructivism as related to acquisition of concepts of Commerce. M.Ed. dissertation (Unpublished), Panjab University, Chandigarh.

Khan, M.S. (1991). *Models of teaching-theory and research*. New Delhi: Ashish Publishing House.

Schutz, W. (1958). FIRO: A three-dimensional theory of interpersonal behavior. New York, NY: Rinehart.

15

Life Long Learning in Science Teacher Education : Issues and Challenges

Selva Ranee Subramaniam

Introduction

The onslaught of information communication technology and the effects of globalization have initiated "new" perspectives in science education. In this context, Malaysia has given utmost priority to the re-development of science education in particular. The significance of science and technology is explicitly documented in government policies namely the New Economic Policy. The science and technology-driven economic policies are stimulus prerequisites for the development of a "learning society". The re-engineering of science and technological education is an enabler to attain an industrialized status in 2020 as envisioned in the country's Vision 2020 document.

The development of science and technology is dynamic and rapid, thus educators have to be "on the toes" during the entire teaching career. Enculturation of lifelong learning is critical for the advancement of the country from an agricultural-based revenue spinner to an industrialized nation. The demand for a skilled workforce in niche areas of science and technology calls upon an urgent need for re-visiting the science teacher education programmes at the various levels. The eventual product of the education system to produce critical and creative human resource should be the ultimate goal.

Lifelong Learning Policy in Science Teacher Education

The Eight Malaysia Plan laid the foundation for transition

from an agricultural-based economy to K-economy. In the education sector, efforts are evident as mega projects in the pipeline are being implemented. Among the projects that contribute to lifelong learning among science teachers is the establishment of Smart Schools in 1999. Smart schools have been identified as the center for the dissemination of the smart school concept, teaching and learning resources, and skills and technology. The Ninth Malaysia Plan formulated for five years (2006 – 2010) is a follow-up of the Eight Malaysia Plan. The long term strategic plan is to adopt strategies to face the challenges of globalization. For this purpose, a substantial amount of the country's budget has been allocated for providing information communication technological facilities and "up-grading" existing infrastructure. The rate of use of computers increased from 1.2% in 1990 to 21.8% in 2005. During this period, the rate of investment increased to 4.7% per annum (Prime Minister's Department 2006).

Education has to be viewed from the spectacle of the current and futuristic market demands. Innovations and values that expand the body of knowledge are contributing factors towards the development of human capital. These elements are determinants for the success of attaining a K-economy nation (Prime Minister's Department, 2006). This statement is realistic and educators must accept and synthesize efforts to adapt to current workplace demands. Efforts are being taken at all levels to make necessary modification, adoption and adaptation at all levels of education, beginning from pre-school to tertiary level in aspects of curriculum and pedagogy, as well as supporting facilities and infrastructure. Educators are given ample opportunities to attend in-service courses of their choice. Educators in the profession may have graduated a decade ago or even more and hence may not have been exposed to ICT courses and application of technology in the teaching-learning process. Thus, it is significant that lifelong learning programmes play a dominant role in teacher education to realize this vision of producing marketable graduates with relevant skills.

Lifelong learning programmes in science teacher education should adopt multiple strategies to encourage the development of "current" knowledge, skills and competencies. Quality innovations which have the potential to be commercialized can emerge from the pursuit of lifelong learning programmes. Curricular and co-curricular activities need to be reviewed at all levels to ensure that the future graduates are prepared for the "school to work" transition.

This paper discusses the implications of lifelong learning policies and strategies implemented in teacher education.

Lifelong Learning Strategic Plan

The teaching profession is subjected to multiple challenges and it is essential that priority and emphasis be given in the areas of teacher training which can be categorized as formal lifelong learning. Non-formal lifelong learning courses are inclusive of up-skilling, re-skilling and multi-skilling courses in the areas of the teaching profession. However, there are factors that need to be given due attention to facilitate the enculturation of lifelong learning in the teaching profession. The significant factors that will be discussed are as follows:

1. **ICT policy in education**
2. **Teacher training and professional support**
3. **Facilities and resources**
4. **Research and development**

The above factors have to complement and supplement each other to pave the way for lifelong learning in teacher education.

ICT Education Policy

ICT in education was catalysed with the implementation of the policy of teaching Mathematics and Science in English since 2003. Schools were allocated with technological facilities namely laptop computers, LCD projectors, science content-based courseware and English proficiency courseware. These supporting facilities initiated "new" learning perspectives among the teachers to cope with the transition. The paradigm shift of adopting English Language in the pedagogical process was reinforced with technological strategies. Thus, teachers automatically engaged themselves in lifelong learning activities. The existing teacher education programmes were revised and refined to incorporate ICT elements in education. Technology becomes obsolete rapidly. The 'Word' and 'Powerpoint' software is continuously evolving with "add-on" features to enable interactive and dynamic presentations. The manipulation of data using technological software *"Excel"* and *"Spreadsheet"* has facilitated analysis, report writing and evaluation. A point to note is that continuous self-initiated learning would enable educators to discover tools that would facilitate and enrich the pedagogical process, which may not be possibly acquired during the courses.

The teacher training programme for the teaching of Science and Mathematics in English is aimed at "up-grading" the ability of teachers in specific areas namely ICT skills in processing words, *Powerpoint* presentations and information search using internet. These lifelong learning initiatives are concerned with a new dimension of technological pedagogical content knowledge. Teachers are assumed to have been equipped with content knowledge, pedagogical knowledge and pedagogical content knowledge upon completion of teacher training programmes. The dimension of technological pedagogical content knowledge is an intervention to cope and juggle with in this technological era. However, with many interventions and technological support tools that could be used in teaching, teachers tend to ponder on the appropriateness of the technological tools in the presentation of a specific content area. Are the technological "hands-on" tools more superior to the laboratory "hands-on" tools? Is the technology appropriate for all types of learners? These are some questions that need to be addressed during lifelong learning teacher education programmes.

Teacher Training and Professional Support

Non-formal lifelong learning programmes take the form of in-service courses. In-service courses have incorporated the ICT component and pedagogical approaches which are meaningful and realistic. However, though teachers are being trained to use technology in the pedagogical process, the specificity of technology use in specific content areas may not be addressed. Lifelong learning in teacher training courses is an "open entry" involving participation from a heterogeneous group of teachers. Certain assumptions are made in the design of lifelong learning "in-service" courses. The training involving technology in the pedagogical process assumes that teachers are able to apply and transfer the non-contextual technological skills to a contextual content specific area. A common scene in the classroom is the use of the fashionable technological tool *Powerpoint*. Notes are prepared on *Powerpoint* slides and displayed on the screen. This is a misconception that a technology-aided lesson can enhance learning abilities. This may have a positive impact in certain cases but with mere notes on the electronic board, the constructive learning process in science is debatable. Teaching practices of this nature may be the outcome of specialised technological training for "up-skilling". Surfing the web for materials is analogous to searching information from hard copy materials in the library. The web is a tool to facilitate the information seeking process and filtering appropriate materials that are essential for the learning process taps upon the critical ability of the students. The technology-assisted learning with critical and creative thinking as a base in the teaching and learning process is significant to ensure that science learning is a constructive and contextual process. Learning science is an active process involving exploration, investigation, and data collection.

Training for up-skilling, re-skilling and multi-skilling are lifelong learning initiatives for consolidating the teaching of science. Science is falsifiable, thus opening doors for continuous exploration and investigation to be carried on. Lifelong learning strategies adopt various shapes in teacher education. There are long distance programmes, post-graduate teacher education programmes and in-service courses. Teaching is not a fixed template to be followed. Thus, teachers have to dwell into simple action research practices to discover the micro-details of the appropriate technology in specific content areas. Action research is an implicit form of lifelong learning endeavour. The continuous action research cycle accumulates learning which could contribute to the body of knowledge. The rapid technological advancement makes it practically impossible for "everything that the teachers need" to be "up-to-date" during these lifelong learning courses. Thus, lifelong learning practices in the form of action research are valuable professional practices that would complement authentic pedagogical practices.

Facilities and Resources

The teaching of Science and Mathematics in English has accelerated the use of ICT in the teaching and learning process. The use of the computer software in the form of CD-ROM, simulations, multimedia, learning modules, and courseware requires appropriate and complete infrastructure. ICT facilities namely LCD projectors, laptop computers, digital camera and multimedia equipment are required for enriching the teaching and learning process.

The question that arises is whether the teachers are skilled in manipulating and operating these technological gadgets. Are the teachers going to rely on the support technical staff, if any exists? Being dependent on the support technical staff would cause "delays" if they are not available or if there is no provision for technical staff. What then should be done? Teachers need to acquire the competency skills in managing these tools. Lifelong learning in science teacher education courses would need to incorporate varied support skills or multi-skills to ensure that the pedagogical process is carried out without any hitch.

Research and Development

ICT is an enabler to facilitate the teaching and learning process. In the context of ICT education, ICT is considered as an enabler to facilitate the teaching and learning process. The key issue is to encourage teachers to use technology in the teaching and learning process. However many questions remain unanswered regarding the use of technology and the "new" direction of science teaching.

Among the questions which raise doubt are as follows:

What is the appropriate technology to be used in the teaching of a particular concept? Is the appropriate technology readily available in the institution or still in the planning stage?

Teachers may uphold conceptions that the use of technology that they were exposed to during lifelong learning courses are significant to be used whenever and wherever possible. Although there would be other emerging technologies, teachers who do not adopt self-initiated learning would implement the same technologies that they were exposed to during the lifelong learning courses. Again, where does this lead to? This leads to "in-grained" teaching practices utilizing technology but "out-dated" in nature.

Time is another factor that needs to be given due consideration in the use of technology-aided teaching and when does technology need to be used? This can be answered by the practitioner who has performed some form of action research practices. The role of the practitioner as a researcher is a lifelong learning process which leads to accumulation of knowledge.

Conclusion

Lifelong learning is significant in science teacher education to improve the quality of the educators in the professional duties. At this juncture, it is important to note that reflections of authentic performance enable educators to continually identify strengths and pitfalls in the teaching and learning process. The evaluating and rectifying process would involve continuous learning, too. In the technological era, knowledge, skills and competencies acquired become obsolete rapidly. Thus, teacher training should operate on a framework of lifelong learning skills, instead of being prescriptive in nature. Lifelong learning courses are not sufficient to equip teachers with skills which are sufficient for their entire career.

The attitude and initiative of the teacher is essential for the success of any intervention in the teaching process. There is always resistance to change but however, it has to be viewed in the light that change will keep us moving with the global changes. Enculturation of life long learning is significant for the sustainable development of science teacher education.

REFERENCES

Prime Minister's Department (2006). Ninth Malaysia Plan 2006 – 2010. Putrajaya: Economic Planning Unit.

16

Issues in Maintaing Continuity and Progression of Students' Learning of Science

Rohaida Mohd Saat

Introduction

Transition is the process through which students leave a phase of his or her life to another. This chapter focuses on the current practice of science teaching and learning at primary level which could influence students' learning in science during the transition of primary to secondary school. This transition period is a critical period as students at this experience with a dissonance of physical, emotional and social changes, together with the stress of moving to new environment. Transition from primary to secondary school affects learning where students often found difficulty in learning especially in science, language and mathematics.

Studies found that there is a decline in students' interest in science and school in general during the transitional period and this phenomenon has been documented since the 1970's (Yager, 1996). Such scenario is not only confined to a certain nation but rather it is a world wide phenomenon. Pell and Jarvis (2001) found both British male and female students' enthusiasm for science declines progressively with age. In Germany, Baumert (1995) used a longitudinal study of nine, 4000 year 7 students to confirm his assumption that students' interest in all school subjects decline. Anderman and Maehr (1994) reviewed major research findings in USA and found that students' attitudes towards school declined in general. In

Australia, Speering and Rennie (1996) found that especially female students were generally disenchanted with the teaching strategies used by their secondary science teachers. The decline in interest towards school is mainly due to students facing transitional issues; i.e., moving from primary to secondary school.

According to Osborne (2007), the present science education fails to attract contemporary youth in developed countries. The ROSE project (Sjoberg & Schreiner, 2005) surveyed students' attitudes to school science across more than 40 countries and found that science was not a popular subject among students in all the developed countries. On the contrary, report of the ROSE project for Malaysian students (Yoong & Aminah, 2005) found that students are generally interested in learning the selected S&T topics and they were very positive about school science learning. This implies that the problem about students' interest in science decline as they enter secondary school is less serious in Malaysia (Yoong & Aminah, 2005). However, micro studies such as carried out by Puziah Mohd. Nawi (2006) reported that students found difficulty in learning science at secondary level despite getting good grades in Science at primary level. In fact, these students scored well in their Science UPSR Chapter (a National Examination at primary level) when they were in primary school but they are struggling learning science at Form 1 level. Osborne and Collins (2001) identified that the negative feature of the curriculum has made teachers to adopt pedagogy of transmission of scientific knowledge, copying notes from the board and lack opportunity for students to engage personally or discursively with the subject. Such practice has made students disinterested in science during this transitional period. If transition is not addressed appropriately, the process could impede continuity and progression of students' learning (Braund & Driver, 2005)

Science Education in Malaysia

Science is taught as a compulsory subject since Year 1 (aged 6-7 years old) till upper secondary school in Malaysia. Specifically, the Malaysian science curriculum comprises three core science subjects and four elective science subjects. The core subjects are Science at primary school level, Science at lower secondary level and Science at upper secondary level. These subjects aim at providing students for scientific literacy and students should be able to apply the scientific knowledge in decision-making and problem solving. In addition to the core science subjects, elective science subjects are offered at the upper secondary level and consist of Biology, Chemistry, Physics, and Additional Science. The elective science subjects prepare students who are more scientifically inclined to pursue the study of science at post-secondary level. These subjects aimed for students who would take up careers in related field of science and technology (Ministry of Education, 2006)

Basically, the emphasis of science education is focused on the acquisition of scientific knowledge, development of scientific skills and the inculcation of scientific attitudes and noble values (Ministry of Education, 2006). Science at primary and lower secondary schools emphasized on providing scientific literacy while at upper secondary schools include the integrated science process skills and the thinking skills.

The basic aim of science education in Malaysia is to provide students with the knowledge and skills in science and technology and enable them to solve problems and make decisions in everyday life based on scientific attitudes and noble values (Ministry of Education, 2006). Students who have followed the secondary science curriculum will have the foundation in science to enable them to pursue formal and informal further education in science and technology. The curriculum also aims to develop a concerned, dynamic and progressive society with a science and technology culture that values nature and works towards the preservation and conservation of the environment.

The Malaysian science curriculum is progressive in nature beginning in Year 1 (Grade 1) to Form 5 (Grade 11) and it adopts the spiral approach. According to Bruner (as cited in Ornstein & Hunkins, 1993) curriculum should be organized according to the interrelationships between the structure of the basic ideas or concepts and learners could grasp these basic concepts and ideas when the concepts and ideas are developed and redeveloped in a spiral fashion. For example the study described in this chapter examines the topic 'Heat'. Heat is introduced in Year 5 (Grade 5) under the second theme 'Investigating Force and Energy'. 'Heat' is again covered under the theme 'Energy' under the Learning Area 'Heat' in Form 1 (grade 7). In Year 5, students are introduced to the concept of heat in relation to temperature and when heat gain, the substance becomes warmer. In Form 1, heat is learnt as a form of energy and students need to differentiate between heat and temperature.

The curriculum advocates the inquiry and discovery approach (MOE, 2006). Teachers should play the role of facilitators in guiding students acquire the scientific knowledge. In doing inquiry activities, students should also develop their scientific skills and scientific attitudes.

Realizing the importance of science and technology for nation building, the Malaysian government has set a target of 60:40 ratio of students taking science and technology related studies to students enrolling in arts related studies. To date, this target is far from reach. Based on the statistics released by Ministry of Higher Learning (2008), there is only 44% of undergraduate students taking science and technical studies in the public universities, and if aggregated with the private higher institutions, the percentage of students taking science and technology related field is 42%. This is illustrated in Table 1.

Based on this current trend in students pursuing tertiary education in science, it can be inferred that science and technology is still not a popular career choice among Malaysian students. Therefore, the current science education has failed to attract more students to pursue science as their career. This could be due to various factors such as the irrelevant of the curriculum or it may be due to the way science is taught in schools.

The Study

In this chapter attention is focused on preliminary findings of a study on transitional issues of students learning science from primary to secondary schools. The study generally aims

Table 1. Number of Undergraduate Students in Public and Private Institutions (MOHE, 2008)

Type of Institution	*Field of Specialization*	*Male*	*Female*	*Total*	*Percent*
Public Higher Institution	Arts	70,484	143,524	214,008	56%
	Science	33,500	55,053	88,553	44%
	Technical	50,492	29,944	80,436	
Private Higher Institution	Arts	92,039	127,255	219,294	60%
	Science	43,544	54,944	98,488	40%
	Technical	37,585	10,473	48,022	
Public & Private Higher Institution	Arts	162,523	270,779	433,302	58%
	Science	77,044	109,993	187,037	42%
	Technical	88,077	40,381	128,458	

to unravel the challenges students faced in learning science when they enter secondary school. The findings of this study is based on the first phase of a three phase project which focuses on the science learning in both primary and early secondary school learning environment. The study employed a qualitative research methodology. The techniques used were interviews with primary and secondary schools students and teachers, classroom observations and analysis of documents. Four primary schools were involved. One science teacher and 10 students from each school were selected in the study. After 10 months, these pupils were re-interviewed; i.e. when they were in the secondary schools. However, since the research is on-going, this chapter will only focus on the scenario of students learning science at the primary level where it was observed science lessons on the topic of "heat" under the Learning Area of 'Investigating Force and Energy' listed in the Curriculum Specification Science Year 5 (pp. 32) and later the investigator interviewed the primary school teachers and students. Pseudonyms are used in this chapter.

Scenario 1: "Where's the Inquiry?"

Mawar Primary school is situated in the vicinity of Kuala Lumpur. The enrollment is approximately 2000 students comprising majority Malay students and a handful number of aborigines' students. The school has one science room or laboratory which is equipped with basic scientific apparatus and a sink. Ms Johana (not her real name) has been teaching science for slightly more than a year and she holds a Bachelor degree in Science with Education.

I observed 5 Bakti class and the class has 36 students. Ms Johana started her lesson by showing the students some graphics from the teaching courseware as portrayed in Figure 1. It was showing a cup of hot coffee and it has some animations illustrating the movement of heat from the coffee to its surrounding. Most of her teaching was conducted in the Malay language and she used English for specific scientific terminologies. Some of the terminologies used were "heat", "heat gained" and "heat loss". She continued teaching using the teaching courseware until it illustrated the set-up of an experiment. The experiment was on 'Heat gain and heat loss'. She explained the experiment that will be carried out. She had also projected on the screen a task sheet that was prepared in MSWord document. She asked the students to copy the questions into their Science note book. The students were then put in groups of four to six and they performed the simple experiment. After completing the experiment, students copied down the results with the guidance of Ms. Johana.

Figure 1. Students listening to the teacher's explanation

This episode raises some questions on the teaching and learning of primary science as implemented by Ms. Johana. The teaching and learning was very dependent on the courseware. Although the courseware had voice-over, students could not understand the language used. The teacher had to repeat the concepts such as "heat is absorbed and the water gets warmer" along with gesture indicating that heat is absorbed. Each concept was given didactically. Although the students were given the opportunity to perform the simple experiment, it was a mere verification of what has been explained to them. Nothing new was discovered through the activity. There was no element of inquiry. As advocated in the Malaysian Science Curriculum (MOE, 2006) inquiry is highly recommended. As pointed out in literature and other science education documents such as the *National Science Education Standards* (National Research Council, 1996), students who use inquiry to learn science engage in many of the same activities and thinking processes as scientists who are seeking human knowledge of the natural world.

Scenario 2: "Demonstration Versus Hands-on"

Kemboja Primary school is situated in Klang Valley in Selangor. The school has a high enrollment reaching almost 3000 students. Majority of the students are of Malay ethnicity and a handful of foreign students, namely, the Indonesian. Although, the enrollment is high, the school is equipped with only one science laboratory. The laboratory has working tables for students to perform activities and it has a sink at the side near the windows. There are only basic scientific apparatus such as measuring cylinders, test-tubes and thermometers available in the room. Due to the limited access to the science laboratory, teachers opted to bring apparatus to classrooms and perform demonstration to students.

The class that was observed by the investigator had a total of almost 45 students. The topic of the lesson was 'Heat'. Mrs. Zaini (not her real name) brought 10 thermometers, a beaker, a tripod and a Bunsen burner to class 5 Merah which was located on the second floor of one of the school buildings. She drew the apparatus and the procedure of the activity and on the board. She also drew a labeled diagram of a thermometer with the scales. She began her class by explaining the meaning of 'heat', definition of temperature and its relationship with hotness and coldness of a certain substance. She then explained to the students how to take temperature using a thermometer. She took a thermometer and showed to the students. She explained the way to take temperature by referring to the thermometer as well as to the labeled diagram of the thermometer on the white board. She cautioned the students that reading must be at the eye level at the meniscus of the mercury in the thermometer. She made reference of meniscus at the diagram of the thermometer on the board. Students listened to Mrs. Zaini's explanation without any questions asked.

Since there were no questions from the students, Mrs. Zaini distributed thermometers beginning with the students in the front row. The students were seated in pairs with their tables joining with each other. The students who got the thermometer examine the thermometer. Most of them looked at the scale on the body of the thermometer and felt the markings with their fingers. They then just passed it to the students behind them. One incidence caught the attention of the investigator, there were these two boys who were sitting far right of the classroom near the windows. When they got the thermometer, they looked curious. They were touching it and trying to get some reading. One of them suddenly put the thermometer into his mouth (see Figure 2), trying to read his body temperature. They then looked left and right as if they were searching for some other things and finally one of them took out his drinking bottle. He opened up the lid and inserted the thermometer into the bottle (see Figure 3). They were taking the temperature of his drinking water!

Figure 2. A boy putting the thermometer into his mouth.

Figure 3. Two boys putting the thermometer into his drinking bottle.

Mrs. Zaini continued teaching as the students were examining the thermometer. She drew a labeled diagram of an experiment set-up which will be done the next lesson, and explained the procedure to the students. The students were then asked to copy the diagram and procedure in their science note book as the class ends.

This second episode clearly illustrate that students are curious about their environment. The two boys needed a real situation for the activity even though the teacher mentioned that they will be performing the experiment in their next lesson. However, the action could harm to both the boys. The thermometer was not sterilized and it was not meant to be used to take body temperature. The teacher failed to provide precautionary action in handling thermometers and these thermometers are not clinical thermometers. Based on this episode, It can be noted that majority of learners at this age (approximately 11 years old) are concrete thinkers, where they need concrete materials or examples in their learning. Through action; such as taken by the two boys, learners at this development stage become increasingly internalized of what they are learning.

ISSUES IN MAINTAINING PROGRESSION AND CONTINUITY IN SCIENCE LEARNING

The two episodes described above illustrate typical science teaching at primary level. In addition to class observations, teachers and students were interviewed and some of the students' work was analyzed. Initial findings showed that learning science at primary schools were more of note-taking, whole class demonstration, using mind-maps, 'recipe-type' of science activities and 'drill and practice'. Such practice concurs with Cheng (1999) where she found that learning science at primary school in many Asian countries focuses on retention of knowledge presented in textbooks and it is the top priority of instruction.

Teachers from both the schools that were involved in this study admitted that they completed their Year 6 (Grade 6) syllabus by the month of June. In order to complete the syllabus, most of them lecture and gave notes during their science lessons. They believed that by giving them notes, students will at least have some concrete materials for them to refer. The notes were sometimes given in the form of mind-maps. After completing the syllabus, the students were given UPSR model science question Chapters as 'drill and practice'. This is to develop students' familiarity with the format and the type of examination questions. When asked whether such strategy was effective, Mr. Ahmad (not his real name) smiled and replied, "...not really. The number of students getting an 'A' is still very low". Later in the year when the UPSR results were released, it it was found that out of the five students who were interviewed in Mawar Primary school, only one managed to get 'A' for the UPSR Science Chapter. The other four students got B for science. When asked why Mr. Ahmad kept carrying out the teaching and learning strategy of give notes and yet his students showed no improvement. He replied that he had to do that due to time factor and pressure given by the school's administrators that require all Year 6 teachers to complete the syllabus by the month of June. This is to enable teachers to do revision.

Besides note-taking and 'drill and practice', teachers also performed whole class demonstration as illustrated in the second scenario. They brought materials and apparatus to class and demonstrated experiments. The students revealed that they hardly went to the Science Room or the laboratory to do activities. It is not only because of the teachers' teaching style but the school's lack of infrastructure in science laboratories. It was impossible to accommodate all the classes for science lessons. The science activity observed in this study was among the few activities that were done in the science laboratory. Other experiments which were commonly performed were on rusting, mould culture on bread and food preservation; which the students usually perform at home and they bring the product to school for class discussion. Some of the students revealed that the whole of Year 5, they remembered that they attended to the science laboratory for about three times.

The teachers also used models such as a globe to illustrate the earth's rotation on its axis. According to the teachers, students could visualize better with such models. These models were available in the science laboratory in both schools. Overhead projectors were also common teaching aids among these teachers. As in the first scenario, teaching coursewares were used in science lessons. According to the teacher, the use of the teaching courseware to help students to understand better since the courseware had animations and the narration was clear enough for the students to understand the concept taught in English. As discussed in the first scenario, the teacher repeated what has been narrated since the students could not comprehend what has been explained to them.

When asked what the students remember about learning science at primary level, particularly at the second level of primary school, most of them remembered about the experiment of 'rusting', preservation of fruits and the concept of 'speed'. Majority of the students expressed that they like science despite being taught didactically and they look forward to learning science in Form 1. They anticipated that science in secondary school will have more experiments.

Based on these findings, it can be concluded that there are three major issues to appropriate teaching and learning science in order to maintain the progression and continuity of students learning science at a higher level. First, is the issue of completing the syllabus for national examination, second, is the lack of science laboratory and lastly, is the issue of the language of instruction.

Issue of Preparing of Students for National Examination

The issue in Malaysia is the current practice of teaching and learning of science in primary school. The current practice of mere imparting knowledge and retention of knowledge through the practice of drill and practice could impede students learning science in secondary school and probably at post-secondary level. There is no doubt that the facts and concepts related to science are important. However, they should be the springboard for students to use as they explore the scientific processes. Scientific processes are mastered using content. These processes and content are fundamentals to learning science at a higher level. In fact this issue is not new. During the 1970's revolution in science education, studies found science courses developed or adapted for use in Malaysia at the upper primary or lower secondary levels of the school system seem rarely to meet criteria of relevance to the future lives of the majority of students (Lewin, 1975). Lewin found that the objectives of many science programmes that aim to promote the understanding and application of scientific principles are often undermined, which tends to favour the rote memorization of factual information. Despite the numerous projects and actions that are being implemented to address the problem, the signs of improvement are still modest in the Malaysian school science education setting. The issue of the decline in interest in science probably starts in late primary school itself due to the current practices.

Issue of Lack of Infrastructure

Some of the teachers reported that their frustration are towards the insufficient infrastructure of the science laboratory. Not many teachers willing to carry apparatus to classrooms to perform any science activities. They would prefer if they could perform them in the science laboratory. Due to lack of infrastructure and appropriate apparatus, teachers tend to opt for a whole class demonstration rather than giving the opportunity for their students to have the hands-on experience in handling the apparatus. Students, as illustrated in the second scenario, were adventurous and curious that they investigated the temperature of things around them. In this case, teachers were unable to conduct science lessons that are of hands-on and minds-on in nature which could enhance their students' scientific processes.

Issue of the Language of Instruction

Teachers from both schools that were involved in this study found difficulty in conducting science lessons in English. The teacher in the first scenario was quite proficient in English, however her students could not follow the lesson. She had to repeat and translate almost every sentence that she uttered. She also had to use gestures to signal the meaning. In class where the students' level of English proficiency is low, this teacher faced the challenge of students not comprehending the lessons taught. The students were not able to understand simple instructions in English and scientific terms used in the lesson. According to Cummins (1980), such type of students might lack the cognitive-academic language proficiency (CALP) and this type of language proficiency needed to comprehend textbooks, to participate in classroom discourse, and to answer tests questions.

The teacher in the second scenario was not as proficient in her English language as compared to the first teacher. Due to her lack of proficiency, there were a couple of misconceptions in her teaching. For example, she mentioned "...as water loses heat, it becomes warmer". Science teaching in these schools is affected by such restriction in the language of instruction. During teaching and learning, interaction between teacher and learners depends on the teacher's ability to communicate fluently and the learners' language proficiency. If teachers are not proficient in the medium of instruction, then it would be rather difficult for them to explain scientific concepts, to be the moderator in their students' discussions, or engage in high level questioning.

This issue of language of instruction is seen less affected the effectiveness of the teaching and learning. Incompetence in the medium of instruction of either the teacher or the students has made the lesson very didactic in nature and the learning environment lack students-teacher interaction.

Conclusion

The initial findings of this study concurs Cheng's (1999) concern where primary science instruction focuses on retention of knowledge presented in the textbooks. Teaching and learning of science was done didactically. Teachers in these schools prepared students for the national examination. No doubt that some students did well in their National Examination UPSR but later faced difficulty in learning science at secondary level (Puziah Mohd. Nawi, 2006). This study found that teaching and learning of science at primary school was more on retention of knowledge rather than influenced the focus on National examination. It is also due to the lack of infrastructure and apparatus and also the medium of language used in the teaching and learning of science, as opposed to the negative curriculum as identified by Osborne and Collins (2001).

The students remembered 'science' as the little experiments and other 'hands-on' science activities they have done. They described science as a subject with experiments and made science enjoyable and they are motivated to learn more science at secondary school. They expect to do more experiments in secondary schools, confirming the findings of other studies (Braund & Driver, 2005; Jarman, 1993)

This study suggests that the students' lack of exposure of 'hands-on' and 'minds-on' activities at primary level. This could lead to students' lack manipulative skills and other scientific skills in handling experiments at secondary level. This scenario might impede learning science at secondary level as one of the factors that influence post transfer regression in science learning is the teaching environments and styles and teachers' language that differs in the secondary school (Pointon, 2000). If transition is addressed appropriately, the process could improve the continuity and progression of students' learning (Braund & Driver, 2005). Unfortunately, students' personal journeys from primary to secondary school through education are often disjointed and discontinuous and this often result in regression in learning (Nicholas & Gardner as cited in Braund & Driver, 2005).

What has been presented in this chapter are only some of the initial findings of this study. It is hoped that a deeper insight of the situation in the secondary school could address some of the concern on the challenges that the students face during the transition to secondary school.

ACKNOWLEDGEMENT

This research has been funded by University of Malaya under the short-term research grant FS116/2007C

REFERENCES

Baumert, J. (1995). *Gender, science interest, teaching strategies and socially shared beliefs about gender roles in seventh graders – A multi-level analysis*. Chapter presented at the annual meeting of the National Association for Research in Science Teaching, San Francisco.

Braund, M. & Driver, M. (2005). Pupils' perception of practical science in primary and secondary school: Implications for improving progression and continuity of learning. *Educational Research, 47*(1), 77-91

Cummins, J. (1980). Teaching English through content-area activities. In P. Rigg and V.Allen (Eds.), *When they don't speak English* (pp. 139-151). Urbana, IL: National Council of Teachers of English.

Jarman, R. (1993). Real experiments with Bunsen burners: Pupils' perceptions of the similarities and differences between primary science and secondary science. *School Science Review, 74*(268), 19-29.

Lewin, K. (1975) *Science Education in Malaysia and Sri Lanka.* IDS Discussion Chapter No. 74. (ERIC Document Reproduction Service No. ED142397)

Ministry of Education (2006). *Integrated Curriculum for Secondary Schools*

Curriculum Specifications: Science Form 5. Kuala Lumpur: Dewan Bahasa dan Pustaka

Ministry of Higher Learning (2008). Retrieved from http://www.mohe.gov.my/web_statistik/statistik_pdf_2008_05/indikator_6-3.pdf

National Research Council, (1996). *The National Science Education Standards*. Washington DC: National Academy Press.

Ornstein, A.C. & Hunkins, F.P. (1993). *Curriculum foundations, principles and issues* (2nd. Edn.). Boston: Allyn & Bacon.

Pell, T. & Jarvis, T. (2001). Developing attitude to science scales for use with children of ages from five to eleven years. *International Journal of Science Education, 23*(8), 847-862.

Pointon, P. (2000). Students' views of environments for learning from primary to secondary school. *International Journal of Educational Research, 33*, 375-382.

Puziah Mohd. Nawi. (2006). *Pengaruh Penggunaan Bahasa Inggeris dalam Pencapaian Sains Tingkatan 2 [The Influence of the Usage of English in Form 2 Science Achievement]*. Unpublsihed MEd Project Chapter. University of Malaya, Kuala Lumpur.

Yager, R. (1996). *Science/technology/society as reform in science education*. NY: State University of New York Press.

Yoong, S. & Aminah Ayob, (2005). *Malaysian students interest in learning science and technological (S&T) topics, their attitudes, perceptions and priorities towards important issues in S&T with international comparisons*. (ROSE Research Project) Penang: University Sains Malaysia, Faculty of Education.

17

Creating a Conductive Environment for Deep Learning in the Classroom : A Framework and Mental Model to Aid Teaches

Tee Meng Yew and Dennis Karney

Introduction

As the above quotes indicate, addressing the problems of the future will require new information, new methodologies, new mental models, new ways of thinking, and creative approaches to make sense of, combine and make use of these information, ideas and methods. If one is keeping track of the amount of information produced daily, there's a good chance that the person would be surprised by the sheer volume. Consider the following: More than a million books are published a year – that's about 3,000 books a day (Worldmapper, 2006). The world's largest library, the US-based Library of Congress, holds about 138 million items, of which 32 million are books and other printed materials (Library of Congress, 2008). It is estimated that there are more than 182 million web sites, currently growing by more than a million new sites a month (Netcraft Web Server Survey, 2008). To put these into perspective, it is estimated that more information has been produced in the last 30 years than in the previous 5,000 years combined (Lyman & Varian, 2004; Wurman, 1989).

We are indeed in the information era. For information to become meaningful, human beings must play a role to make sense of the information to render it useful. Peter Drucker

(2001) refers to this role as being a knowledge worker or technologist, as opposed to being a manual worker that relies minimally on making use of emerging information.

From an educational standpoint, teachers must facilitate learning that helps students develop the ability to differentiate the relevant from the irrelevant when accessing information in today's world, and then to use it to solve problems. In order to develop and internalize this ability, the student must cultivate the capacity to analyze, evaluate, and critique information as it emerges. The student must then be able create a synthesis of new knowledge, to problem-solve, and communicate ideas or solutions when the need arises. These are critical foundations to a thinking society that will likely face unprecedented number of complex and even "wicked" problems (Camillus, 2008; Rittel & Webber, 1973; The Arlington Institute, 2008). More than ever, citizens of nations and members or employees of organizations will need these skills to respond to an ever increasing complex world. These base skills and abilities can be cultivated in the educational setting if students are given the opportunity to experience conditions and processes that promotes deep learning. In order to do so, teachers need to begin considering how his or her learning environment can be designed and created so that it becomes a more conducive place to hone communication, analytical, critical, and creative problem-solving skills and to help the student more quickly internalize these skills.

This change is needed because the classrooms of today can still be too focused on knowledge transmission with not enough time spent on creating learning conditions that promote deep learning (Cole, 2000; Herrington & Oliver, 2000; Marton & Saljo, 1976; Resnick, 1987; Whitehead, 1929). As the volume of information continues to explode, numerous education systems have fallen into the trap of trying to do too much in too short a time, leaving students little time to reflect on and internalize what they are attempting to learn. In an ensuing vicious cycle, teachers feel they have no choice but to give directed instruction or lecture—as John Dewey (1938, p. 102) puts it, "knowledge already organized" and "ladled out in doses"—so that they can cover the syllabus within the given time. In exam-oriented educational cultures, this practice is further magnified as teachers strive to teach to exams often at the expense of meaningful learning (Beech, 2006; Chong, 2008).

In a previous paper (Tee & Karney, 2007), we proposed a model for creating a conducive learning environment based on Nonaka's SECI model of knowledge creation, with actions that teachers can take to create and energize a conducive classroom environment, or a *ba*, for deep learning. Here, we want to further develop this framework along with a corresponding mental model and suggest additional ideas and approaches needed to create and energize this *ba*. The suggestions offered here are drawn in large part from a naturalistic research (Lincoln & Guba, 1985) conducted by the first author in an online graduate-level strategic management course (Tee, 2004) coupled with an examination of years of teaching by the second author in the world of business in four countries across the globe, with common insights attained during a stint of co-teaching together. The collective courses drawn on cover a wide span of business topics, with students from all levels of business education (undergraduate, graduate and working professionals) and diverse ages (17-65). As these courses have a common theme of developing practice professionals, who in our context happen to be in the business domain, they have much in common with courses in the fields of education, engineering, law, social work, counseling as well as many of the medical professions.

A Framework for Deep Learning

Nonaka's model of SECI and his concept of *ba* provide important guidance toward a more holistic framework for the integration of learning activities and an environment that can lead to deeper understanding. Essentially, Nonaka examines four key processes by which knowledge is created and the shared context in which these processes come alive. He refers to these processes as socialization, externalization, combination and internalization or SECI in short, which are most stimulated in a *ba*. *Ba,* loosely translated from Japanese, means "shared context."

Nonaka and his colleagues hold that there are four types of knowledge conversion. The first type of conversion is from tacit knowledge to tacit knowledge. This occurs through the socialization process that often includes conversation, observation, imitation and practice. The second conversion is from tacit knowledge to explicit knowledge. This occurs through the externalization process and consists of articulating, giving voice to the knowledge in the form of symbols, language, concepts, models, hypotheses, metaphors, vignettes and analogies. The third conversion is from explicit knowledge to explicit knowledge. This occurs through the combination process, which draws on the synthesis of various bodies of explicit knowledge. The fourth conversion is from explicit knowledge to tacit knowledge through an internalization process—including reflection and action—by the learner. All these key processes must be present to fuel one another and to create deep learning. They are energized and brought to life within a corresponding *ba*.

A *ba* is essentially a place with a unifying form where knowledge can be stimulated, shared, created and utilized, punctuated by the necessary energy, quality, and medium to perform the individual knowledge conversions in an on-going and interacting spiral of socialization, externalization, combination and internalization (Nonaka & Konno, 1998; Takeuchi & Nonaka, 2004). This place can be physical, like a classroom or a field site. It can be virtual, like an online meeting place or through video conferencing. It can be mental, through shared experiences, values and ideals. Or it can be through a relationship of people sharing common learning goals and aspirations.

The Framework in Action

As it is described above, this cycle of socialization, externalization, combination and internalization may mislead readers into thinking that it is a neatly or sequentially packaged cycle of learning. It is not. The first key point is this: It is when all four processes interact with one another—both in a personal and collaborative context, involving various knowledge sources—that the "spiral" of knowledge creation becomes hyper active, a positive reinforcing cycle in Senge's (1990) terms. The greater the interaction, the more active the spiral; the richer the environment the better the opportunities for new knowledge creation. With each spiral, the depth of knowledge or understanding—at the individual, group and class level—becomes deeper.

The second key point: Merely building a learning environment (*ba*) is not enough to activate the knowledge-creating spiral. It needs to be "energized" to give motion and meaning to the learning process, driven by both implicit and/or explicit purposes, direction, interest, and mission (without which the learning and creative energy in the classroom cannot be directed effectively). A learning environment can be significantly energized when provisions are made to enable conditions such as autonomy; fluctuation and creative chaos; requisite variety; and trust and commitment.

So what does it take to create a conducive *ba* to enhance the SECI cycle in our classroom? The below is a synthesis of findings based on research and decades of practice wisdom, with an illustrative summary towards the end of this chapter (refer to Figure 1):

***Creating a conducive* ba *for socialization*. The main purpose of socialization is the sharing of tacit knowledge, for example values, beliefs, context-specific language, experiences, and ways of communicating, thinking or doing things. Tacit knowledge can be conveyed from one individual to another and from individuals to groups through conversations or dialogues, through experiments and creating experiences. This in itself is not a novel goal for educators facilitating learning in the classroom since encouraging open and relevant conversations in the classroom often improve the quality of the class.**

However based on research and practice wisdom, the authors found that the greatest likelihood to be successful is to create a *ba*—in this case, a learning environment—that has distinctly informal and low-stakes characteristics. For example, the second author takes great effort in all his classes to let his students know that "this will not be education as usual," while peppering comments with tongue-in-cheek statements to fuel a lively discussion. "Here we will have to talk and discuss, and learn together. I know, every teacher says this on first day, and then goes off and lectures forever. But I really mean it!" he would say. "I will expect you to know things from previous lectures, other classes...I know, I know... it is against classroom rules of what is expected in the class...as negotiated by the 'union.' I know you are not use to talking and sharing your questions, ideas and experiences in class, but we will be different." He would go on to assure them that he will not talk down on them, or penalize them for sharing alternative perspectives. In fact, in his syllabus he notes: "My promise to you is to create an environment in which you can learn, to be as prepared as possible, and to respect each of you and your opinions. I expect the same from you in all dealings with respect to this course, with me, or with your fellow classmates." He goes out of his way to reinforce conversations with the students in the class, treating each question or point raised with respect and care.

Similar things were observed in the study by the first author in a virtual setting, leading to open discussions, inquiries or explorations. For example, in separate messages from the professor to the online students, he encouraged them to "apply the knowledge you've gained from all your previous courses, as well as your knowledge of strategic and entrepreneurial thinking," and to "to make connections between the ideas/concepts in the textbook, your own personal experience, and what goes on in the real world of business and strategy."

In other words, the teacher needs to make a great effort to create this environment, often going out of his way to break old rote learning habits and in the mean time, create a more open environment for inquiry, sharing and discussion. It doesn't have to be a formal exercise. In fact, socialization can begin with a simple introduction and some icebreakers. It can include a simple but meaningful sharing of each person's hobbies or where they came from, and over time, their professional interests, perspectives, and experiences. The teacher takes the time to ask questions to draw out the different personalities, eventually getting to questions such as: Besides it being required (or needing an elective), why are you in this class? What do you hope to learn? In your mind, what will make this course a success? What is something we all need to know about you to better understand you? How do you think this content relates to your future career? What do you plan to do when you graduate?

The teacher creates multiple opportunities for students to share contextually relevant experiences through open discussions, sometimes leading them down a meandering path to emphasize the significance of the content of the course to their lives. Whenever possible, he encourages storytelling so that richness can begin to emerge. He shares his own stories to illustrate points and to show he is a learner too, making mistakes, being human and hopefully growing. Over time, the classroom can evolve into a learning space where honest opinions and experiences can be shared. At its most effective level, the socialization process will allow for a free flow of ideas and questions.

Commenting on the value of class discussions—characterized by informality and diverse opinions and experiences—students report that they could not have learned from more formal sources what they learned from the discussions because the discussions were richer contextually as they were unedited, first-hand accounts of fellow students' experiences. The key to this process is to develop some form of shared experience, without which it is extremely difficult to identify with another individual's thinking process. The mere transfer of information will often make little sense if it is devoid of emotions or contexts embedded in shared experiences.

Creating a conducive ba *for externalization.* Creating a culture of openness based on trust and mutual respect paves the way for learners to begin to articulate and make sense of what is up to this point mostly tacit knowledge. This is what Nonaka refers to as externalization. When knowledge is made more explicit, sharing with the other learners becomes easier.

Through more effective and efficient sharing, students begin to discover with greater certainty what they do and don't know about their own knowledge bases.

Through activities that encourages students to use metacognition (to think out loud) and to reflect (orally and in writing), they begin to develop a "common language," metaphors and analogies to begin to grapple with what is being learned. Writing activities and development of proposals, models or prototypes for more focused discussions can begin to "concretize" previously loose understandings of the concepts being studied. The teacher takes the time to ask questions that relate course content to their own lives (How does this relate to what you hear at home, read in the papers, see on TV or even YouTube? How might it relate to your future career?), carefully leading them down deeper and more probing questions and discussions (How does this relate to other things you learned? How does it relate to your personal and other educational experiences? Explain...tell us more. What is another way to explain that? How is this different than what we discussed last week?). He creates multiple opportunities for sharing contextually relevant experiences through open and facilitated discussions and group-oriented activities. Ultimately, students are beginning to engage in sense making and articulation of ideas, perspectives, experiences and ways of doing things. Implicit within these processes, students learn to critique and respond to critiques.

The externalization process is characterized by greater formality and precision compared to socialization, often revolving around questions or reflections regarding practicality or feasibility. For example, one of the students said that it required a measure of discipline to relate her experiences to concepts that were being discussed, but felt that it was a worthy exercise because it forced her to think things through with greater detail so that she could confidently share it with others. Other students talk about the deepening of their own understanding, either as a result of somebody else's explanation or by having to talk about their own experiences in relation to a real-life situation, concept or theory.

Creating a conducive ba *for combination.* As the learning environment develops, dialogues become more meaningful and written reflection begins to take a more informed characteristic. As this begins to happen, each student should begin to draw knowledge and understandings from different sources—including required readings, notes from other courses, their professional and personal experiences, or interactions from within and without the classroom—to cultivate "new" knowledge. Students are further challenged to consider if these related sources support or contradict with the ideas being considered and to explain their rationale. They are also asked to consider what questions they may have at the particular point. This process of synthesis is referred to as combination. At this stage, learners are given the opportunity to organize and share their new understanding in a more systematic context that may be more formal and are of higher stakes (e.g. higher grade weightage). Besides discussions and typical writing assignments, this may come in the form of formal project presentations, papers or other deliverables, or exams.

Again, these options of learning activities or evaluations are not in it of itself unique. What are unique are the accompanying activities that take place in order to complete these activities. Students meet within their working groups either face-to-face or online, with external informants or to consider whatever knowledge sources needed to seek out potential solutions to the issues they are facing. The teacher also takes the time to ask for progress reports, to meet students individually or in groups, functioning more like a facilitator or consultant than a teacher most of the time. Here the key role is primarily to help students learn to ask questions, to identify beneficial sources, to begin to process information and do analysis, to begin to break down and order the activities in doable steps i.e. to help with both content development and skill development. If students are unable to find answers immediately, the teacher nudges them towards knowledge sources that can help them. If students are having group issues, he can offer counsel on how to affectively deal with the issue, even intervening in extreme cases. Students can become somewhat uneasy with this process, but with proper guidance, many will find their footing and more importantly begin to develop the ability to learn independently.

The combination process can be characterized by a greater need for organization of knowledge, so that it can be transferred with greater clarity and fidelity. For example, in doing a major group assignment, each group of students dedicates a significant amount of time to collecting and sharing explicit knowledge, proposes and considering ideas in different media, and finally consolidating everything into a rational and coherent document. The content of this document can then be shared through a formal presentation with a question-and-answer session, or a more informal inter-group discussion to consider the difference in approaches utilized by each group.

Creating a conducive ba for internalization. The learning is not quite complete yet. The student must make the knowledge his own, or in other words, personalize it. This can be achieved by creating numerous activities for reflection and action, many of which would have occurred in some shape or form in the socialization, externalization and combination process. For instance, the teacher can ask at the end of assignments or discussions, "what did you learn from this exercise? How does it relate to other things in this class? How might you apply this in your own day-to-day living?" Or periodically throughout the class, the assignment can be to reflect on everything to date and identify the two or three most important things one has learned and why they are important. In the naturalistic study, it was observed that internalization was most apparent when students were continuously and fully engaged in the simulation game, particularly in situations where each team had to deal with a common problem, analyze the situation, discuss possible solutions, and eventually act on an agreed upon decision and be ready to respond to what transpired.

Essentially, by creating engaging and interactive authentic or simulated conditions, learners are given opportunities to act on their new understanding. In doing so, the individual begins to gain insights, or as several students described as developing an understanding that enables a person to see a once inert concept "come to life." When knowledge becomes one's own (personalizing), he can begin to explain and use it in his own creative ways. Additional activities such as reflection papers and *kaizen* (continuous improvement discussions, even if the suggestions/recommendations to improve the offering of the course stand to benefit only future students) can help stimulate the internalization further.

Internalization is generally a personal process, but it also happens in a group context, such as when a group of people who have stayed together for a period of time internalizing a unique culture that is only apparent to the individuals of the group. Either way, the act of doing that leads to internalization usually involves an ongoing culmination and refinement of one's knowledge through interplay of reflection and action.

Integrative not linear. In practice, the above four steps are not linear but blend and reinforce each other. Often an activity may contain pieces of all four processes. Take for example the "current event" activities used by the second author. He first asks each student to identify a current event and submit it with a brief write-up summarizing the key points of the event, why he chose it (externalization) and how it relates to the course (combination). These are collected, read and grouped into common themes related to the course by the teacher. Then, the themes are introduced and students are asked to discuss and share their current event with the class based on a particular theme (socialization) and the teacher may make additional observations about how the course materials are closely related to the current news (combination) and how these themes relate or compare to one another (combination). Finally, the teacher summarizes the day to illustrate how "we are living the class in the real world" and asks them to reflect on their learnings for the day (internalization). Students have reported at the end of the semester that this should be done more often during the term and one even said, "finally I can understand what they are trying to say in the Wall Street Journal!"

Learning environment as a living system. The effect of implementing a *ba* so that the SECI spiral can remain active must be seen from an overall context because the whole function of the learning environment is larger than the sum of the isolated elements. The "glue" that holds this elements together is the ethos of the learning environment, as guided by the mental model of the teacher as a facilitator of learning. In other words, teachers can be seen as designers and creators of living ecologies for learning. Each class is like an ecology in itself. Indeed, the teacher can decide or influence to a significant extent what each class session will look and feel like for the purpose of deep learning yet still let the learning process emerge and evolve. The teacher helps create the ethos that can hold the *ba* together and energize it as further discussed below.

Characteristics that Energizes the *ba*

To Nonaka, Toyama and Konno (2000), a *ba* must be energized by providing the necessary ethos and conducive quality to the SECI process. From the standpoint of learning environment, these include 1) Autonomy – this is likely to increases each person's motivation to seek and understand valuable information and to create new knowledge. Not only can self-organization increase the commitment of individuals, but it can also be a source of unexpected knowledge; 2) Love, care, trust and commitment – are feelings needed among members of a classroom to stimulate and give form to a knowledge sharing and creation foundation. These feelings simply make it easier to share and create knowledge; 3) Redundancy – refers to the intentional overlapping of information during learning activities and about the class as a whole, often in relation to individual responsibilities within the class. While this may seem a waste of time, it should speed the knowledge sharing and creation process in two manners. Firstly, sharing redundant information promotes sharing of knowledge that may be more tacit in nature as individuals begin to detect what the others are trying to articulate. Secondly, it helps learners to better understand their role, which in turn functions to influence their thoughts and action paths; 4) Creative chaos – stimulates the interaction between the learners, the group they belong to, and the class as a whole, in relation to a bigger and broader external environment. It is different from complete disorder in that it is intentionally introduced in the learning environment to evoke a sense of crisis, which in turn sets the conditions to think and to change. Creative chaos, together with the notion of requisite variety, usually helps to focus members' attention and motivate them to transcend existing boundaries in dealing with a problem and solving it. Note that the benefits of creative chaos are constructive only if individuals can reflect on their actions, especially within the context of their group and classmates.

This is where a teacher's mental model can affect the kind of learning that takes place in and outside the classroom. As a beginning point, consider how applying the following energizing ethos and conducive quality in your classroom to encourage the SECI processes:

> *Autonomy, with love, care, trust, and commitment.* Throughout the class, the teacher's main intent is to enable and empower students to learn on their own. He doesn't simply teach – he creates a trusting and mutually respectful environment, coaching his students to learn to ask questions, and guiding if not cajoling them occasionally to consider different means to find answers or explanations. Indeed this is probably more important than any fact that is covered in the class. Consistent with other research, students tend to respond with greater commitment to a positive and autonomous learning environment (Bain, 2004; Tan, 2005).

However, the teacher must be prepared to detect issues and facilitate when the need arises. For example, in cases where a member of a group fails to fulfill his or her responsibilities, it compromises the group's performance and certainly the climate of trust and commitment. It can also be demoralizing when fellow students choose to do the bare minimum, while others are striving hard to contribute. In a classroom context, teachers will have to expect some tension to exist between fostering this climate of love, care, trust and commitment and giving students autonomy. In this case, the instructor may be able to help teams develop good team habits, skills to address issues as they arise and an appropriate work ethic by providing mentoring and engaging with students on a regular basis. Ultimately, this is to simply make it easier to share and create knowledge and to develop skills for the future.

Fluctuation and creative chaos. When students are learning to be empowered learners, one must expect for conditions to become ambiguous and stressful at times. Language to make the implicit explicit is always cumbersome, even more so for those who are attempting it for perhaps their first time in a particular domain area. This awkwardness should not only be welcomed, but deliberately designed into the broader learning environment and openly discussed. For example—in the study done by the first author—a sense of crisis was evoked in a team trying to recover from a potentially debilitating performance in the simulation game they were playing. There was also significant room for ambiguity that forced some of the students to work and think beyond their conventional capacity as members of a classroom, and as a result there were some positive breakdowns of set routines learned from more structured educational experiences. As other researchers have found, working with novel problems can help students to learn to more effectively deal with uncertainty (Bransford, Brown, Cocking, & National Research Council, 2000; Tan, 2005).

Redundancy and requisite variety. Students are often inclined to ask the teacher for the right answers, without attempting to work one out themselves. The teacher must learn to turn to the class and ask them questions such as the following: "What do you think? How do you answer this or at least begin to answer this? What did you learn in class that may help? What does theory tell you?" There will be overlaps or redundancies in these discussions, but this creates valuable opportunities to break down a problem and consider different potential solutions. In addition, it helps each student to better understand where they stand in the class, and that is often used as a guide for each individual's thinking and action.

The simulation game, noted above, is an excellent example of redundancy as the game is designed with an abundance of information that "forced" students to begin to understand how to discriminate the most critical information from the generally important information. An excellent example of variety occurs in one of the second author's classes, when he assigns his students to read a business novel rather than a traditional textbook. After a certain number of chapters, he would facilitate the discussion asking questions like: if you were the main character, given all the variables described in the book, how would you solve the problem? What might help? How do you at least start? Additional variables may be added—either intentionally or otherwise—so that there's a requisite variety, where the internal diversity of the learning environment comes close to matching the variety and complexity of the external environment (Nonaka, Toyama, & Byosiere, 2001).

Relationship of SECI Model to Problem Solving

It is worth noting that there are also strong parallels between the SECI processes and effective problem solving strategies. For instance, early in the process of identifying a problem, it is not unusual for the process to start with a feeling or hunch that something is wrong, but words are lacking to describe it. At this stage—in the midst of discussions—analogies are often used and experiences shared to try and communicate to others the potential nature of the problem (S&E). At some point, as awareness and understanding grows, there is a progression into seeking better ways to articulate the issue and to really understand the problem that needs addressing (E).

After a reasonable problem statement is agreed upon, the process shifts to the gathering and sifting through of information, looking to identify pertinent information and/or common threads, and seeking to combine this information and threads even to the point of creating new frameworks to shed light on the issue and/or to generate possible courses of action (E&C). This is followed by selecting a course of action, making a change and seeing if the change is effective (E&C). When a solution is being implemented, there's a valuable opportunity to reflect and discover for themselves, individually or as a group, the strengths and weaknesses of the initial thinking (I).

Given these links between the SECI processes and those of problem solving, the more the student can experience the processes of SECI in their education, (in addition to the increased opportunity to experience deeper learning and to develop improved critical thinking), the easier it will be for them to transfer and apply these processes in the area of problem solving. To this end, by way of summary, we suggest a path forward in the section below.

A Path Forward

The framework discussed above essentially incorporates what Bransford and his colleagues at the National Research Council (2000) refer to as the four basic elements of a healthy learning environment that brings together a knowledge-centered, learner-centered, assessment-centered and community-centered approach to learning.

The SECI processes, as described in this chapter, are a knowledge-centered element concerned with processes of knowledge sharing and creation. After all, the practical goal of creating learning ecologies can ultimately be framed with this question: are students able to take what he or she has learned to facilitate future learning, thinking and action? It is a pragmatic approach that creates diverse and numerous situations that make it difficult for learners to depend only on memory without understanding. Socialization, externalization, combination and internalization are essentially exercises of creating greater understanding – both at the individual and group levels. Both traditional and alternative means of assessment can be used to ascertain if the quality and outcome of learning can be used to facilitate future learning, thinking and action.

The possibilities of fostering greater understanding can be increased by energizing the *ba* as a learning environment – concepts very similar to Bransford's approaches of learner- and community-centeredness. The *ba* for socialization—sometimes referred to as the originating *ba*—is basically a low-stakes and informal setting to encourage open and contextually-rich knowledge sharing and discussions. The *ba* for externalization—or dialoguing *ba*—is a mid-stakes setting as discussions, sense-making and idea articulation become more focused. The *ba* for combination—or systemizing *ba*—usually takes place in a higher-stakes and more formal settings where "shareable" synthesized knowledge is shared, presented or even put to the test. The *ba* for internalization—or exercising *ba*—is perhaps the most tricky to create in the classroom because the goal is help students begin to embody or personalize their understanding through a series of reflection and action.

An illustrative summary of this discussion is provided in Figure 1.

One of the challenges in implementing this framework is the time needed to establish ways of communicating and working together in what is usually a three or four-month semester. The teacher will also have to plan his time carefully as in-class and out-of-class socialization activities can consume significant amount time. In the more advance stages of the SECI spiral, the role of the teacher as a coach will also demand significant time and attention to detail. In the authors' experience, teaching three classes of 30-plus-students-each with this framework can already be pushing the limits. Our suggestion is experiment with one class first, and then expand to the others as one becomes more comfortable and more skilled in teaching this way.

The other challenge is for teachers to expand their toolbox. Many teachers would not readily have all the capacity needed—such as skills to facilitate and coach, or identifying or creating rich contexts in the form of simulation, case studies or field activities—so work in the time to build the necessary repertoire. In international settings (where students are from a different country than the teacher), the teacher may not even be aware of the learning models and/or teaching approaches that the students are accustomed to. Time and effort will be needed for the teacher to make necessary adjustments. Indeed, the second author has found that even just focusing on energizing the originating and dialoging *ba* can expedite the understanding on the teacher's part and learning on the students' part, especially if the teacher is willing to actively engage the students in addressing this issue. In these situations, time invested early in the course to discuss and discover together the difference in the approaches used in the classroom as well as some basic cultural difference can pay huge dividends. For example, American students tend to love to have examples to illustrate a point early in the learning process. On the other hand, French students tend to look for theory at the beginning. So when

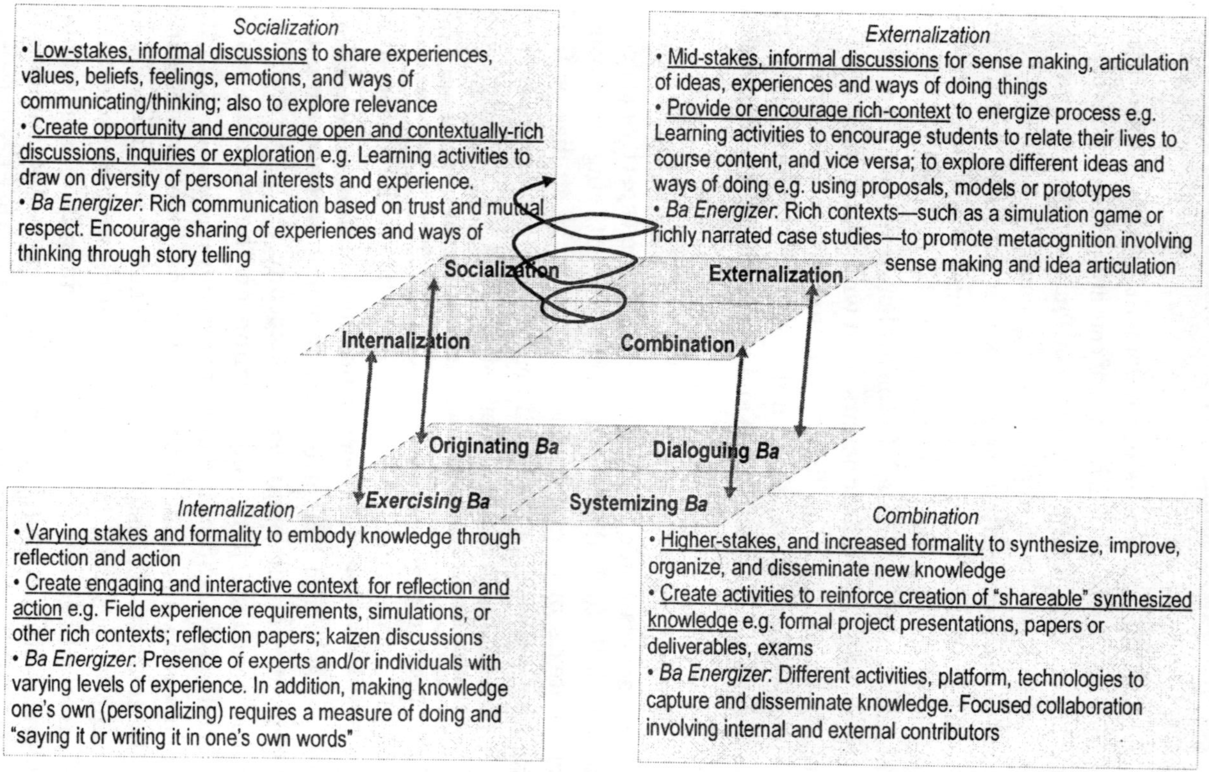

Figure 1: Creating a conducive learning environment for deeper learning

teaching in France, even when asked to teach the "American" way, it is not unusual for students to say something like 'yes you have given us some examples we didn't know but we have learned nothing new because there was no theory.'

Finally, perhaps the most significant challenge is mindset – both that of the teacher and the students. If one is used to the lecture format in the class, this can become a very uncomfortable experience. If this is the case, our suggestion is to take incremental steps. Perhaps, begin with learning how to facilitate an open class discussion – learn to draw the students out of their old classroom habits, learn to build trust, and perhaps most of all, learn to develop mutual-respect. The next possible step could be learning to implement collaborative learning activities, and so on. For example, ask the students what the main points of the chapter were? What did they learn and how does it relate to other things they know? Organize them in small groups of 4 to 6 to discuss these questions and have one person speak for the group. This helps to reduce fear, can save face, and helps the shy students be a little more comfortable contributing. Explain afterwards why you are doing this. This can improve the chances for success. The authors have also found belonging to communities of practice can also help in the development process as well as bringing into the classroom content experts to share their knowledge and experiences. Don't be afraid to spend a little time afterward with the students to discuss the learnings and help them see the ties to the class.

Conclusion

More than seventy years ago, Whitehead (1929) criticized traditional formal education for teaching inert facts rather than helping students develop meaningful knowledge. More recently, Resnick (1987) and Cole (1990) noted that the hallmark of traditional school and university learning have been the separation between knowing and doing – basically, extracting essential principles, concepts and facts, and teaching them in an abstract and decontextualised form. But what we have found is that when learning is properly contextualized and *ba* is created and energized, it creates opportunities for deep learning. Contextualizing should be integrated into the basic fabric of the classroom – the learning environment. As a teacher, you have significant influence in the way the classroom as a learning environment functions, looks and feels. This holistic framework can be used to consider and experiment with the design of your learning environment so that it can be more effective at promoting deep learning in your classrooms and to better ensure your students are better able to function in the world they will live in. It is our hope that this chapter has energized you to learn more and experiment in your classroom. We would love to hear of your efforts so that we too can become better teachers.

REFERENCES

Bain, K. (2004). *What the best college teachers do.* Boston: Harvard University Press.

Beech, H. (2006). School daze [Electronic Version]. *Time* from http:/ /www.time.com/time/asia/features/asian_education/cover.html.

Bransford, J., Brown, A. L., Cocking, R. R., & National Research Council. (2000). *How people learn : brain, mind, experience, and school* (Expanded ed.). Washington, D.C.: National Academy Press.

Camillus, J. C. (2008). Strategy as a wicked problem. *Harvard Business Review*(May), 98-106.

Chong, W. L. (2008). *Learning beyond schooling: Bringing out children's true potential.* Subang Jaya, Selangor: Pelanduk Publications.

Cole, R. A. (2000). *Issues in Web-based pedagogy : a critical primer.* Westport, Conn.: Greenwood Press.

Dewey, J. (1938). *Experience and education*. New York,: The Macmillan company.

Drucker, P. (2001). The next society [Electronic Version]. *The Economist*. Retrieved October 22, 2008 from http://www.economist.com/surveys/displaystory.cfm?story_id=E1_SSDRTJ.

Herrington, J., & Oliver, R. (2000). An instructional design framework for authentic learning environments. *Educational Technology Research and Development, 48*(3), 23-48.

Library of Congress. (2008). About the library: Fascinating facts. Retrieved October 30, 2008, from http://www.loc.gov/about/facts.html

Lincoln, Y. S., & Guba, E. G. (1985). *Naturalistic inquiry*. Beverly Hills, Calif.: Sage Publications.

Lyman, P., & Varian, H. R. (2004). How much information. Retrieved September 10, 2004, from http://www.sims.berkeley.edu/how-much-info-2003

Marton, F., & Saljo, R. (1976). On qualitative differences in Learning I: Outcome and process. *British Journal of Educational Psychology, 46*, 4-11.

Netcraft Web Server Survey. (2008). Web server survey archives: October 2008. Retrieved October 30, 2008, from http://news.netcraft.com/archives/web_server_survey.html

Nonaka, I., & Konno, N. (1998, Spring). The concept of "ba": Building a foundation for knowledge creation. *California Management Review, 40*, 15.

Nonaka, I., Toyama, R., & Konno, N. (2000, Feb). SECI, ba and leadership: A unified model of dynamic knowledge creation. *Long Range Planning, 33*, 5-34.

Resnick, L. (1987). Learning in school and out. *Educational Researcher, 16*(9), 13-20.

Rittel, H. W. J., & Webber, M. M. (1973). Dilemmas in a General Theory of Planning. *Policy Sciences, 4*(2), 55–69.

Senge, P. M. (1990). *The fifth discipline : the art and practice of the learning organization* (1st ed.). New York: Doubleday/Currency.

Takeuchi, H., & Nonaka, I. (2004). *Hitotsubashi on knowledge management*. Singapore: John Wiley & Sons (Asia).

Tan, A. G. (2005). *What matters in learning?* Singapore: Marshall Cavendish.

Tee, M. Y. (2004). *Sharing and cultivating tacit knowledge in an e-learning environment: A naturalistic study.* University of Kansas, Lawrence.

Tee, M. Y., & Karney, D. (2007). *Creating a conducive environment for deep learning in the classroom.* Paper presented at the International Conference on Teaching & Learning 2007, Putrajaya, Malaysia.

The Arlington Institute. (2008). World's biggest problems. Retrieved October 30, 2008, from http://www.arlingtoninstitute.org/wbp/portal/home#

Whitehead, A. N. (1929). *The aims of education and other essays.* New York: Macmillan.

Worldmapper. (2006). Books published: Map no. 343. Retrieved October 29, 2008, from http://www.worldmapper.org/display.php?selected=343

Wurman, R. S. (1989). *Information anxiety* (1st ed.). New York: Doubleday.

SECTION 5 : SCIENCE EDUCATION AND TECHNOLOGY

18

Construction of Mathematical Knowledge : Usage of Technology

Prof. Dr. Noraini Binti Idris

Introduction

Technology such as graphing calculators and Geometer's Sketchpad can be used to enable students to investigate and apply mathematical ideas in a way not easily achieved by other means. It was also found that students are actively involved in problem solving and talk about mathematics they are learning. As the goals of education begin to change to reflect new social and educational needs, teaching strategies also change, and so, consequently, do strategies for integrating calculator into teaching and learning of mathematics (Noraini Idris, 2006). Two of the current words in the field of mathematics education are constructivism and usage of technology. Technology- based resources include an enormous amount of useful instructional materials and constitute an exciting new medium that stimulates students to think about concepts rather than just follow procedures. Graphing calculators and Geometer's Sketchpad can be used to enable students to create and explore mathematical ideas where irrelevant details are eliminated. In this chapter, author will share about the usage of technology in the teaching and learning in the mathematics classroom and how it's stimulate thinking, and will demonstrated an examples to illustrate the constructivist approach to technology.

Attempts to realize Malaysia's Vision 2020 and fast technological advancement pose great challenges to mathematics educators in Malaysia. Changes for improvement and development have to be undertaken to be prepared in dealing with such enormous challenges. Its curriculum implication is that, there is a need to keep abreast of these technological trends to become relevant in the present and in the future. In secondary mathematics, this would mean that the order and treatment of most topics would need to change.

An emerging technological society and economy makes mathematical knowledge and problem solving both essential and advantageous for students as they position to join the workforce. In Malaysia, the cultivation of a mathematically competent and mathematically literate Malaysian workforce anchors on the concomitant improvement of mathematical achievement in Malaysian students in order to possess the mathematical knowledge to produce, use, and manipulate new technologies. In secondary mathematics, this would mean that the order and treatment of most topics would need to change.

Mathematics relies on logic and creativity, and it is pursued both for a variety of practical purposes and for its intrinsic interest. The essence of mathematics lies in its beauty and its intellectual challenge. In many parts of the world there has been a considerable interest in the teaching and learning potential of scientific calculators. Malaysia intends to transform its educational system into a technologically literate teaching and learning system for the next century. Transforming the educational system will entail changing the culture and practices of Malaysia's primary and secondary schools students. This will move away from memory based learning designed for the average student to an education system based on technology such as scientific calculators and graphing calculators that will stimulate thinking whilst catering individual abilities and learning styles. This will require students to exercise greater responsibility for their own education.

How is mathematics learned and constructed? This important question has no simple answer. A current viewpoint that seems ubiquitous in mathematics education is constructivism, the theory that learners actively construct their own knowledge through interaction with their environment and usage of

Technology. Meaningful learning is an integral part of constructivism. What does it mean for students to construct their mathematical knowledge? The construction of mathematical knowledge cannot be passive; it must be active on the part of the learner. Thus, in this chapter, the author will discuss about using a constructivist approach - the social and Technology learning approach. In the lesson designed, the author has provided numerous opportunities for reflection on the ideas at hand including through usage of graphing calculator and Geometer's Sketchpad. The communicative aspects of the lesson (group work and writing assignments) also bring to mind the theory of Vygotsky - that learning is essentially a social activity, that depends upon the use of language.

The process of learning has been a source of amazement, fascination, and study for centuries. The *Curriculum and Evaluation Standards for School Mathematics* (NCTM, 1989) encouraged students to create, invent, construct, or use of Technology that are meaningful for them. Much learning and understanding can be gained from constructing knowledge. This is evident in the *Standards* (NCTM, 1989, p. 17) illustrated by the use of many behaviorally oriented verbs - such as explore, justify, represent, solve, construct, discuss, use, investigate, describe, develop, and predict. Each of these verbs encourages critical thinking and requires an active role for children in doing and eventually learning mathematics.

As we walk into a classroom, responsible for helping a group of children learn mathematics make us often ask the following questions:

(1) What mathematical knowledge will the children in our classroom have as they started the year?

(2) What mathematical ideas do they need to learn?

(3) What are we expected to teach?

From those questions, we can outline specific objectives to be accomplished, organize instructional materials, and plan daily lessons effectively. Whatever the age level of our students, we will probably have several goals:

(1) To help children learn specific mathematical content (facts, skills, and concepts)

(2) To help children learn how to apply mathematical ideas to solve problems

(3) To help children learn how to construct mathematical knowledge

(4) To foster a positive attitude toward learning of mathematics.

How is mathematics learned and constructed? This important question has no simple answer. In fact, every instructional activity within the classroom expresses the teacher's view of learning. Early in the twentieth century, John Dewey asserted that learning comes from experience and active involvement by the learner. A current viewpoint that seems ubiquitous in mathematics education is constructivism, the theory that learners actively construct their own knowledge through interaction with their environment. Mathematics can and should make sense. If it does, it has meaning and is understood as a discipline with order, structure, and numerous relationships. Meaningful learning is an integral part of constructivism. Constructivism is a view of learning that says learners use their experiences to actively construct understanding by having it presented in an already organized form.

TI-84 PLUS GRAPHING CALCULATOR IN TEACHING AND LEARNING OF MATHEMATICS

The TI-84 Plus Graphing Calcualtor is easy-to use and powerful hand-held tool that can be easily learnt by teachers, students, and those interested. All commands are placed in neatly arranged pull-down menus, and in the event that one cannot find the commands, the calculator's catalog gives an alphabetically arranged list of all the commands. The keys have also been strategically arranged in functional groups for easy access to the user, for example the arithmetic keys are together and so are the trigonometry keys.

TI-84 Plus can handle real and complex numbers, matrices and even strings. Its features for trigonometry, calculus, and simple algebra in the form of an equation solver will also meets the needs of most secondary school curriculum.

In addition, TI-84 Plus Graphing Calculator can carry out list-based one- and two-variable statistical analysis. The descriptive statistics and linear regression models are applicable to Malaysian secondary school curriculum, whilst the calculator's advanced hypothesis testing, confidence intervals and distributions.

The TI-84 Plus Graphing Calculator also has an added accessories that can further enhance its usability and practicality for classroom usage. For example, it has a calculator-to-calculator link cable that can transfer data from one calculator to another. This feature can be very useful for teachers wanting their classes to investigate the same set of data for purposes of teaching mathematical concepts. With a common set of data, teaching can be more focused and more effectively executed.

According to Cobb (1988) a unifying theme in many contemporary theories of learning is that knowledge and cognitive structures are actively constructed by learners. This belief is derived directly from Piaget's work. This construction cannot be passive; it must be active on the part of the learner. Davis (1984) sees children who understand mathematics as having developed a large number of ideas that are connected in networks that provide a context for meaning. Conceptual knowledge grows through the construction of relationships among individual bits of information.

What does it mean for students to construct their mathematical knowledge?

The construction of mathematical knowledge cannot be passive; it must be active on the part of the learner. Resnick (1987) has noted that successful learners understand that the real task to be done is to construct meaning.

Noddings (1990) believes that:

(1) Knowledge is not passively received; rather knowledge is actively created or constructed by students.

(2) Students construct new mathematical knowledge by reflecting on their physical and mental actions. They observe relationships, recognize patterns, and make generalizations and abstractions as they integrate new knowledge into their existing mental structure (Dienes, 1960)

(3) Learning reflects a social process in which children engage in dialogue and discussion with themselves as well as others as they develop intellectually (Bruner, 1986).

Vygotsky's (1978) theory of mathematical development has been widely used in contemporary literature of cognitive development and education. He emphasises the importance of social interaction as an important mediator of cognitive development. Children learn by internalizing activities conducted in the world around them, their social world, which is the source of all their concepts, ideas, facts, skills, and attitudes. According to him, the zone of proximal development is the activity setting in which the child can learn with the greatest development effects. This zone is constructed in the cooperation between the child and the teacher on the basis of what the child gets from the teacher. Learning within the zone of proximal development obviously makes sense for the child, because the need for this learning emerges from the activity the child wanted to be involved in.

Research suggests that learning activities that fall within a child's zone of proximal development have a high probability of success, whereas engaging in activities outside of the zone have much less likelihood of success.

Piaget found that cooperative learning is an important factor in development. Cooperative learning, in which students work in groups toward a common goal, has proven to be a powerful instructional tool to promote improvement in achievement (Slavin, 1990). Most studies find equal benefits of cooperative learning for high, average, and low achievers (Slavin, 1995). Further, cooperative learning promotes critical thinking, higher-level thinking, and problem-solving (Artzt & Newman, 1997). It also encourages development of intergroup relations, acceptance of those with disabilities, improved self-esteem, contributing to the internal locus of control and improved classroom behaviour (Slavin, 1995). Perhaps most importantly, cooperative learning tasks provide students the opportunity to engage in mathematical activity and be able to construct mathematical knowledge in the classroom (Artzt & Newman, 1997).

Technology such as graphing calculator can be used to enable students to investigate and apply mathematical ideas in a way not easily achieved by other means. As we that knowledge and ideas emerged only from a situation in which learners had to draw them out of experiences that had meaning and importance to them. These situations had to occur in a social context, such as a classroom. Graphing calculator also give an opportunity for creating and exploring mathematical ideas where irrelevant details are eliminated. Graphing calculator has the ability to draw and analyze graphs, carry out complex computations, numerically solve equations, perform matrix arithmetic, statistical analysis and plotting a graph as in Figure 1.

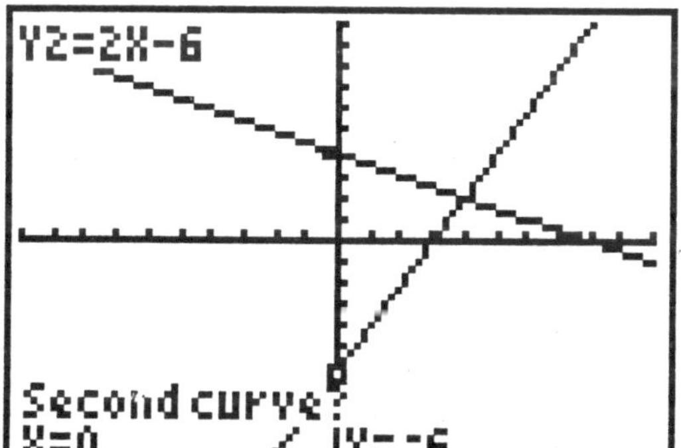

X	Y1	Y2
0	4	-6
1	3.5	-4
2	3	-2
3	2.5	0
4	2	2
5	1.5	4
6	1	6

X=0

Figure 1: Plotting a Graph

Graphing calculator can help students learn mathematics. For example, with calculators and computer students can examine more examples or representational forms than are feasible by hand, so they can make and explore conjectures easily. The graphic power of TI 84 Plus graphing calculator affords access to visual models that are power but that many students are unable or unwilling to generate independently. The computational capacity of technological tools extends the range of problems accessible to students and also enables them to execute routine procedures quickly and accurately, thus allowing more time for conceptualizing and modeling.

Students curiosity are enhanced when activity relates directly to students personally and when active participation in the lesson helps maintain it over time. When solving problems students may be involved in creative process such as searching for alternative methods of solving a problem, creating and recognizing patterns, experimenting with different ways of communicating mathematical and science ideas, creating personal hypotheses, and generating problems.

Calculators are just tools for performing computations. They have great potential as instructional aids for the development of mathematical/science concepts and understandings. The TI-84 Plus graphing calculator is a relatively new technology that was developed as an aid in arousing curiosity. It has the ability to draw and analyze graphs, carry out complex computations, numerically solve equations, perform matrix arithmetic and statistical analysis.

The graphing calculator offers teachers and students a rich learning aid. Its potential is great and as yet untapped both in developing concepts and in developing positive attitudes and persistence in problem solving. As stated in NCTM's *Curriculum and Evaluation Standards for School Mathematics,* "the thoughtful and creative use of technology greatly improves the quality of the curriculum and the quality of children's learning" (1989, p. 21).

Author would like to share one of her researches in the usage of graphing calculator. The purpose of this research was to investigate the use of TI-84 Plus graphing calculator as a tool in enhancing teaching and how its help in creating a climate for success.

Specifically, the research questions are:

(1) How does the students involvement in the process of learning in the classroom?

(2) What are the perceptions of students towards the use of the graphic calculator and how its help creating a climate for success?

The finding of the study is as follows:

Students Involvement in the Process of Learning in the Classroom

Attitude Toward Learning : Some students view and belief that learning using Technology as opportunities to acquire new abilities and skills. Others consider learning using Technology as presenting competitive situations in which their existing abilities and skills are challenged. As the observation and interview data were analyzed, it became clear that the students beliefs that the use of the Technology helps them to visualize and self discovery tool.

Self-Confidence : The amount of effort students are willing to invest in a mathematical task is dependent not only on the value they recognize in the task but also on their perception of the likelihood that they will successfully complete the task (Ames and Ames 1985). Problem solving, discovering relationships, proving theorems, analyzing situations, and interpreting mathematical communications are all cognitive tasks requiring students to work through perplexing moments. Those who are not confident in their own mathematical abilities tend to stop working on a task as soon as they become perplexed; more-confident students tolerate perplexity longer and are more likely to continue with the task.

In this study majority of the students are motivated to achieve learning goals that they consider relevant to their needs. Students usually aim to achieve goals that they perceive as interesting. As we know that mathematics students often need time to think about the problem before gaining an insight into possible solutions. In this study, students in the experimental group were given similar opportunities. Students' insight opened up further possibilities for creative endeavour.

Communication Skills. Mathematics lessons typically require students to *receive* messages (e.g., by *listening* to the teacher and to one another and *reading* explanations, examples, and directions appearing in textbooks, on visual classroom displays, worksheets, computer screens, and tests). Schools typically provide students with extensive exposure to lessons targeting general communications skills (reading, writing, speaking, and listening). Most of the students in the experimental group agreed that "...efficient communicators present coherent and meaningful messages". In this study, it was found that the students were able to sequence messages in ways that allow students to interpret the intended meaning correctly. It was observed that with the help of Technology, students in the experimental group emphasize important and relevant aspects of mathematics and also established positive relationship with each other and teacher. Teacher who focus on efficient communication skills are better able to develop effective teaching styles.

GEOMETERS' SKETCHPAD IN TEACHING AND LEARNING OF MATHEMATICS

In Malaysia, geometry is taught in primary and secondary schools levels. According to several Malaysian textbooks, the topics of triangles and quadrilaterals are covered from primary to secondary schools. Thus, the students identify triangles and quadrilateral since Year One. However, according to Noraini Idris (1999) from her clinical interviews conducted on 13 and 14-year-old students from public school in Kuala Lumpur, Malaysia, it was found that the words "square" and "rectangle" were not part of their normal vocabulary.

Geometric concepts are often neglected in elementary and middle schools in favour of teaching computational skill (Cox, 1985). Various reasons related to the mathematical system itself, curricular materials, instructional practices, and cognitive development have been proposed to explain students' difficulties with geometry.

As students are introduced to increasingly abstract concepts and exposed to relational operators such as equal, congruent, and similar, their mental models of the relationships among concepts require continual restructuring (Mc Donald, 1989). From the perspective of the van Hiele model of the development of geometric thought, the student moves from observing and identifying the figure to a recognition of it properties, and then to understanding the interrelationships of the properties of the figures and the axiomatic system within which they are placed.

Geometry was defined as a basic skill by the National Council of Supervisors of Mathematics (NCSM, 1980) and the National Council of Teachers of Mathematics (NCTM, 1989).

Learning geometry may not be an easy and a large number of them fail to develop an adequate understanding of geometry concepts, geometry reasoning, and geometry problem solving skills (Battista, 1999; Mitchelmore, 2002). The lack of understanding in learning geometry often causes discouragement among the students, which invariably will lead to poor performance in geometry. A number of factors have been put forward to understand why geometry learning difficult – geometry language, visualization abilities, and ineffective instruction.

Teaching and Learning of Mathematics

Memorization has been a major method in teaching mathematical definitions, and teachers still use this method. Teacher's beliefs about mathematics influence techniques chosen by them to teach mathematical topics. Teachers draw on their own experiences as students in mathematics classrooms (Borko, Eisenhart, Brown, Underhill, Jones & Agard, 1992). Elementary and middle school teachers generally depended heavily on their texts to supply definitions and methods for teaching geometric concepts. Students memorized text definitions but seemed generally not to use this definition when they described figures in their own words (Battista & Clements 1990). A study was conducted with two groups of students learning geometry. Both received the same classroom instructions, but one group also used Logo, a geometry software package. "Even after being taught the standard textbook definition, most of the non-Logo students' definitions of angles reflected mainly the influence of common languages uses" (p.15). Students often are expected to give answers with no justification; multiple-choice tests, fill-in-the-blank, and matching tests found in test banks are prime examples of this fact. This expectation results in students being concerned only with answers, not procedures (Glatzer & Glatzer, 1989). The authors suggested using worksheets, which did not ask for specific answers, but for statements about the answer. For example, a triangle that had an 80° vertex angle and two sides marked as being congruent was drawn. A question mark was placed at one base angle. Some possible student conjectures were:

1. The sum of the measures of the angles of a triangle is 180°, so the missing two angles measures must have a sum of 100°.
2. The triangle is isosceles.
3. The base angles of an isosceles triangle have equal measure.
4. Each base angle must have a measure less than 60°. (p. 39)

The advantage of using these techniques was that students were forced to think about the fundamental concepts related in the figure, rather than immediately reaching for some numerical answer, which may or may not make sense.

Manipulatives have been used in the primary grades as a bridge between concrete and abstract learning. However, evidence by research by Suydam and Higgins (cited in Parish & Weiss, 1988) claimed that the use of manipulatives increased the chances of mathematics achievement, and that achievement was intensified "across a variety of topics at every grade level (K-8) with the use of manipulatives" (p. 26).

Drawings of geometry relationships also help in teaching concepts other than geometry ones. The pie chart was referred to when teaching fractions and division of 3 into 2 (Graeber & Baker, 1992). Two pizzas were divided among three people: this was depicted by two circles separated three congruent sectors each, with the names assigned to two pieces per person.

Teachers sometime fail to consider the importance of reading comprehension and vocabulary when teaching mathematics. Assumptions about prior knowledge of students have been made every time a worded problem is assigned. The teachers own instruction may be mainly verbal, making little if any use of diagrams, graphs and manipulatives (Long & Ben-Hur, 1991). The interview technique was used in assessing a fourth- grade student's understanding of a picture of a fraction circle with one- half, one-third, and one-sixth parts shaded different colors. The student being interviewed verbally described the parts as one-half, a third, and a small third, while at the same time writing the fraction 1/3 for each part of the circle. The responses indicated that the student, who could add fractions, had little understanding of the meaning of fractional parts of a circle.

Similarity of geometric figures has not received appropriate consideration in the present mathematics curriculum (Woodward, Gibbs & Shoulders, 1992). Woodward et al. claimed that similarity needs to be taught in the elementary curriculum with everyday applications, such as graphs, blueprints, models, maps and photographs. Without an understanding of similarity, student will not have the prerequisite background for further study of geometry in a more formal setting. Manipulative used in the teaching unit discussed were cut-out of similar figures, laminated strips hinged with paper fasteners, geo boards, and dot-paper pictures. To make similar shapes from worksheets, it was suggested that the teacher use a copy machine and reduce or enlarge the originals. Students' reactions to the unit were enthusiastic and they made interpretations about similarity beyond the expectations of researchers. Included were relations between similarity and congruence, and ratios of the areas of similar figures. Again, the importance of the use of manipulative was stressed as well as verbal communication among students working in a small group.

Area and perimeter have been taught in primary schools with manipulative but this two usually have been abandoned by the third or fourth year. The formulae have simply been given to students, and the students were expected to apply them. In several published workbooks, both perimeter and area formulae were not justified at all, but simply shown to the student in the form of calculative keys the students was to punch. For example, the area of a square was indicated by the following set of symbols: "A= s x s. These formulae were immediately followed by a set of numerical problems to answer using a calculator. This approach did not indicate any reasoning at all on the part of the student; it only afforded the student the chance to use a particular type calculator and plug numbers into a given procedure. Students persistently confuse perimeter to the area due to the lack of understanding of the concepts.

Tiling activities have been supplementary topics in elementary school texts for years, but have not been appreciated for their true value in construction fundamental relationships (Wheatley, 1992). Senechan (cited in Wheatley, 1992) stated that studying shapes formed a central element in mathematics education which not only enriched mathematics but also sciences and the arts. In the act of tiling, students seem to build relationships and understanding of congruence, translations, rotations, and even place-value. The constructions of new unit shapes with simpler shapes indicated a connective progression just as thinking in days is a profession over thinking in hours or in minutes. Not only were several different tiling patterns produced, built the use of symmetry and color patterns result in true works of arts by the students. Several students used both regular and non-regular hexagons as a basic for their designs; this results in a deeper familiarity with the shape than the cursory attention usually given to the simple regular hexagon in everyday classes.

Computer technology has been recommended as an aid to teaching geometry. As mentioned before, Battista and Clements (1990) used Logo to help students learn about angles. Results of extended studies of second-grade students using Logo yielded two major recommendations for teaching. Recognitions of importance of visual imagery in reasoning should be stressed. Visual imagery as a mode of thinking should be respected, and students should be encouraged to use this mode to analyze and persuade themselves of the actuality of geometry ideas. Visual reasoning should be discussed with students, and students' clarified. Teachers should make use of a variety of examples of sizes and shapes in non-standard orientations.

The absence of spatial activities in textbooks was clear evidence that imagery was believed to be unnecessary in school mathematics. Most students rarely have the chance to use imagery in their school mathematics classes. What shapes students see is greatly affected by their previous experience with the shape. In a study by Brown and Wheatley (cited in Wheatley, 1991), six fifth-grade students were chosen. Three of these students had high spatial ability and low performance on standardized tests, and three low spatial ability but average to high achievement on standardized test. Those with low spatial ability seemed to attach infinitesimal meaning to mathematical concepts and could not work non-trivial problems, while those with high spatial ability solved the same problems, often creatively. It was concluded that imagery was useful in understanding geometric shapes and their properties, but also in performing numerical tasks and in problem solving.

Parents attitude have operated under the idea that students must master the academic content at each level before a student may climb to the next level (Mayberry, 1981). As a result, many poorer students are required to stay at lower levels of classes until they are able to memorize arithmetic facts. Yet memory may be one of the weakest skills for these students. Hence the at-risk students are handicapped by the system. They are never allowed to see the exciting parts of mathematics, such as probability and geometry, which justify the need for recalling arithmetic facts.

Vocabulary and Geometry Ability

According to the National Council of Teachers of Mathematics (1989), communication in mathematics is one of the primary standards toward which all mathematics teachers must strive. This involved speaking and writing mathematics, not only as part of the communication between teacher and student, but between student and student. Mathematics is not just numbers. It is thinking, analyzing, computing, and reporting the results of all of these processes; it is not computation alone. The verbal ability of a student in mathematics greatly affected his or her ability to reason, to communicate, and ultimately, to learn.

The first step in increasing vocabulary was basic word recognition, when students became familiar with both the language and the mathematical symbols. Next, the student decoded these words and connected a literal meaning to the symbols. Third, the new term was interpreted by the learner. At the highest level of reading, the student applied this interpretation of the literal meaning of the symbols encountered on the written page or in conversation. Before understanding occurred, the learner must have recognized the mathematical symbols and pronounce the words involved. For example, parallel lines are difficult for students to describe without using models, such as two fingers held side-by-side. The word parallel is difficult for young people to learn to say. It often comes out as "pallarel" until the student become more familiar with the term. Hence the student may use phrase like, "go in the same direction," "be side-by-side," or " be the same distance apart." Of these, the last phrase indicates a deeper understanding of the relationship, since one of the theorems about parallel lines states that parallel lines are everywhere equidistant.

Kirshner (1985) studied the psychological basis of syntactical skills by examining the ability of 517 students to evaluate standard algebraic syntax versus a nonce, or artificial, algebraic notation designed to show the deep structure of algebraic expressions. Language syntax was discussed first, and then standard algebraic syntax was reviewed. The students varied widely in age groups and educational level, from ninth-grade first-year algebra to fourth-year engineering students. Most (93.6%) of the students were competent using regular algebraic notation, but fewer (66.3%) succeeded with more complicated nonce algebra items. If the symbols were physically closed, the nonce notation proved more difficult than the more widely spaced notation (Kirschner, 1985). No matter what language was used, the symbols used affected the success rate of the learner, until the symbols were familiar once more.

Bradley (1988) argued that two serious problems were present in mathematics education: a lack of meaning in mathematical knowledge, and inability of the student to communicate appropriately using proper mathematical language and ideas. She administered a mathematics achievement and a mathematics language test to a group of junior-high school students. The statistical tests indicated that there was a significant interaction between language facility and procedural knowledge of mathematics. For above-average children, higher language ability indicated successful conceptual achievement.

Many mathematics educators have stressed the need for teaching mathematical literacy and for broadening the curriculum to include language development (Mayberry, 1981; Fauvel, 1988; Burton, 1988; Ciani, 1981; Fuys, Geddes, & Tischler, 1988, Noraini Idris, 2006). As an extra credit assignment in a high school algebra course, Jur (1991) had her students write word problem poems. She stated that poetic mathematics problems were popular in the Middle Ages in India, and she wanted to expose her students to both the historical aspect of the project and to the literary aspect.

Extend the idea of poetry in mathematics a bit further: Henry Wadsworth Longfellow was a famous poet, and few realize that he was also an accomplished mathematician. He composed beautifully worded mathematical problems which should pique the interest of the non-mathematically minded students. The language used in the following indicates the verbal imagery which might be found in a well-phrased algebra problem.

A tree one hundred cubits high is distant from well two hundred cubits; from this tree one monkey descends and goes to the well; another monkey takes a leap upwards, and descends by the hypotenuse; and both pass over as equal space. Find the height of the leap.

Teaching terms providing additional language meaning, such as similar, different, both, neither, but, and also helped in teaching many concepts. Tables or line graphs relating topics were a big help in teaching both vocabulary and structure of the concept being studied. For example, students were requested to convert information found in tables of data into sentences by reading across a row. Pairs of columns or rows were compared or contrasted using like or unlike sentence structure. Line graphs were used to illustrate class inclusion, conditional relations, and rating or ranking schema. Students were requested to describe the relationship found there in a well-developed paragraph. Mohan (1986) suggested that tables and line graphs should be used as an aid to comprehending and writing text and as a general introduction to, or summary of, content.

Mohan (1986) divided the verbal expressions used to convey the composition of knowledge into three levels of probable difficulty. The simplest was the language used when learners explain what a graphic means. This level involved interrelationships in class membership or class attributes. Using the words is and have were natural ways to express those relationships in English. Conditional relations were expressed using if, then, so, and because. Later students used more complicated terminology, including attribute or factor. The second level of difficulty was needed when students talked about a graphic or occupied themselves with thinking processes required to discuss or invent a graphic. This level contained methods of sharing information, such as questions and assertions of fact by the student. The third and highest level of language usage was required when students interpreted a graphic in the form of a written paragraph. In this stage, it was necessary that the student know how to link sentences and how to explain and concentrate information into complex sentence form using subordinate clauses.

Curcio (1987) studied ability of fourth- and seventh-grade students to comprehend graphs of several types. He found that reading and mathematical achievement, plus prior knowledge, mathematics content, and the type of graph were unique predictors were the same as before except that prior knowledge and the form of the graph were not include. A regression analysis was done and the combination of three factors of gender, reading, and mathematical achievement was significant ($p<.01$). Each factor was entered separately for both Grade 4 and Grade 7. Again, they were significant ($p<.01$). The author suggested that young children should actively collect real world data and makes their own graphs. Verbalization of relationships and patterns noticed in the data should be stressed. In this manner, applications of mathematics to the student's everyday environment might improve the comprehension of implicit mathematical associations shown in graphs.

A scheme proposed by Cummins (1986) suggested only two major factors: cognitive involvement and context supported language proficiency. If a child's language was highly context-embedded, performance in mathematics and other topics which require reduced dependence on context would be poor. One big mistake made by teachers was attributing the academic failure of such students to a low cognitive ability, whereas the failure was due to a low position on the contextual scale.

One problem which has not yet been resolved concerning mathematics and language is which comes first- the thought or the language? Piaget and Vygotsky disagreed on the order. While Piaget claimed that thought preceded language, Vygotsky claimed that formal thought was a product of language growth. If a person were asked to think about a triangle, chances are that the metal image was a generic triangle, unless the questioner asked if the triangle was isosceles, equilateral, or scalene. More than likely, the words forced a closer examination of the mental image, which changed as the adjectives changed. Here, the concept preceded the language. However, if a person were asked to visualize a decagon, the image would probably be a fuzzy form of a many-sized regular polygon, with the thinker aware that ten sides were needed. The regular polygon would be imagined since few irregular or non-convex decagons are shown in mathematics books at any level in elementary or high school. In this case the language inspired a previously learned specific concept. At a specific instant, the mind is probably operating in several divergent patterns.

Instructional Activities Using Geometers' Sketchpad

Geometers' Sketchpad is dynamic software that enables students to investigate, explore, and understand mathematics in ways that are simply not possible with traditional tools or with other mathematics software programs. The following information on the Geometers' Sketchpad can be found in the following website http://www.keypress.com/sketchpad/product_info.html. Instructional activities based on Geometers' Sketchpad as shown in activity 1 – 3 are to help the students in upgrading their understanding, improving their learning, attitudes and attain higher mathematical achievements. These activities allowed the students to explore, investigate, discover, reflect, and visualize the concepts of sum of the angles in a triangle equal to 180 degrees, translation and circumscribe of a circle and sine rule.

These activities also helped to enhance the logical and critical thinking of the students and would also be able to improve their abilities in using technology in communication and problem solving.

Activity 1 The sum of the interior angles in a triangle equal to 180 degrees

Objective

To assist students to explore the sum of the interior angles in a triangle equal to 180 degrees.

Learning outcome

After this activity, the student should know that the sum of the interior angles in any triangle equal to 180 degrees.

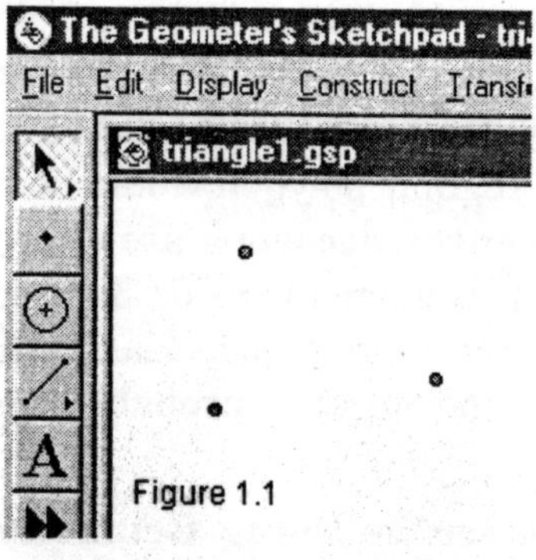

Figure 1.1

Jot down whatever you have observed while you are constructing the objects.

1. Create 3 points and label it with A, B and C. (Figure 1.1)

   [Use the mouse to select *Compass Tool* . Click (anywhere) on the window to form the three points. Select the *Text Tool* A to label the points.]

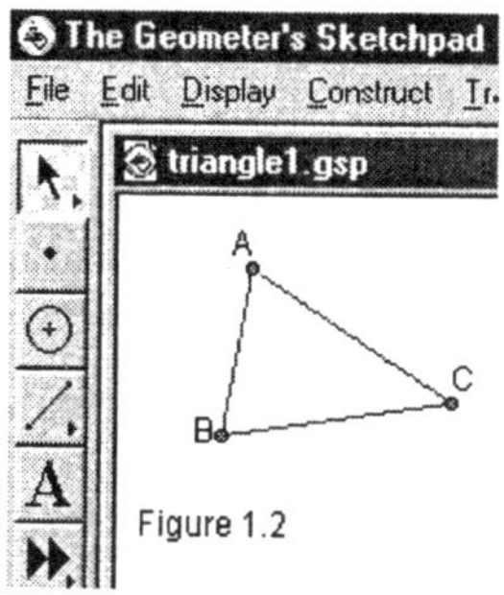

Figure 1.2

2. Select all the points and construct line segments. (Figure 1.2)

   [Use the mouse to select *Arrow Tool* . Select all the points then click on the Construct menu to select Segment to construct the segment.]

3. Measure the angles of ABC, BCA and CAB. (Figure 1.3)

   $\angle ABC$ = ________________

   $\angle BCA$ = __________

   $\angle CAB$ = ________________ .

   [Use *Arrow Tool* to select the points A, B and C to measure the angle ABC. Repeat the same steps to measure the angles BCA and CAB.]

4. Calculate the sum of the angles ABC, BCA and CAB. (Figure 1.4)

   $\angle ABC + \angle BCA + \angle CAB$ = ____________________

   [Click on the Measure menu to select Calculate to calculate the sum of interior angles of a triangle.]

5. Move the point A, what is happening to the sum of the angles?

____

____

____

6. Move the point B, what is happening to the sum of the angles?

____

____

____

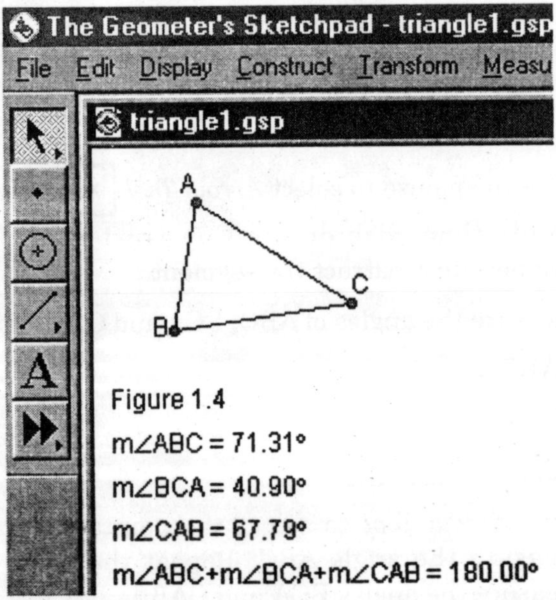

7. Can you guess what is the sum of the interior angles in a four segments polygon?

____

____

____

8. Can you guess what is the sum of the interior angles in a five segments polygon?

 ____

 ____

 ____

9. What relationships can you discover about the various segments and legs of the triangles?

Discussion, Conclusion and Implication

As a learning tool, technology can be seen as a catalyst for students' achievement. Several studies have attempted to compare overall achievement between experimental group for whom the technology is being use in instruction and control groups whose taught in traditional way. Quesada and Maxwell (1994) and Smith and Shotsberger (1997) found significant different in the achievement between experimental group and control group.

To support classroom teaching and learning effectively, teachers must build a community in which students will feel free to express their ideas and create a climate for success. Student who obtain lower grades need help from teachers in order to share mathematical ideas with one another in way that are clear enough for other students to understand. In this study, learning to see things from other people's perspectives is a challenge for students. Students should gradually take more responsibility for participating in whole-class discussions and responding to one another directly. They should become better at listening, paraphrasing, questioning, and interpreting others' ideas. For example, students in the secondary schools are often reluctant to stand out in any way during group interactions.

Despite this fact, teachers can succeed in creating communication rich environments in mathematics classrooms by using Technology as tool in his/her teaching. By the time students completed from secondary school, they should have internalized standards of dialogue and argument so they always aim to present clear and complete arguments and work to clarify and complete them when they fall short. Modeling and carefully posed question can help clarify age-appropriate expectations for student work. It is observed that in a positive climate students are treated as competent individuals capable of learning and understanding the need to learn.

Research on the use of Technology in the mathematics classroom seems to indicate that, to date, calculators have positive effect on the learning of mathematics. The results of the study suggest that the use of Technology in teaching and learning is beneficial in terms of students' level of understanding, communication skills, and achievement. The study also showed that the key to create a climate for success is involvement, which means that students are attending and are actively participating in the learning activity. With the use of Technology, students are not only promoted to involvement but also encouraged students to participate in classroom discussion, asking for explanations and justification for answers and thus creating a climate for success.

Students, who have succeeded on a task, be able to connect mathematics and science to their lives is usually eager to do more of the same kind of task. They are motivated to achieve learning goals that they consider relevant to their needs (Noraini Idris, 2001). Mathematics and science can be a creative activity involving intuition and intervention.

When students perceive learning to be interesting, fun, personally meaningful, and relevant and the context supports and encourages personal control, motivation to learn and self-regulation of the learning process occur naturally. Learning activities and experiences that students find interesting and stimulating are usually inherently motivating.

Among other things, students learn more and behave better when they understand and appreciate what is being conveyed. Students learning activities are influenced by teaching that either hinder or facilitate information processing in students.

The introduction of several technologies such as graphing calculator and geometer's Sketchpad offer great opportunities for the advancement of mathematics education. But the new technology is not magic solution for the problems of mathematics teaching and learning. This technology can support the introduction of a reform process at all levels by favoring the design and putting into practice of experiences tat question the traditional vision of teaching and learning mathematics. Technology enables students to investigate and encourage a process of discovery in which students first visualize and then make conjectures before attempting a proof. According to van Hieles, the learner assisted by appropriate instructional experiences passes through the five levels. Van Hiele-based instructional materials and the use of Geometers' Sketchpad played a special role in helping students to progress within a level or t a higher level of thinking.

To take advantage of the vast potential of graphing calculator and geometer's sketchpad for all students, teachers will need to make significant changes in their pedagogy. They will need to form working relationships with students that allow for creative, higher order thinking to emerge. They will need to break traditional barriers that impose restrictions on the potential benefits to be realized from technology in classrooms, and they will need to be willing to make ongoing efforts to be successful in the implementation process.

Changing pedagogy expects that teachers will be proficient at using graphing calculator and geometer's sketchpad. In addition, teachers may no longer follow the well-traveled road of traditional education, but must be visionary in the potential opportunities for learning and their shift from teacher to guide and facilitator. The teachers need to structure mathematics lessons differently. They have to change in terms of the entire process, focus, and outcomes of educational expectations. Teachers are not only transferring knowledge to students but they are also engaging in different roles as students experience different processes of learning.

REFERENCES

Ames, C., & Ames, R. (Eds.) (1985). *Research on motivation in education: Vol. 1. Student motivation.* Orlando, FL: Academic Press.

Artzt, A. F., & Newman, C. M. (1997). *How to use cooperative learning in the mathematics classroom.* Reston, VA: NCTM.

Battista, M. T. (1999, February). The mathematical miseducation of America's youth. *Phi Delta Kappan*, 425-433.

Battista, M.T. & Clements, D.H. (1990). Student's understanding of three-dimensional

Rectangular arrays of cubes. *Journal for research in Mathematics Education,* 27(3), 258-292.

Borko, H., Eisenhart, M., Brown, C., Underhill, R., Jones, D., & Agard, P. (1992, May). Learning to teach hard mathematics: Do novice teachers and their instructors give up too easily? *Journal for Research in Mathematics Education, 23*, 194-222

Brophy, J. (1987, October). Synthesis of research on strategies for motivating students to learn. *Educational Leadership*, 40 -48.

Brophy, J. (1990). Teaching social studies for understanding and higher order application. *The Elementary School Journal, 90*, 351 - 418.

Bruner, J. (1986). *Actual minds, possible worlds*. Cambridge, MA: Harvard University Press.

Cairncross, A. (2000). *The fostering of teaching-learning situations which promote the development of students into learners at Universities.* Paper presented at 25th International Conference. The University of the Future and the Future of Universities: Learner-centred Universities for the New Millennium.

Calfee, R. (1986). *Those who can explain teach.* Paper presented at the annual meeting of the American Educational Research Association. San Francisco.

Cobb, P. (1988). The tension between theories of learning and instruction in mathematics education. *Educational Psychologist*, *23*(2), 87-103

Cox, P. (1985). Formal geometry: More is needed. *Mathematics Teacher*, *78*, 404-405.

Cummins, J. (1986). Empowering minority students: A framework for intervention. *Harvard Educational Review*, *56*(1), 18-36.

Davis, R. B. (1984). *Learning mathematics: The cognitive science approach to mathematics education.* Norwood, NJ: Ablex.

Dienes, Z. P. (1960). *Building up mathematics.* London: Hutchinson

Fauvel, J. (1988). Cartesian and Euclidean rhetoric,. *For the learning of mathematics,* 8, 25 -29.

Fuys, D., Geddes, D., & Tischler, R. (1988). The van Hiele Model of Thinking in Geometry among adolescents. *Journal for Research in Mathematics Education, NCTM Monograph 3*

Glatzer, D. J., & Glatzer, J. (1989, December). Math connections. *Teaching Children Mathematics*, 60.

Graeber, A. O., & Baker, K. M. (1992). Little into big is the way it always is. *Arithmetic Teacher*, April.

Jur, B. (1991). The poetry of mathematics: Writing Problems as Poetry. *Primus,* vol 1, no. 1, pp 75 -81.

Kirshner, D. (1985). The visual syntax of algebra. *Journal for Research in Mathematics education,* 20(3), 274 -287.

Long, M. & Ben-Hur, M. (1991, February). Informing learning through the clinical interview. *Teaching Children Mathematics*, pp. 44-46

Mayberry, J.W. (1981). *An investigation of the van Hiele levels of geometric thought in Undergaraduate preservice teachers.* Unpublished dissertation, University of Georgia, UMI Publication.

McDonald. J. (1989). Formal operations and the ability of students to structure geometric content. Paper presented at the annual meeting of the Jean Piaget Society, Philadelphia.

Meng, K. & Patty, D. (1991). Field dependence and contextual organizers. *Journal of Educational Research, 84(3), 183 - 190.*

Mitchelmore. M.C. (2002). Prediction of developmental stages in the representation Of regular space figures. *Journal for Research in Mathematics Education,* 11, 83-93.

National Council of Teachers of Mathematics. (1989). *Curriculum and Evaluation Standards For School Mathematics.* Reston, VA: NCTM.

NCSM. (1980). *The teaching of geometry.* Washington, DC: National Academy Press.

Noddings, N. (1990). Constructivism in mathematics education. In R. B. Davis, C. A. Maher & N. Noddings (Eds.), *Constructivist views on the teaching and learning of mathematics*. JRME Monograph, Reston, VA: NCTM.

Noraini Idris. (1999). Students' intellectual growth in geometry. *Jurnal Pendidikan, 20*, 71- 82.

Noraini Idris. (2001). *Encouraging motivation to learn: Usage of Technology in Mathematics classroom.* Paper presented at International Conference on Challenges and Prospects in Teacher Education. Kuala Lumpur.

Noraini Idris (2006). Teaching and learning of Mathematics: Making sense and Developing Cognitive. Kuala Lumpur: Utusan Publication.

Parish, J. & Weiss, V. (1988). *Teaching and Evaluation Scheme.* Addison Wesley.

Quesada, A. R., & Maxwell, M. E. (1994). The effects of using graphing calculators to enhance college students' performance in precalculus. *Educational Studies in Mathematics, 27*(2), 205 – 215.

Resnick, L. B. (1987, December). Learning in school and out. *Educational Researcher,* 13-20.

Rosenshine, B. (1987). Explicit teaching. In D. Berliner & B. Rosenshine (Eds.), *Talks to teachers.* New York: Random House.

Saracho, O. (1990). The march and mismatch of teachers' and students' cognitive styles. *Early Child Development and Care, 54, 99 - 109.*

Slavin, R. E. (1990). Student team learning in mathematics. In N. Davidson (Ed.), *Cooperative learning in math: A handbook for teachers.* Boston: Allyn & Bacon.

Slavin, R. E. (1995). *Cooperative learning: Theory, research and practice.* Needham Heights, MA. Simon & Schuster.

Smith, K. B. & Shotsberger, P. G. (1997). Assessing the use of graphing calculators in college algebra: Reflecting on dimensions of teaching and learning. *School Science & Mathematics, 97(7).*

Vygotsky, L. (1978). *Mind in society: The development of higher psychological processes.* Cambridge: Harvard University Press.

Wheatley, G. H. (1991). Enhancing mathematics learning through imagery. *Arithmetic Teacher, 39*(1), 34-36.

Woodward, E., Gibbs, V., & Shoulders, M. (1992, April). A fifth-grade similarity unit. pp. 22-25

19

Theoretical or Conceptual : Exploring Frameworks in Mathematics Education Research

Sharifah Norul Akmar bt Syed Zamri

Introduction

The notion of a framework, either theoretical or conceptual is an integral ingredient in research regardless of disciplines or programs. It is one of the criteria that journal editors and referees look for in research. It is a well known fact that one of the reason why manuscript for journals were rejected outright is because there was no theoretical framework or 'the theory base was missing' (Smith et. al., 1993). Despite its importance, the use of frameworks in research may be the least understood aspect of the whole research process. My personal experience supervising post graduates students revealed that there was widespread misunderstanding of the definition and concepts of a theoretical or conceptual framework in research. In addition, their knowledge about theories involved seemed to be quite limited and shallow. In this context, Lester (2005) blamed certain graduate program's failure to prepare graduates with adequate knowledge on theory and he also attributed the problems on research journals for not insisting on using the underlying theory to explain research findings reported in the journals. Review of literature reveals that there are variations in the conceptual and theoretical framework used in mathematics education research. The choice of either conceptual or theoretical framework was partly influenced by the epistemological perspectives of the individual researchers involved and thus we can expect considerable diversity in the conceptual/theoretical frameworks chosen to conceptualize research in mathematics education.

Definition of Framework

There are a number of definitions of framework in the literature. Metaphorically, some researchers refer to it as a "scaffold erected to make it possible for repairs to be made on a building, encloses the building and enables workers to reach otherwise inaccessible portions of it" (Lester, 2005). Morse (1994) defined framework as a mechanism to help a researcher to focus and set limits or boundaries besides as a guide for data collection. Lester (2005) used a refined version and describe research framework as *a basic structure of ideas (i.e., abstractions and relationships) that serve as the basis for a phenomenon that is to be investigated (p.458).* In this perspective, a framework provides structure for conceptualizing and designing research studies. Liehr and Smith (2001) defined research framework as a guide to conceptualize and determine *the nature of the research questions asked, the manner in which questions are formulated, the way concepts, constructs, and processes of the research are defined and the principles of discovery and justification allowed for creating new findings about the topic under study*

Nature of Theoretical and Conceptual Framework

Eisenhart (1991) identified three types of research frameworks: theoretical, practical and conceptual, each with its own characteristics and role in mathematics education research. Theoretical framework guides research activities by its reliance on a formal theory or full blown theory that has been developed by using an established, coherent explanation of certain sorts of phenomena and relationships such as Piaget's theory of intellectual development and Vygotsky theory of socio-cultural constructivism claimed by many researchers as the most dominant theory in mathematics education (English & Sriraman, 2005). A theoretical framework can also be thought of as a ready-made map or travel plan (Lier and Smith, 2001; Sinclair, 2007). Sinclair (2007) elaborated the idea as follows:

When planning a journey in unfamiliar country, people seek as much knowledge as possible about the best way to travel, using previous experience and the accounts of others who have been on similar trips. 'Survival advice' and 'top tips' enable them to ascertain the abilities, expectations and equipment that may help them to have a successful journey with good outcomes, to achieve their objectives and return to base safely.(p. 39)

Lester (2005) reported that there are four misconceptions associated with the use of a theoretical framework. The misconceptions are related to the belief that theoretical framework force the researcher to explain their results by 'decree' rather than evidence (*data fit theory*), the *data have to be stripped of context and local meaning in order to serve the theory,* not functional outside the academic discipline-irrelevant to the experience of practitioners) and the absence of triangulation (especially using a single theoretical perspective to frame one's research.

Practical framework on the other hand is a mechanism to guide research by using 'what works' (Scriven, 1986). This framework is not based on formal theory but by accumulated practice knowledge of practitioners and administrators, the findings of previous research, and often the viewpoints offered by public opinion. Research questions are derived from this knowledge base and research results are used to support, extend or revise the practice.

The third type of research framework, conceptual framework is a structure of concepts and/or theories which are pulled together as a map for the study. Eisenhart (1991) described conceptual framework as "a skeletal structure of justification, rather than a skeletal structure of explanation" (p.210). As such, a conceptual framework is an argument that the concepts chosen for investigations, and any anticipated relationships among them will be appropriate and useful given the research problem under investigation. Conceptual framework are based on previous research and built from an array of current and possible far-ranging sources. The framework used may be based on different theories and various aspects of practitioner knowledge, depending on what the researcher can argue will be relevant and important to address about a research problem.

Despite the definitions given, there are still gray areas between conceptual and theoretical framework. Liehr and Smith (2001) clearly described the difference between theoretical and conceptual framework in a simple yet meaningful diagram (See Fig 1). From this figure, researcher needs **to create** a structure to guide research in conceptual framework but only **identify** a full blown structure/theory to guide research for theoretical framework.

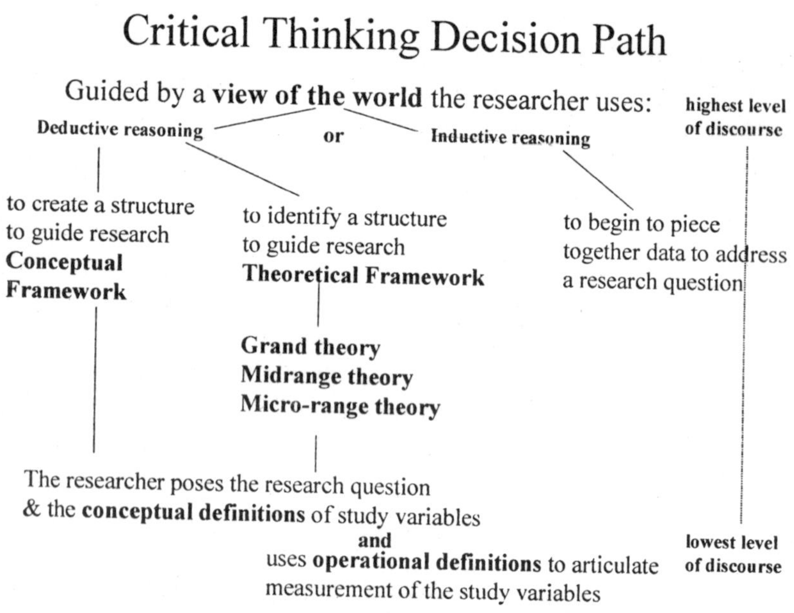

Figure 1. Liehr and Smith (2001) Critical thinking decision path.

Theoretical and Conceptual Frameworks in Mathematics Education Research

Mathematics education in general is experiencing an expansion of scope and diversity of research frameworks. English and Sriraman (2005) reported that *diverging, epistemological perspectives about what constitutes mathematical knowledge* (p. 170) and the heavy influence of cultural, social and political forces on mathematics education are among several explanations for the diverse phenomena. For the past two decades, theoretical frameworks in mathematics education research were very much influenced by psychology and mathematics, however, towards the end of the 80's, social related theories took center stage with the increase in number of research towards social aspects of mathematical learning that perceived mathematics as a *social product* (Lerman, 2000). The adoption of frameworks from other fields such as sociology, philosophy, history and anthropology is also a common phenomena during that period (Boaler, 2002; English & SriRaman, 2005). An example of framework diversity in mathematics education research can be seen in the research on values in mathematics education (Bishop, 2001; Chin & Lin, 2001; Nik azis, 2007; Chang et.al, 2002) (See Table 1). It was reported that weak theoretical foundation and the absence of a common framework were reported to be the major constraints in conducting research on affect such as values and beliefs. As a result, interpreting and comparing research on affect could prove to be a problem.

Table 1. Research on values and diverse theoretical frameworks

Research	*Theoretical frameworks*
Teaching of values in Malaysian Primary Education (Chang et.al., 1997, Sharifah Norul Akmar, 2002)	Social related theories focusing on the general educational values which which the school/education system aims to inculcate in pupils.
Values development in the secondary school mathematics and science education in Malaysia (Nik Azis et. al., 2007)	Universal integrated theory which can be divided into three domains: context (general values, specific values, procedural values and intrinsic values), nature (philosophical and practical) and status (absolute or relative).
The values and Mathematics Project (Bishop et. al, 2001)	Based on the original work of White (1959), a renowned culturologist, who proposed four components technological, ideological, sentimental/attitudinal and sociological to explain cultural growth

Research	Theoretical frameworks
Study on values in mathematics education in Taiwan (Lin & Chin, 1998)	Based on Rath's approach of value clarification and Vygotsky's notion of inner speech and social speech. Investigate the extent to which teachers involved are able to clarify their own value positions and study forms of teacher-student value interaction in mathematics teaching.

Example of Theoretical Framework and Conceptual Framework Employed in Research

Baiduriah (2003) investigated 14 year old students' development of graphical concepts using graphic calculator. The theoretical framework adopted in her study was based on two broad interpretations of Vygotsky's *zone of proximal development* (ZPD). The following excerpt briefly explain the rational for adopting the theoretical framework.

(The theoretical framework) is built upon Vygotsky's notion of knowledge construction, specifically his notion of zone of proximal development (ZPD). ...Vygotsky's model of knowledge construction is used in this study as it helps to account for the following issues in the context of leaning graphing with graphing calculators:

(i) The interaction process in classrooms, in particular the student-teacher interaction

(ii) The use of language, educational tools and symbol systems, and

(iii) The development of knowledge in teaching and learning" (p. 56)

In another study, Nur Riza (2007) adapted the Input-Process-Output (IPO) conceptual framework to model quality in education. She refined and adapted conceptual framework used in previous research, and proposed a new IPO-based model for her study (Refer to Fig.2)

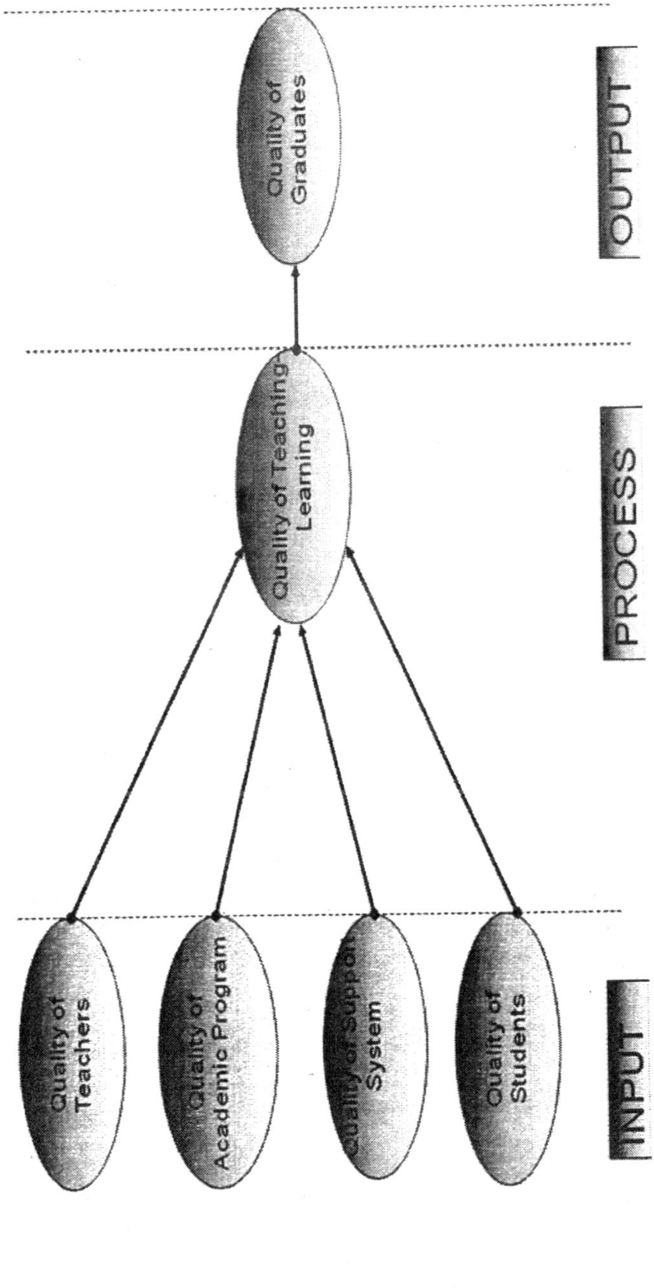

Figure 2. Nur Riza's initial IPO-based framework (p. 30)

Concluding Remark

Identification of either conceptual or theoretical framework is a very important element in the research process. Theoretical and conceptual framework provides a structure for conceptualizing and designing mathematics education research The choice of a particular framework helps in determining the nature and formulation of research questions asked, the way the appropriate concepts, constructs and procedures are defined, the way data are interpreted and conclusions drawn and justified. As mentioned earlier in this paper, the choice of either a theoretical or conceptual framework was among others influenced by the researchers' epistemological background and belief. Thus, we can find expanding range of frameworks being employed in mathematics education research such as radical constructivism, socio-cultural theory, information-processing psychology, and situated cognition. Theoretical fields other than psychology and/or mathematics influencing mathematics education research include philosophy, evaluation, ethnography, sociology and history. In this context, Boaler (2002) cautioned that too much framework diversity would resulted in lack of focus in mathematics education research.

> *In the past, mathematics educators drew largely from psychological frameworks and theories, but contemporary researchers are increasingly demonstrating the insights that may be learned from additional frameworks. Central among the frameworks now drawn upon are sociology.., socio-cultural theory.., politics.., mathematics.., philosophy.., history.., anthropology. But scholarship is anything but simple, and whilst we may agree that breadth of thinking is critical to the evaluation of ideas, and that different frameworks should be considered and employed, we must also be wary that mathematics education is a relatively new and young field and that too much breadth will cause a scattering of focus and preclude opportunities for consolidation and identity(p. 31)*

Nevertheless, despite the diversity, mathematics education

researchers have been able to collaborate with each other and thus the different frameworks have become a rich ground for further theoretical development. Some research studies can benefit more than others from having a strong theoretical base. Baiduriah's (2003) choice of Vygotsky zone of proximal development has allowed her to study the mediating role of technology in mathematics learning. The extent to which a theory is valuable depends upon the specific purposes and type of research being conducted.

REFERENCES

Baiduriah Yaacob (2003). *Graphing calculators and the zone of development: A study of fourteen year olds Malaysia students development of graphical concept with technology.* Unpublished PhD thesis, Institute of Education (IOE), United Kingdom.

Bishop, A.J., Fitz Simon, G., Seah, W. T., Clarkson, P. C.(2001). *Exploring issues of control over values teaching in the mathematics classroom.* Paper presented at the 2001 Annual conference of the Australian Association for research in Education, Freemantle, Australia.

Boaler, J.(2002). Exploring the nature of mathematical activity: Using theory, research and 'working hypotheses' to broaden conceptions of mathematical knowing, *Educational studies in mathematics*, 51(1),3-21.

Chang Lee Hoon et.al (2003). *Teaching of values in Malaysian primary education: Phase 1,* Intensified Research in Priority Area(IRPA) Report, University of Malaya.

DeBellis, V. A.. & Goldin, G. A.(1997). The affective domain in mathematical problem solving. In E. Pehkonen (Ed.). *Proceedings of the 21st conference of the International group for the Psychology of Mathematics education*, Vol. 2 (pp. 209-216). Finland: University of Helsinki.

Eisenhart, M.A.(1991). Conceptual frameworks for research circa 1991: Ideas from a cultural anthropologist; Implications for mathematics education researchers. *Proceedings of the 13th annual meeting of the North American Chapters of the International Group for the Psychology of Mathematics Education* (Vol. 1, pp. 220-239). Blacksburg, VA.

English, L.& Sriraman, B. (2005). Theories of Mathematics Education. In Chick, H.L. & Vincent, J. L. (Eds.). *Proceedings of the 29th Conference of the International Group for the Psychology of Mathematics Education*, Vol. 1, pp. 170-202.Melbourne:PME.

Lerman, S. (2000). The social turn in mathematics education research. In J. Boaler (Ed.) *Multiple Perspectives on Mathematics Teaching and Learning* (pp. 19-44). Westport, CT: Ablex.

Lester, F.K. (2005). On the theoretical, conceptual, and philosophical foundations for research in mathematics education, *ZDM* Vol. 37(6)pp. 457-467).

Liehr, P. & Smith, M.J. (2001). Frameworks for Research, In G. LoBiondo-Wood & J. Haber (Eds.), *Nursing Research: Methods, Critical Appraisal and utilization* (4th Edition) St. Louis: Mosby.

Lin, Fou.-L., & Chin, C. (1998).*Study on values in mathematics education in Taiwan*: Unpublished manuscript, National Taiwan Normal University and National Tsing Hua University, Taiwan.

Mc Leod, D. B. (1992). Research on affect in mathematics education: A reconceptualization. In D. A. Grows (Ed.) *Handbook of research on mathematics teaching and learning* (575-596). New York: Macmillan.

Morse, J. M. (1994). Designing funded qualitative research. In N.K. Denzin & Y. S. Lincoln (Eds.) *The handbook of qualitative research* (pp. 220-235). Thousand Oaks, CA: Sage

Nik Azis Nik Pa (2008). *Research on values in mathematics and science education*, Paper presented at the National Seminar on Values development in Mathematics and Science education, Faculty of Education, University of Malaya, 1-2 August, 2008.

Nur Riza Suradi (2007). *Modeling quality education in a higher education institutions based on the IPO (input-process-output) framework*, Unpublished PhD thesis, Institute of post graduate studies, University of Malaya.

Scriven, M. (1986). Evaluation as a paradigm for education research. In E. House (Ed.), *New directions in education evaluation* (pp.53-67). London: Falmer Press.

Sharifah Norul Akmar bt Syed Zamri (2002), Teaching of values in Malaysian primary mathematics Education, paper presented at the Convention of values, Monash University, Australia.

Sinclair, M. (2007). Editorial: A guide to understanding theoretical and conceptual frameworks. *Evidence based midwifery* 5(2): 39.

Smith, M.U., Wandersee, J.H., & Cummins, C.L.(1993). What's wrong with this manuscript?: An analysis of the reasons for rejection given by *Journal of Research in Science Teaching* reviewers, *Journal of Research in Science Teaching*, 39(2), 209-211.

20

Science Teaching in the Constructive Paradigm

Jasim Ahmad

Education is a process of development through which an individual's physical, mental, emotional and social development takes place. Education makes an individual adaptable to changing nature and needs of society. Education instils in an individual all those competencies through which he or she can occupy a suitable place in the society. Education is that which make an individual worthy of himself, his family and the society as a whole. An educated person is capable of adapting as per the change and demands in the dynamic society. If an individual does not develop these abilities despite having degrees and diplomas of formal education, he cannot be considered as educated.

Science Education

The vast changes that we see during the pre-historic, ancient, medieval periods and modern age in all spheres of life are mainly the products of science and technology. We are living in the age of science and technology. In fact science and environment has become synonymous. For example, we are wearing clothes, using pens, pencils, shoes, slippers, socks, various types of oils, dyes, rings, and other ornaments, watches, etc., all these thing which we use in our daily life are the product of science and technology. Artists cannot show their arts, painters cannot paint, poets can't write poems, writers cannot write, without the aid of science. In fact, science has become the heart and soul of life. There is no any activity or area of work or profession in which science is not involved.

Knowing about science has been the basic instinct and motivation of mankind. From time immemorial man has been trying to explore, control and exploit the environment and the natural forces.

Science develops thinking ability, reasoning ability, curiosity, creativity, open-mindedness, positive attitude and problem solving approach. These are the abilities and qualities that must be developed in every citizen of the world. This needs the development of basic knowledge and understanding of science in all global citizens'. This global necessity leads to the development of the concept of scientific literacy at global level i.e. global scientific literacy, scientific attitude and training in scientific method to all citizens of the world.

Scientific Literacy

It is globally accepted that every individual should acquire the basic knowledge and understanding of science. Scientific literacy is the minimum level of scientific understanding which is required to be achieved by all citizens and is an obligation on the state to provide it to all of its citizens. This is the reason that India's National Policy of Education (1986) and National Curriculum Framework for School Education (2000) have agreed to take, science as a core subject from class one to class tenth to promote scientific literacy, scientific temper as well as scientific attitude. It is an effort to develop universal scientific literacy so that every citizen acquires the minimum levels of basic scientific and technological knowledge, understanding and skills.

Types of Scientific Literacy

1. ***Practical Scientific Literacy*:** It covers those aspects of scientific knowledge and understanding which helps in solving practical problems of day-to-day life. Population control, Conservation of energy and other resources like water, petroleum, forest, soil fertility; eradication of polio, AIDS and other communicable diseases; balanced diet, environmental pollution etc comes under this category.

2. ***Civic Scientific Literacy*:** It refers to the aspects of scientific literacy, which contributes to the awareness of science

and science related issues of civic importance like HIV-AIDS, developing nuclear energy, solar panels, etc.

3. *Cultural Scientific Literacy*: It includes knowledge and achievement of science as a human enterprise. Green revolution,

White revolution, life saving drugs and its development, information technology, media, multi-media, internet etc are the examples of cultural scientific literacy.

Qualities of a Scientifically Literate Person

Science teachers should try to develop in themselves and in their students such qualities which make an individual a scientifically literate person. According to Arons (1983) and Hodson (1988), the following qualities must be developed in a scientifically literate person:

- Interest in the areas of science, nature and natural resources.
- An inclination and appreciation towards science and technology and its use in day-to-day life.
- Knowledge and understanding of the relationship between science, technology and society (STS).
- General level of understanding and application of the common concepts, principles, laws and processes of science.
- The ability to assimilate and apply technical information.
- Rational thinking, logical decisions and unbiased attitude.
- Interest in applying the findings of scientific research in improving the quality of life.

Scientific Attitude

One of the most important objectives of science teaching at school level is the development of scientific attitude in the growing children and trains them in scientific method so that they can address their day-to-day problems scientifically. It is a set of attitudes and values possessed by an individual, which are commonly used in solving scientific problems or solving problems in a scientific way. It is a kind of positive attitude towards life. The set of values and attitudes constituting the scientific attitude are underneath.

- **Believing in cause and effect relationship:** It is the feeling and understanding that there is always a perfect natural explanation for everything. To believe that every effect has some causes is the most important attributes of a scientific attitude. It leads to the aversion of superstition and automatic preference to scientific explanation
- **Objectivity:** It refers to the unbiased attitude of an individual towards everything. All decisions taken by the individual are totally rational and logical in his approach.
- **Curiosity and imagination:** It is the inquisitiveness on the part of the individual to go into the imagination to find the reality and knowing the unknown things.
- **Empiricism:** It is the characteristics which demands that the opinion should be based on evidence. It should be based on observation, especially self-observation.
- **Scepticism:** It is the belief that nothing is final and permanent. Alternatives are available and there is always scope for innovation.
- **Empathy for human conditions:** It is the attitude of putting oneself in others situations and considering the needs of other people.
- **Critical thinking:** It is the thinking which involves analysis, assessment and evaluation to find out strength and weakness with the intention to bring further improvement.
- **Suspended judgment:** It is the attitude of generalizing once finding only if it is proved from different ways and through many experiments and observations.
- **Open-mindedness:** It is the ability to face the facts as they are, regardless of what one has previously thought. It includes the ability to accept new and sometimes even

distasteful ideas. One must expect many failures and be willing to try again. The mind cannot be made up once and for all. New knowledge may make a change in thinking process and direction. What is accepted as true often is relatively, and not absolutely, true. A scientific truth offers an explanation that is acceptable only in the light of what is known at a particular time. Simply, it is 'ready to change opinion' if adequate evidences are available. It leads to the respect for the views of others.

- **A belief that problems have solutions:** This aspect of scientific attitude makes an individuals' thought that there is no problem in the world which can't be solved. If there is a problem, there is also solution for that.
- **Parsimony:** It refers to the preference of simple explanation to the complex one.

A science teacher should reflect and practice these attitudes. He should set himself as an example to the students and nurture these attitudes and values in his pupils.

In the current scenario of pedagogy of teaching and learning "constructivist approach" is widely discussed, praised and accepted by the educationists around the globe. This approach is instrumental in developing creativity and scientific attitude among students. It has the potential to train students in using problem solving method or scientific method in sorting out problems of daily lives.

Meaning of Constructivism

Constructivism is based on the philosophy that there is no knowledge independent of the meaning attributed to experience or constructed by the learner. Knowledge construction implies that the learners construct their own knowledge through the active participation in the process of teaching and learning by seeking to find their own meaning in their experiences. In other words, learners construct or develop meaning in their subjective experiences, and this result into his knowledge development. According to constructivists, each individual's subjective experience is just as valid as anyone else's, and no one has privileged viewpoint. It reflects that there are no objective criteria for what constitutes knowledge. Knowledge to one may not be knowledge for others, because no two persons necessarily have the same basic skills and mechanism or mental process of constructions.

Constructivists replace the position of a teacher from the center of knowledge (objective), with the learner (subjective). Independent of the teacher, each student's subjective experience has a special and unique meaning in constructivism.

Constructivist learning has emerged as a forceful approach to teaching and learning in this millennium. This is based on the work of John Dewey, Jean Piaget, Jerome Brunner, Montessori, and Lev Vygotsky. It represents a paradigm shift from behaviorist teaching-learning to education based on cognitive theory. Behaviorists' epistemology focuses on intelligence, domains of objectives, levels of knowledge, and reinforcement. Constructivist epistemology assumes that learners construct their own knowledge on the basis of interaction with their environment. Four epistemological assumptions constitute the heart and soul of the constructivist approach of learning which are given underneath.

1. Physical construction of Knowledge: Knowledge is physically constructed by learners who are involved in active learning.
2. Symbolic construction of Knowledge: Knowledge is symbolically constructed by learners who make their own representation of actions.
3. Social construction of Knowledge: Knowledge is socially constructed by learners who convey their meaning making to others.
4. Theoretical construction of Knowledge: Knowledge is theoretically constructed by learners who try to explain things they don't completely understand.

Epistemology in Constructivism

Knowledge and its construction have varied meaning in constructivism, which may be understood from the following assertions.

1. Knowledge is always an interpretation which depends on individuals' ability, intelligence, previous experiences, past and prevailing situation, creativity, level of thinking etc. Therefore, knowledge is always open to uncertainty. It varies with time. It is never permanent as it is always open to question

2. Knowledge is a way of making sense of experiences. The same process or product may be experienced by many. But knowledge about that process or product may vary for all individuals as they all may sense and perceive them differently. Knowledge is not something concrete outside the individual which may be swallowed and digested as we feed something.

3. Learning and knowledge is a personal and private activity.

4. Knowledge is a construction of reality. According to Taylor (1993), "Human knowledge is a process of personal cognitive construction, or invention undertaken by the individual who is trying to make sense of his social or natural environment".

5. Knowledge acquisition or learning is not the transfer of "nuggets of truth" (as referred by Kelly in 1995) to the individual but a personal construction.

6. Learning is determined by the interplay among learners existing knowledge, social context, teaching-learning environment and the problem that is to be solved.

There are various theories of constructivism but all have two major similarities as identified by Cunningham and Duffy. These are:

(i) Learning is an active process of constructing rather that acquiring it.

(ii) Teaching is a process of supporting that construction rather than communicating or transmitting knowledge or information.

Types of Constructivism

Various theories or approaches of constructivism share some common core characteristics regarding knowledge development and learning. These are:

- It is constructed rather than transmitted or acquired.
- The construction of knowledge takes place through the process of reflective thinking and reflective abstraction.
- It is facilitated by learners' cognitive structures.
- Learners' cognitive structures develop continuously.
- Knowledge Construction or learning is facilitated by constructivists' method and pedagogy of learning.

A brief description of the important types of constructivism is discussed underneath.

1. Cognitive Constructivism

It is based on the research findings of Jean Piaget. It discusses the cognitive structure of human beings and its developmental process. It elaborates the development, acquisition and constriction of knowledge with the help of cognitive structure. It explains the mechanism of the construction and reconstruction of cognitive structure which develops an individual's cognitive abilities and influences the whole personality. It accepts intellectual structures and capabilities as an individually constructed approach. It gives stress on personal meaning making. This considers learning as an active process in which children construct new ideas or concepts based on their previous experiences. This involves assimilation, accommodation, equilibration and adaptation. With the help of these processes children derive their own meaning and construct knowledge which is unique to them.

It is the duty of teachers to facilitate cognitive change by presenting new ideas, new concepts, and difficult situations that pose challenge to students to trigger multidirectional thinking.

2. Social Constructivism

There are two parts of knowledge, one is individual and the other is society. These two cannot be seen independently as both influence each other.

Social constructivism takes two approaches. One is 'situated cognition' and the other is 'sociocultural cognition'. Both forms highlight the importance of meaningful, integrated learning in the context of the environment. It believes that knowledge construction takes place in a certain social setting.

Situated cognition advocates that transformation of knowledge is done in the context of social environment. Both the individual and the environment change as a result of interaction. It focuses on meaningful integrated teaching-learning. It states that the learning tasks must be organized in such a way which contains a variety of subject areas and their social context.

3. Cultural Constructivism

Culture is one of the most important determinants of personality development. Every new learning is based on prior experiences and learning. Previous learning includes various concepts of the concerned subjects and culturally dependent assumptions about the world, called as world view. As per the cultural constructivism, learning is influence by world view, which varies from individual to individual. We observe in daily life that different persons observing the same event report it differently. This difference in reporting is due to the different world view or perspectives or different individuals.

4. Cybernetic Constructivism

Cybernetic constructivism is based on the concept of *autopoiesis* (self-formation) which was formulated by the Chilean cell-biologists Maturana and Varela (1980, 1987). An autopoietic system is a system which is "organized as a network of processes of production (transformation and destruction) of components that produces the components (i) through their interactions and transformations continuously regenerate and realize the network of processes (relations) that produced them; and (ii) constitute it ...as a concrete unity in space which they (the components) exist by specifying the topological domain of its realization as such a network".

An autopoietic system is a self-contained and a self-referential unity which is identified by the following six criteria (Mingers, 1995)

- It is identifiable through its border.
- Analyzable through its components.
- The interacting components obey the general physical laws (like a natural system).
- Boundary of the system is self-maintained by preferential neighborhood relations (it can stabilize its own boundary).
- The system is contained within and producing the boundary.
- It is a self-productive system. It reproduces self by using its own components or by transformed imported material.

Autopoiesis was originally developed to describe biological cells. But now it has been applied to a variety of disciplines covering physical, cognitive, and psychic systems (Mingers, 1995; Maturan & Varela, 1987). Particularly interesting is Luhmann's application of autopoiesis in social, communication, and legal systems (Luhmann, 1989-90, 1995.)

Autopoiesis' constructivist character is evident at the level of the closure of the nervous system implying that action and cognition depend on each other without any outside system of reference. According to von Foerster, "my nervous system does not, indeed, cannot, tell me what is 'out there,' not because of mechanical but because of logico-semantic reasons. My nervous system cannot tell me anything because it is 'me': I am the activity of my nervous system, all my nervous system talks about its own state of sensory-motor activity" (Von Foerster, 1993). At another place, von Foerster (1984) advocates that all sensory receptors (visual, auditory, tactual, etc.) send physically indistinguishable 'responses' to the cortex and that, therefore, the 'sensory modalities' can be distinguished only by keeping track of the part of the body from which the responses come, and not on the basis of 'environmental features.' From this observation Von Glasersfeld concludes that "contemporary neurophysiological models may be compatible with a constructivist theory of knowing but can in no way be integrated with the notion of transduction of 'information' from the environment that any realist epistemology demands" (Von Glasersfeldhttp://www.math.upatras.gr/~mboudour/Chapters/constr.html - Glasersfeld%20%281989%29 1989).

Learning Design in Constructivism

The constructivist learning design emphasizes the following six important elements in the process of teaching and learning.

1. **Creating a situation:** Teacher is required to create a suitable situation for students about the process of their learning.
2. **Grouping:** Teacher is required to select a process for grouping of students and the learning materials to be used.
3. **Bridging:** Teacher has to develop a bridge between students' previous learning and the learning task i.e. what the teacher want them to learn.
4. **Questioning:** Teacher should have command on questioning skill. He should anticipate questions to be asked to the students for their answers without giving any explanation for them.
5. **Exhibiting:** Teacher should motivate students to exhibit a record of their thinking by sharing it with their class mates and teachers.
6. **Reflecting:** Teacher is required to solicit reflection of students on their learning. It also helps in students' evaluation and effectiveness of on going teaching learning process.

Five E's of Constructivism

In the constructivist learning design, all learners are subjected to construct their own knowledge and understanding. The idea underlying constructivism has been deeply studied and explained by educationist like Jean Piaget, Eleanor Duckworth, George Hein, Lev Vygotsky and Howard Gardener. The Principal Investigator of Biological Science Curriculum Studies (BSCS), Bybee, has developed an instructional model for constructivism, called as "Five Es". The five 'Es' are discussed underneath.

1. **Engage:** Students first encounter and identify the learning task. Students are encouraged to make a link between their previous experiences and the current learning task. Foundation is laid down for the organizational ground work for the activities to be performed and students are induced to involve in these activities. Students' attention is drawn and they are encouraged to participate in the learning process and in the activities being organized. This is done with the help of questioning, and applying the scientific approach of teaching.
2. **Explore:** This is the stage at which learners get directly involve with the phenomena under study and materials being used. This results into the development of a grounding of experience with the phenomenon. Each student builds a base of common experience developed as a result of sharing of ideas and communication among the members of the group. Teachers act as a facilitator, guide, friend, motivator, material provider, and stage setter. The inquiry from students' side drives the teaching-learning ahead during the exploration.
3. **Explain:** Multidirectional explanation is needed for effective teaching and learning. At this stage, first of all students explain the phenomena according to their understanding. This explanation may be at the individual level, between two students, among students of a group, between two or many groups and finally students explain to the facilitator. The facilitators then explain in their own words with proper labeling of the technical terms.
4. **Elaborate:** Students make connections among various correlated concepts which they have already learned and apply their understanding in day-to-day lives. In this way students are expanding or elaborating their current learning with those they have learnt in the past. They

make connections among them and these connections often lead to further inquiry and innovation in their ideas and understandings.

5. **Evaluate:** This is the diagnostic process that allows the teacher to find if the learner has attained the desired level of cognitive knowledge and understanding of concepts. It may occur continuously during the teaching-learning process. A few important tools that may be used for this purpose are: rubrics (quantified and prioritized outcome expectations), observation schedule, check list, student interviews, portfolio designed with specific purposes, project and problem based assignment etc. It gives the indication of the level of effectiveness of teaching and learning and serves to guide the teacher in further lesson planning and for modification or change of direction. If a teacher perceives clear evidence of misconception, then he can revisit the concept to enhance better understanding. If students show deep interest in any specific direction of inquiry, the teacher can consider refocusing the investigation to take the advantage of students' high level of interest and motivation.

The continuous and comprehensive process of evaluation gives the constructivist approach a cyclic structure. The learning process is open-ended and can be changed as per the needs, aspirations and understanding difficulties of the students. There is an ongoing loop where questions lead to answers but more questions and teaching-learning instructions are driven by both, predetermined lesson design and the process of inquiry.

Constructivist Classroom, Teacher, and Lesson

The foundation of constructivism lies in the philosophy that students should be made capable to construct their own knowledge. Teachers are not the transmitter, supplier, or a ready made knowledge provider for the students. Teacher should help students in right kind of learning or constructing right knowledge through right methods. Hence the nature of classroom, role of the teacher and lesson structure and presentation needs deviation from the conventional approaches of teaching and learning.

It is very important for the teacher to interpret students learning difficulties in a consistent manner. Learning is viewed as active construction by the learner. For this to happen it is very essential for the teacher to take students belief and conceptions (mainly wrong belief and misconceptions) seriously which leads to the development of student's self construction of knowledge pedagogy. It requires focusing on the students' interest, needs, intelligence, creativity, thinking ability, reflection and skills of learning. It is very essential to move form the cramming of facts, concepts, principles, theories and laws to construct the understanding of these in the minds of the learners. If this happens only then it may be called as education and especially biological science learning. The students should also understand the ways in which biology or science learning is helpful to him and the society as a whole, not only on occasional basis but on daily-life basis. Constructivism is a very strong tool to attain the objectives of 'scientific literacy' and movement like 'science for all', which can make knowledge of science and its various branches more meaningful.

The classroom and the teacher's role in constructivist approach of teaching and learning need to be redefined as compared to the conventional outlook. It requires to be created a very specific type of learning environment, which Strommen and Lincoln (1992) called a "child-driven learning environment". Only this type of environment can provide students the opportunity to create their own ideas and knowledge. In addition to this there is a need to create an atmosphere in the classroom in which students collaborate their ideas with one another, share ideas with peer group and have a good discussion on these ideas in a very healthy environment. Every child should be given an opportunity to reflect upon their ideas and the child who is not reflecting should be compelled to reflect through encouragement and motivation by the teacher.

Constructivist Classroom

The following characteristics may be considered as a constructivist classroom.

- A very interactive class. The interaction between teacher and students, between two groups of students and among various students must be encouraged in a healthy environment and in a much disciplined manner.
- The classroom philosophy should be based on 'knowledge sharing' between teacher and students rather than 'knowledge imparting' by the teacher to the students.
- The activeness of teacher and students should be balanced. It is not good that the teacher is very active and students are passive or vice-versa.
- For proper conduction of class, demonstration, classroom management, procuring community resources to the class, responsibilities must be shared among students and teachers.
- The size of the class should preferably be small to be able to transact it properly.
- The class should be heterogeneous in nature. It should carry the concept of 'inclusive education' with it. A heterogeneous group will bring more and diverse ideas to the class and will give the opportunity of constructive discussion among students.
- Hands-on-experiences should be provided to the learners.
- Each student of the class should feel thirst of knowledge, should be curios, motivated to ask questions and give responses. Every student should put their ideas to the teacher and to their classmates without any hesitation.
- Teaching goals and objectives should be negotiated and not imposed.
- Evaluation should serve as a self-analysis tool.
- Classroom environment should be such which help pupils interpret the multiple perspectives of the world.

- It is must to create real-world environment that employ the context in which learning is relevant.

Constructivist Teacher

A constructivist teacher's personality should have the following characteristics:

We require conventional teaching approach to command on teaching subject

- Understanding of other subjects which are correlated to his subject. For example, a biology teacher, in addition to having command on biology, he should have a considerable level of understanding of chemistry, physics, statistics, mathematics, geography, environment etc.
- Ability to correlate topics of his subject with other subjects of students' choice. As the choices of students are diverse, the teacher must have high potential to relate his subject with most of the school teaching subjects.
- The teacher must be able to integrate the teaching content with the real environment, nature and society-what the students observe in their daily lives. It is the extension of teaching and learning beyond the class and school.
- The teacher should act as a guide and facilitator in instruction and learning, depending on the knowledge level of the children.
- It is very important to know the previous knowledge, entry behaviour and understandings of students. Students use prior knowledge to help make sense of the new knowledge being constructed. This helps pupils think critically and make informed decisions. The teacher should have command in using the skill of *testing previous knowledge*, *eliciting students' thought process* and *bringing their misconception on the surface* so that it can be discussed and reconstructed.
- A constructivist teacher should act as a 'prime resource center' for students; he should not only be the primary source of information.

- The teacher should engage students in experiences that challenge the previous conceptions of their existing knowledge. This will help teacher to identify students' misconception and will provide an opportunity to re-build them.
- Consideration of individual differences and giving individual attention to all students as far as possible.
- Encouraging students to express their ideas without hesitation.
- Allowing students responses to lead the lessons on and seek elaboration of student's initial responses.
- Seeking students' ideas before presenting self (teacher) ideas or before studying ideas from textbooks or other sources.
- Encouraging students to challenge one another's conceptualization of ideas in a very healthy environment and with the attitude of 'learning to learn more', and 'learning by cooperation and discussion'.
- Allowing students time for thinking after posing questions.
- Encouraging the spirit of questioning by asking thoughtful and open-ended questions.
- Using cognitive terminologies like 'classify', 'analyze', and 'create' when framing tasks.
- Promoting student leadership, collaboration, location of information and taking actions as a result of the learning process.
- Encouraging students' autonomy and initiative.

Constructivist Lesson

Considering the above discussion about constructivist classroom and the role of teacher, it becomes easy to reflect upon the lesson and its presentation in a constructive way. Every teacher has his own potentialities and by the virtue of this he or she can plan a constructivist lesson accordingly. A constructivist teacher must be an expert in teaching skills, especially constructivist teaching skills. Following is the strategies for implementing a constructivist lesson, a modified version of the strategies given by Yager (1991).

Step 1: Introduction

It includes the following

- Questioning to the class.
- Listening and considering the possible responses of the class.
- Noting the unexpected answers, phenomena, misconceptions etc.
- Identifying situations where pupils' perceptions are different.
- Observing the whole environment for points to questions.

Step 2: Lesson Development and its Continuation

It includes:

- Elicitation of ideas
- Brainstorming the possible alternatives
- Engaging students in focused discussion and play.
- Looking for information (if any).
- Experimentation (if any).
- Observing the phenomena.
- Designing the model, collecting and organizing data.
- Using problem solving strategies.
- Choosing appropriate resources.
- Students discuss solution with peer group.
- Students design and conduct experiment.
- Students evaluate and debate choices.
- Pupils identify risks and consequences.
- Defining parameters of an investigation.

Step 3: Propdsing Explanation and Solutions

It includes:

- Communicating information and ideas.
- Constructing explanation of model.
- Constructing a new explanation.
- Review and critique of the solutions given.
- Applying peer evaluation.
- Assembling appropriate closure.
- Integrating the developed solution with existing knowledge and experiences.

Step 4: Action Taking

It includes:

- Decision making.
- Applying knowledge and skill constructed in this lesson.
- Transferring and integrating knowledge and skills developed.

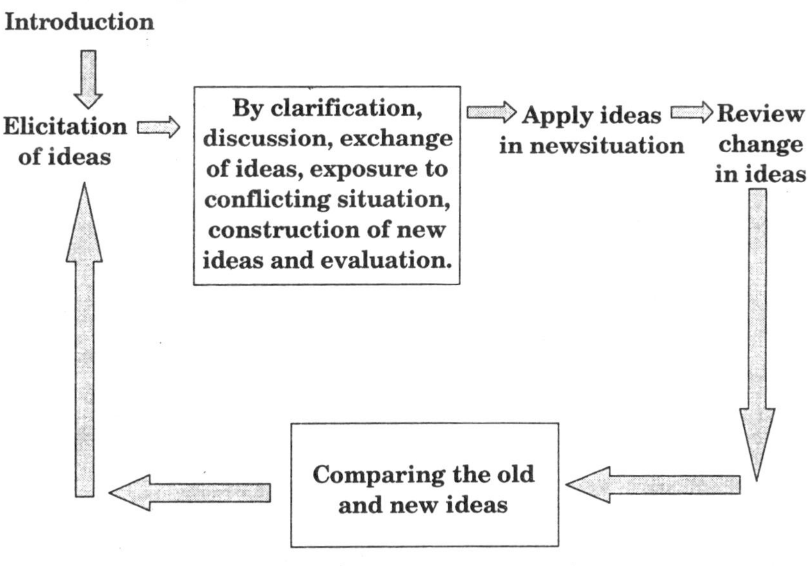

Figure 1: Constructivist teaching sequences (based on Rosalind Driver, 1989, 88)

- Sharing information and ideas.

- Asking new question and new problems.
- Developing products and promoting ideas.
- Using models and ideas to elicit discussions and gaining acceptance by others.

A constructivist teaching sequence is given in figure 1, adapted from Rosalind Driver (1989, 1988). The figure depicts that the students are provided with many opportunities to develop their own ideas and experiences and to construct their own meaning of the phenomena or concept observed or studied.

REFERENCES

Bybee, R. (1993). *Reforming Science Education*. Teachers College Press, P.O. Box 2032, Colchester.

Foerster, H. Von (ed.) (1984). *Observing Systems*. Salinas: Intersystems Publications.

Foerster, H. Von (1993). *Wissen und Gewisse,*. Frankfurt: Suhrkamp.

Glasersfeld, E. Von (1989). Cognition, Construction of knowledge and Teaching. *Synthese, 80(1),* 120-140.

Kelly, A.E (1995). The researcher's human face: A review of Investigating mathematics teaching: A constructivist enquiry. *Journal for Research in Mathematics Education, 26 (5),* 498-502.

Luhmann, N. (1989). *Ecological Communication*. Cambridge: UK, Polity Press.

Luhmann, N. (1990). *Essays in Self-Reference*. New York: Columbia University Press.

Luhmann, N. (1995). *Social Systems*. Stanford: Stanford University Press.

Maturana, H., and F.Varela (1980). *Autopoiesis and cognition: The Realization of the Living*. Dordrecht:Reidel.

Maturana, H., and F.Varela (1987). *The tree of knowledge: Biological roots of human understanding*. Boston: Shambhala.

Mingers, J. (1995). *Self-Producing systems: Implications and applications of autopoiesis*. New York: Plenum.

Piaget, J. (1952). *The origins of intelligence in children*. New York: International University Press.

Report of the commission on the Reorganizatiion of Secondary Schools USA; Teaching, Schools, and Society; Evelina Orteza Y Miranda and Romulo F Magsiño; published by Routledge; The Falmer Press, 1990.

Taylor, P.J. (193). Mathematics Achievement: A Question of Ages with GC Leder, *Research Briefs, 8,* 26-29.

Thakur, N. N. (1993). *Gandhian Philosophy of Education and Contemporary World.* New Delhi: Creative Books.

Yager, R.E. (1991). The Constructivist Learning Model: Toward Real Reform in Science Education. *The Science Teacher, 58 (6),* 52-57.

SECTION 6 : CONTEMPORARY FIELDS OF EDUCATION

21

Art Education : The Quadrant Model

Daryl S. Paulson

Introduction

Many approaches have been used over the years to interpret literature, and these same approaches can be used to interpret art in art education. Interpretation is not merely a nicety in life; it is a process each person employs just to survive. It was Heidegger (1962) who first made humans face their temporality by facing life directly. This requires a constant and on-going process of directly interpreting one's world. Humans are not neutral observers "in" this world but instead are frighteningly affected by every event, specifically negative events – massive lay-offs, SARS epidemics, disease, war, terrorist attacks, events in their communities and in their own neighbourhood. Humans simply cannot escape interpreting every event in the world of which they become aware relative to its impact on them.

Throughout the ages, art has offered a tremendous resource for interpreting the depicted situation, and that is so today. Through art, one can plumb the depths of the collective unconscious to clearly say that which cannot be said in formal concrete ways (Jung, 1964; Richter, 1965). That is, art allows one to describe what cannot otherwise be described. It is involved with feelings and visions. The artist involves him/herself beyond intellect to feeling, living, seeing, and memory in his/her own unique way.

Some postmodern art critics argue that contemporary art cannot be interpreted, for it is what it is, just another aspect of a senseless life. But a "senseless life" is an interpretation, not a true or false statement. Most viewers, from an authentic perspective, do not subscribe to this nihilist view. Instead, they want to better understand and "interpret" the artwork, given it means something. From this perspective, works of art are forms of communication that can be interpreted via multiple dimensions. For example, art may be interpreted in terms of its representation of the objective world, "being in the world," visions, or even an imaginary world. An artwork can be understood better through its elemental forms: mass, shapes, planes, textures, colors, tensions, balance, symbols, flow, and rhythm. These attributes can be compared and contrasted within the artwork or with other artwork styles.

Art may also be understood based on the "artist's intention" in making the piece. Was the portrayal conscious or not to the artist? What was the artist portraying: a feeling, a concept, a fear, a pleasure, an event? Or, the artwork can be interpreted by the "viewer." What do I see, think, and feel about this piece? Finally, art can be interpreted within the context of time or history.

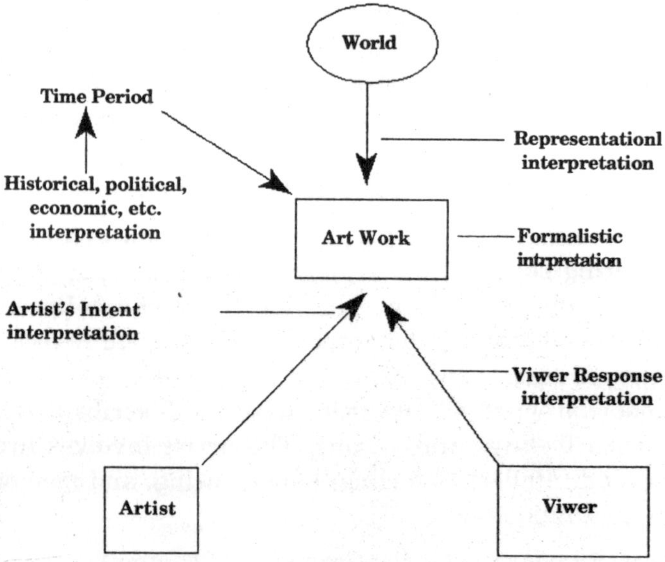

Figure 1. Multi-Perspectives of Art Interpretation

All these forms of interpretation can be manifest or latent. A manifest perception is one of surface meanings, and latent is one of depth. To fully understand what is being seen, both are necessary. Figure 1 portrays these five art interpretive approaches in a form similar to M. H. Abram's (1953) schema for literary interpretation.

As we can see, art interpretation is, to a large degree, communication – an artist expressing a concept or pattern to which another can relate. It is, at its essence, a very preliterate and post-literate way of contacting oneself and others (Newton, 1990). Let us look more closely at these interpretive approaches, individually, as they apply to art.

Representational Interpretations

Representational art interpretation can be valuable in comparing the artwork to the actual world, or an idea or concept about it. In its most basic form, it answers the question: "how well does the artwork represent some aspect or concept of the world," or perhaps more precisely, "being in the world?" That is, how close is the map in representing the territory? Hence, the technical ability of the artist to represent a natural, imaginary, or subjective phenomenon is critical (Scholes, 1982). Objective representational art dates back to Paleolithic times. For example, the limestone sculpture, *Venus of Willendorf* (28,000-23,000 BC), represents not just a heavy-breasted, wide-hipped woman, but a symbol of fertility, i.e., "Life." The power to bring forth new life must have been awesome to our forebears in Paleolithic times. And there was a clear association between heavy breasts and wide hips and child-bearing capabilities. There are no biologically "natural" shapes or features on the sculpture, and the emphasis is clearly upon revered female reproductive capabilities, a magical power that ensured continued survival of the group. The breasts, hips and belly are dramatically exaggerated and "ball-shaped," much more so than seen in actual pregnant and/or lactating women. The arms, in contrast, are "stick-like," and no facial features are present. Despite the lack of detail in the figure as a whole, the pubic triangle appears to be emphatically etched into the limestone sculpture. Clearly, women must have been viewed as imbued with a mystical power to bring forth new life. Perhaps as a number of anthropological mythologists have suggested, this type of art contained magical powers that tribal members believed influenced and promoted fertility (Campbell, 1959; Gebser, 1985).

Some major Paleolithic art finds have been discovered in the deeper recesses of caves — "the bowels of the earth" — used by early humans in parts of France and Spain (Gardiner, 1996; Gebser, 1985). Arguably, the most famous are the cave wall paintings found at the Lascaux cave complex in Dordogne, France. In one chamber is found an assortment of animals — bison, ibex, and other species — drawn onto the cave walls in areas certainly not lived-in. It is probable that these areas were designated magical power spaces where tribal initiates gained control over these animal food sources through magic-inducing rituals (Campbell, 1959; Eliade, 1964; Neumann, 1973). There are spear-point marks scoring many of the painted animals, suggesting that by spearing the paintings, tribe members would be assured a successful hunt, for a painted animal representation and the actual animal were one and the same. They were not differentiated. Many other similar representational art forms and styles found throughout Mesopotamia, upper Egypt, and the Indus Valley may have been used similarly (Gardiner, 1996; Paulson, 2005).

In historical times, representational art portrayed aspects of the lived world and, hence, were copies of it. This form of art was not valued by all, particularly Plato (Selden, 1988). For example, in *The Republic* (Hamilton & Cairn, 1963), representational art carried a negative connotation. According to Plato, representational art was an inferior "copy" of aspects of the natural world. The natural world, itself, was but an imitation of the true "archetypal," or Platonic world.

Much later in history, in the modern and, particularly, postmodern eras, pursuit of representational art has been severely criticized for attempting to produce an exact copy of an object, particularly an object in the natural world (e.g., portraits, landscapes, etc.). Although representational art can represent a "mirror reflection" of an object, it usually points beyond an exact copy to include more complex facets concerning the obvious object (e.g., symbolic, a certain perspective or idea, an image superimposed on the object).

Shortly after Plato's criticism of representational art, Aristotle championed it, arguing that it fulfilled a basic human need, and categorized it in terms of its means (art form) and its manner (presentation perspective) (Frye, 1957; Selden, 1988; Toynbee, 1995). According to Aristotle, one can imitate by "means" of paint and brush, and through song, dance, orchestration, mime and writing. These imitative processes are not simply mirror reflections but contain additional, unique factors termed "emergents." Perhaps this is why a superbly-done painting of a landscape, a temple, or a person often seems to reveal more than a photograph. The painting seems to incorporate an "over time" emergent richness that a photograph does not. Perhaps this is due to the many sittings a painter employs to depict the object: a multi-time portrayal instead of a snapshot moment. Secondly, imitation requires of the artist a rigorous process of specifically selecting and magnifying those "objects" that are worth representing. Representational art also incorporates a specific, unique "manner" of presenting the portrayed object – for example, the time of day depicted by subtle contrasts between light and dark areas of the painting not only seen but felt. In short, it is the unique way in which an artist uses his/her tools (paint, line, texture, color mixes, perspective, medium, etc.) to represent an object. An artist, then, does not merely provide an exact copy of an object, but selectively constructs a coherent visual and felt setting in which to place the object of the work. And, truly valued artworks nearly always represent some universal human theme (e.g., love, yearly seasons, death, war, victory, defeat, motherhood, childhood, God, religion, etc.).

Plotinus, from a slightly different view, argued that representational art did not imitate the material world, but represented ideas and concepts. A sculptor carving a statue of Zeus does not represent a god-person, but the concept of power and majesty. Let us look at some examples.

The Gods represented in ancient Indian art were for devotional and instructive purposes. They acknowledge in us our divinity. The Ramayana describes Mainaka, a mountain prince and the son of Himavan, appearing in human form on his mountain peak in order to address Hanuman, the monkey God. One of the most striking examples is Himavan accompanied by his queen, Mena, giving his daughter, Uma, in marriage to Shiva (Sivaramamurti, 1977). Notice that they are surrounded by many spirits and relatives. These two are presented large and centered in the carving with others not fully carved in detail. Their value can be immediately realized.

Representational art includes religious and spiritual themes as well. The Lascaux cave paintings were as spiritual to early humanity as the Cathedral of Pisa was to medieval Italians.

Modern abstract art also may represent spiritual concepts (Conze, 1967; Craven, 1934). Reportedly, Helena Petrovna Blavatsky, co-founder of the Theosophical Society in New York, motivated a number of abstract artists to break new ground (Lipsey, 1988; Regier, 1987). For example, her influence on Wassily Kandinsky is apparent when reading his book, *Concerning the Spiritual in Art* (1982). For him and other artists of the time, Blavatsky and Theosophy brought "food in a time of famine." Recall science and philosophy of that time were deconstructing the authority of the church, as well as the concept of a universal Grand Design and Designer. The world, to many intellectuals, seemed to look like a mistake without purpose. And without purpose, there can be no grounding. Many promising artists across Europe and America were influenced by the "Ancient Wisdom," providing them a "path of inner wisdom." This inner wisdom was direct and not dependent on a religious bureaucracy and an intermediary deciding what was and what was not truth. Roger Lipsey (1988) went so far as to state that "without Cezanne and Theosophy, there would be no modern art."

Italian painters are not immune to representation, but are not known for it. For example, Tracey Emin exhibited a collection of material she called *My Bed*. It consisted of a rumpled, unmade, unadorned plain bed with white sheets and pillow case. Resting on the floor by the bed are various paraphernalia she used during the course of a represented week. There are several books strewn on the floor, a used bottle of vodka, as well as other bottles of various sizes and shapes, cigarette butts, condoms and handkerchiefs. She is representing her life in her art work. It is not special, holds no idealism, is not above or below a set cultural standard; it just is.

Formalistic Interpretation

From a formalistic perspective, artwork's meaning – usually unconscious – is found in the relationships between forms and patterns within the artwork itself. Theophile Gautier's phrase, "art for art's sake," written in the preface to *Mademoiselle de Maupin* (1835), describes this position (Malraux, 1953). Generally, the forms of an artwork are interpreted based on their "aesthetic" contributions, not just on personal, subjective likes or dislikes. And, aesthetic satisfaction is grounded in universal themes.

For example, both Kandinsky and Piet Mondrian were interested in C. W. Leadbeater's and Annie Besant's clairvoyant work with "thought forms" and expressed those forms in their paintings (Regier, 1987). Formal interpretation, then, is based upon the form elements within the artwork (e.g., lines, shapes, contrast, color, texture), as well as the organization of these form elements within the work (e.g., unity, balance, rhythm, proportion). Many computer graphics programs are able to display extremely pleasing abstract patterns of pixels, many based on specific complex mathematical functions. Huge amounts of formalistic study have been conducted on color, pattern, and size placements, showing that form appreciation is not just learned but actually is hardwired into the human genome. Certain patterns explained by geometry – for example, the golden mean – are observed in many natural structures, including sea shells, naturally-formed landscapes, and foliage patterns (Huntington, 1985).

Time Period (Historical) Interpretation

Time period interpretation acknowledges that many art works have been influenced by economic, political, social, cultural and religious occurrences that affected the artist making the work; that is, influences on the artist by forces outside of him/herself. For example, the Mahabhasha of Patanjali tells of the palaces build for Brahmanic deities like Rama and Kesava (Craven, 1997). There are many early inscriptions expressing salutations to Rama and Kesava in which Rama appears as a human with a single pair of arms and a turban on his head. This emphasizes the vulnerability felt by most ordinary citizens encountering their world. I wonder what his view would be in the opening years of the twenty-first century?

In the United States, Isaac Sayer's painting, the *Employment Agency* (1937), depicts the agony of the unknown felt by ordinary unemployed people, particularly during the hard economic times of the Great Depression. Sayer portrays the employment agency's waiting room as a place where downtrodden people enter initially hoping for a better future – a job – only to realize that bettering their situation is hopeless. The painting expresses vividly the anguish, depression and agonizing fear humans feel without a job, unwanted by the world.

The difficulties in pursuing an authentic spiritual path in a modern age are clearly expressed in Reginald Machell's painting, *The Path* (1895), which portrays the evolution of the human soul in aspiring to full spiritual self-consciousness (Blavatsky, 1979; Chaudhuri, 1965). The supreme condition of the soul is expressed in this work by the Great Figure, whose head, in the upper triangle, is lost in the glory of the sun above, and whose feet are in the waters of space, symbolizing spirit and matter in the lower triangle. His wings, filling the middle region of the painting, represent the motion or pulsation of cosmic life, while elements presented within an octagon portray the various planes of consciousness through which humanity must rise to attain perfection. Depicted are various motifs, including spiritual initiation, steadfastness, and one-pointedness, ever moving toward the master of one's being, the Soul. The path's difficulty is represented by the rocky trail, and the many obstacles that can arise to deflect one from one's path (laziness, lust, avarice, greed, etc.), by the slain dragon. Many individuals are shown to have fallen or been distracted from their path, but not the aspirant, who truly is "a spiritual warrior." Such a warrior will unceasingly pursue the "path" toward Self-realization, in spite of adversity in the world (Besant, 1972; DePurucker, 1935).

Intentional Interpretation

Intentional interpretation attempts to answer the question, "what was the artist's intention in creating the artwork?" Because, in many cases, the artist does not comment on his/her intention, it must be interpreted. It is, in a very real sense, an interpretation (viewer) of the artist's interpretation of his/her subject. Even if the artist does state a conscious intent, depth psychologists – Freudians and Jungians – claim the "real" intent of the artist is unconscious (Brenner, 1973). For them, artist intent must be uncovered through a psychological analysis of the artwork.

Intentionality presents itself at several levels: surface and deeper ones. The artist is aware (or can be, with a little introspection) of surface levels, as often is the viewer. Deeper intentions, however, are increasingly unconscious to the artist and, at some point, unknown, because of lack of self-awareness and the overt operation of psychological defence mechanisms.

The intent of an artist is certainly influenced by his/her life experiences, cultural and sub-cultural worldviews, various interpersonal relationships, and relationship with oneself. As depth psychologists report, one very effective way of interpreting artistic intent is to treat the artist's works (the artwork, personal writings, journal entries, etc.) as a dream. The interpretation can then be made, addressing levels (surface to deep) of awareness, and attempting to integrate them into a final and inclusive interpretation (Gadet, 1986). For example, if an artist has painted a couple picnicking by a stream on a bright, colorful spring day, the conscious intention of the painter may have been to depict a young couple as they fall in love, beginning a new relationship in a time of growth — spring. At a deeper (unconscious) level, the artist may have been expressing an experience s/he had with someone years ago and a hoped-for love that did or did not bloom.

However, care must be taken – interpretation can very quickly become a creation of "fantasy." It is important, then, that interpretation, particularly at a deep level, be *grounded* in reliable knowledge of both the artist's inner and outer life. And, as integral philosopher Ken Wilber (1995, 1996, 1997) has pointed out, in interpreting an artist's deep, unconscious intentions, one is faced with two issues. First, "is the proposed interpretation really true?" And, second, "if it is true, is it the whole truth or is it partial, concealing yet deeper truths?"

Often, artistic intent may be spiritual (Lipsey, 1988). For example, Paul Klee stated that an artist is expressing the deepest, most secret place within, where the primal power resides. In 1939, he painted a work entitled *Omphalo-Centric Lecture*, a visualization of his thoughts and insights about life. The abstract figure in the painting faces the viewer and holds in its hand a glowing navel that represents the divine light from whence all knowledge comes. The navel also symbolizes the womb, birth, creation and the continuity of life. Although much of the artistic expression originates from the artist's personality, glimpses of their Soul's intent can be intuited.

Much more likely in today's art circles, an artist wishes to transgress established norms of art. They tend to test and challenge shared cultural values of morals, laws, society, and art, itself. Some clearly focus on the absolute defiance of shared values in other ways. I do not know if this happens in India, but in the United States, I remember the metal-covered "sex" book by Madonna. While some argued Madonna had something to say, others said the quality was so bad, it would have been better to have had monkeys do the type-setting. But nevertheless, the life style of bondage, sadism, and masochism are there; they are real and present. So are the horrors of protracted cancer, and the pain and disfigurement it wreaks upon its victims before they die. And the massive injustices people incur in life, while some are born with silver spoons, never really having to do anything to contribute. Instead, they take and use whatever and whenever they choose. Others work hard to advance their lot, but find it gets them nowhere.

Viewer Response Interpretation

The viewer obviously contributes to art interpretation. Viewer responses contain multiple levels of interpretation, both surface (conscious) and deep (unconscious). The vast majority of viewer response interpretation requires that a viewer be "competent" in art evaluation. Competent viewers often compare the works of an artist to his/her other works and those of other artists, as well as interpret the "cultural" message of the work. Viewer responses traditionally are not "naive" responses based on one's likes or dislikes. But this cannot be entirely so, because viewers have power and influence over artists, in that they buy the art. Andy Warhol picked this up right away. He stated in his magazine interview that "business art is the step that comes after art. I started as a commercial artist, and I want to finish as a business artist. After I did the thing called "art," or whatever it is called, I went into business art. I wanted to be an Art Businessman or a Business Artist." Warhol concluded "being good at business is the most fascinating art."

In my opinion, a method I term the "authentic" viewer interpretation seems to be the most useful. It is based on one's own subjective impressions. Although each of us responds to art through the lens of our culture, we also have our own views and perceptions, resulting in a wholly individual interpretation. For example, Edvard Munch's *The Scream* (1893) represents to me at a surface level the tremendous amount of pain, suffering, and cruelty found in the world. However, through Jungian dream interpretation and guided imagery, I discovered a deeper response level that tapped memories of experiences I had during combat as a Marine infantryman in the Vietnam war. At this deeper level, the bridge or walkway upon which Munch's screaming person stands represents to me the "conveyor belt" on which I rode. I had no control over what battles I fought, whether I was killed, wounded, hurt, alone, etc. The "conveyor belt" took me where it wanted. The red, fiery sky in the artwork represents the red-orange glow of the mortar-flares we sent up to illuminate the areas beyond our trenches, the fire zones, the more easily to shoot attacking Viet Cong or North Vietnamese Army Regulars. The screaming person represents me, bent, overwhelmed, terrified with eyes wide open, having seen too much death at the age of 20.

Let us spend more time on postmodern interpretation and consider that there may be no real art interpretation, because any attempt to interpret the painting (signs) leads only to sliding constructed signifiers forever – i.e., deconstruction. In this view, art interpretation is meaningless. Like everything else, it is just an event.

While this is a popular and radical interpretation of postmodern deconstruction, I cannot find in Derrida and Foucault's writings that meaninglessness is not their position. Their actual presentations are that no signifier – painting, sculpture – can completely represent – signify – its subject. There is always something left out and something more to reveal. Art, like the map of a territory – no matter how detailed – can never completely encompass that territory, and hence, can never be completely interpreted. Certain key structures of the art piece – a smile, a form, a pattern, a depiction of torment or suspicion, or a pastoral setting – is what points to the meaning, and this must be interpreted – always partial, never complete. Meaning in art, like meaning in language, depends on signs or codes a viewer recognizes and makes sense of, interprets. The art structures – signifiers – represent meaning through recognition of the signified by the viewer, an unavoidably incomplete interpretation. Interpretations are rooted in shared signs or referents. But a referent, say, a smile, is not enough to portray meaning; a context is also required, one that builds a relationship between the rest of the artwork's components. Context, imitative or expressive, includes form (flowing, angular, diagonals, vertical-horizontal lines, scale) and colors, in their many variations of brightness, hue, apposition. Each and all of these variables provide cues for individual viewer interpretation. And where this is authentic interpretation, there forms a relationship between the viewer's being in the world and the art piece.

An Integral Perspective

In the United States, things tend not to be integrated for most individuals. Sociology is not related to science; feelings are different from thoughts. This is a horrible mistake, and perhaps it can be remedied by a country like India that can bring unrelated things to integration.

In order to better and more completely interpret the meaning(s) of visual art (painting, drawing, sculpture, wood carvings, and photography), it is important to have an integral way of organizing and perceiving its multiple dimensions. Art interpretation processes, like other integral processes, have both whole and part aspects. A specific artwork is "a part" of a larger whole, the culture of shared values, as well as the social setting of the world-at-large. Both subjective and objective components are common to the whole and the parts. A specific artwork medium consists of stone, paint, wood, bronze, etc. The artwork, itself, is a physical (objective) depiction of the artist's intention (subjective). The whole consists of a social setting in the "objective" world, as well as the subjective domain of culturally shared values. And, finally, for each whole/part, subjective and objective, there is a histographic "time-line" component.

These phenomena can be presented in a quadrant model. Recall, no quadrant dimension (objective, subjective, unit, and whole) in this model can be completely reduced to any other dimension, and each dimension is of importance equal to the others, as well as interrelated with and connected to them. The quadrant model, then, applied to art criticism and interpretation contains five dimensions (Figure 2).

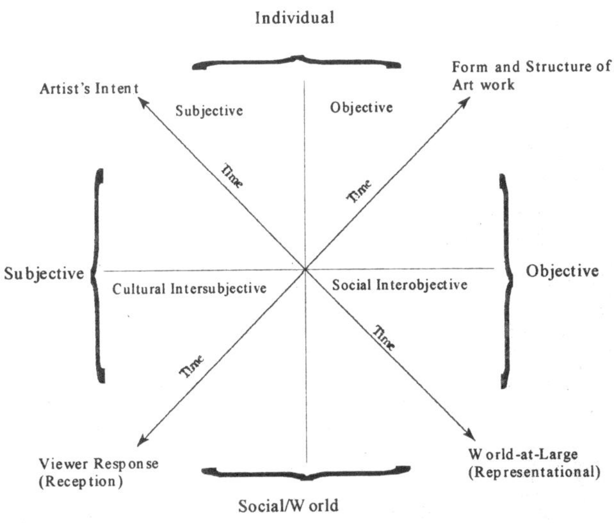

Figure 2. Quadrant Model with Historical Time Dimension

The quadrant model, with a histographic time dimension, provides the five-dimensional perspective by which to understand and interpret art in an integrated way. The dimensions include the representational view of the world, both real and imaginary (lower right quadrant), the artwork itself (upper right quadrant), the artist's intent in creating the work (upper left quadrant), and the viewer's response to the artwork (lower left quadrant). Within each quadrant, the diagonal line represents historical influences over time. Let us now look more closely at these five dimensions.

World-at-Large (Lower Right Quadrant)

The world-at-large is the domain of representational art interpretation. As previously discussed, the artwork portrays some "thing" found or imagined in or about the objective world. This dimension, an objective one, can represent a specific scene or "snapshot" of a portion of the world. However, it can just as easily represent a universal theme such as family, death, war, love, sickness, etc. Artwork that stands the passage of time and continues to be valued, more than likely, represents a universal theme easily identified by viewers.

Form and Structure of the Art Work (Upper Right Quadrant)

This dimension, the "Formalistic Interpretation" dimension, interprets art for art's sake. Here, the main value is the artwork's form, including elements such as the lines, shapes, contrast, light and dark, color and texture that compose the work, and how these are physically organized (e.g., unity, plane, balance, rhythm, tension, space and proportion).

Artist's Intent (Upper Left Quadrant)

Artist's intent, or "Expressive Interpretation," has already been discussed. But it is important to realize that, like all humans, the artist is influenced by his/her life experiences and reactions to them – psychological growth, long-term frustrations and traumatic events, emotional sensitivity, religious feelings, age-wisdom, etc. Each of these facets influences, in a combined way, the artist's intent, both consciously and unconsciously. Because artist intent cannot be known directly by a viewer, it must be interpreted. Through background research, one can ground one's interpretation in facts, but one can never be sure that the interpretation is the whole truth. There can always be deeper, unconscious intentions left undiscovered. Of particular importance in this type of interpretive practice are the depth psychologies of Jung (Analytic Psychology) and Freud (Psychoanalysis). However, not all interpretations stem from depth; some are from "height," or spiritual influences (Aurobindo, 1971; Lipsey, 1988; Regier, 1987).

Viewer Response (Lower Left Quadrant)

Finally, as previous discussed, viewers contribute to art interpretation collectively and are greatly influenced by the "shared values" of scholars and art critics (Eco, 1979; Hirsch, 1976; Hoy, 1978). All viewer art interpretations are colored by such shared values – cultural influences and personal bias – and viewers cannot and do not respond to artwork without these (Selden, 1988). However, the viewer's experiences, likes, dislikes, psychological make-up, sensitivity, level of cognitive/ moral development, and other personal particularities, can particularly color subjective valuing. For the most part, viewer responses are bound within their interpretation of their being relative to cultural shared values, beliefs, ideologies, worldviews, and expectations. As existential philosopher Hans-George Gadamer stated, we, as life participants, viewers, cannot impartially view life events or symbols without the enmeshing of our human condition, nor the temporality of our human existence.

Time Period Influence s (45° Onward-moving Time Lines in Each Quadrant)

As previous discussed, time period influences — political, cultural, social, scientific and spiritual phenomena— affect the artist's presentation. Because there are four quadrants, there are four moving time lines affecting the qualities of each quadrant. Each of the time lines, except the viewer response, must be "calibrated." That is, they must be matched to one another. For example, looking at Figure 3, and using the quadrant model to interpret Van Gogh's *The Rectory Garden in the Winter* (1884), one must adopt a perspective in each quadrant consistent with the 1884 period.

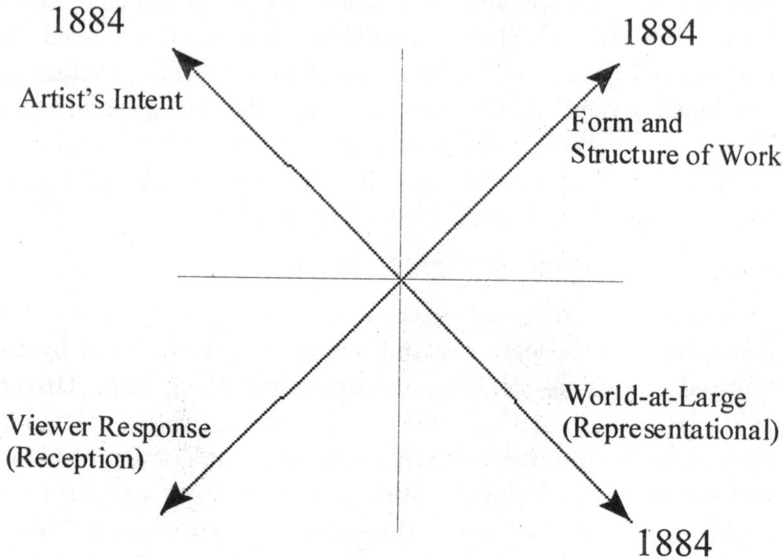

Figure 3. Quadrant Model of Interpreting

The Rectory Garden in the Winter

What was Van Gogh's experience prior to this time period, and what was he attempting to present in this drawing at that specific time (upper left quadrant)? What type of formal structures had evolved at a time period within the artist's cultural purview (upper right quadrant)? What was occurring in the world-at-large, as reported by historians of the day? What political, socio-economic, scientific and/or religious influences are at work in this piece (lower right quadrant)? And, finally, what is the viewer's perception of the work based on present cultural worldviews (lower right quadrant)? Remember that this is 2008, the viewer can "act as if" s/he were a nineteenth century viewer and try to determine how the work would have been received in that time period from a cultural perspective. More than likely, there are available historical texts that can be of assistance in this "retrospective" evaluation process. Of course, viewer reception need not be one or the other, "then" or "now;" it can be a combination of both "then" and "now."

Conclusion

To understand art more fully, to allow it to speak to us, to reveal its soul, to appreciate its enchantment and its magic, requires that we reframe art interpretation from one dimension to multiple dimensions. As T. S. Eliot (1963) wrote:

"We shall not cease from exploration

And the end of all our exploring

Will be to arrive where we started

And know that [artistic] place for the first time."

REFERENCES

Abrams, M. H. (1953). *The mirror and the lamp*. New York: Oxford University Press.

Aurobindo. (1971). *The foundations of Indian culture*. Pondicherry, India: Sri Aurobindo Ashram.

Besant, A. (1972). *The ancient wisdom*. Adyar, Madras, India: Theosophical Publishing House.

Blavatsky, H. P. (1979). *The secret doctrine*. 3 vol. Adyar, Madras, India: Theosophical Publishing House.

Brenner C. (1973). *An elementary textbook of psychoanalysis*, Revised ed. Madison, CT: International University.

Campbell, J (1959). *The masks of god: Primitive mythology*. New York: Viking.

Chaudhuri, H. (1965). *Integral yoga*. London: George Allen & Unwin.

Conze, E. (1967). *Buddhist thought in India*. Ann Arbor: University of Michigan Press.

Cranston, S. (1993). *H.P.B.* New York: Tarcher/Putnam.

Craven, R. C. (1997). *Indian art: A concise history*, Revised ed. New York: Thanes & Hudson.

Craven, T. (1934). *Modern art*. New York: Simon & Schuster.

DePurucker, G. (1935). *The esoteric tradition*. 2 vols. Pasadena, CA: Theosophical University Press.

Eco, U. (1979). *The role of the reader*. Bloomington: Indiana University Press.

Eliade, M. (1964). *Shamanism*. Princeton: Princeton University Press.

Eliot, T. S. (1963). *Collected poems: 1909-1962*. New York: Harcourt Brace Jovanovich.

Frye, N. (1957). *Anatomy of criticism*. Princeton: Princeton University Press.

Gadet, F. (1986). *Sassure and contemporary culture*. London, UK: Century Hutchinkson LTD.

Gardiner, H. (1996). *Gardiner's art through the ages*, 10th ed. New York: Harcourt Brace.

Gebser, J. (1985). *The ever-present origin*. Athens: Ohio University Press.

Hamilton, E., & Cairns, H. (1963). *Plato: The collected dialogues*, Bollinger Series LXXI. Princeton: Princeton University Press.

Heidegger, M. (1962). *Being and time*. New York: Harper Collins.

Hirsch, E. D. (1976). *The aims of interpretation*. Chicago: University of Chicago Press.

Hoy, D. C. (1978). *The critical circle*. Berkeley: University of California Press.

Huntington, S. L. (1985). *The art of ancient India*: New York: Weatherhill.

Jung, C. G. (1964). *Man and his symbols*. New York: Doubleday.

Kandinsky, W. C. (1982). *Concerning the spiritual in art*. New York: DeCapo.

Lipsey, R. (1988). *An art of our own*. Boston: Shambhala.

Malraux, A. (1953). *The voices of silence*. Garden City: NY: Doubleday.

Neumann, E. (1973). *The origins and history of consciousness*. Princeton: Princeton University Press.

Newton, K. M. (1990). *Interpreting text*. New York: St. Martins.

Paulson, D. S. (2005). *Interpreting Indian and Chinese art: A multiple perspective*. Wales, England: Warnborough University.

Regier, K. (1987). *The spiritual image in modern art*. Wheaton, IL: Theosophical Publishing House.

Richter, G. (1985). *Art and human consciousness*. Spring Valley, NY: Anthroposophic Press.

Scholes, (1982). *Semiotics and interpretation.* New Haven, CT: Yale University Press.

Selden, R. (1988). *The theory of criticism from Plato to the present.* Essex, England: Longman House.

Sivaramamamurti, C. (1977). *The art of India.* New York: Harry N. Abrams, Inc.

Toynbee, A. (1995). *A study of history.* New York: Barnes & Noble.

Wilber, K. (1995). *Sex, ecology, spirituality.* Boston: Shambhala.

Wilber, K. (1996). *A brief history of everything.* Boston: Shambhala.

Wilber, K. (1997). *The eye of spirit.* Boston: Shambhala.

22

Physical Education in Enhancing Health-Related Fitness : A Malaysian Perspective

Shabeshan Rengasamy

The status of health-related fitness among the American population is not very satisfactory (Corbin, 1987; U.S Department of Health and Human Services 1996[USDHHS]. Many educators and experts believe that being physically inactive is one of the reasons for being overweight, thus attributing to risk factors for cardiovascular diseases among the adult population thus contributing to health problems among the population (Blair et al., 1989; Blair et al., 1996; Young & Steinhardt, 1995; USDHHS, 1996). In a developed country like United States, more than 60% of the adult population is not regularly active and 25% of the adult population is totally physically inactive (USDHHS, 1996).

In Malaysia, latest trend reflect that cardiovascular mortality which was the third cause of death in the 1950's, became the number one killer in the country since the 1970's through the middle of the 1990's (Ministry of Health, Malaysia, 1995). In 1989, mortality rate of cardiovascular disease increased to 16.5 times from 1.8% in 1950 to 29.6% in 1989 (Khoo, Tan & Khoo, 1991). The mortality incidence of cardiovascular disease, which is ranked first with reference to total death from 1985 to 1994, is coronary heart disease (Ministry of Health, Malaysia, 1995). This is due to the fact that many Malaysians are not engaging in any physical activity and further they do not have the knowledge to translate the health-related fitness concepts into practice (Jayamalar, 1991; Khoo et al., 2000). Studies in Malaysia have indicated that, population under study have showed risk factors to cardiovascular diseases and a decline in health-related fitness components (Arjunan, 2007; Arokiasamy & Gan, 1995; Lim et al. 2000; Kasmini et al. 1997 Khoo et al.1991; Khoo et al. 2000; Rengasamy 2003; 2008). They further add that, the occurrence of the disease and the decline of health-related fitness components are due to the fact of improved socio-economic status and the changing life style of the population. To a large extent, it reflects the emerging trend in a developing country, but one should not stop blaming the developing trends alone that contribute to the alarming statistics on health status of our population in our country. One has to go beyond this, by tackling the root cause of the problem that many are not actively engaging themselves in any physical activity due to the fact, many lack the knowledge on fitness and its importance to individuals (Jayamalar, 1991; Khoo et al., 2000).

In Malaysia, one of the objectives of physical education is to educate and enhance health-related fitness among the school population. These health-related fitness components are enhanced through teaching of games skills (Ministry of Education, 1998). Keeping in view of this problem, the present author intends to look into the role of health-related fitness among the Malaysian school population. In this chapter, author specifically addresses the question of what health-related fitness and its components, the importance of it, the current trend of teaching health-related fitness in Malaysia and the role of physical education in overcoming the present health problems in the country.

Health Related Fitness

Physical fitness is defined as the capacity of the heart, blood vessels, lungs and muscles to function at optimum efficiency (Pate, 1993). The above definition covers a broad area as with greater emphasis in performance related fitness. But health-related fitness in the present context refers to the physical and the physiological components of fitness that impact more directly on health status of the individual. According to Bouchard

(1990), health-related fitness refers to the state of physical and physiological characteristics that define the risk levels for the premature development of disease or morbidity conditions presenting a relationship with sedentary mode of life. In addition, having good state of physical and physiological state enhances the ability of the individual to carry out daily activities with vigor without undue fatigue, and have enough energy to enjoy leisure time pursuit (MaClynn, 1993). Health-related fitness include the physiological functions of the body that protects the individual from sedentary life style. Health-related fitness concerns with the physiological make up that offers some protection to coronary heart disease associated with being overweight, a variety of muscle and joint ailments and physiological complications to our response to stress (Blair et al., 1989; Cooper et al., 1976). The components of health-related fitness are cardio respiratory endurance, muscle strength and endurance, flexibility and percentage of body fat.

Cardio respiratory endurance refers to the ability of an individual to deliver oxygen and nutrients to all the vital organs and the working muscles during an exercise period. (Fox,1996). The greater the ability to deliver 0xygen to the working muscles, the higher is the cardio respiratory fitness level. Cardio respiratory endurance involves the circulatory system that includes the heart, lungs, the vessels and the blood. To improve the cardio respiratory system, one must perform continuous activity at least fifteen minutes at a frequency of three times a week at the required target heart rate (American College of Sport Medicine [ACSM], 1998).

Muscular strength is defined as the maximum force produced when a muscle group is activated to overcome any resistance or overload and muscular endurance is the ability of the group to exert any force over a period of time (Wescott, 1995). Muscular strength is essential for individual, as they need to carry out a variety of daily activities. Muscle strength is a relative factor but some argue that minimum strength is needed by all individuals (Faigenbaum, Milliken, Loud, & Burak, 2002; Fox.1996; McGlynn, 1993; Wescott, 1995). To develop strength, one must employ resistance type of training using either weights or any form of resistance with lower repetitions and the development is governed by the intensity of the exercise or activity. As for muscular endurance it can be developed through proper weight training with a moderate workload with higher repetitions (Faigenbaum et al., 2002; McGlynn 1993; Plowman & Smith 1997; Wescott 1995)

Flexibility is a measure of the ability to move a joint through its normal range of motion (Howley, 2001). Flexibility is not only important to high performance athletes but also to general population and among school population (Faigenbaum, 2002). A decrease in flexibility may limit joint movement and may lead to an injury to the individual (Faigenbaum et al., 2002; Wescott, 1995).

Body composition or percentage of fat typically describes the amount of fat relative to the body mass (Howley, 2001). A recommended proportion of body fat for man is approximately is 12-17 percent; and for woman is in region of 19-24 percent (MaGlynn, 1993).

Health benefits mentioned above can be stimulated through a safe and progressive application of training principles (MarArdle et al. 1996; Plowman & Smith 1997; Pollock et al., 1995). Although higher intensities may be associated with rapid improvements in health benefits, but a combination of moderate intensity with longer duration or increased frequency do elicit comparable health benefits (ACSM, 1998; Fox, 1996; MacArdle et al.,1996; Plowman & Smith, 1997).

Principles of Training

Exercise is defined as 'a single acute bout of bodily exertion or muscular activity that requires an expenditure of energy above the resting level and generally results in voluntary movements' (Plowman & Smith, 1997, p5). Exercise is planned, structured and repetitive bodily movements, which are performed to improve or maintain health fitness. Researchers in exercise physiology studied exercise routines in controlled experiments applying training principles of intensity, duration and frequency to adaptations and benefits among individuals. The improvement of an individual's cardio respiratory system depends on the sound application these training principles (MacArdle et al. 1996; Plowman & Smith, 1997; Howley, 2001; ACSM, 1998).

ACSM (1998), with scientific evidence, recommended that to elicit any measurable training effect on the physiological system, intensity or the exercise bout should be at least 60%-90% heart rate maximum (HR_{Max}), with a duration of 20 – 30 minutes of continuous activity, exercising three times a week. Intensity is the stress or the load that stresses the individual's cardio respiratory system in an exercise bout; frequency is the number of sessions per week; and duration is the number of minutes the activity or exercise is carried out (Plowman & Smith, 1997).

Benefits of Health-Related Fitness

The components of health-related fitness play a vital role in improving personal health among the population. If engaged in regular physical activities, with proper intensity, duration and frequency, the benefits one receives are that it makes the heart stronger and more efficient in pumping blood out (MacArdle et al., 1996; Plowman & Smith, 1997; Scheuer & Tipton, 1977). A stronger heart improves coronary circulation and this decreases the chance of heart attack. In addition, it would lower the blood pressure by expanding to more capillaries and acts as a strong resistance to atherosclerosis (hardening of the arterial wall). Further regular exercise also reduces body fat and increased lean body mass which indirectly improves personal appearance (Ratliff & Ratliff, 1994). Another important aspect is that regular exercise would improve muscular strength and endurance which acts to resist fatigue (Wescott, 1995). On the whole, if the population is exercising, risk factors to heart diseases and other health-related diseases would be lowered and health status of the population would be enhanced and further lowering medical cost in the country (Jayamalar, 1991).

Current Trends in Malaysia

The benefits of regular exercise are well documented. But the current statistical figures available in the country show that the mortality rate locally in relation to cardiovascular disease is alarming (Ministry of Health, 1995; 2005). One has to critically analyze the local data to draw the conclusion that the level of health-related fitness and the knowledge among the local population are not at a satisfactory level (Arjunan, 2007; Balakrishnan, 2003 Jayamalar, 1991; Khoo et al.2000; Rengasamy, 2003; 2006; 2008; Singh, 2005). The problem of low fitness level in our country is further compounded by electronic conveniences and the automation that came by due to modern technology which avoided physical activity. Malaysia has developed from a third world country in the 60's to a developing nation in the 1990's. With that came along the conveniences of life and it has given a new way of life to most Malaysians. Malaysians have become more sedentary due to the nature of the job and this has increased the health problems in the country (Jayamalar, 1991; Ministry of Health, 1995; 2005). Compounded further, as some experts believe, is that the type of life style Malaysian lead. This indirectly reflects to the type of education and especially the type of physical education one underwent during the schooling years (Jayamalar, 1991; Khoo et al., 2000; Rengasamy, 2008). Data indicate low mean scores for cardiovascular endurance and other health-related fitness components among Malaysian school going children (Arjunan, 2007; Balakrishnan, 2003; Rengasamy, 2006; 2008; Singh, 2005; Sinnapan, 2006). One of reasons put forward for the decline among Malaysian school population is the reduction of frequency of teaching the subject in schools.

In Malaysia, the total time allocated for physical education is 80 minutes a week and is divided into two 40 minutes sessions carried out on alternate days (Ministry of Education, 1989). In practice, most schools in the country carry out their physical education classes in a reduced frequency of once a week for a total of 80 minutes due to the introduction of flexi-timetable in 1996 by the Ministry of education (Rengasamy, 2002). Since most schools in the country carry out their physical education classes once a week and this is a direct contrast to the minimum training principles of 2 or 3 times a week as suggested by ACSM (1998). Studies abroad using different frequencies have reported that training less than 2 days a week does not generally result in a meaningful increase in cardiovascular endurance (Gettman et al., 1976; Shepherd, 2001; Wenger & Bell, 1988) Studies conducted locally at the school environment implementing once a week of physical education schedule, have also reported similar findings (Arjunan 2007; Balakrishnan, 2003; Rengasamy 2003, 2006; 2008; Sinappan, 2006).

The teaching of physical education in Malaysian schools should comply with the minimum standard outlined by ACSM (1998). If physical education programs are effective in Malaysian schools, students would have received the message of health benefits and engage in regular exercise to keep healthy. Children need to know about fitness and understand the concepts of fitness (Ratliff & Ratliff, 1994). By understanding health fitness concepts early in life that is through physical education, then they would develop attitudes to value fitness, which indirectly would lead to a healthy life style (Dennison et al., 1998).

Importance of Teaching Physical Education

Getting students engaged in fitness activities incorporated with health concepts should be part of health and physical education programs in schools. This approach is important, as the subject does teach health-related activities and learning experiences incorporated through the learning of sports skills. By doing so it would improve health-related components of the students and at the same time students have fun in the learning environment. A strong push for health-related fitness is important, as we know that the health benefits that we derive from fitness activities. Physical education is the only subject that offers and provides the learning experiences of fitness and the knowledge of health concepts in physical education. It is the subject that prepares and gives practical knowledge of maintaining good health for the future (Corbin, 1987; Jayamalar, 1999; Ratliff & Ratliff, 1994).

At present little importance is given to the subject in Malaysian schools. The reduced frequency of teaching the subject, allowing untrained teachers in the field to teach the subject and poor implementation of the program as a whole has led to the decline of health-related fitness levels (Arjunan, 2007;

Rashid, 1994; Rengasamy 2006; 2008; Singh 2005; Sinnapan, 2005)

School administrators and physical educators should play a vital role in promoting quality physical education programs and ensure effective teaching and implementation of the subject. There should be proper time allotment, sufficient frequency and trained teachers should be placed in the teaching of the subject. These teachers can translate educational goals in an operational manner using effective instructional methodologies. By doing so at an early age, attitudes can be modified and there is a strong chance these positive attitudes could have a strong carry over effect (Dennison et al., 1998). As we know, good health is the ultimate goal, but one has to know the process to attain it.

Conclusion

In conclusion, Malaysian health status is in the decline. On the other hand, improved health status especially health-related fitness reduces the risk factors of coronary heart disease and other related illness indirectly reduces health problems in the country. Health-related fitness concepts should be taught in Malaysian physical education classes and it is the only subject that plays an important role in improving health-related fitness. Students ought to be told of the benefits of health- related fitness components and why they should maintain a certain level of fitness. By imparting the knowledge of health fitness, students would be able to plan their own fitness activities or programs and even carry out these activities outside school environment as this would achieve the nation's goal of healthy nation.

REFERENCES

Abdul Rashid Salleh (1994). The physical education curriculum in Malaysia.

Unpublished master's thesis, University of Manchester, England.

American Academy of Pediatrics. (2001). Strength training by children and adolescents. *Pediatrics, 107*(6), 1470-1472.

American College of Sports Medicine [ACSM]. (1998). Position stand: The recommendedquantity and quality of exercise for developing and maintaining cardiorespiratory and muscular fitness and flexibility in healthy adults. *Medicine and Science in Sports & Exercise. 22*, 265-274.

American Heart Association. (1992). American Heart Association Council on Clinical cardiology Committee on Exercise and cardiac Rehabilitation. Statement of Exercise: Benefits and recommendation for physical activity programs for all Americans: A statement for health professionals. *Circulation, 86*, 340-344.

Arjunan, R.(2007). Effectiveness of circuit training towards cardiovascular endurance among Form One students. Unpublished master's thesis, University of Malaya, Kuala Lumpur, Malaysia.

Arokiasamy, J. T., and Gan, C.Y. (1985). A blood pressure profile of Malaysians 12 Years and above in a rural community. *Journal of Malaysian Health,* 5(2), 17-24.

Balakrishnan. M. (2003). The Impact of 80 Minutes Physical Education a week in enhancing Health Related fitness Among School Children. Unpublished master's thesis. University of Malaya, Kuala Lumpur, Malaysia

Bouchard C. (1990). *Exercise, fitness and health: The consensus statement.* (Ed). pp. 3-28. Champaign, IL:Human Kinetic.

Blair, S., Kempert, J., Kohl, H. Balow, C., Macera, C. Paffenbarger, R., & Gibbons, L. (1996). Influences of cardiorespiratory fitness and other precursors on cardiovascular disease and all-cause mortality in men and women. *JAMA*, 276, 205-210.

Blair, S.N. Kohl, H.W., Paffenbarger, R.S, Clark, D.G., Cooper, K.H., & Gibbons, L.W. (1989). Physical fitness and all cause mortality: A prospective study of healthy men and women. *JAMA*:262, 2395-2401.

Cooper, K. H, Purdy, J, G., Friedman, A., Bohannon, R. L., & Arrends, J. A.1975). An aerobic conditioning program for the Fort Worth, Texas School district. *Research Quarterly,* 46, 345-350.

Corbin, C.B. (1987). Youth fitness, exercise and health: There is much to be done. *Research Quarterly for Exercise and Sports, 58* (4), 308-314.

Dennison, B., Straus, J., Mellits, D., & Charney, E. (1988). Childhood physical fitness test: Predictor of adult physical activity level? *Pediatrics,* 82(3), 324-329.

Faigenbaum, A. D., Milliken, L.A., Loud, R.L., & Burak B.T. (2002).

Comparison of 1 and 2 days per week of strength training in children. *Research Quarterly for Exercise and Sport, 73*, 416-424.

Fox, E. L. (1996). *Sports physiology*. 3rd. ed. CBS College Publishing.

Howley, E.T. (2001). Absolute verses relative intensity of physical activity in a dose response context. *Medicine and Science in Sports & Exercise,* 33(6), 298-302.

Jayamalar. R. (1991). Coronary artery disease in Malaysia: A Perspective. *Medical Journal of Malaysia*, 46(1),1-6.

Kasmini, K., Idris., M. N., Fatimah, A., Hanafiah, S., Iran, H., & Asmah Bee, M. (1997). Prevalence of overweight and obese school children aged between 7-16 years amongst the 3 major ethnic groups in Kuala Lumpur, Malaysia. *Asia Pacific Journal of Clinical Nutrition, 6*(3), 172-174.

Khoo, K.L., Tan, H., & Khoo, T.H. (1991). Cardiovascular mortality in peninsular Malaysia: 1950-1989. *Medical Journal of Malaysia, 2,* 11-17

Khoo, K.L., Tan, H., Liew, Y, M., Sambhi, J. S., Aljafri, A. M., & Hatijah, A. (2000). Blood pressure, body mass index, heart rate and levels of blood cholesterol and glucose of volunteers during national heart week, 1995-1997. *Med. J. Malaysia,* 55(4), 506-509.

Lim, T.O., Ding, L. M., Zaki, M., Suleiman, A. B., Kew, S. T., Ismail. M., et al. (2000). Distribution of blood total cholesterol in a national sample of Malaysian adults. *Medical Journal of Malaysia,* 55(4),476-79.

MacArdle, W. D., Katch, F. I., & Katch, V. I. (1996). *Exercise physiology, energy, nutrition and human performance.* Philadelphia: Lea.

McKenzie, T. L., Marshall, S. L., Sallis, J. F., & Conway, T. L. (2000). Student activity levels, lesson content, and teacher behaviour during middle school physical education. *Research Quarterly for Exercise and Sport, 71*, 249-259.

McGlynn, G. (1993). *Dynamics of physical fitness, A practical approach* (3rd.). Dubuque, Iowa: WCB Brown and Benchmark publishers.

Ministry of Education, Malaysia, (1998). *Form four syllabus for physical education. Curriculum development center*: Kuala Lumpur, Malaysia.

Ministry of Health, Malaysia, (1995). *Annual report*. Kuala Lumpur, Ministry of Health.

Ministry of Health, Malaysia, (2005). *Annual report*. Kuala Lumpur, Ministry of Health.

Pangrazi, P., & Darst, P. W. (1991). *Dynamic physical education forsecondary school students: Curriculum and instruction* (2nd edn). New York: Macmillian.

Pate, R.R. (1993). A new definition of youth fitness. *Physical and Sports Medicine,* 11(4), 77-88.

Plowman, S.A., & Smith, J. (1997). *Exercise physiology for health fitness and performance*. Allyn & Bacon.

Ratliff, T., & Ratliff, L. (1994). *Teaching children fitness: Becoming a master teacher,* Champaign, IL: Human Kinetics.

Rengasamy, S. (2002). The frequency of conducting physical education in secondary schools. [Unpublished raw data].

Rengasamy, S. (2003). The impact of four exercises in a form of a circuit towards some health related measures among college students. Chapter Presented at *The 4th. International Congress of Health Physical Education Recreation Sport and Dance* (ICHPER.SD – ASIA CONGRESS), Bangkok, Thailand, 20-23, March.

Rengasamy, S. (2006). The effect of regular physical education towards cardiovascular endurance. *Journal of Education, 26*, 61-70.

Rengasamy, S. (2008). *The effect of a physical fitness intervention program on health-related fitness components among Malaysian Form four students* Unpublished doctoral thesis, University of Malaya, Kuala Lumpur.

Scheuer, J. & Tipton, C. M. (1977). Cardiovascular adaptations to physical training *Annual Review of physiology,* 39, 221-251.

Singh, M. (2005). *The effect of an intervention program on the health related physical fitness of lower secondary school boys.* Unpublished doctoral thesis, University Science Malaysia, Kelantan.

Shephard, R. J. (2001). Absolute versus relative intensity of physical activity in a dose-response context. *Medicine & Science in Sports & Exercise,* 33(6), S400-418.

Sinnapan, R. (2006). Effectiveness of an intervention program on physical fitness among primary school children. Unpublished master's thesis, University of Malaya, Kuala Lumpur..

U.S. Department of Health and Human Services [USDHHS], (1996). *Physical activity and health: A report of the surgeon general.* Atlanta, GA: USA..

Wenger, H. A., & Bell, G. J. (1986). The intractions of intensity, frequency and duration of exercise training in altering cardiorespiratory fitness. *Sports Medicine,* 3, 346-356.

Westcott, W. (1995). *Strength fitness: Physiological principles and training techniques* (4th ed.). Dubuque, IL: Brown.

Young, D. R., & Steinhardt, M. A. (1995). The importance of physical fitness versus physical activity for coronary artery disease risk factors: A cross–sectional analysis. *Research Quarterly For Exercise and Sports, 64*(4), 377-384.

23

Educating Community Through Social Capital

S.A. Shahab

Introduction

Harvard political science professor Robert Putnam in his study on "civic engagement", a survey of 26,200 people in 40 American communities, summarized his findings in his best-selling book *Bowling Alone* (2000), that multiculturalism does not make vibrant communities but defensive ones. In other words, in ethnically diverse communities there is a decrease in trust and cooperation. This was not only counter-intuitive but rather explosive, according to Putnam, especially in light of efforts by the US government and civic groups to create a more tolerant ethnically diverse but integrated plural society. Putnam was horrified when he began receiving hundreds of e-mails from "racists and anti-immigrant activists" congratulating and applauding him for speaking on their behalf. So Putnam is engaged in a world-wide project to develop proposals to compensate for the negative effects of diversity, through his social capital community benchmark surveys. THE SAGUARO SEMINAR: CIVIC ENGAGEMENT IN AMERICA is an ongoing initiative of *Professor Robert D. Putnam* at the *John F. Kennedy School of Government* at *Harvard University*. The project focuses on expanding what we know about our levels of trust and community engagement and on developing strategies and efforts to increase this engagement.]

What Does "Social Capital" Mean?

The central premise of social capital is that social networks have value. Social capital refers to the collective value of all "social networks" [who people know] and the inclinations that arise from these networks to do things for each other ["norms of reciprocity"]. Social capital refers to those stocks of social trust, norms and networks that people can draw upon to solve common problems. Networks of civic engagement, such as neighborhood associations, sports clubs, and cooperatives, are an essential form of social capital, and the denser these networks, the more likely that members of a community will cooperate for mutual benefit. Social capital is productive, since two farmers exchanging tools can get more work done with less physical capital; rotating credit associations can generate pools of financial capital for increased entrepreneurial activity; and job searches can be more efficient if information is embedded in social networks. Social capital also tends to cumulate when it is used, and be depleted when not, thus creating the possibility of both virtuous and vicious cycles that manifest themselves in highly civic and uncivic communities.

By analogy with notions of physical capital and human capital—tools and training that enhance individual productivity—the core idea of social capital theory is that social networks have value. Just as a screwdriver (physical capital) or a college education (human capital) can increase productivity (both individual and collective), so too social contacts affect the productivity of individuals and groups. Whereas physical capital refers to physical objects and human capital refers to properties of individuals, social capital refers to connections among individuals—social networks and the norms of reciprocity and trustworthiness that arise from them. In that sense social capital is closely related to what some have called "civic virtue." The difference is that "social capital" calls attention to the fact that civic virtue is most powerful when embedded in a dense network of reciprocal social relations. But a society of many virtuous but isolated individuals is not necessarily rich in social capital.

There is one very important connotation of the notion of social cohesion which dates way back to the 14th century. This was Ibn Khaldun's concept of *asabiya*. Khaldun advocated the role of cohesion in his cyclical theory of history. He documented that North African dynasties typically began as desert tribes poor in everything but rich in *asabiya* or social solidarity. Their willingness to sacrifice for each other made them formidable in battle. But once they conquered a civilized state along the coast, the inevitable growth in inequality began to weaken their *asabiya*, until after several generations their growing divisiveness allowed another cohesive clan to emerge from the desert and overthrow them.

Five hundred years after Ibn Khaldun, the Frenchman Alexis de Tocqueville wrote that much of America's success was due to its "forever forming associations. There are not only commercial and industrial associations in which all take part, but others of a thousand different types—religious, moral, serious, futile, very general and very limited, immensely large and very minute. Nothing, in my view, deserves more attention than the intellectual and moral associations in America."

How does Social Capital Work?

The term social capital emphasizes not just nice and happy feelings, but a wide variety of quite specific benefits that flow from the trust, reciprocity, information, and cooperation associated with social networks. Social capital creates value for the people who are connected and - at least sometimes - for bystanders as well.

Social capital turns out to have forceful, even quantifiable effects on many different aspects of our lives. Our schools and neighborhoods don't work so well when community bonds slacken, that our economy, our democracy, and even our health and happiness depend on adequate stocks of social capital.

Social Capital Works through Multiple Channels

Information flows (e.g. learning about jobs, learning about candidates running for office, exchanging ideas at school, etc.) depend on social capital norms of reciprocity (mutual aid) and are dependent on social networks. Bonding networks that connect folks who are similar sustain particularized (in-group) reciprocity. Bridging networks that connect individuals who are diverse sustain generalized reciprocity. Collective action depends upon social networks, although collective action also can foster new networks. Broader identities and solidarity are encouraged by social networks that help translate an "I" mentality into a "we" mentality. What are some examples of social capital? When a group of neighbors informally keep an eye on one another's homes and their children, that's social capital in action? "Gotong-royong" in the rural "sawah padi" is social capital in action, and so too are e-mail exchanges among members of a cancer support group. Social capital can be found in friendship networks, neighborhoods, mosques and churches, schools, old people's clubs, civic associations, and even bars. Social capital can be found in places "where everybody knows your name".

A well-connected individual in a poorly connected society is not as productive as a well-connected individual in a well-connected society. And even a poorly connected individual may derive some of the spillover benefits from living in a well-connected community. If the crime rate in my neighborhood is lowered by neighbors keeping an eye on one another's homes and children, I benefit even if I personally spend most of my time on the road and never even say hello to another resident on the street.

Social capital can thus be simultaneously a "private good" and a "public good." Some of the benefit from an investment in social capital goes to bystanders, while some of the benefit fulfill the immediate interest of the person making the investment. For example, service clubs, like Rotary or Lions, mobilize local energies to raise scholarships or fight disease at the same time that they provide members with friendships and business connections that pay off personally.

Social connections are also important for the rules of conduct that they sustain. Networks involve (almost by definition) mutual obligations; they are not interesting as mere "contacts." Networks of community engagement foster strong norms of reciprocity: I'll do this for you now, in the expectation that you (or perhaps someone else) will return the favor. Sometimes, as in these cases, reciprocity is *specific:* I'll do this for you if you do that for me. Even more valuable, however, is a norm of *generalized* reciprocity: I'll do this for you without expecting anything specific back from you, in the confident expectation that someone else will do something for me down the road. The Golden Rule is one formulation of generalized reciprocity.

A society characterized by generalized reciprocity is more efficient than a distrustful society, for the same reason that money is more efficient than barter. If we don't have to balance every exchange instantly, we can get a lot more accomplished. Trustworthiness lubricates social life. Frequent interaction among a diverse set of people tends to produce a norm of generalized reciprocity. Civic engagement and social capital entail mutual obligation and responsibility for action. Dense social ties facilitate gossip and other valuable ways of cultivating reputation—an essential foundation for trust in a complex society.

Physical capital is not a single "thing," and different forms of physical capital are not interchangeable. An eggbeater and an aircraft carrier both appear as physical capital in our national accounts, but the eggbeater is not much use for national defense, and the carrier would not be much help with your morning omelet. Similarly, social capital — that is, social networks and the associated norms of reciprocity — comes in many different shapes and sizes with many different uses. Your extended family represents a form of social capital, as do your Sunday school class, your college roommates, the civic organizations to which you belong, the Internet chat group in which you participate, and the network of professional acquaintances recorded in your address book.

Sometimes "social capital," like its conceptual cousin "community," sounds warm and cozy. Networks and the associated norms of reciprocity are generally good for those inside the network, but the external effects of social capital are by no means always positive. It was social capital, for example, that enabled Timothy McVeigh to bomb the Alfred P. Murrah Federal Building in Oklahoma City. McVeigh's network of friends, bound together by a norm of reciprocity, enabled him to do what he could not have done alone. Similarly, urban gangs, and power elites often exploit social capital to achieve ends that are antisocial from a wider perspective. Social capital, in short, can be directed toward malevolent, antisocial purposes, just like any other form of capital. (McVeigh also relied on physical capital, like the explosive-laden truck, and human capital, like bomb-making expertise, to achieve his purposes.) Therefore it is important to ask how the positive consequences of social capital—mutual support, cooperation, trust, institutional effectiveness—can be maximized and the negative manifestations—sectarianism, ethnocentrism, corruption—minimized. Toward this end, scholars have begun to distinguish many different forms of social capital.

Some forms involve repeated, intensive, multistranded networks—like a group of technicians who meet for drinks every Friday after work and see each other at the mosque, or the church mass on Sunday—and some are episodic, single stranded, and anonymous, like the faintly familiar face you see several times a month in the supermarket checkout line. Some types of social capital, like a Parent-Teacher Association, are formally organized, with incorporation Chapters, regular meetings, a written constitution, and connection to a national federation, whereas others, like an impromptu football game, are more informal.

Of all the dimensions along which forms of social capital vary, perhaps the most important is the distinction between *bridging* (or inclusive) and *bonding* (or exclusive). Some forms of social capital are, by choice or necessity, inward looking and tend to reinforce exclusive identities and homogeneous groups. Examples of bonding social capital include ethnic fraternal organizations, ethnic-based women's culinary groups, and fashionable country clubs. Other networks are outward looking and encompass people across diverse social cleavages. Examples of bridging social capital include the civil rights groups, many youth service groups, and religious organizations.

Bonding social capital is good for enhancing specific reciprocity and mobilizing solidarity. Dense networks in ethnic enclaves, for example, provide crucial social and psychological support for less fortunate members of the community, while furnishing start-up financing, markets, and reliable labor for local entrepreneurs. Bridging networks, by contrast, are better for linkage to external assets and for information diffusion. Economic sociologist Mark Granovetter (1983) has pointed out that when seeking jobs—or political allies—the "weak" ties that link me to distant acquaintances who move in different circles from mine are actually more valuable than the "strong" ties that link me to relatives and intimate friends whose sociological niche is very like my own. Bonding social capital is, as Xavier de Souza Briggs puts it, good for "getting by," but bridging social capital is crucial for "getting ahead." (1998).

Bonding social capital constitutes a kind of sociological superglue, whereas bridging social capital provides a sociological lubricant. Bonding social capital, by creating strong in-group loyalty, may also create strong out-group antagonism. Nevertheless, under many circumstances both bridging and bonding social capital can have powerfully positive social outcomes? In short, bonding and bridging are not "either-or" categories into which social networks can be neatly divided, but "more or less" dimensions along which we can compare different forms of social capital.

At the conclusion of the twentieth century, for example, ordinary Americans shared a sense of civic apathy. They were reasonably content about their economic prospects, hardly a surprise after an expansion of unprecedented length, but they were not equally convinced that they were on the right track morally or culturally. Of baby boomers interviewed in 1987, 53 percent thought their parents' generation was better in terms of "being a concerned citizen, involved in helping others in the community," as compared with only 21 percent who thought their own generation was better. Fully 77 percent said the nation was worse off because of "less involvement in community activities." In 1992 three-quarters of the U.S. workforce said that "the breakdown of community" and "selfishness" were "serious" or "extremely serious" problems in America. In 1996 only 8 percent of all Americans said that "the honesty and integrity of the average American" were improving, as compared with 50 percent who thought they were becoming less trustworthy. Those who said that people had become less civil over the preceding ten years outnumbered those who thought people had become more civil, 80 percent to 12 percent (Putnam: 1996). In several surveys in 1999 two-thirds of Americans said that America's civic life had weakened in recent years; that social and moral values were higher when they were growing up, and that the society was focused more on the individual than the community. More than 80 percent said there should be more emphasis on community, even if that put more demands on individuals (Putnam: 2000). Americans' concern about weakening community bonds may be misplaced or exaggerated, but we should not underrate public opinion; instead we should explore the issue more thoroughly within our own social context.

Is life in communities as we enter the twenty-first century really so different after all from the reality of world communities in the 1950s and 1960s? One way of curbing nostalgia is to count things. Are club meetings really less crowded today than yesterday, or does it just seem so? Do we really know our neighbors less well than our parents did, or are our childhood recollection of neighborhood activities filled with a golden glow of wishful recollection? Are friendly soccer games less common now, or is it merely that we have become bystanders and onlookers rather than active players? Are strangers less trustworthy now? Are the baby boomers and generation X'ers really less engaged in community life? Perhaps the younger generation today is no less engaged than their predecessors, but engaged in new ways.

Of course, social change, like climatic change, is inevitably uneven. Life is not lived in a single dimension. We should not expect to find everything changing in the same direction and at the same speed, but those very uncertainties may contain important clues to what is happening. The forms of our social capital—the ways in which we connect with friends and neighbors and strangers—are varied. We need to examine in greater depth the trends in our participation in politics and public affairs; we must look at the institutions of our communities—clubs and community associations, religious bodies, and work-related organizations, such as unions and professional societies. Then we explore the varieties of informal ties that link members of our society—soccer groups, music bands, bars and clubs, picnics and parties, volunteer groups, parents and teachers, golf clubs, business and merchant groups, small groups, social movements, and Internet chat groups, and numerous others. Next we examine the changing patterns of trust and altruism—philanthropy, volunteering, honesty, reciprocity.

Here is Putnam's view of what has happened in America: For the first two-thirds of the twentieth century a powerful tide bore Americans into ever deeper engagement in the life of their communities, but a few decades ago — silently, without warning — that tide reversed and we were overtaken by a treacherous rip current. Without at first noticing, we have been pulled apart from one another and from our communities over the last third of the century. (Putnam, 1996).

Putnam has several ideas about why Americans are disengaging which include pressures of time and money, mobility and sprawl, technology and mass media, and generational changes. (Putnam, 2000). The most common explanation for the disengagement of Americans is busyness. However, Putnam found that relating busyness to disengagement is much more difficult than he originally suspected. For instance, "the number of weekly hours of market work per person in the United States has been roughly constant since World War II" and "the last three decades have seen no general decline in free time in America that might explain civic disengagement" (p. 190). However, importantly, "dual-career families are more common and are spending more time at work each week in 1998 than 1969" (p. 191). Therefore, well-educated middle class parents, who have provided a great proportion of community service in the past, actually are experiencing a time bind. Furthermore, even if everyone has hours to spend volunteering, if everyone's free hours are not the same, coordinating schedules for group activities is almost impossible. Therefore, it is possible to show that time could be a reason that group forms of civic engagement have declined more rapidly than individual forms. However, after many contradicting facts, Putnam concludes that while busyness may be a contributing factor to disengagement, it cannot be the sole cause.

Putnam also examines money as a possible cause of the disengagement. More financial worries often lead to less volunteering but "economic good fortune has not guaranteed continued civic engagement" (p. 194). However, when people work outside of home, they have more opportunity to become engaged but less time to take advantage of the opportunities. Putnam decides that money is also not the primary cause of civic disengagement. "The central exculpatory fact is that civic engagement and social connectedness have diminished almost equally for both women and men, working or not, married or single, financially stressed or financially comfortable" (p. 203).

Mobility and sprawl were the next possible causations that Putnam examined. He immediately discounted mobility as a factor because it has not increased in the past fifty years (p. 205). However, sprawl causes more social segregation which leads to less involvement and disrupts community boundedness (p. 214). However, Putnam again comes to the conclusion that sprawl cannot account for more than a small fraction of the decline because civic disengagement exists in smaller towns and rural areas that have not yet been affected by sprawl (p. 215).

After sprawl, Putnam attempted to see if technology and the mass media could be the main cause of disengagement. Putnam was able to find a strong correlation between dependence on television for entertainment and civic disengagement. However, rather than causation, this relationship could be interpreted as "people who are social isolates to begin with gravitate toward the tube as the line of leisurely least resistance" (p. 235). Putnam states that without a true experiment instead of just case studies, entertainment cannot be proven the cause of disengagement. If television does reduce civic engagement, there are three possible ways:

1. Television competes for scarce time.
2. Television has psychological effects that inhibit social participation.

3. Specific programmatic content on television undermines civic motivations

Putnam concludes that the evidence is powerful but circumstantial. However, he believes that true experiments would prove that entertainment is a main cause of civic disengagement.

Putnam's final possible idea for a cause of civic disengagement is generational succession. Putnam's facts show that the older generations are much more involved in civic life. Nevertheless, he states that generational succession has "not contributed equally powerful to all forms of civic and social disengagement" (p. 265). Declines in church attendance, voting, political interest, campaign activities, associational membership, and social trust are almost entirely attributed to generational succession, but declines in things like card playing and entertaining at home are society wide changes (p. 266). Putnam concludes by saying that much of the decline "is attributable to the replacement of an unusually civic generation by several generations...that are less embedded in community life" (p. 275).

Putnam reviews all of the possible causes that he previously discussed, and talks about how much each cause is responsible:

1. Pressures of time and money: 10 percent
2. Sprawl, suburbanization, commuting: 10 percent
3. Entertainment: 15 percent
4. Generational change: 35 percent
5. Entertainment and generation both: 15 percent
6. Other: 15 percent

Putnam shows that the disengagement of Americans has a negative effect on education, child welfare, safe and productive neighborhoods, economic prosperity, health, happiness, and democracy. These are all major parts of American society, and continuing disengagement could have disastrous consequences. These negative effects show that civic disengagement is a real problem that affects everyone.

Putnam presents some possible ideas on how the trend of civic disengagement can be stopped or even reversed. He believes that we need "an era of civic inventiveness to create a renewed set of institutions and channels for a reinvigorated civic life that will fit the way we have come to live" (p. 401). Putnam has several suggestions that he sets out for the American public (which we can also consider for our social context):

1. The level of civic engagement in all parts of our society among current generations should match that of their grandparents when they were that same age, and that at the same time bridging social capital will be substantially greater than it was in their grandparents' era (p. 404).
2. The workplace should be substantially more family-friendly and community-congenial, so that workers will be enabled to replenish stocks of social capital both within and outside the workplace (p. 406).
3. People should spend less time traveling and more time connecting with their neighbors. There should be more integrated and pedestrian-friendly areas, and that the design of our communities and the availability of public spaces should encourage more casual socializing with friends and neighbors (p. 408).
4. People should be more deeply engaged in one or another spiritual community of meaning, while at the same time becoming more tolerant of the faiths and practices of others (p. 409).
5. People should spend less leisure time sitting passively alone in front of glowing screens and more time in active connection with fellow citizens. There must be new forms of electronic entertainment and communication that reinforce community engagement rather than forestalling it (p. 410).
6. People should participate more in (not merely consume or 'appreciate') cultural activities from group dancing to songfests to community theater to cultural festivals. They

must discover new ways to use the arts as a vehicle for convening diverse groups of fellow citizens (p. 411).

7. Many more people should participate in the public life of our communities-running for office, attending public meetings, serving on committees, campaigning in elections, and even voting (p. 412).

If implemented, these solutions could prove beneficial to our communities. It seems like it would be difficult to argue against any of Putnam's ideas. If we even made a dent in the problem of disengagement in our communities by examining these ideas, progress would be made.

REFERENCES

Briggs, X. de S. (1998). Brown Kids in White Suburbs: Housing Mobility and the Many Faces of Social Capital. *Housing Policy Debate* 9(1), 177-221.

Coleman, J. (1990). *Foundations of Social Theory.* Cambridge: Harvard University Press.

de Tocqueville, A. (2000). *Democracy in America.* In Harvey C. Mansfield and Delba Winthrop (Eds.), University of Chicago Press.

Fukuyama, F. (1995). *Trust: The Social Virtues and the Creation of Prosperity.* New York: Free Press.

Granovetter, M. (1983). The Strength of Weak Ties: A Network Theory Revisited. *Sociological Theory*, 1, 201-233.

Reprinted in P.V. Marsden & N. Lin (eds.) 1982, *Social Structure and Network Analysis*, Sage Publications.

ibn Khaldun. (1980). *The Muqaddimah*, trans: Franz Rosenthal, 2nd ed. Bollingen Series XLIII: Princeton Univ. Press.

Putnam, R. (1993). The Prosperous Community: Social Capital and Public Life. *The American Prospect* 13 (Spring), 35-42.

Putnam, R. (1996). The Strange Disappearance of Civic America. *The American Prospect* 24 (Winter).

Putnam, R. (2000). *Bowling Alone.* New York: Simon & Schuster.

Verba, S., Schlozman, K. & Brady, H. (1995). *Voice and Equality: Civic Voluntarism in American Politics.* Cambridge: Harvard University Press.

24

Self-Advocacy : An Essential Component in Special Education

Yeo Swee Lan and Loh Sau Cheong

ABSTRACT

The needs of persons with learning disabilities can be more effectively addressed when they advocate for themselves. For this very reason, self-advocacy groups are formed so that persons with learning disabilities can unite their voice to represent themselves in society. A recent research on the Self-Advocacy Movement in Malaysia found that self-advocacy has positive impact on the lives of persons with learning disabilities. It was found that self-advocacy can be taught to help persons with learning disabilities develop independent skills. The research concluded that self-advocacy should be taught in schools and other institutions to equip persons with learning disabilities to face with life after school. This proposal was affirmed by 25 special education teachers and coordinators at a seminar held at the Special Education Department of Malaysia. This Chapter will give an overview on the importance of self-advocacy. It will also discuss some recommendations on how self-advocacy can be taught to equip persons with learning disabilities to lead a more independent life.

What is Self-Advocacy?

Self-advocacy, according to Walmsley (2002:29) is about people with learning disabilities advocating for their own needs rather than having their needs represented by others. Self-advocacy enabled people with learning disabilities to speak up and to be heard by others.

Referring to the definition of People First, the only organisation in London that is run and controlled by persons with learning disabilities, Aspis (1997:648) noted that self-advocacy includes: Speaking up for yourself; standing up for your rights; making choices; being independent; and taking responsibilities for one self.

Test, Fowler, Wood, Brewer and Eddy (2005:6-7) did a comprehensive study on the definition of self-advocacy and aptly concluded that components of self-advocacy include: Knowledge of self; knowledge of rights; communication; and leadership.

Test, Fowler, Wood, Brewer and Eddy had rightly used the term 'communication' instead of 'speaking up for yourself' in their definition of self-advocacy. Communication can be expressed verbally or non-verbally and therefore, self-advocacy is not only for those who have verbal skills but it is also for persons with severe learning disabilities who do not have verbal skills. Tan (1996:3), included persons with severe learning disabilities in his quote of the term 'self-advocacy':

> Given the right, many persons with learning difficulty can and will self-advocate. A person with mild learning difficulty self-advocates by voicing out his or her views. A person with severe learning difficulty self-advocates by his or her presence in a public meeting. Their inherent right to be in and part of society must be seen and upheld by us.

The term 'self-advocacy' in this chapter refers to persons with mild, moderate or severe learning disabilities expressing their thoughts, feelings as well as their views, standing up for their rights, making choices, being independent and taking responsibilities as an individual and as a group.

Who are Persons with Learning Disabilities?

The term 'learning disabilities' is sometimes referred to as "learning difficulties" or 'intellectual disabilities' by different countries and authors. The operational definition for 'learning disabilities' in this Chapter adheres to the definition used by the Malaysian Ministry of Education, which include students with Down Syndrome, mild Autism, Attention Deficit Hyperactive Disorder, Mild Mental Retardation and Specific Learning Disabilities such as Dyslexia (Maklumat Pendidikan Khas 2006). The choice of term is also in alignment with the Malaysian legislature, Section 3 (1) of the Education Act (Special Education) Regulations 2 of the Regulation 1997 which defines "students with special needs" as those with "visual impairment, hearing impairment or with learning disabilities".

As agreed by experts in the field of study on learning disabilities, individuals with learning disabilities are a heterogeneous population. Lerner (2003:14) noted that "Many different characteristics are associated with learning disabilities, but each individual is unique and will present only some of these characteristics".

The Development of Self-Advocacy Movement

Atkinson (2002:123), an expert in the history of learning disabilities recorded that the self-advocacy movement was founded in Sweden and then in the US in the late 1960's. Today, the self-advocacy movement has grown into an international movement in 43 countries. In the United States alone, there are more than 800 self-advocacy groups. Citing Simons (1992), Goodley (2000:21) revealed that by 1992 there were about 500 self-advocacy groups in the UK.

In the Asia region, it was reported that there are about 245 self-advocacy groups in Japan that are supported by Inclusion Japan, a parents support movement (Yeo, 2007:23). Chosen Power is the only self-advocacy group that is led by people with learning disabilities in Hong Kong. Chosen Power was established in 1995.

In Malaysia, the first self-advocacy group was founded in 1993. Today, there are 13 self-advocacy groups all over Malaysia. There are four self-advocacy groups in Selangor, one in Kuala Lumpur, two in Perak, one in Penang, one in Sabah, two in Sarawak and one in Kelantan. Except for United Voice that has become a registered society in 2005, the other groups are rather small with an average membership of less than 20 and they are under the sponsorship of other organizations. United Voice is the first society in Malaysia that is led by persons with learning disabilities.

A recent research (Yeo, 2007) discovered that education on self-advocacy has impact on persons with learning disabilities to develop independent skills through knowledge of self-awareness and awareness of rights. However, the research also found that only a small fraction of people who are involved in the education and services for persons with learning disabilities in Malaysia are aware of the positive impact of self-advocacy.

The above mentioned research showed that persons with learning disabilities can voice up and represent themselves when given the training, support, exposure and opportunities. The key concern is that many persons with learning disabilities in Malaysia have yet to learn to self-advocate. The research strongly recommended that self-advocacy should be a component of the Special Education curriculum for students with learning disabilities (Yeo, 2007:97). This recommendation was affirmed by 25 educators of Special Education in a seminar on Self-Advocacy held at the Department of Special Education, Putrajaya on 11th April 2008 (United Voice, 2008). The recommendation to teach self-advocacy in school is a vital issue to be addressed since its impact in the lives of students with learning disabilities is significant.

Situation in Malaysia

Self-advocacy is an unknown term to many Malaysians. It appears that many Educators of Special Education in Malaysia are not aware of the impact of self-advocacy in the lives of persons with learning disabilities. This lack of awareness could be due to the fact that self-advocacy is not formally introduced as a subject in the Malaysian Special Education Curriculum for Primary and Secondary Schools *(Jabatan Pendidikan Khas, 2003; Jabatan Pendidikan Khas, 2004).*

Abidin, a senior officer at the Department of Special Education, Ministry of Education Malaysia noted that the term 'self-advocacy' is not used in the curriculum and most teachers have no knowledge of the term 'self-advocacy'. As a special educator for the past 10 years and currently pursuing a doctorate degree, specializing in a field of Special Education, Abidin affirmed that self-advocacy is a very important subject as it will "help students with learning disabilities become independent persons and be aware of their rights and teach them to seek help from appropriate channels when needed." However, she stressed that self-advocacy can only be successfully introduced to students when teachers are educated on what self-advocacy is all about. (N. Z. Abidin, personal communication, September 8, 2005.)

Study shows that students who learnt self-advocacy early in school tend to cope with post school life more confidently (Janipa & Costenbader 2002:465; Test, Fowler, Wood, Brewer & Eddy, 2005:2). Self-advocacy should be taught in school to instill awareness and build the competence in students with learning disabilities to voice up for themselves.

Chang, the Coordinator of Malaysian CARE Services for People with Special Needs, a Non-Governmental Organisation that has helped to establish six Employment Training Centers in Malaysia, confirmed that self-advocacy has yet to be introduced formally in the vocational training programmes used by these centers. Most service centers do not have formal training on self-advocacy skills for students with learning disabilities as it is not included as a subject in their curriculum. Chang however, noted that it was only recently that there is more awareness on the urgency for self-advocacy to be taught in a formal approach to equip students to know their rights, to exercise their rights by making decisions and voicing up for themselves to help them live a more independent life. Acknowledging the importance of self-advocacy in the lives of persons with learning disabilities, Malaysian CARE is in the process of developing training programme on self-advocacy as part of the curriculum in their Job Training Programme (Chang, F. C., personal communication, September 7, 2005).

Observation shows that parents who are aware of the importance of self-advocacy are almost insignificant. This could be due to lack of awareness. Some could be apprehensive that their children could be trained to advocate for themselves in this society where people with learning disabilities are still deprived of quality education and active participation in the community.

The lack of awareness and education on self-advocacy is obviously shown in the lives of adults with learning disabilities in Malaysia. Jamali, a self-advocate and a leader of United Voice expressed that it is difficult to be a self-advocate in Malaysia, "We are not given the freedom to speak up in our community in general. People are not interested to listen to us. People think we are immature and they do not trust us to do things for ourselves. People must learn to trust us." He further stressed that, "We need to speak up so that the public know us and do not look down on us. The government should hear us and help us in the aspect of education, employment and accommodation" (J. Jamali, Personal communication, 2005, September, 22).

Situation is however changing where there is beginning to be more collaboration between United Voice, the first self-advocacy society of persons with learning disabilities in Malaysia with other disability groups. Their collaboration includes advocacy efforts and awareness programmes. The Ministry of Women, Family and Community Development has recently appointed a member of United Voice to be one of the Council Member of the Disability Act National Council. These openings for persons with learning disabilities to advocate for themselves can lead to positive changes in the welfare of people with learning disabilities in Malaysia. To equip and to encourage more people with learning disabilities to voice up for themselves and to integrate as participative individuals in the society, self-advocacy skills should be imparted effectively.

The Impact of Self-Advocacy

Many studies have shown that self-advocacy has significant impact in the lives of persons with learning disabilities (Aspis, 1997, 2002; Atkinson, 1999, 2002; Beart, Hardy, & Buchan, 2004; Goodley, 1996, 1997, 1998, 2000; Ramcharan, McGrath, & Grant, 1997; Ward, 1999). Self-advocacy has helped persons with learning disabilities to be more independent and take up challenges beyond the expectations of their own and others.

Atkinson and Goodley (Atkinson, 1999, 2002; Goodley, 1996, 1997, 1998, 2000;) two renowned researchers on self-advocacy movement in the UK, have recorded many life stories of how self-advocacy had impact in the lives of individuals. Many self-advocates learnt to voice out for themselves and develop skills to negotiate with parties involved in their daily experiences – be it at home, in institutions or centers, at work or within the community in general. Independent living became a reality for some after joining a self-advocacy group. The most powerful impact of this movement is raising a group of self-advocates who are able to challenge policies or legislations and take part in policy making that involves persons with learning disabilities (Aspis, 2002:5).

Atkinson (2002:123) observed that the self-advocacy movement has moved people with learning disabilities to the forefront. The awareness of self-advocacy and the training received in speaking up has trained some self-advocates to be effective advocates and valuable resources in the researches on issues related to people with learning disabilities.

Goodley (2000:85) highlighted the life stories of five "top self-advocates" which revealed many stories on how involvement in self-advocacy groups affect the lives of these five persons with 'learning difficulties' (a term preferred by most of these five narrators). Lloyd Page for example, testified that his involvement in the self-advocacy movement has given him the opportunities to participate and contribute in organisations and committees such as Central Council for Education Training and Social Work, Equal Opportunities Committee and Open University. He even had the opportunity to be present at the Houses of Parliament to fight for the civil rights of people with learning disabilities in UK.

This review has given us a glimpse of how involvement in self-advocacy activities have significant impact in the lives of individuals with learning disabilities from being reserved and shy to being more confident and bold. Some have learned to be outspoken and have been given opportunities to speak their minds in public places.

Many people with learning disabilities in Malaysia are not informed or taught how to self-advocate (Yeo, 2007). They have been depending from others to speak up for them. They do not realize that they have the right to speak up for themselves. Aspis (1997:648) strongly emphasized that in order for people with learning disabilities to advocate they need to learn skills. He noted that in UK, courses are now conducted by service providers, adult training centers, special schools and colleges on how to make choices, taking responsibility and how to speak up.

It was strongly suggested by Aspis (1997:647, 2002:5) that in order for self-advocacy to have a lasting impact in bringing permanent change, persons with learning disabilities need to be informed of their rights and know how to use their rights. The emphasis on self-determination and self-advocacy in the pre-vocational and transition programmes offered in the US and the UK special education curriculums perhaps have contributed to the rapid growth of self-advocacy movement in these countries.

Ronald (2000:458) did a comprehensive study on the impact of legislation in the development of persons with learning disabilities. He noted that in the US legislation on vocational education and transition for students with disabilities began in the 80's. By 1997, the re-authorisation of the Individuals with Disabilities Education Act requires transition planning to begin no later than age 14. A review on two most widely used transition curriculum in the US, The Life-Centered Career Education (LCCE) and The Kent Transition Implementation Model showed that self-advocacy is emphasized in these curriculums (Brolin, 1995:64-68).

This short review indicates that self-advocacy has helped persons with learning disabilities to be more independent and it has led them to be active contributors of an inclusive society. Since self-advocacy is an acquired skill, informal and formal education is necessary to help persons with learning disabilities to develop this skill that can lead to a better quality of life.

Recommendations

The Biwako Millenium Framework for Action of Economic and Social Commission for Asia and the Pacific (ESCAP) (2002:5) stated:

> Persons with disabilities are the most qualified and best equipped to support, inform and advocate for themselves and other persons with disabilities. Evidence suggests that the quality of life of persons with disabilities, and of the broader community, improves when disabled persons actively voice their concerns and participate in decision-making...

To date, the education for persons with learning disabilities for all levels, from early intervention to vocational education is still far from satisfactory. Pre-vocational Training and Transition has yet to be introduced in the curriculum of Special Education for students with learning disabilities. There is only one vocational training school run by the government that offers training courses for persons with learning disabilities. Employment opportunities for persons with learning disabilities are way below the needs. There is little effort to provide adequate housing for adults with learning disabilities who are interested in independent living. For a better future, it is vital for persons with learning disabilities in Malaysia to stand up for their rights and make their voice heard.

Studies have shown that persons with learning disabilities can voice up and represent themselves when given the support, exposure, training and opportunities. Education on self-advocacy should be emphasized in the Special Education for children, youth and adults with learning disabilities. Such a move will gradually help them strengthen their voice for an inclusive society.

The following are some recommendations how people with learning disabilities in Malaysia can be equipped to self-advocate.

National Policies

Every government owes its disabled citizen a just and impartial society. The government in Malaysia can strengthen the national policies to protect persons with disabilities from discrimination. Hurst's (Hurst 1995:534) suggestion for anti discrimination legislation for liberation should be considered.

The Parliament has finally enacted the Disability Act 2008. It is yet to be seen how effective this Act is in enforcing its commitment in improving the quality of life of people with disabilities. At present, support by the government for the self-advocacy movement is minimal. The researcher is confident that the government is open to know more about self-advocacy and support the move if it is clear to them that such a movement will enhance the quality of life of persons with learning disabilities. The promises made in the 8th and 9th Malaysian Plan give hope to people with disabilities that the government is making an effort to improve their quality of life. The government seems interested to help people with disabilities to reach their full potential and to live a dignified and fruitful life.

Ronald's (2000:458) recorded that the US legislation on vocational education and transition for students with disabilities began in the 80's. By 1997, the re-authorisation of the Individuals with Disabilities Education Act requires transition planning to begin no later than age 14. Such a move could be considered to improve the Malaysian Special Education Curriculum.

Legislation to include Transition and Pre-Vocational in the special education curriculum will strengthen the self-advocacy movement in Malaysia. A national policy that protects the rights of persons with disability is desperately needed by persons with learning disabilities in Malaysia so that their quality of life will improve with better education, better opportunity for employment, housing and benefit provision that enable them to live an independent life.

The Ministry of Education should invest more in researches that will strengthen the Special Education. More collaboration between the government and NGOs is necessary to synergise the available expertise and resources. In the implementation of introducing self-advocacy in school, more funds would be needed to build up the necessary resources.

More study and consultation are needed in regards to introducing Pre-Vocational Training and Transition in the curriculum of Special Education in Malaysia. These are two important subjects that include vocational skills and self-advocacy as key focus. The right expertise from within the country and overseas should be consulted for strategy planning, action plan and training. More research is needed for fruitful planning.

The legislation of Transition and Pre Vocational Education to be taught in school and should be included in the section on Education for persons with learning disabilities of the Disability Act 2008.

Self-advocacy in the Special Education Curriculum

Aspis (1977:648) strongly emphasized that persons with learning disabilities need to learn skills to advocate. Aspis (1997:647, 2002:5) also stressed that for self-advocacy have a lasting impact in bringing permanent change, persons with learning disabilities need to be informed of their rights and know how to voice their rights.

At present, self-advocacy is neither taught in the government run Special Schools nor in Private Schools or Centers run by NGO's. Jelas's (SUHAKAM, 2004:200-205) Chapter, Access to Quality Education for the Disabled was informative about the current situation of the Special Education in Malaysia. Much emphasis was on Inclusive Education. In her attempt to report on the teaching programmes of Special Education of all the various disability groups, there was no mention at all on Pre-vocational Training, Transition and the need to introduce self-advocacy.

Though United Voice has existed for more than 10 years and progressed actively as a self-advocacy group, no effort has yet been made to challenge that self-advocacy should be taught in school. This is due to the fact that even within United Voice there is limited knowledge about how self-advocacy should be taught and at what age persons with learning disabilities should learn about self-advocacy. Lack of research, exposure, man-power, resources could have led to this delay in discovering this urgent need.

As Malaysia progresses in modernity, greater emphasis should be given to improve the education for persons with disabilities. Chiam (2004:32) aptly quoted The Convention On The Rights of The Child (CRC) Chapter 23, and emphasized:

> Children with disabilities have the same right as children without disabilities. They have the right to non-discrimination, the right to development, freedom of expression, the right to healthcare and so forth..a mentally or physically disabled child should enjoy a full and decent life, in conditions which ensure dignity, promote self-reliance, and facilitate the child's active participation in the community.

To help children with learning disabilities to enjoy the right to development, freedom of expression, self-reliance and active participation in the community, it is urgent to teach them self-advocacy skills in school. Education on self-advocacy will help them to be aware of their rights and equip them to express or voice up for themselves, be self-reliant and participate in the community.

The Human Rights Commission in Malaysia (SUHAKAM, 2004:309) in its observation on the Proceedings of the Conference on Human Rights and Education held on Malaysia Human Rights Day 2002 stated that, "Human right education should be targeted to vulnerable and minority groups and aims at changing their human rights situation. The minority groups could be..people with disabilities.."

The above statement clearly supports the idea of teaching persons with learning disabilities to self-advocate while they are still in school. The school is the best place to educate the grassroots on human rights and about the self-advocacy. The school can also educate the educationists and parents about self-advocacy when the subject becomes part of the system.

To improve the quality of life of persons with learning disabilities, self-advocacy must be introduced to persons with learning disabilities in school to ensure that all persons with learning disabilities are taught to self-advocate at a young age. Such practice will help persons with learning disabilities assimilate this independent skill in their daily life so that they can become more self-reliant and have more active participation in the society. When self-advocacy becomes a formal subject in school, the public, including the parents and practitioners will also gradually be educated to give persons with learning disabilities their rightful place in the society.

The Ministry of Education has to first of all recognize the importance of self-advocacy being introduced and taught in school. When support from the Ministry of Education is approved, forming a think-tank group is essential to study the strategy of introducing self-advocacy in school. A decision has to be made as at which level should self-advocacy be introduced.

Training programmes for special education teachers trainees in the universities and colleges have to be revised to include self-advocacy as a subject. University programmes in Special Education should also introduce self-advocacy as a subject so that practitioners under training will be informed and educated on the importance and the know-how of self-advocacy.

Research to develop a syllabus on self-advocacy that can be introduced in the curriculum of Special Education is vital. Consultation with special educationists from overseas who are experts in this area is needed to help facilitate this research. There should also be consultations with local NGOs that are experienced in this field. They can share their experiences in the Malaysian context.

Sufficient funds should be allocated to carry out the necessary research, consultations, training and developing the syllabus and materials necessary to teach self-advocacy in school.

The Role of Non-Governmental Organisations (NGOs)

Established NGOs that provide services for persons with learning disabilities are observed to focus on early intervention and vocational training programmes. However, it was found that many are lack of awareness on the importance of self-advocacy and the lack of know-how about self-advocacy (Yeo,

2007). There isn't any strategy just yet on educating persons with learning disabilities on self-advocacy. Some effort has been made by United Voice to promote self-advocacy groups but there are hardly any adequate manuals and teaching tools available for those who are interested to form their own self-advocacy groups. There is only one basic manual that is produced by Dignity & Services Bhd: *"Self-advocacy" - A brief introduction on self-advocacy and basic guidelines on forming a self-advocacy group* (Tan, 1996:5-7).

The lack of training materials, resources and know-how, has affected the growth of the movement. The lack of knowledge on what is self-advocacy and how to teach persons with learning disabilities to self-advocate hinders the self-advocacy groups from progressing effectively.

Lack of strategy and know-how in emphasizing self-advocacy in their teaching programme indicates that NGO centers are lack of knowledge on the importance of self-advocacy. Besides financial constraints, the lack of expertise and training materials are the main reasons that have hindered support from NGOs in this movement (Yeo, 2007). Self-advocacy is an unheard of or a new concept to most caregivers and practitioners. Training manuals and practical training are needed to equip more NGOs to teach self-advocacy at their centers, to establish self-advocacy groups and to be involved in supporting self-advocacy groups effectively.

Collaboration between the Ministry of Higher Education, Special Education Department, the Social Welfare Department and the NGOs is necessary to improve on the above situation. The Ministry of Higher Education need to include training programmes that will prepare educationists to teach self-advocacy in schools. The Social Welfare Department should introduce courses on Self-Advocacy to the Community Rehabilitation Centers (CBRs). There are currently about 379 CRls all over Malaysia (Welfare Department of Malaysia, 2008). More investment is needed in research and in equipping trainers.

Joint effort of the above parties is also necessary to work on training manuals on self-advocacy that are useful for all levels. Training manuals should be available not only for trainers but also for self-advocates. There should be manuals that can help them understand what self-advocacy is and how to practice self-advocacy which could include independent skills, communication skills, public speaking and leadership skills.

Training seminars and conferences should be organized periodically to create awareness and educate parties involved in educating persons with learning disabilities. Parents should be included in such training as self-advocacy is practiced in daily living. What is learned in school or training centre should be enhanced at home.

Social Model of Disability

The awareness and the impact of Social Model of Disability movement is generally weak in Malaysia. The Social Model of Disability approach which is often adopted by advocacy supported and autonomous groups has proven to have a greater impact in developing an inclusive society as seen not only in the developed countries but also in United Voice and Mutiara Voice Club in Malaysia (Yeo, 2007). This indicates that Social Model of Disability is applicable if persons with learning disabilities in Malaysia are given an opportunity and an environment that adopt an inclusive setting. But, much work is needed to educate the public in general and those involved in services for persons with learning disabilities on the concept of Social Model of Disability. The society has to change their attitude towards persons with learning disabilities. They need to accept their disability and acknowledge their rights to have an active participation in the society. Creating a right-based and inclusive society requires a national reform.

NGOs should awaken to the fact that the way forward for persons with learning disabilities is to equip them to stand up for themselves. The Social Model of Disability should be practiced to promote empowerment. Training manuals on self-advocacy should include information on the models of disability and the structure of self-advocacy groups. This will help educate those who are involved to know the effect of the various approaches and will perhaps influence their choice of approaches that best suit each group.

National bodies for the disabled such as the Malaysian Council of the Disabled should educate NGOs that are involved in advocating or providing services for persons with learning disabilities to equip persons with learning disabilities in voicing up for themselves and taking up leadership responsibilities. Persons with learning disabilities should be represented in public meetings. Individuals that are invited to represent organizations for persons with learning disabilities should make it a point to ensure that persons with learning disabilities are included. Inclusion should begin with the movements advocating for persons with disabilities. This effort, together with active promotion on self-advocacy will eventually encourage more self-advocacy groups and societies to develop throughout Malaysia.

Family Support

Mitchell's (1997:47) observation that independence of persons with learning disabilities from parents and families seems more difficult for Asians appeared to be true in Malaysia. Jones and Wallaces (1992) observed that the adulthood of persons with learning disabilities is only "socially confirmed" if they are independent of financial support from their families.

Since the mindset of parents or guardians is discovered to be a big influence in supporting their child's involvement in self-advocacy groups, more effort should be made to educate parents and guardians on self-advocacy. The right information and life stories will help parents see the relevance of self-advocacy groups.

In our Asian culture, speaking up is sometimes seen as being rude. Parents have to be educated on the importance of allowing their children who have learning disabilities to voice their opinions. As suggested by Barnes (1997:73), the interdependence approach should be encouraged to help parents realise that self-advocacy is not promoting rebellion and alienation from families, but promotes an interdependence culture. This may encourage parents who have difficulty in letting go to see the positive outcome of self-advocacy.

It is observed that most parents do not know the rights of their children. They should be informed and be encouraged to teach their children about their rights. Parents should also be informed how self-advocacy can lead to policy change that can improve the quality of life for persons with learning disabilities. Parents should know the purpose of self-advocacy groups and the possible outcomes and impact the group can have on their children.

Parents support organisations can play an important role in the development of the self-advocacy movement. As practised in Japan, self-advocacy groups were established with the support of a parents support movement, Inclusion Japan. It was reported that the self-advocacy groups compiled a resolution at the end of each annual conference to be submitted to the Welfare Measures of Tokyo Metropolitan Government (JICA Rehabilitation Course Report, 2006). Their resolution implied that self-advocates in Japan are informed of their rights and the national policies for persons with disabilities. Nevertheless, support from parents support movement will better enhance the self-advocacy movement if self-advocacy groups that have the potential are eventually given the liberty to become an independent bodies or societies of persons with learning disabilities.

There is currently no national parents support movement for persons with learning disabilities in Malaysia. As noted by Jayasooria (2000:104-105), only a minority group of parents are involved in advocacy. Many parents are ignorant on the rights of persons with disability and their family. They lack knowledge on how advocacy can improve the current situation of persons with learning disabilities in Malaysia. Such ignorance could have contributed to the slow development in nearly all sectors for persons with learning disabilities in this country.

Family support is important for the development of self-advocacy movement. The support from parents for the self-advocacy movement is generally weak due to lack of awareness on advocacy and self-advocacy (Yeo, 2007). The absence of active parents support movement could be one of the reasons self-advocacy movement in Malaysia is slow in its progress.

More awareness campaigns for parents regarding the importance of self-advocacy are necessary. Parents of school-going children, school-leavers or adults should be educated on the role and impact of self-advocacy.

If self-advocacy is introduced as a subject in school, parents will be more aware of the importance of self-advocacy. Parents-Teachers Associations in schools are good platforms to educate parents on this subject.

Training should be provided for parents to know how to enhance what their children have learned in schools or centres or groups regarding self-advocacy. NGOs should conduct workshops and seminars to create awareness amongst parents on the need to strengthen the self-advocacy movement and their role in strengthening this movement.

Parents need to be concerned about what life is after school for their children. They need to be informed that self-advocacy groups provide social and moral support for school leavers. It is also a place where they can unite their voice and make their presence felt in the society.

Public Attitude

Public attitude is a big obstacle for persons with learning disabilities to integrate in society. The government can play an important role in changing this attitude and create an inclusive society.

SUHAKAM (2004) has compiled several Chapters that are focused on Human Rights and Education. It was strongly advocated that Human Rights should be taught in school to change the mindset of our society towards the underprivileged. Wu (2004:25), from Hong Kong observed student's attitude towards disabilities,

> On disabilities, students tended to pay attention only to the constraints and held erroneous perceptions of person with disabilities. Persons with disabilities were perceived as pitiful, deviant, accident prone and appropriate for repetitive work...

Such attitude is observed to be true in the Malaysian schools and in the general public. Public awareness through media, public meetings and campaigns will help educate the public and change mindsets. But, a more effective approach for long-term change would be to educate students about human rights and social responsibilities. Wu (2004:26) further emphasised,

> Many persons with disabilities are still largely excluded socially from the mainstream, and students viewed this exclusion as normative. This leads to a vicious cycle of further misunderstanding and hesitance to treat them equally as members of society..education must be built on diversity and equality. People are different but they are equal; and education and textbooks must act as catalysts for change.

Wu's suggestion is vital if a society desires to see a change of mindset and attitude towards people with disabilities. Such a view should be seriously considered taken into serious consideration by the Ministry of Education. Inclusive Education should be adopted which promotes integration of students with and without disabilities. SUHAKAM (2004:316) applauded the view of the former Prime Minister of Malaysia, Tun Mahathir Mohamad that the school environment plays a critical role in students' understanding of human rights and their belief that human rights is an essential element to the quality of life.

Public attitude towards persons with learning disabilities can change through education and public awareness. School plays an important role in educating students about persons with learning disabilities. Students should be encouraged to include students with learning disabilities in school activities. Such interaction can create a better awareness and understanding of persons with learning disabilities. Attitude towards persons with learning disabilities may change when there is a better understanding of their needs. With better awareness people might be more willing to listen when persons with learning disabilities speak up.

NGOs in Malaysia play an important role in creating public awareness. Nadason (2004:179) observed that NGOs in

Malaysia have undertaken various programmes to enable the masses to understand human rights and increase their awareness about these rights.

Jayasooria (2000:193) suggested there is a need for a strategy and action plan to create equal opportunities for persons with disabilities in education, employment and in developing a society without barriers. NGOs such as United Voice should make every effort to work together with their counterparts to create more public awareness about persons with learning disabilities and their potentials. United Voice (United Voice, 2005) used various ways to create awareness, including Medias like airing through radio station for nationwide publicity. Publicity for persons with learning disabilities should be strengthened through visual medias such as internet, television and promotions through VCDs (Video Compact Disks).

The government has the power to change the mindset of the society through awareness campaigns and policies (Yeo, 2002:14). The Malaysian government has developed pro-active campaigns such as "A Caring Society" to promote awareness and care for persons with disabilities. However, such a campaign has to be ongoing and creatively presented to create an impact.

Public prejudice towards persons with learning disabilities can be changed by creating awareness to help the public understand persons with learning disabilities and to see their potential instead of focusing on their disabilities. The role of the government in changing public attitude towards persons with learning disabilities is vital.

The Ministry of Education should speed up effort on educating mainstream students about persons with learning disabilities in schools to clear misconceptions. Campaigns that help students to be aware and understand the characteristics of learning disabilities will help students appreciate their school-mates with learning disabilities better. A healthy integration environment should be fostered through school activities.

More educational TV and Radio programmes should be produced to help the public understand persons with learning disabilities. NGOs should be encouraged to create informative websites and produce brochures to educate public about learning disabilities.

The public should be aware that persons with learning disabilities can contribute in the society when necessary support is given them. Publicity that focuses on their contributions and abilities should be promoted.

Employers should be encouraged to hire persons with learning disabilities by giving them guidebooks that will help them understand persons with learning disabilities and ways to assist them work more effectively. Corporate Social Responsibilities (CSR) campaigns should highlight not only contribution on monetary support but should also motivate community to include persons with learning disabilities in society. Corporate companies and the government sector should take the lead in creating employment for persons with learning disabilities within their set-up. Through partnership with United Voice in recruitment, GCH Retails (M) Sdn (is this the real name for the company? has now become an exemplary corporate sector in employing persons with learning disabilities to work in their supermarket outlets throughout Malaysia. Kandiah, Senior Manager of GCH reported that about 100 adults with learning disabilities in Klang Valley (45), Seremban (6), Johor (30) and Ipoh (20) were employed by GCH to work in their Giant and Cold Storage outlets within a year since first recruitment in October 2007 (personal communication, Kandiah, N., 24 October 2008). According to Kandiah, more will be recruited from other states by end of 2008. Such exemplary CSR approach should be awarded by the government.

Conclusion

The welfare of persons with learning disabilities in Malaysia is observed to have improved over the last 10 years. However, more efforts need to be made to improve the education system for persons with learning disabilities in order to help them "live with dignity and self-respect" as pledged in the 9th Malaysian Plan.

Self-advocacy may not have the answer to solve all the needs of persons with learning disabilities. But, the testimonies of members of United Voice (Yeo, 2007) showed that persons with learning disabilities can advance in independent skills with the awareness on self-advocacy. Self-advocacy has helped them to have more friends, to improve in their communication skills, to make choices, to stand up for their rights, to take up leadership responsibilities and to move towards independent living. We would deny them a great opportunity to develop themselves if we do not teach them to self-advocate. They could be deprived of good moral support and social life by not being part of a self-advocacy group as testified by a member of United Voice, "If I am not involved in United Voice, I would probably be stuck at home and miss out all the opportunities. I would not have so many friends that I do now."

Based on the findings of this study, awareness and education on self-advocacy is strongly proposed to be introduced in the special education programmes. More self-advocacy groups should develop in every district in Malaysia to empower and impact more persons with learning disabilities. Collaboration between the government sectors and NGOs should be strengthened to support the self-advocacy movement.

REFERENCES

Aspis, S. (1997). Self-advocacy for people with learning difficulties: Does it have a future? *Journal of Disability & Society, 12*(4), 647-654.

Aspis, S. (2002). Self-advocacy: Vested interest and misunderstandings. *British Journal of Learning Disabilities, 30,* 3-7.

Atkinson, D. (1999). An old story. In S. French and J. Swain (Eds). *Therapy and Learning difficulties: Advocacy, participation and partnership (p. 11-21).* Oxford: Butterworth Heinemann.

Atkinson, D. (2002). Self-advocacy and research. In B. Gary & R. Jackson (Eds.),

Advocacy and learning disability (p. 120-136). London and Philadelphia: Jessica Kingsley Publisher.

Barnes, M. (1997). Families and empowerment. In Ramcharan P., Roberts, G., Grant, G., and Borland J. (Eds.). *Empowerment in everyday life: Learning disability (p. 70-87).* London: Jessica Kingsley Publishers.

Beart, S., Hardy G., & Buchan L. (2004). Changing selves: a grounded theory account of belonging to a self-advocacy group for people with intellectual disabilities. *Journal of Applied Research in Intellectual Disabilities, 17,* 91-100

Borland, J., & Ramcharan, P. (1997). Empowerment in informal settings. In Ramcharan P., Roberts, G., Grant, G., and Borland J. (Eds.). *Empowerment in everyday life: Learning disability (88-97).* London: Jessica Kingsley Publishers.

Brolin, D. E. (1995). *Career education: A functional life skills approach.* USA: Prentice-Hall, Inc.

Chiam, H. K. (2004). Human rights from the Window of Children. In Human Rights Commission of Malaysia, *Persidangan Kebangsaan Pendidikan Hak Asasi Manusia Di Sekolah (23-36).* Kuala Lumpur: Haji Jantan Sdn Bhd

Economic and Social Commission for Asia and the Pacific (ESCAP). (2002). *Biwako Millennium Framework for Action Towards an Inclusive, Barrier-Free and Rights Based Society for Persons with Disabilities in Asia and the Pacific.* United Nations Economic and Social Council. (p. 5)

Goodley, D. (1996). Tales of hidden lives: a critical examination of life history research with people who have learning difficulties. *Journal Disability & Society, 11*(3), 333-348.

Goodley, D. (1997). Locating Self-advocacy in Models of Disability: understanding disability in the support of self-advocates with learning disabilities. *Journal of Disability & Society, 12*(3) 367-379.

Goodley, D. (1998). Supporting people with learning difficulties in self-advocacy groups and models of disability. *Health and Social Care in Community 6*(6), 438-446.

Goodley, D. (2000). *Self-advocacy in the lives of people with learning difficulties.* Buckingham: Open University Press.

Hurst, R. (1995). Choice and empowerment – lessons from Europe. *Disability and Society, 10*(4), 529-534

JICA Rehabilitation Course Report (2006). Rules of Honninbukai/ Yuuaikai. [Online] Retrieved September 30, 2006, from http:// www.jicafriends.jp/vocational/gi2006/material/resume/yuai/ index.html

Janipa, S. J., & Costenbader, V. (2002). The transition from high school to post-secondary education for students with learning disabilities: A survey of college service coordinators. *Journal of Learning Disabilities Austin, 35(5),* 462-468

Jayasooria, D. (2000). *Disabled people: Citzenship & social work, The Malaysian experience.* London: ASEAN Academic Press.

Jones, G., & Wallace, C. (1992). *Youth, family and citizenship.* Buckingham: Open University Press.

Learner, W. L. (2003). *Learning Disabilities: Theories, Diagnosis, and Teaching Strategies.* Boston:Houghton Mifflin Company.

Maklumat Pendidikan Khas. (2006). Jabatan Pendidikan Khas, Kementerian Pendidkan Malaysia (p.2).

Mitchell, P. (1997). The impact of self-advocacy on families. *Journal of Disability & Society, 12*(1), 43-56.

Nadason, M. (2004). The Impact of NGOs in Promoting Human Rights. In SUHAKAM's Observation, Recommendations and Conclusion, *Proceedings of the Conference on Human Rights and Education, Malaysia Human Rights Day 2002 (175-187).* Kuala Lumpur: Watan Sdn. Bhd

Ramcharan, P., McGrath, M., & Grant, G. (1997). Voices and choices: Mapping entitlements to friendships and community contacts. In Ramcharan P.

Roberts, G., Grant, G., and Borland J. (Eds.). *Empowerment in everyday life: learning disability (48-69).* London: Jessica Kingsley Publishers.

Ronald, L. T. (2000). *Assessment of exceptional students: Educational and psychological procedures.* United States: Allyn and Bacon (p. 458-465).

Simons, K. (1992) "Sticking up for yourself": Self-advocacy and people with learning difficulties. Community Care publication in association with the Joseph Rowntree Foundation. In Goodley, D. (2000). *Self-advocacy in the lives of people with learning difficulties.* Buckingham: Open University Press.

SUHAKAM (Human Rights Commission in Malaysia) (2004). SUHAKAM's Observation, Recommendations and Conclusion. In *Proceedings of the Conference on Human Rights and Education, Malaysia Human Rights Day 2002 (309-316).* Kuala Lumpur: Watan Sdn. Bhd.

Tan, C. S. (1996). *Self-Advocacy - by persons with learning difficulties.* Malaysia: Dignity and Services Bhd.

Test, D. W., Fowler, C. H., Wood, W. M., Brewer, D.M., & Eddy, S. (2005). A conceptual framework of self-advocacy for students with disabilities. *Remedial and Special Education Austin, 26*(1), 6-7, 43-54.

United Voice (2005). [Online] Retrieved on March 6, 2006, from http://www.unitedvoice.com.my

United Voice Newsletter (2006) April. Malaysia Wamsley, J., (2002). Principles and types of advocacy. In B. Gary & R. Jackson (Eds.), *Advocacy and learning disability (p. 29)*. London and Philadelphia: Jessica Kingsley Publisher.

Ward, L. (1998). *Innovations in advocacy and empowerment for people with intellectual disabilities*. Lancashire, England: Lisieux Hall Publications.

Welfare Department of Malaysia (2008). [Online] Retrieved on October 30, 2008, from http://www.jkm.gov.my/

Wu, H. A. (2004). Equalizing Education Opportunities for Human Development. In SUHAKAM (Human Rights Commission in Malaysia), *Proceedings of the Conference on Human Rights and Education, Malaysia Human Rights Day 2002* (21-37). Kuala Lumpur: Watan Sdn. Bhd.

Yeo, S.L. (2002, November 7). *A Learning Experience*. The STAR, Section 2, p. 14.

Yeo, S. L. (2005, March 3). *Special Challenge*. The STAR, Star Two, Malaysia, p.25.

Yeo, S. L. (2007) Self-Advocacy Movement of Persons with Learning Disabilities: A Case Study in the Malaysian Context. *A Dissertation Submitted to the Faculty of Education, University of Malaya in Partial Fulfilment of the Requirements for the Degree of Master of Education.*

25

Parental and Social Influence on Career Choice

Swaha Bhattacharya

Introduction

Every individual in the modern and fast changing world is trying to seek for those careers which would ultimately led them to achieve fairly in life. Each and every individual is coping with dynamic world and its demands. Therefore to choose the career which provide them fair chance in life, success, satisfaction and approved from both family and society is in prime focus. However, the choice of career by an individual is influenced by various factors and among them parental and social influence is very important. Career development is a life long process of engaging the work world through choosing among employment opportunities made available to them. Each individual undertaking the process is influenced by many factors, including the context in which they live, their personal aptitude and educational attainment (Bandura et al. 2001).Sometimes it seems that greater level of psychological distress predicted higher levels of career in decision which in turn, was associated with lower career certainty and greater perceived family conflict (Constantine & Flores, 2006). Assessing influential factors in the family related to career decision-making is consistent with evolving post-modern approaches to career counselling. However, the change for measuring family influence is technically demanding considering the ongoing revolutionary changes in the structure of the family (Chope, 2005). The relationship between specific parental behaviour and career development of young adolescents was assessed by Keller and Whiston (2008). Regression analysis revealed that parental behaviour did relate to the career development of middle school students, after controlling for student's grade level and gender. Parental behaviours tended to relate more to career decision-making self-efficiency than to career maturity and general psychological parenting behaviours appear to be more salient than career focused parent behaviour. On the other hand, career choice is also depend upon social influences, viz., teachers, peer groups, economic status, media as well as whole society. It was found that the viewer of the participants, in terms of how they thought decisions should be made and how they were approaching their own decisions were consistent with models of career decision-making that include notions of interdependence, experience, intuition and emotion (Bubani et al, 2008). Besides this, identity status was also related to career decision, self-efficacy and differentiation of interests but it was not associated with consistency of interest (Nanta & Khan, 2007). Considering the above, the present investigation has been designed to parental and social influence on career choice as perceived by the students of four renowned colleges of Kolkata City.

Objectives

1. To study the parental and social influence on career choice as perceived by the students of four renowned colleges of Kolkata City.
2. To study whether economic conditions take important role in this regard.
3. To study whether gender difference has a significant role in this context.

Hypotheses

Hypothesis I: Parental influence on career choice of students belonging to families of income level Rs. 5001 to Rs 10000, Rs 10001 to Rs 20000 and Rs.20001 to Rs 30000 vary significantly.

Hypothesis II: Social influence on career choice of students belonging to families of income level Rs. 5001 to Rs 10000,

Rs 10001 to Rs 20000 and Rs.20001 to Rs 30000 vary significantly.

Hypothesis III : Parental and social influence on career choice of students belonging to families of income level Rs. 5001 to Rs 10000, Rs 10001 to Rs 20000 and Rs.20001 to Rs 30000 are differentially associated with gender difference.

METHOD

Participants

A group of 600 students (300 male and 300 female) of four renowned colleges of Kolkata City were selected as participants who were willing to respond. The pertinent characteristics of the participants are as follows :

(a) Age : 18 to 22 years

(b) Education : College students of First year, Second Year and Third Year.

(c) Monthly family income :

(i) Rs 5001 to Rs. 10000 (Group A)

(ii) Rs. 10001 to Rs. 20000 (Group B)

(iii) Rs. 20001 to Rs 30000 (Group C)

Tools

1. General Information Schedule : It consists of items like name, address, age, sex, education, monthly family income etc.

2. Perceived parental influence Questionnaire : It consists of twenty statements in connection with parental influence on career choice answerable in a five point scale from strongly agree to strongly disagree where high score indicates high parental influence on career choice and vice-versa. Odd-even split-half reliability is 0.81

3. Perceived Social Influence Questionnaire : It consists of twenty statements in connection with social influence on career choice answerable in a five point scale from strongly agree to strongly disagree where high score indicates high social influence on career choice and vice-versa. Odd-even split-half reliability is 0.83.

Procedure

The General Information Schedule, Perceived Parental Influence Questionnaire and Perceived Social Influence Questionnaire were administered to the students by giving proper instruction. Data were collected and properly scrutinized. Scoring was done with the help of scoring key. Tabulation was done for male and female group separately. Frequency and percentages were calculated for general information schedule

Data Analysis

Mean and S.D. were calculated for perceived parental and social influence questionnaire. Comparison was made by applying t-test.

RESULTS AND INTERPRETATION

General characteristics data inserted in Table –1 reveals the characteristic features of the students, under study.

Table 1 : General characteristics features of the students

General Characteristics		*Male N= 300*	*Female N= 300*	*CombinedN = 600*
Age (Mode Value)		20.81 years	21.11 years	20.93 years
Rs. 5001—Rs. 10000		32%	33 %	32.5 %
Rs. 10001—Rs. 20000		36 %	32 %	34.0 %
Rs. 20001—Rs. 30000		32 %	35 %	33.5 %
Education :	Ist year	33 %	32 %	32.5 %
	2nd year	34 %	35 %	34.5 %
	3rd year	33 %	33 %	33.0 %

Data inserted in Table – 2A and 2B reveal the significant impact of parental influence on career choice as perceived by the students and also a comparative picture in connection with students belonging to families of three income levels. It can be said from the findings that the more the income level, the more is the parental influence on career choice of students. Not only this, parental influence is more predominant upon male groups in all the three groups of income level. When comparison was made between the three groups of income level separately with each other, significant difference was observed except for the male group belonging to families of income level of Group B and Group C. Analysis of data also reveals that parental influence upon career choice are mainly due to social status, stable and security of jobs which they know well and future orientation. Thus the **"Hypothesis I which postulates, : Parental influence on career choice of students belonging to families of income level Rs. 5001 to Rs 10000, Rs. 10001 to Rs 20000 and Rs.20001 to Rs. 30000 vary significantly." – is accepted** except for the male group belonging to Group B and Group C.

Table 2A : Perceived parental influence on career choice score

	Gr. A			*Gr. B*			*Gr. C*		
	Male	*Female*	*Comb.*	*Male*	*Female*	*Comb.*	*Male*	*Female*	*Comb.*
Mean	67.12	62.87	64.99	73.29	68.06	70.67	75.89	72.13	74.01
S.D.	8.76	9.55	9.02	10.21	9.88	10.03	9.23	8.67	8.91
N	100	100	200	100	100	200	100	100	200

Score range : 20 to 100, High score indicates high parental influence and vice-versa.

Table–2B : Comparative picture of perceived parental influence on career choice

	Male	*Female*	*Combined*
Group A vs Group B	4.60**	3.78**	5.97**
Group B vs Group C	1.89*	3.11**	3.55**
Group C vs Group A	6.90**	7.23**	10.13**

*Difference is nonsignificant , ** $p < 0.01$

Data inserted in Table–3A and 3B reveals the social influence on career choice as perceived by the students and also a comparative picture in connection with students belonging to families of three income levels. Here also it can be said that the more the income level the more is the social influence on career choice. Watching TV, internet facilities, interaction with friends, neighbours and college mates, advertisements, role model of a person etc. are the significant factors in this context. When comparison was made between the income levels separately with each group, significant difference was observed except for the female group belonging to families of income level Group A and Group B. Thus the **Hypothesis – II which postulates, "Social influence on career choice of students belonging to families of income level Rs. 5001 to Rs. 10000, Rs. 10001 to Rs. 20000 and Rs. 20001 to Rs. 30000 vary significantly" – is accepted** except for the female group belonging to Group A and Group B.

Table 3A. Perceived social influence on career choice score

		Gr. A			Gr. B			Gr. C	
	Male	Female	Comb.	Male	Female	Comb.	Male	Female	Comb.
Mean	70.56	67.88	69.22	74.33	70.69	72.51	78.97	74.33	76.65
S.D.	9.16	9.55	9.27	10.56	11.23	10.89	10.65	9.88	10.01
N	100	100	200	100	100	200	100	100	200

Table 3B. Comparative picture of perceived social influence on career choice

	Male	*Female*	*Combined*
Group A vs Group B	2.71 ***	1.91*	3.25 ***
Group B vs Group C	3.11 ***	2.44 **	3.98 ***
Group C vs Group A	6.01 ***	4.70 ***	7.74 **

* Difference is nonsignificant , ** $p < 0.05$, *** $p<0.01$.

Comparison was also made between the male and female group of students belonging to families of three income levels in terms of perceived parental and social influence on career choice. In all the three comparisons, significant difference was observed. Besides this, it can be clearly said that parental and

Table 4. Comparison between male and female group in terms perceived parental and social influence on career choice

Income	Parental				Social			
	Category	Mean	S.D.	t-value	Category	Mean	S.D.	t-value
Gr. A	Male	67.12	8.76	3.29**	Male	70.56	9.16	2.03*
	Female	62.87	9.55		Female	67.88	9.55	
Gr. B	Male	73.29	10.21	3.68**	Male	74.33	10.56	2.36*
	Female	68.06	9.88		Female	70.69	11.23	
Gr. C	Male	75.89	9.23	2.98**	Male	78.97	10.65	3.22**
	Female	72.13	8.67		Female	74.33	9.88	

* $p < 0.05$, ** $p < 0.01$.

social influence is more predominant upon the male group than that of the female group. Thus the **Hypothesis - III which states, "Parental and social influence on career choice of students belonging to families of income level Rs. 5001 to Rs. 10000, Rs. 10001 to Rs. 20000 and Rs. 20001 to Rs. 30000 are differentially associated with gender difference." is accepted in this investigation**.

Conclusion

In conclusion it can be said that there is a significant impact of parental and social influence on career choice of students belonging to families of three different income levels, viz., Rs. 5001 to Rs. 10000, Rs. 10001 to Rs. 20000 and Rs. 20001 to Rs. 30000 respectively. The factors behind the parental influence are mainly due to social status, security and stability of the job and future orientation. On the other hand, the significant factors regarding the social influence are internet facilities, interaction with friends, neighbours and class mates, advertisements, and watching TV etc. Each and every student have personal likings, personal interests and preferences to choose his or her career but present findings reveal more impact of parental and social influence on career choice of students. This is the time to think about the right career choice of students which would be beneficial for the students, family and also for the society at large.

REFERENCES

Bandura, A., Barbaranelli, C. Caprara, G.V. and Pastorelli, C.(2001). Self-efficacy beliefs as shapers of children's aspirations and career trajectories. *Child Development*, 72, 187-206.

Bubany, S.T., Krieshok, T.S., Black, M.D. and McKay, R.A. (2008). College students" perspectives on their career decision. *Journal of Career Assessment*, 16(2), 177-197.

Chope, R.C. (2005). Qualitatively assessing family influence on career decision-making. *Journal of Career Assessment*, 13(4), 395-414.

Constantine, M.G. and Flores, L.Y. (2006). Psychological distress, perceived family conflict and career development issues in college students of colour. *Journal of Career Assessment*, 14(3), 354-369.

Keller, B.K. and Whiston, S.C. (2008). The role of parental influences on young adolescents' career development. *Journal of Career Assessment*, 16(2), 198-217.

Nanta, M.M. and Kahn, J.H. (2007). Identity status, consistency and differentiation of interest and career decision self-efficacy. *Journal of Career Assessment*, 15 (1), 55-65.

26

Error Analysis and Learner Errors

Mariam Mohamed Nor

Introduction

Error Analysis (EA) consists of a set of procedures for identifying, describing and explaining learner errors. Technically errors can occur in both comprehension and in production but comprehension errors are difficult to detect as it is often impossible to locate the precise linguistic source of an error. Thus, EA is the study of the errors that learners make in their speech and writing. Error evaluation (EE) is a set of procedures for assessing the relative seriousness of learner errors.

Errors and Mistakes

Explaining errors involves determining their sources in order to account for why they occurred. One obvious reason why learners make errors is the difficulty they experience in accessing their L2 knowledge when communicating. If L2 forms have not yet been automized, they require controlled processing, which places heavy demand on learners' information-processing systems.

Errors and mistakes can be distinguished by checking whether the learner fails to use the correct form of the simple past tense which constitutes a mistake rather than an error, because other forms are correctly marked. The best way to determine a particular deviation of an error is by consulting the learner. If the learner is able to self-correct the deviant form, it can be classified as a mistake.

Researchers found many learners' errors were beyond the structures found in the native language. Not only did errors occur that were not predicted by the theory but also there was evidence that predicted errors did not occur.

Some of the assumptions of the Contrastive analysis hypothesis are (Selinker, 1972, p. 219).

1. Language learning is habit formation.
2. The major source of errors is the native language (L1)
3. Errors can be accounted for by comparing the L1 and L2.
4. The greater the differences, the more errors will occur.
5. What is dissimilar between the languages is what must be learnt.
6. Difficulties and ease in learning are due to similarities and differences respectively.

Corder (1967) makes an important distinction between mistakes or performance errors and, true errors or markers of a learner's transitional competence. Sentences containing errors would be characterized by systematic deviancy. While the learners correct sentences do not necessarily give evidence of the rules that the learner is using or of the hypothesis he is testing. In fact, his errors suggest the strategies he employs to work out the rules of the new language and the language he has developed at given stages of his language development.

One-third of the deviant sentences from second language learners could be attributed to language transfer. The conceptualization and role of errors took a different role with the publication of an article by Corder (1967) titled "the significance of learners errors". They started to be viewed as an indication of a learners attempt to figure out some system; that is, to impose regularity on the language the learner is exposed to. As such they are evidence of an underlying rule-governed system.

Error analysis as the name suggests is a type of linguistic analysis that focuses on the type of errors that learners make. Unlike contrastive analysis, the comparison made is between

the errors a learner makes in producing the TL and the TL form itself. It is similar to the weak form of contrastive analysis in that both start from learner production data; however in contrastive analysis the comparison is made with the L1, whereas in error analysis the comparison is made with the L2.

Intralingual interference refers to items produced by the learner which reflect not the structure of the L1, but generalizations based on partial exposure to the L2. In an analysis of English errors produced by speakers of a multitude of unrelated languages representing several language families, Richards noted subcategories of error types which seem to be common to speakers of diverse languages as they develop hypothesis about the structure of English. Like first language learners, the second language learner tries to derive the rules behind the data to which he has been exposed, and may develop hypothesis that correspond neither to the L1 nor the L2.

Certain errors appear to be universal, reflecting learners' attempts to make the task of learning and using the L2 simpler (Ellis, 1997). Use of past tense suffix '-ed' for all verbs is an example of overgeneralization. These errors are common in the speech of second language learners, regardless of their mother tongue.

Facility and economy of effort may explain why first learned structures tend to be overused and may resist replacement by later taught items. This is often the case with simple present/ present continuous. Once the present continuous is introduced it is used more frequently than necessary. Likewise an early learned question form may replace all other learned question forms in the learner's speech, despite constant exposure to all other types of question forms. Words with broad semantic extension may become overused in preference to more specific vocabulary. A linguist looking for an understanding of the learners' language learning process can contribute a lot to language teachers.

Many teachers complain that their students are incapable of using linguistic forms that they are taught. According to Lengo (1995) this situation is due to the teacher's mistaken impression that output should be an accurate representation

of input. This belief ignores the function of intake the knowledge of language the students internalize. Intake may be different from the teacher's syllabus being subject to be internalized.

Another notion that should be introduced at this point is that fossilization, which, according to Ellis (1997), is the cessation of the language learning process somewhere short of target language competence.

For instance, Malay second language learners of English have the following fossilization in their target language.

He *played* tennis.

He *goed* to school.

He *putted* the bag in the car.

He *taked* the pencil just now.

They *catched* the thief.

Keshavarz (1997) maintains that an error-based analysis can give reliable results upon which remedial materials can be constructed. In other words, analysis of second language learners' errors can help identify learners' linguistic difficulties and needs at a particular stage of language learning. It is essential for a syllabus to provide with the training for learning appropriately and errors are important evidence for that.

Harmer (1998) suggests three steps to be followed by the teacher to correct learners' errors. The teacher first listens to the students, then identifies the problem, and puts it right in the most efficient way. Corder (1971) states that knowledge of being wrong is only a starting point. Skill in correction seems to lie in determining the necessary data to present to the learner and what statements, descriptive or comparative, to make about it. What Corder points out below summarizes the view of error correction in language

Teaching (1971):

Language learning is not parrot learning; we do not 'learn' or 'practice' examples. They are the data from which we induce the system of the language. Skill in correction of

> *errors lies in the direction of exploiting the incorrect forms produced by the learner in a controlled fashion (p. 82)*

A great deal of work using error analysis has been carried out in the classroom context. The goal was clearly one of pedagogical remediation). Corder (1967 & 1971) identified a model for error analysis which included three stages.

1. Data collection: Recognition of idiosyncrasy
2. Description: Accounting for idiosyncratic dialect
3. Explanation (the ultimate object of error analysis).

Similarly, Gass & Selinker (1994, p. 67) provide a more through model:

1. Data needs to be collected. This is typically done with written data.
2. Identifying errors. (Into word classes etc.)
3. Classify errors (Overgeneralization, tense etc.)
4. Quantifying errors (how many overgeneralization errors occur? How many tense errors occur?)
5. Analyzing source of error. (Interlingual, intralingual due to a certain teaching method)
6. Remediating for errors. (Pedagogical intervention)

There are two main types within an error analysis framework: Interlingual and intralingual. **Interlingual** are those that can be attributed to the L1 (they involve cross-linguistic comparisons). **Intralingual** errors are those which are due to the language being learned, independent of the L1. One would therefore expect similar intralingual errors to occur from speakers from a wide variety of languages.

The types of errors can be categorized into two: Descriptive and surface structures.

Types of Errors

Error Categories

A. Descriptive

1 Noun phrase

2 Verb phrase

(a) subject-verb agreement

(b) Simple Past Tense

3 Complex sentence

B. Surface structure

1 Omission

2 Addition

3 Misinformation

4 Misordering

5 Blends

One example of a semantic error, which is also commonly made by Malaysians in speech and writing, is due to a lack of understanding of the distinction between the verbs *borrow* and *lend:*

Ask your friend to *borrow* you money.

Ask your friend to *lend* you money.

In English the word *borrow* contains the meaning '+*take*' and the word lend contains the meaning '+*give*'. In BM, however, both meanings are covered by the verb *pinjam* and the distinction in meaning can be created by word order.

Thus, this is clearly an interlingual error, and is caused by the interference of Bahasa Malaysia (BM).

The use of unmarked forms instead of marked forms is far more frequent, as can be seen in the examples below:

I had so much fun talking to my dad last night as he *pack* the computer into the boxes.

I had so much fun talking to my dad last night as he *packed* the computer into the boxes.

I knew I *need* to settle my credit card problem immediately.

I knew I *needed* to settle my credit card problem immediately.

In the past, to use the MAS Golden Lounge, we *have* to go to the Satellite terminal after the train.

In the past, to use the MAS Golden Lounge, we <u>*had*</u> to go to the Satellite terminal after the train.

One possible cause of these errors is the fact that in BM verbs are not marked for tense. Tense is indicated by addition of *sudah* (already).

Intralingual causes can also be posited as the source of verbal errors. Verbs undergo more subtle variation (tense, agreement) than the other word classes in English. This makes their acquisition by all learners, regardless of native language a difficult task.

Subjects also exhibited errors in subject-verb agreement as is shown in the examples below:

It all depends on how a person *perceive* "sexy".

It all depends on how a person *perceives* "sexy".

He *know* me so well.

He *knows* me so well.

I don't even pay frequent *visit* to the canteen.

I don't even pay frequent *visits* to the canteen.

The omission of the third person "-s" can be attributed to the fact that BM does not require verbs to agree with subjects. However, as indicated by Dusková (1984), the ending free form is generalized for all persons to make the learning task easier and this is a common intralingual made by people with diverse native languages.

Some errors, like the one below, cannot be attributed to interference:

I spent the *just-over* weekend at Island Redang Island.

I spent *last* weekend at Island Redang.

This is an intralingual error where the learner uses the communicative strategy of creating a term he is not familiar with by using terms he already knows.

Some of the errors involving prepositions are due to omission:

They are searching solution from the web

They are searching *for* solutions from the web)

Once a while we buy groceries from the supermarket.

Once *in* a whilewe buy groceries from the supermarket.

The omission of prepositions as shown in the examples above cannot be explained by examining the structure of BM as similar structures (prepositions) exist in the language. However omission is often used as a simplification strategy by learners to lessen the learning load.

Articles too, were omitted often by the subjects:

We waited for few minutes.

We waited *a* few minutes.

If I'm late I can't go to gym.

If I'm late I can't go to *the* gym.

These omissions, unlike the ones involving prepositions can be attributed to the fact that BM doesn't use articles like those used in English. Along with the influence of the tendency of learners to simplify the learning task, interference from the L1 can account for the higher frequency of article-omission errors as opposed to preposition omission-errors.

Most of the errors concerning nouns involve an error in the distinction of 'mass nouns' and 'count nouns':

The PTA seeks to raise *fund* for the poor students.

The PTA seeks to raise *funds* for the poor students.

In the example above the subject fails to realize that *'fund'* is a count noun unlike *water*. The distinction between mass and count words does not exist in BM. Thus this can be treated as an interlingual error.

Causes and Sources of Errors

Interlingual errors are the result of mother tongue influences. Learners transfer/borrow some forms but not others due to two factors such as proto-typicality and language distance (Kellerman, 1979). Malay learners of English commonly make errors in negative sentences.

For example:

Adryna no coming today.

[Adryna tak datang hari ini].

Such errors are common in pre-verbal negation using *no*, the same negative construction as in their L1. In order to determine whether transfer is the cause for the occurrence of errors, James (1998) demonstrates that learners with a particular L1 make an error that those with a different L1 do not. He provides a useful summary of these strategies:

1. False analogy
2. Misanalysis
3. Incomplete rule application exploiting redundancy
4. Overlooking co-occurrence restrictions
5. System-simplification

It is not clear which strategy is responsible for a particular error. Errors can also be viewed as 'natural' or as 'induced'. For example:

He *played* football yesterday.

He *goed* home at six.

He *drinked* milk.

He *eated* dinner.

He *sleeped* at eight.

The description of errors is a comparative process, the data being the original erroneous utterances and the reconstructed utterance (Corder, 1974). Thus, description of learner errors involves specifying how the forms produced by the learner differ from those produced by the learner's native-speaker counterparts. It focuses on the surface properties of learner utterances. The two steps involved are:

1. Developing a set of descriptive categories for coding the identified errors.
2. Recording the frequency of the errors in each category.

James (1998) stated that there are two kinds of taxonomy used:

1. Linguistic taxonomy
2. Surface structure taxonomy

A linguistic taxonomy is usually based on categories drawn from a descriptive grammar of the target language. Such a grammar will include general categories relating to basic sentence structure, the verb phrase, verb complementation, the noun phrase, prepositional phrases, adjuncts, coordinate and subordinate constructions and sentence connection.

Dulay, Burt, and Krashen (1982), postulated that surface structure taxonomy is based on 'the ways surface structures are altered' in erroneous utterances/sentences. They noted four principal ways in which learners modify the target forms:

1. Omission (for example, omission of copula *be* in the utterance *My sisters very pretty*. [*My sisters are very pretty]*.
2. Addition (i.e. the presence of a form that does not appear in a well-formed utterance). This is sub-categorized into:
   (a) Regularization (for example, *eated for ate; taked for took; putted for put and goed for went*)
   (b) Double-marking (for example, *He didn't came; She didn't went.*)
   (c) Simple additions (i.e. additions not describable as regularizations or as double-markings)
3. Misinformation (i.e. the use of the wrong form of the morpheme or structure):
   (a) Regularization (for example, *Do they be happy?*)
   (b) Archi-forms (for example, the learner uses *me* as both a subject and object pronoun).

      Me go with you tomorrow;

      You and me can wash the car.)

   (c) Alternating forms (for example, *Don't* +v and *No*+v).

      Don't sleep- No sleep.

4. Misordering (i.e. errors characterized by the incorrect placement of a morpheme or group of morphemes in an utterance as in *She fights all the time her brother; She very unresponsible to let water drip all day long.*).
5. Blends (i.e. errors that reflect the learner's uncertainty as to which of two forms required). This can result in over-inclusion as in the sentence, *We can go shop at the Jusco supermart.*

To conclude, learners' errors are noted by noticing how they have simplified, added, misinformed or misordered elements in their utterances and writings.

Significance of Learner Errors

According to Corder (1967), learner errors are significant in three ways:

(1) Pedagogic purpose to show teachers what learners have learned and what they have not yet mastered;

(2) Research purpose to provide evidence about how languages are learned and acquired.

(3) Learning purpose to act as devices by which learners can discover the rules of the target language.

To conclude, learners' errors are a part of the learners' language learning process. Hence, teachers should not penalize students for the errors thèy made. Instead, teachers should note those errors and devisé ways to assist learners to overcome their problems in language learning.

It is difficult to decide whether grammatically or acceptability should serve as the criterion for error analysis. If grammatically is chosen, an error can be defined as 'breach of the rule of the code' (Corder, 1967). Defining errors in terms of grammatically also necessitates giving consideration to the distinction between overt and covert error.

An error is said to be *overt* if it can be detected by inspecting the sentence/utterance in which it occurs. An error is *covert* if it only becomes apparent when a larger stretch of the discourse is considered. Acceptability is more dependent on the subject evaluation of the researcher but determining acceptability also involves attempting to identify a situational context in which the utterance in question might fit.

In the field of methodology, there are two schools of thought with regard to learners' error. Firstly, the school which maintains that if we were to achieve a perfect teaching method, the errors would have never be committed and therefore the occurrence of errors is merely a sign of inadequacy in our teaching techniques. The philosophy of the second school is that we live in an imperfect world and consequently errors will always occur in spite of our very best teaching and learning methods.

One effect has been perhaps to shift the emphasis away from a preoccupation with teaching towards a study of learning.

The differences between the two are clearly defined: that the learning of the mother tongue is natural, whereas, we all know that there is no such inevitability about the learning of a second language; that the learning of the mother tongue is part of the whole maturational process of the child, whilst learning a second language normally begins only after the maturational process is complete.

A child's incorrect utterances can be interpreted as being evidence that he is in the process of acquiring language and the errors provide these evidences. Brown and Frazer (1964) point out that the best evidence a child possesses construction rules is the occurrence of systematic errors, since when the child speaks correctly, it is quite possible that he is only repeating something that he has heard.

In the case of the second language learner it is known that we do know some knowledge of what the input has been which we call as the syllabus. The simple fact of presenting a certain linguistic form to a learner in the classroom does not necessarily qualify it for the status of input, for the reason that input 'is what goes in', not 'what is available' for going in, and we may reasonably suppose that it is the learner who controls this input. This may well be determined by the characteristics of his language acquisition mechanism and not by those of the syllabus.

It was suggested that educational planners should take more account of the learners' needs when planning the syllabuses, however this has not led to any indept researches. Teachers can create a problem-solving situation for the learner in which he must find, by enquiring either of the teacher or a dictionary appropriate verbal response for solving the problem.

The use of the term systematic in this context implies that there may be errors which are random. We are immediately aware of them when they occur and can correct them with more or less complete assurance. It would be quite unreasonable to expect the learner of a second language not to exhibit such slips of the tongue or pen, since he is subject to similar external and internal conditions when performing in his first or second language. Therefore, we must make a distinction between those errors which are the product of such chance circumstances and those which reveal his underlying knowledge of the language or as we may call it his transitional competence.

The errors of performance are unsystematic, whereas the errors of competence are systematic. Errors or performance are referred as as mistakes.

The term *error* refer to the systematic errors of the learner from which we are able to reconstruct his knowledge of the language (Miller, 1966). Mistakes are insignificant to the process of language learning. However, it is problematic to differentiate between a learner's mistake and a learner's error. The utterance of a correct form cannot be taken as proof that the learner has learned the systems since he may be merely repeating a heard utterance, in which case we should class such behaviour, not as language. Spolsky, (1966) refers such utterance as 'language-like behaviour'. The situational context will determine whether his utterance was an error or not.

To conclude, in language teaching we may be able to allow the learner's innate strategies to specify our practice and determine our syllabus.

Specifically, teachers may learn to adapt ourselves to learner's needs rather than impose upon him/her our preconceptions of *how* he ought to learn, *what* he ought to learn and *when* he ought to learn it.

Classroom Application

Below are two pieces of spoken language produced by speakers of English. Identify the ***mistakes*** on each sample and suggest what might have caused them. As an English teacher suggest how would you rectify the mistakes.

(a) I and my mother goed to market yesterday to buy one tail fish.

(b) We very lucky because we get visited at the beautiful place.

(c) I very happy because get suck up air and I no feel tired.

(d) We reach to the house inside o'clock 2.30 pm.

(e) We not stop scream because so fear.

(f) After that, we raise a bus for went to the famous in history.

SUMMARY

- **Error:** a systematic deviation made by learners who have not yet mastered the rules of the L2.
- **Error analysis**: the study of kind and quantity of error that occurs in language
- **Interlingual errors**: errors traced to L1 interference
- **Intralingual errors**: similar errors found in all L2 learners regardless of their L1
- A learner's errors provide evidence of the system of the language that he is using at a particular point in the course. They are significant in three different ways.

1. Informs the teacher how far towards the goal the learner has progressed and, consequently, what remains for him to learn.
2. Informs the researcher evidence of how language is learned or acquired, what strategies or procedures the learner utilizes in his discovery of the language.

Error	*Reconstruction*	*Linguistic Description*	*Surface Structure Description*
The big of them ...	The bigger of them	Noun phrase; adjectives; comparative form	Misinformation – regularization
..was watching...	..were watching...	Verb phrase; subject-verb agreement (plural)	Misinformation – regularization
..was in this corner...	..who was in this corner...	Complex sentence– relative clause– relative pronoun (who)	Omission
..whistle...	..whistled...	Verb phrase– simple past tense– regular verb	Misinformation – regularization
..escape...	..escaped...	Verb phrase– Simple past tense– Regular verb	Misinformation – regularization
..stop...	..stopped...	Verb phrase– simple past tense– regular verb	Misinformation – regularization
..contain...	..contained...	Verb phrase– simple past tense– regular verb	Misinformation – regularization

An example of error description

3. Informs the learner himself that the making or errors is a device the learner uses in order to learn. It is a way the learner has of testing his hypotheses about the nature of the language he is learning.

To conclude, the making of errors is a strategy employed both by children acquiring their mother tongue and by those learning a second language.

REFERENCES

Brown, R. W., & Fraser, C. (1964). The Acquisition of Syntax. In Ursula Bellugi and Roger Brown (eds.), *The Acquisition of Language. Monograph of the Society for Research in Child Development*, 29, No.1.

Carroll, J. B. (1955). *The Study of Language*. Cambridge.

Corder, S. P.(1967). The significance of Learners' errors. *International Review of Applied Linguistics,* 5, 161-70.

Corder, S. P. (1971). Idiosyncratic dialects and error analysis. *International Review of Applied Linguistics*, 9, 2.

Dulay, H., & Burt, M.K. (1972). You Can't Learn Without Goofing: An Analysis of Children's second Language Errors.

Dulay, H., Burt, M. & Krashen, S. (1982). *Language Two.* New York: Oxford University Press.

Dusková, L. (1984). Similarity-An aid or hindrance in foreign language learning. *Folia Linguistica, 18*(1-2), 103-115.

Ellis, R. (1997). *Second language acquisition*. New York: Oxford University

Ellis, R. & Barkhuizen. (2005). *Analyzing Learner Language*. Oxford. Singapore.

George, H. V. (1971). English for Asian Learners: Are we on the right road?' *English Language Teaching, XXV*, 270- 77

George, H. V. (1972). *Common Errors in Language Learning*. Rowley, Massachusetts.

Harmer, J. (1998). *How to teach English*? Essex, Longman.

Jain, M. (1969). Error Analysis of an Indian English Corpus. unpublished paper, University of Edinburgh.

James, C. (1998). *Errors in Language Learning and Use: Exploring Error Analysis.* London. Longman

Kellerman, E. (1979). Transfer and non-transfer: where are we now? *Studies in second language acquisition*, 2, 37-57.

Keshavars, M.H. (1997). *Contrastive analysis and error analysis*. Tehran: Rahmana Pub. Press.

Lengo, N. (1995). What is an error? *English Teaching Forum*, 33(3), 20-24.

Miller, G. A. (1966). Language and Psychology. In E.H. Lenneberg (ed.). *New Directions in the study of Language*. Boston.

Richards, J. C. (1984). *Error Analysis: Perspectives on Second Language Acquisition* Longman. New York.

Selinker, L. (1972). Interlanguage. *International Review of Applied Linguistics,* X (3), 219-231

Spolsky, B. (1966). A Psycholinguistic Critique of Programmed Foreign Language Instruction. *International Review of Applied Linguistics,* 4.2, 1966, 119-29.

Stenson, B. (1974). Induced Errors. In J.Schumann and N. Stenson (eds.): *New Frontiers in Second Language Learning*. Rowley, M A: Newbury House.

Index

N